PRINCIPLES OF

PARALLEL PROGRAMMING

Calvin Lin

Department of Computer Sciences
The University of Texas at Austin

Lawrence Snyder

Department of Computer Science and Engineering
University of Washington, Seattle

PEARSON

Addison
Wesley

Boston San Francisco New York
London Toronto Sydney Tokyo Singapore Madrid
Mexico City Munich Paris Cape Town Hong Kong Montreal

Executive Editor: *Michael Hirsch*
Acquisition Editor: *Matt Goldstein*
Editorial Assistant: *Sarah Milmore*
Senior Production Supervisor: *Marilyn Lloyd*
Text Designer: *Gillian Hall*
Cover Designer: *Barbara T. Atkinson*
Cover Image: *Flip Nicklin/Hinden Pictures (Orca whales)*
Media Producer: *Bethany Tidd*
Senior Media Buyer: *Ginny Michaud*
Marketing Manager: *Christopher Kelly*
Senior Manufacturing Buyer: *Carol Melville*
Production Services: *Gillian Hall, The Aardvark Group Publishing Services*
Illustrations: *Donna Ellison*
Copyeditor: *Kathleen Cantwell, C4 Technologies*
Proofreader: *Holly McLean-Aldis*
Indexer: *Jack Lewis*

Access the latest information about Addison-Wesley titles from our World Wide Web site:
http://www.aw.com/computing

Many of the designations used by manufacturers and sellers to distinguish their products are claimed as trademarks. Where those designations appear in this book, and Addison-Wesley was aware of a trademark claim, the designations have been printed in initial caps or all caps.

The programs and applications presented in this book have been included for their instructional value. They have been tested with care but are not guaranteed for any particular purpose. The publisher does not offer any warranty or representation, nor does it accept any liabilities with respect to the programs or applications.

Library of Congress Cataloging-in-Publication Data

Snyder, Lawrence.
 Parallel programming / Lawrence Snyder, Calvin Lin. -- 1st ed.
   p. cm.
 ISBN 978-0-321-53134-6
 1. Parallel programming (Computer science) I. Lin, Calvin. II. Title.
 QA76.642.S667 2008
 005.2'75--dc22   2008000970

ISBN-13: 9780321487902
ISBN-10: 0-321-48790-7
1 2 3 4 5 6 7 8 9 10—CRW—11 10 09 08

To Mom and Dad
(Josette and Min Shuey)

To Julie, Dave, and Dan

Preface

Welcome!

For readers who are motivated by the advent of multi-core chips to learn parallel programming, you've come to the right place. This book is written for a world in which parallel computers are everywhere, ranging from laptops with two-core chips to supercomputers to huge data-center clusters that index the Internet.

This book focuses on scalable parallelism, that is, the ability of a parallel program to run well on any number of processors. This notion is critical for two reasons: (1) Most of the techniques needed to create scalable parallel computations are the same techniques that produce efficient solutions on a multi-core chip, and (2) while multi-core chips currently have a modest number of processors, typically 2–8, the number of cores per chip promises to increase dramatically in the coming years, making the notion of scalable parallelism directly relevant. Thus, while today's multi-core chips offer opportunities for low latency communication among cores, this characteristic is likely a short-term advantage, as on-chip delays to different parts of the chip will become increasingly apparent as the number of cores grows. So, we focus not on exploiting such short-term advantages, but on emphasizing approaches that work well now and in the future. Of course, multi-core chips present their own challenges, particularly with their limited bandwidth to off-chip memory and their limited aggregate on-chip cache. This book discusses these issues as well.

First, we discuss the principles that underlie effective and efficient parallel programs. Learning the principles is essential to acquiring any capability as sophisticated as programming, of course, but principles are perhaps even more important for parallel programming because the state of the art changes rapidly. Training that is tied too closely to a specific computer or language will not have the staying power needed to keep pace with advancing technology. But the principles—concepts that apply to any parallel computing system and ideas that exploit these features—lead to an understanding that is timeless and knowledge that will always be applicable.

But we do more than discuss abstract concepts. We also apply those principles to everyday computations, which makes the book very practical. We introduce several parallel programming systems, and we describe how to apply the principles in those programming systems. On completion, we expect readers to be able to write parallel programs. Indeed, the final chapter is devoted to parallel programming techniques and the development of a term-long parallel programming capstone project.

Audience

Our intended audience is anyone—students or professionals—who has written successful programs in C or similar languages and who describes himself as a programmer. It is helpful to have a basic idea of how a computer executes sequential programs, including knowledge of the fetch/execute cycle and basics of caching. This book was originally targeted to upper level undergraduate computer science majors or first year graduate students with a CS undergraduate degree, and it continues to be appropriate for that level. However, as the book evolved, we reduced the assumed knowledge and emphasized pedagogy in the belief that if some explanations cover knowledge the reader already has, it's easy to skip forward.

Organization

Because parallel programming is not a direct extension of sequential programming with which the reader is doubtless familiar, we have organized this book into four parts:

Foundations: Chapters 1–3

Abstractions: Chapters 4–5

Languages: Chapters 6–9

Looking Forward: Chapters 10–11

To enable you to select intelligently from these parts, we now explain their goals and content.

Foundations. In Chapter 1 we discover the many issues that parallel programmers must address by showing how difficult it is to implement a computation that is trivial when written for sequential computers. The example focuses our attention on issues that concern us throughout the entire book, but it also emphasizes the importance of understanding how a parallel computer operates. Chapter 2 introduces five different types of parallel computers, giving a few details about their architecture and their ability to scale to a larger size. There are two key conclusions from the chapter: First, unlike sequential computing, there is no standard architecture. Second, to be successful at spanning this architectural diversity we need an abstract machine model to guide our programming. And we give one. With the architectures in mind, Chapter 3 covers basic ideas of concurrency, including threads and processes, latency, bandwidth, speedup, and so forth, with an emphasis on issues related to performance. These foundations of Part 1 prepare us for an exploration of algorithms and abstractions.

Abstractions. As an aid to designing and discussing parallel algorithms, Chapter 4 introduces an informal pseuodcode notation for writing parallel programs in a language-independent way. The notation has a variety of features that span various programming models and approaches, allowing us to discuss algorithms without bias toward any particular language or machine. To bootstrap your thinking about parallel algorithms, Chapter 5 covers a series of basic algorithmic techniques. By the end of Part 2, you should be able to conceptualize ways to solve a problem in parallel, bringing us to the final issue of encoding your algorithms in a concrete parallel programming language.

Languages. There is no single parallel programming language that fulfills the role that, say, C or Java plays in sequential programming, that is, a language widely known and accepted as a baseline medium to encode algorithms. As a result, Part 3 introduces three kinds of parallel programming languages: thread-based (Chapter 6), message-passing (Chapter 7), and high-level (Chapter 8). We cover each language well enough for you to write small exercises; serious computations require a more complete language introduction that is available through online resources. In addition to introducing a language, each chapter includes a brief overview of related languages that have a following in the parallel programming community. Chapter 9 briefly compares and contrasts all of the languages presented, noting their strengths and weaknesses. There is benefit to reading all three chapters, but we realize that many readers will focus on one approach, so these chapters are independent of one another.

Onward. Part 4 looks to the future. Chapter 10 covers a series of new, promising parallel technologies that will doubtless impact future research and practice. In our view, they are not quite "ready for prime time," but they are important and worth becoming familiar with even before they are fully deployed. Finally, Chapter 11 focuses on hands-on techniques for programming parallel machines. The first two sections of the chapter can be read early in your study of parallel programming, perhaps together with your study of abstractions in Chapters 4 and 5. But the main goal of the chapter is to assist you in writing a substantial program as a capstone design project. In this capacity we assume that you will return to Chapter 11 repeatedly.

Using This Book

Although the content is presented in a logical order, it is not necessary to read this book front to back. Indeed, in a one term course, it may be sensible to begin programming exercises before all of the topics have been introduced. We see the following as a sensible general plan:

- Chapters 1, 2
- Chapter 11 first section, Chapter 3 through Performance Tradeoffs; begin programming exercises
- Chapters 4, 5

- One of Chapters 6–8, programming language chapters
- Complete Chapter 3 and 11, begin term project
- Complete remaining chapters in order: language chapters, Chapters 9, 10

There is, of course, no harm in reading the book straight through, but the advantage of this approach is that the reading and programming can proceed in parallel.

Acknowledgments

Sincere thanks are due to E Christopher Lewis and Robert van de Geijn, who critiqued an early draft of this book. Thanks also to the following reviewers for their valuable feedback and suggestions:

David Bader, Georgia Institute of Technology

Purushotham Bangalore, University of Alabama, Birmingham

John Cavazos, University of Delaware

Sandhya Dwarkadas, University of Rochester

John Gilbert, UC Santa Barbara

Robert Henry, Cray Inc.

E Christopher Lewis, VMWare

Kai Li, Princeton

Glenn Reinman, UCLA

Darko Stefanovic, University of New Mexico

We thank Karthik Murthy and Brandon Plost for their assistance in writing and running parallel programs and for finding bugs in the text, and we are grateful to Bobby Blumofe, whose early collaborations on a multi-threaded programming course are evident in many places in the book. We recognize and thank the students of the Parallel Programming Environments Seminar (CSE590o) at the University of Washington in autumn quarter, 2006 for their contributions to the text: Ivan Beschastnikh, Alex Colburn, Roxana Geambasu, Sangyun Hahn, Ethan Katz-Bassett, Nathan Kuchta, Harsha Madhyastha, Marianne Shaw, Brian Van Essen, and Benjamin Ylvisaker. Other contributors are Sonja Keserovic, Kate Moore, Brad Chamberlain, Steven Deitz, Dan Grossman, Jeff Diamond, Don Fussell, Bill Mark, and David Mohr.

We would like to thank our editor, Matt Goldstein, and the Addison Wesley team: Sarah Milmore, Marilyn Lloyd, Barbara Atkinson, Joyce Wells, and Chris Kelly. Thanks to Gillian Hall who has been especially tolerant of our antics.

Finally, we thank our families for their patience through the writing of this book.

Calvin Lin
Lawrence Snyder
February 2008

Contents

Any sufficiently advanced technology
is indistinguishable from magic.

—Arthur C. Clarke
Profiles of the Future, 1961

Foundations

We begin our study of parallel programming by building a solid foundation. The most important goal is to clarify the difference between the sequential and parallel programming worlds. In sequential computing, operations are performed one at a time, making it straightforward to reason about the correctness and performance characteristics of a program. In parallel computing many operations take place at once, complicating our reasoning about correctness and performance, and as a result, modifying our programming approach. This part explains the main consequences of this distinction.

Our introduction to parallel computation in Chapter 1 begins by solving a simple problem of counting the number of occurrences of 3 in a 1-dimensional array. This trivial task requires four attempts before we create a program with reasonable performance. Even then, we find that our maximum hoped-for speedup can't be realized. While working through the example, we introduce a series of basic concepts of parallelism.

Chapter 2 describes the basic architectural features of parallel computers. It is an interesting topic in its own right, because challenging problems such as interprocessor communication have a multitude of potential solutions, and the techniques that architects use to address them exhibit considerable ingenuity. The main conclusion of our tour of parallel machines will be that they are extremely different. Because programmers need to know certain properties of the underlying machine to write quality programs, it will be necessary to find a machine model that unifies the disparate architectures. We introduce such a model as the basis for our subsequent study.

With a clear idea of how parallel computers work, Chapter 3 characterizes the many conceptual issues surrounding parallel performance. We introduce key ideas including latency, bandwidth, speedup and efficiency. Certain facets of programming, such as dependences, are highlighted as being a source of interference among parallel threads. Once these foundational ideas have been introduced, we will be prepared to move on to the algorithmic ideas presented in Part 2.

1

Introduction

Parallel computation is a fundamental technique by which computations can be accelerated, so the increasing availability of parallel hardware represents a tremendous opportunity. But implementing a parallel solution presents certain conceptual and programming challenges that this textbook is designed to address. To place the opportunities and challenges in perspective, this chapter sets the context and introduces basic ideas.

The Power and Potential of Parallelism

Parallelism arises frequently in everyday life. More importantly, parallelism has contributed in many ways to the steady performance improvement in computers over the past several decades. And now, new opportunities are available. Let's look closely.

Parallelism, a Familiar Concept

Parallelism is a familiar concept. Juggling is a parallel task that humans can perform. House construction is a parallel activity, because several workers can perform separate tasks simultaneously, such as wiring, plumbing, and furnace duct installation, and so on. Most manufacturing—cars, hairdryers, frozen dinners—is performed in parallel using an assembly line, or pipeline, in which many units of the product are under construction at once. A call center, where many employees service customers at the same time, is another organization that applies parallelism.

Although familiar, these forms of parallelism are different. The call center, for example, differs from house construction in a fundamental way: Calls are generally independent and can be serviced in any order with little interaction among the workers. In construction, some tasks can be performed simultaneously—wiring and plumbing—while others are ordered—framing must precede wiring. The ordering restricts the amount of parallelism that can be applied at once, limiting the speed at which a construction project can complete. The ordering also increases the degree of interaction among the workers. Manufacturing pipelines are different still, because they generally have strict ordering constraints with the separate stages often being performed sequentially; the parallelism comes from having many instances of the product in the pipeline at once. And juggling is an instance of event-driven parallelism, where an event—a falling ball—causes the execution of operations— catching, throwing—in response to the event. Such familiar forms of parallelism will also arise in our consideration of parallel computation.

Parallelism in Computer Programs

The main motivation for executing program instructions in parallel is to complete a computation faster. But most programs today are incapable of much improvement through parallelism, because they were written assuming that the instructions would be executed in order, one at a time, that is, *sequentially*. The semantics of most programming languages embed sequential execution, and the resulting programs typically rely so heavily on this property for their correctness that it is rare to find significant opportunities for parallel execution. To be sure, there are some opportunities, as when the expression (a+b)*(c+d) must be evaluated; assuming these are simple variables, the subexpressions (a+b) and (c+d) are independent of each other, so they can be computed simultaneously. Such opportunities are an example of Instruction Level Parallelism (ILP).

Indeed, one reason that we have continued to write sequential programs is because computer architects have been so successful at exploiting parallelism. They have used the steady improvements in silicon technology to add several kinds of parallelism, including ILP, into sequential processor design. First, architects provide separate wires and caches for instructions and data. The separation allows instruction and data memory references to execute in parallel without interfering. Second, instruction execution is pipelined, fetching and decoding future instructions while the current instruction is being executed and while the results of past instructions are still being written to memory. Furthermore, the processors issue (initiate) more than one instruction at a time, they prefetch instructions and data, they speculatively perform operations in parallel even if they cannot be sure that they will be needed, and they use highly parallel circuits to perform basic arithmetic operations. In short, modern processors are highly parallel systems.

The key point for programmers is that all of this parallelism has been transparently available to sequential programs. We call this *hidden parallelism*. Such parallelism, together with increasing clock speeds, has allowed each succeeding generation of processor chip to execute programs faster, while preserving the illusion of sequential execution. But the prospects for finding new opportunities to apply parallelism while preserving sequential semantics are becoming limited. More seriously, existing techniques for exploiting ILP have largely reached the point of diminishing returns, in terms of both power consumption and performance. So, given current technologies, sequential program execution may be approaching its maximum speed.

To continue achieving significant performance improvements, we must move beyond the single sequence of instructions typical of existing programs. We need programs that have multiple instruction streams that operate simultaneously. This approach will require new programming techniques, which is the topic of this book.

Multi-Core Computers, an Opportunity

Though performance improvements for a single processor may be reaching a limit, the prophecy of Moore's Law continues to deliver improved transistor densities. Chip manufacturers have used this opportunity to place more than one instruction execution engine, together with its caches, on a single chip. This structure has rapidly acquired the name *core*, because it represents the core components of a typical sequential processor. Early chips had 2, 4, or 8 cores, but this number increases with each generation.

The advent of the first multi-core chips in 2005/2006 prompted a community-wide discussion about the "end of the free lunch." The key observations of the discussion were as follows:

- Software developers have enjoyed steadily improving performance for decades—the "free lunch"—thanks to advances in silicon technology and architecture design (hidden parallelism), as just described.
- Programmers, not needing to be concerned with performance, have changed their techniques and methodologies little over the years (the object-oriented paradigm is a notable exception).
- Existing software generally cannot exploit multi-core chips directly.
- Programs that cannot exploit multi-core chips do not realize any performance improvements now and they will not in the future.
- Most programmers do not now know how to write parallel programs.

The uncomfortable conclusion was that programs need to change, and to make that happen, programmers do, too.

Though the conclusion might be viewed by some as bad news, there was corresponding good news. Specifically, if a computation is rewritten to be parallel and if the parallel program is also *scalable*, meaning that it is capable of using progressively more processors, then as silicon technology advances and more cores are added to future chips, the rewritten program will stay on the performance curve. Non-scalable parallel programs, though, will not enjoy the continued benefits of silicon technology advances. It is important, therefore, to achieve scalable parallelism.

Some observers, especially in the graphics community, no doubt find the discussion of the need for parallel computation curious, because they have been using parallelism for years. Graphics processing units (GPUs), a.k.a. graphics cards, have been the standard technique for accelerating the rendering pipeline. Though the GPU might seem like a niche co-processor of little interest for general computer applications, advances in silicon technology have enabled the notion of GPGPU, *general-purpose computing on graphics processing units*. With a generation cycle of roughly 18 months, the GPU has steadily become increasingly general with each generation, and parallel programmers have applied them to a long list of compute-intensive non-graphics applications. Like multi-core chips, exploiting the potential of GPUs requires knowledge of parallel programming.

Even More Opportunities to Use Parallel Hardware

The opportunities to use parallelism discussed so far involve a small number of processors. But there are many opportunities that are more ambitious.

Supercomputers. The problems of interest at the national research labs, the military, and large corporations have traditionally required supercomputers, which by definition are the world's fastest computers. Twenty years ago, supercomputers were custom-made single-processor systems (generally with vector processing capabilities), but single-processor systems last appeared on the Top 500 List of fastest computers in November 1996, when just three appeared, ranking #265, #374, and #498. Today, the Top 500 List is dominated by parallel computers with many thousands of processors. In many ways, supercomputer programmers form the largest, most experienced community of parallel programmers.

Clusters. It is often observed that no matter how fast a single computer is, connecting two or more of them together produces a faster computer in the sense that the combined machine can execute more instructions per unit time. Of course, well-written parallel programs are needed to exploit the added power. Clusters have been popular since the 1990s because they are relatively inexpensive to build from commodity parts. The low price not only makes them attractive for small groups—labs or small firms—but also gives them a tremendous price/performance advantage over other forms of high-end computing. In the June, 2007 Top 500 List (www.top500.org), clusters represented 74.6 percent of the list.

Servers. The expansion of the Internet and the popularity of remote services, such as searching, have created huge installations of networked computers. In terms of total number of instructions executed per second, these centers represent a huge computational resource. The typical computations—the processing of search queries, for example—are independent of each other; furthermore they use distributed—as opposed to parallel—programming techniques (see the next section, *Parallel Computing versus Distributed Computing*). Nevertheless, these huge networked systems are being used to analyze the features of their workload and to perform other data-intensive computations; the solutions also apply parallel programming techniques.

Grid Computing. Generalizing still further, the collection of computers need not be in the same location, nor administered by the same organization; after all, the computers connected by the Internet represent an enormous computing resource. By analogy with the power grid, a computing grid seeks to provide a single convenient computing service, even though the underlying computer typically consists of physically dispersed machines governed by multiple administrative organizations. Many technical issues remain before grids become commonplace, but they are a topic of active research.

We see then, that there are ample opportunities to use a parallel program beyond the few processors on a single silicon chip. These large computer systems also motivate us to write scalable parallel programs.

Parallel Computing versus Distributed Computing

As suggested above, distributed computing and parallel computing are different.

The goal of parallel computing has traditionally been to provide performance—either in terms of processor power or memory—that a single processor cannot provide; thus, the goal is to use multiple processors to solve a single problem. The goal of distributed computing is to provide convenience, where convenience includes availability, reliability, and physical distribution (being able to access the distributed system from many different locations).

In parallel computation the interaction among processors is generally frequent, typically fine grained with low overhead, and assumed to be reliable. In distributed computation the interaction is generally infrequent, heavier weight, and assumed to be unreliable. Parallel computation values short execution time; distributed computation values long uptime.

Of course, parallel computing and distributed computing are closely related. Some features are a matter of degree—frequency of interaction among processors—and we haven't specified the crossover point. Some features are a matter of emphasis—speed versus reliability—and we know that both properties are important to both types of systems. It follows then, that the two kinds of computing represent distinct, but nearby points in a multidimensional space. The more one knows about parallel computation (or distributed computation, but that's not the emphasis of this book), the more easily one can move around in the parallel-distributed space. Learning the basics of parallel computation will be valuable even for programmers with no need to improve performance.

System Level Parallelism

Return for a moment to our earlier argument that to enjoy the benefits from parallelism we must move beyond a single sequence of instructions. This argument is relevant within a single application. When we view a desktop computer's software from a system level, however, we see many tasks executing at once. The operating system orchestrates their concurrent execution, which heretofore meant that several tasks were juggled at once, with only one executing at a time, a technique known as multitasking.[1] An obvious question is, "Why not simply run these separate tasks on the extra processors?" It makes sense because their concurrent design ensures that whatever interactions are required among them will be handled safely.

> **Concurrency and Parallelism.** Though these terms are closely related, history influences how we use them. Concurrency is widely used in the operating systems and database communities to describe executions that are logically simultaneous, while parallelism is typically used by the architecture and supercomputing communities to describe executions that physically execute simultaneously. In either case, the codes that execute simultaneously exhibit unknown timing characteristics. For example, an operating system might execute just one code segment at a time, but because the execution can context switch at any point in time to another code segment, the issues are the same as if they were physically executing simultaneously. Similarly, with physical parallelism, the timing relationships among the code segments is unpredictable, forcing the assumption that any timing is possible. Thus, the issues for program correctness are the same for both concurrent and parallel computation, and in a sense, they are endpoints on a spectrum of varying parallel resources. In this book, we will use the terms interchangeably to refer to logical concurrency.
>
> *Definition*

The first answer is that for the large-scale parallelism just described, there are not nearly enough tasks to keep large processors busy. But, for small amounts of parallelism as is typical of today's multi-core chips, the separate tasks can be run on separate processors. Indeed, it has been suggested that continuously executing tasks such as security software (or the OS itself!) would be good candidates for the extra processors. But there may be fewer opportunities than might at first appear. First, many applications don't stress the hardware even now—word processors perform spell-checking continuously in the background and never fall behind the typist. Second, much of the multitasking in an operating system comes from switching to a new task when the currently executing task requests a time-consuming, external operation, such as a page fault, disk I/O, or network I/O. Suppose that task A blocks on such a request. On a single processor system, some task B could execute while A blocks, providing good utilization of the processor, but on a multi-processor system, task B may have already completed execution on a separate processor, forcing the processor that executes task A to simply remain idle.

The main reason that running multiple tasks on the separate parallel processors is not a silver bullet, however, is because it doesn't usually improve the performance of an individual application. And in those cases where improved performance is needed, it is essential that there are multiple streams of cooperating instructions that use multiple processors effectively.

---

[1]Because certain I/O devices like disk controllers are typically separate from the main execution engine, there has long been true parallel execution among the processor and its external devices.

Convenience of Parallel Abstractions

Finally, there is one reason to exploit parallelism besides performance: Some computations are more easily expressed as parallel computations. For example, user interfaces are typically best written as a collection of threads, with one thread responsible for interacting with the user: The thread waits for user input and dispatches other threads to respond appropriately. With such an organization, the code that displays a widget is greatly simplified because, for example, it needn't concern itself with the responsibility of polling for a user mouse click that might come at any time.

As we shall see, the abstractions used to organize and manage parallel computations make it convenient and safe to use multiple instruction streams. When flow of control is unpredictable, parallelism can help even when the resulting instruction sequences are not executed simultaneously. Thus, while we emphasize the fast solution of a problem, we acknowledge that there are other uses of parallelism.

Examining Sequential and Parallel Programs

The previous sections have emphasized the potential advantages available in hardware. We have asserted that existing sequential programs cannot take advantage of, say, multi-core computers, so it's time to consider ways to realize the benefits of parallel hardware.

Parallelizing Compilers

Knowing that a compiler translates the programs that we write into the machine instructions of the computer that we use, and not knowing (at least for most of us) how this magical translation is done, it is reasonable to wonder why someone doesn't just write a compiler that translates existing programs into a form suitable for parallel execution. After all, the sequential program specifies the computation, and all that needs to be done is to transform the same operations into a parallel form. This idea to compile sequential programs for parallel machines was among the first approaches tried, and it continues to be a dream. Unfortunately, the dream seems beyond reach, despite over three decades of intense research.

The reason for pessimism is that scalable parallel algorithms are generally qualitatively different from the sequential algorithms found in existing programs. We will describe this situation by saying that the parallel solution typically requires *a paradigm shift* in the solution approach. Since compilers transform programs in ways that preserve their correctness, they do not change the essential features of the algorithm. (Figure 1.1 illustrates the phases of a generic compiler.) Compilers change the form of the program code; they can remove unnecessary instructions, as for example, when 0 is added to a variable; they can add helpful instructions, say, to check that array indices are in bounds; they can move instructions around, say hoisting them out of loops when the value computed isn't affected by the iteration;

and they can perform other amazing transformations. But the general algorithm is preserved. Whether it was sequential or parallel in the source form, the algorithm will remain fundamentally the same in the object form.

Thus, although automatic parallelization by compiler would be wonderful, we must consider other approaches. First, consider how sequential and parallel algorithms for the same task might differ.

A Paradigm Shift

To make it clear that sequential and parallel algorithms are different, compare alternative algorithms for finding the sum of a sequence of numbers. This example is sufficiently simple that there *are* compiler techniques to identify it and generate a more parallel solution, but we choose it because it is a simple illustration of the conceptual difference between a sequential solution and a parallel solution.

To begin, we assume that the sequence has n data values,

$$x_0, x_1, x_2, ..., x_{n-1}$$

and that these have been stored in an array, x.

Iterative Sum. Perhaps the most intuitive solution is to initialize a variable, call it sum, to 0 and then iteratively add the elements of the sequence. Such a computation is typically programmed using a loop with an index value to reference the elements of the sequence, as follows:

```
1   sum = 0;
2   for(i=0; i<n; i++)
3   {
4      sum+=x[i];
5   }
```

This computation can be abstracted as a graph showing the order in which the numbers are combined (see Figure 1.2). Such solutions are intuitive because most of us first learn programming in this style.

Of course, addition over the real numbers is an associative and commutative operation, implying that its values need not be summed in the order specified, least index to greatest index. We can add them in another order—perhaps one that admits more parallelism—and get the same answer.

Nonassociativity. Strictly speaking, addition is not associative on the fixed precision representation of a floating point numbers, because they only approximate real numbers. For some sequences of values, different orders of addition will produce different answers. We ignore such issues and reorder computations to improve performance, reasoning that a) under most circumstances the sequence's order was arbitrary in the first place, and, b) in those cases where it is not arbitrary *and* numerical precision is a potential issue, error management is required throughout the computation.

Note

Figure 1.1
Generic compilation process. In the first phases, the source program is scanned (lexical analysis) and parsed (syntactic analysis), resulting in a program representation known as an Abstract Syntax Tree. In this form the program is type-checked to ensure, for example, that variables are declared. Next, the program is transformed into a linear sequence of simple instructions known as 3-address code. The resulting intermediate representation is improved (grandly called optimization). The resulting code is transformed into machine-specific assembly code. It is then trivial to transform the result into binary code and to assign virtual addresses.

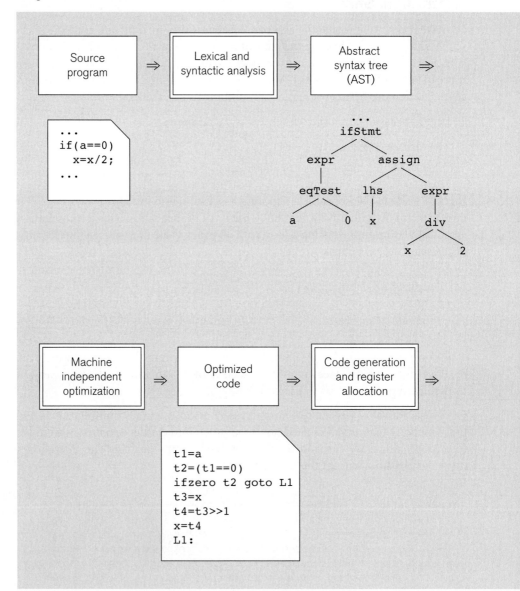

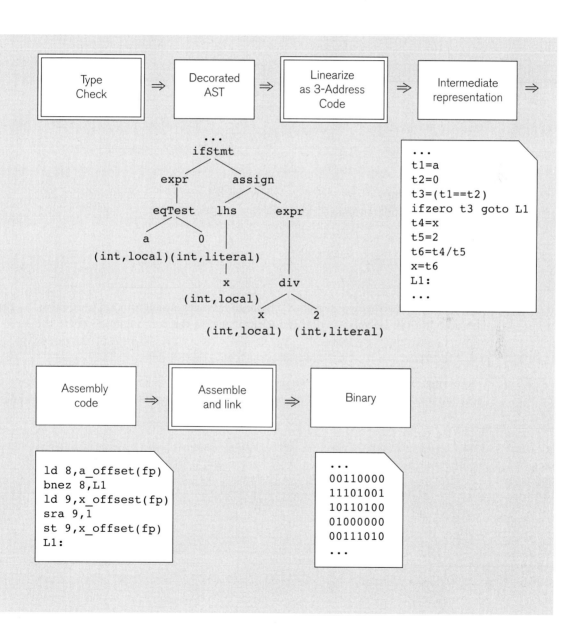

Figure 1.2
Summing in
sequence. The order
of combining a
sequence of numbers
(7, 3, 15, 10, 13, 18,
6, 4) when adding
them to an accumula-
tion variable.

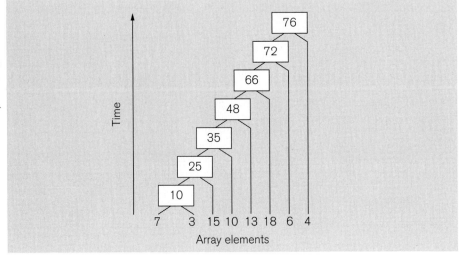

Pair-Wise Summation. Another, more parallel order of summation is to add even/odd pairs of data values yielding the intermediate sums,

$$(x_0 + x_1), (x_2 + x_3), (x_4 + x_5), (x_6 + x_7), \ldots$$

which are added in pairs,

$$((x_0 + x_1) + (x_2 + x_3)), ((x_4 + x_5) + (x_6 + x_7)), \ldots$$

yielding more intermediate sums, which are themselves added in pairs, and so on. This solution can be visualized as inducing a tree on the computation, where the original data values are leaves, the intermediate nodes are the sum of the nodes below them, and the root is the overall sum (see Figure 1.3).

Comparing Figures 1.2 and 1.3, we see that because the two solutions require the same number of operations and the same number of intermediate sums, there is no

Figure 1.3
Summing in pairs.
The order of combin-
ing a sequence of
numbers (7, 3, 15,
10, 13, 18, 6, 4) by
(recursively) combin-
ing pairs of values,
then pairs of results,
and so on.

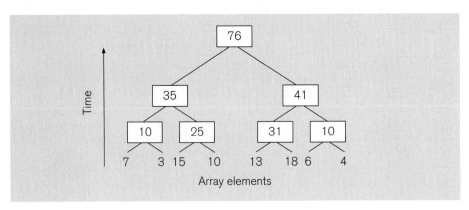

time advantage to either solution when using one processor. However, with a parallel computer that has at least $P = n/2$ processors, all of the additions at the same level of the tree can be computed simultaneously, yielding a solution with time complexity that is proportional to log n. The strategy is a significant improvement over the linear time sequential algorithm. Like the sequential solution, the pair-wise approach is a very intuitive way to think about the computation.

Expressing Parallel Sum. The iterative summation was illustrated using C code, but the pair-wise summation was not. If we are not concerned about writing code for an arbitrary length array, we might write it as follows to highlight the binary tree structure of the computation:

```
1   t[0]=x[0]+x[1];
2   t[1]=x[2]+x[3];
3   t[2]=x[4]+x[5];
4   t[3]=x[6]+x[7];
5   t[4]=t[0]+t[1];
6   t[5]=t[2]+t[3];
7    sum=t[4]+t[5];
```

The first four assignments can be performed in parallel; after they are complete, the next two (5, 6) can also be performed in parallel.

Parallel Prefix Sum

Closely related to the sum is the prefix sum, also known as *scan* in many parallel programming languages. It begins with the same sequence of n values,

$$x_0, x_1, x_2, ..., x_{n-1}$$

but the desired computation is the sequence

$$y_0, y_1, y_2, ..., y_{n-1}$$

such that each y_i is the sum of the first i elements of the input, that is,

$$y_i = \sum_{j \leq i} x_j$$

Solving the prefix sum in parallel is less obvious than summation, because all of the intermediate values of the sequential solution are needed. It seems as though there is no advantage to, nor much possibility of, finding better solutions. But in fact the prefix sum can be performed in parallel.

The observation is that the summation by pairs approach can be modified to compute the prefix values. The idea is that each leaf processor storing x_i could compute the value, y_i, if it only knew the sum of all elements to its left, that is, its prefix; in the course of summing by pairs, we know the sum of all subtrees (see Figure 1.3), and if we save that information, we can determine the prefixes without directly summing them. To do so, we start at the root, whose prefix—that is, the sum of all elements *before* the elements of the sequence—is 0. This is also the prefix of its left subtree, and the total for its left subtree is the prefix for the right subtree. Applying this idea inductively, we get the following set of rules:

- Compute the grand total at the root by pair-wise sum, as before.
- On completion, imagine the root receiving a 0 from its (nonexistent) parent.
- All non-leaf nodes receive a value from their parent, relay that value to their left child, and send their right child the sum of the parent's value and their left child's value that was computed on the way up; these are the prefixes of their child nodes.
- Leaves add the prefix value from above and the saved input.

The values moving down the tree are the prefixes for the child nodes (see Figure 1.4, where downward moving prefix values are shown in the white square).

The computation is known as the parallel prefix computation. It requires an up sweep and a down sweep in the tree, but all operations at each level in a sweep can be performed concurrently. At most two add operations are required at each node, one going up and one coming down, plus the routing logic. Thus, the parallel prefix also has logarithmic time complexity. Many seemingly sequential operations yield to the parallel prefix approach.

An essential difference between the sequential and parallel algorithms is that we organized the parallel algorithms to change the order of the computation.

Figure 1.4
Computing the prefix sum. The gray node values, computed going up the tree, are from the pair-wise sum algorithm; the white values, the prefixes, are computed going down the tree by a simple rule: send the value from the parent to the left child; add the sum from the left child (that came up) to the value from the parent and send it to the right child.

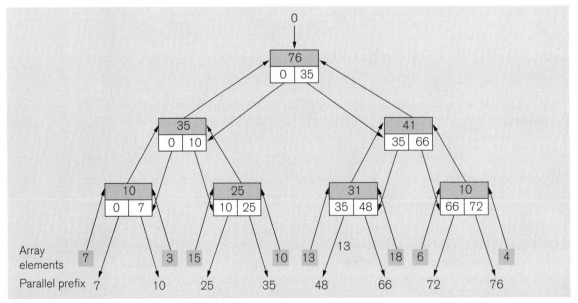

Parallelism Using Multiple Instruction Streams

In this section, we illustrate the complexities of parallel programming by developing a parallel program that solves a trivial problem. It will take us four tries to get a satisfactory result.

We begin by describing one way to conceptualize an instruction stream.

The Concept of a Thread

A *thread*, or thread of execution, is a unit of parallelism. As we will discuss in Chapter 3, a thread has everything needed to execute a stream of instructions—a private program text, a call stack, and a program counter—but it shares access to memory with other threads. Thus, multiple threads can cooperate to compute on global data.

For example, the iterative summation loop previously discussed could be the basis for a thread if we rewrote it as follows:

```
1   for(i=start; i<end; i++)          Caution: Incomplete Solution
2   {
3       sum+=x[i];
4   }
```

The loop index i would be local to the call stack, while the variable sum and the array x would be shared. By assigning each thread a different set of start and end values, multiple threads can work on the problem at once, introducing a form of parallelism.

A Multithreaded Solution to Counting 3s

To understand the obstacles to writing correct, efficient and scalable threaded programs, consider the problem of counting the number of 3s in an array. This computation can be trivially expressed in most sequential programming languages; what is required to solve it using threads?

The Parallel Computer. To make matters concrete, let's assume that we will execute our parallel program on a parallel computer with eight processors, as shown in Figure 1.5. Consider the two processors labeled P0 and P1. Each is shown adjacent to its private Level 1 *cache*, labeled L1. A cache is fast (compared to the RAM) memory for storing instructions and data while a program runs. Each pair of processors (P0 and P1, P2 and P3, and so on) shares a Level 2 cache, which is even larger but slower than the L1 caches. Finally, all eight processors share the Level 3 cache, which is larger and slower than the L2 cache but still faster than RAM. Data can be shared among the processors by exchanging information in the L2 and L3 caches.

Figure 1.5
Organization of a multi-core computer system on which the experiments are run. Each
processor has a private L1 cache; it shares an L2 cache with its "chip-mate" and shares an
L3 cache with the other processors.

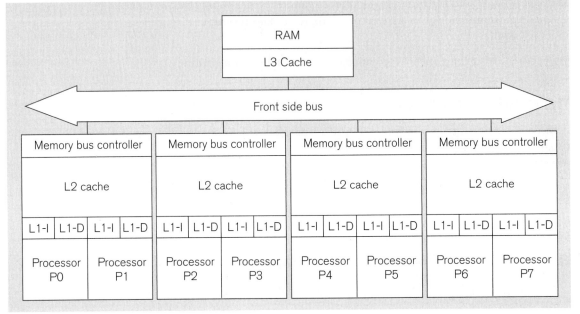

First Solution: Try 1. We will use a threads programming model in which each
thread executes on a dedicated processor, and the threads communicate with one
another through shared memory (including the caches). Thus, each thread has its
own process state, but all threads share memory and file state. The serial code to
count the number of 3s follows:

```
 1   int *array;
 2   int length;
 3   int count;
 4
 5   int count3s()
 6   {
 7      int i;
 8      count=0;
 9      for(i=0; i<length; i++)
10      {
11         if(array[i]==3)
12         {
13            count++;
14         }
15      }
16      return count;
17   }
```

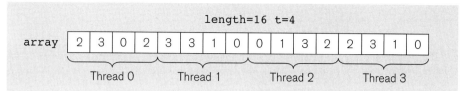

Figure 1.6
Schematic diagram
of data allocation to
threads. Allocations
are consecutive
indices.

To implement a parallel version of this code, we can partition the array so that each thread is responsible for counting the number of 3s in 1/*t* of the array, where *t* is the number of threads. Figure 1.6 shows graphically how we might divide the work for *t*=4 threads and *length*=16.

We can implement this logic with the function `thread_create()`, which takes two arguments—the name of a function to execute and an integer that identifies the thread's ID—and spawns a thread that executes the specified function with the thread ID as a parameter. The resulting program is shown in Figure 1.7.

```
1   int t;                      /* number of threads */
2   int *array;
3   int length;
4   int count;
5
6   void count3s()
7   {
8      int i;
9      count = 0;
10     /* Create t threads */
11     for(i=0; i<t; i++)
12     {
13        thread_create(count3s_thread, i);
14     }
15
16     return count;
17  }
18
19  void count3s_thread(int id)
20  {
21     /* Compute portion of the array that this thread
          should work on */
22        int length_per_thread=length/t;
23        int start=id*length_per_thread;
24
25     for(i=start; i<start+length_per_thread; i++)
26     {
```

Figure 1.7
The first try at a
Count 3s solution
using threads.

(continued)

Figure 1.7
(*continued*)
The first try at a
Count 3s solution
using threads.

```
27      if(array[i]==3)
28      {
29          count++;
30      }
31    }
32  }
```

Unfortunately, this seemingly straightforward code will not produce the correct answer because there is a *race condition* in the statement that increments the value of count on line 29. A race condition exists when the result of an execution depends on the timing of two or more events. In this case, the problem arises because the statement that increments count is typically implemented on modern machines as a series of primitive machine instructions:

- Load count into a register
- Increment count
- Store count back into memory

Thus, when two threads execute the count3s_thread() code, these instructions might be interleaved, as shown in Figure 1.8. The result of the interleaved executions is that count is 1 rather than 2. Of course, many other interleavings are possible, some yielding correct results and others yielding incorrect results, but the fundamental problem is that the increment of count is not an *atomic operation*, that is, it is interruptible.

Second Solution: Try 2. We can solve this problem by using a *mutex* to provide *mutual exclusion*. A mutex is an object that has two states—locked and unlocked—and two methods—lock() and unlock(). The implementation of these methods ensures that when a thread attempts to lock a mutex, it checks to see if it is locked or unlocked. If it is locked, it waits until the mutex is in an unlocked state before locking it. By using a mutex to protect code that we wish to execute atomically—often

Figure 1.8
One of several possible interleavings of references to the unprotected variable count, illustrating a race condition.

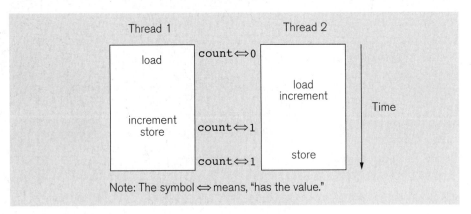

Note: The symbol ⟺ means, "has the value."

referred to as a *critical section*—we guarantee that only one thread accesses it at any time. For the Count 3s problem, we simply lock a mutex before incrementing count, and we unlock the mutex after incrementing count, resulting in our second try at a solution (see Figure 1.9).

Terminology. Mutual exclusion and atomicity are related terms to describe an uninterrupted transformation.

Mutual exclusion. A piece of code executes with mutual exclusion if at most one thread can execute that code at any time.

Atomicity. The term atomicity comes from the database community, where a set of operations is atomic if either they all execute or none executes. Thus, there is no way to see the results of a partial execution.

Definition

With this modification, our second try is a correct parallel program. Unfortunately, as we can see from the graph shown in Figure 1.10, the solution is much slower than our original sequential code. With one thread, execution time is more than four times slower than the original serial code, so the overhead of using the mutexes is drastically harming performance. Worse, when we use two threads, each running on its own processor, our performance is even worse than with just one thread; here *lock contention* degrades performance, as each thread spends additional time waiting for the critical section to be unlocked.

Third Solution: Try 3. Recognizing the problem of lock overhead and lock contention, we implement a third version of our program that operates at a larger granularity or unit of sharing. Instead of accessing a critical section every time count

```
1    mutex m;
2
3    void count3s_thread(int id)
4    {
5      /* Compute portion of the array that this thread
            should work on */
6      int length_per_thread=length/t;
7      int start=id*length_per_thread;
8
9      for(i=start; i<start+length_per_thread; i++)
10     {
11       if(array[i]==3)
12       {
13         mutex_lock(m);
14         count++;
15         mutex_unlock(m);
16       }
17     }
18   }
```

Figure 1.9
The second try at a Count 3s solution showing the count3s_thread( ) with mutex protection for the count variable.

Figure 1.10

Performance of our second Count 3s solution.

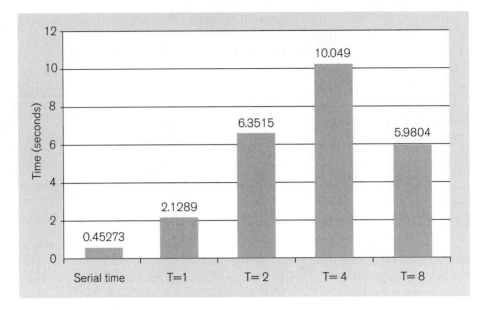

must be incremented, we can instead accumulate the local contribution to the over-all count in a private variable, `private_count`, and only access the critical section for updating count once per thread. Our new code for this third solution is shown in Figure 1.11.

In exchange for a tiny amount of extra memory, our resulting program now exe-cutes considerably faster, as shown by the graph in Figure 1.12.

We see that with one thread our execution is close to the time of the serial code, so our latest changes have removed most of the locking overhead. However, with two threads there is still significant performance degradation. This time, the perfor-mance problem is more difficult to identify by simply inspecting the source code. We also need to understand some details of the underlying hardware. In particular, our hardware uses a protocol to maintain *coherent caches*, that is, to ensure that both processors "see" the same memory image. If processor 0 modifies a value at a given memory location, the hardware will invalidate any cached copy of that memory location that resides in processor 1's L1 cache, thereby preventing processor 1 from accidentally accessing a stale value of the data. This cache coherence protocol becomes costly if two processors take turns repeatedly modifying the same data, because the data will repeatedly bounce between the two caches.

Fourth Solution: Try 4. In our code, there does not seem to be any shared mod-ified data. However, the unit of cache coherence is known as a cache line, and for our machine the cache line size is 64 bytes. Thus, although the threads on processors P0 and P1 have exclusive access to either `private_count[0]` or `private_count[1]`, the underlying machine places them on the same 64 byte cache line; because cache coherence is maintained at the granularity of a cache line,

Figure 1.11
The `count3s_thread()` for our third Count 3s solution using
`private_count` array elements.

```
 1   private_count[MaxThreads];
 2   mutex m;
 3
 4   void count3s_thread(int id)
 5   {
 6     /* Compute portion of array for this thread to
          work on */
 7     int length_per_thread=length/t;
 8     int start=id*length_per_thread;
 9
10     for(i=start; i<start+length_per_thread; i++)
11     {
12       if(array[i] == 3)
13       {
14         private_count[id]++;
15       }
16     }
17     mutex_lock(m);
18     count+=private_count[id];
19     mutex_unlock(m);
20   }
```

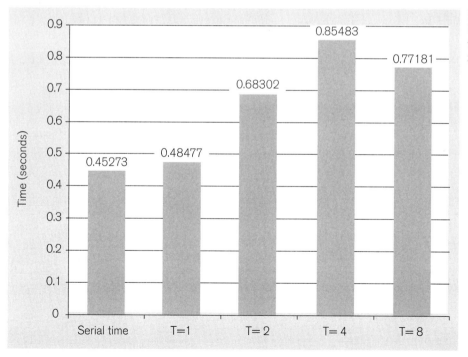

Figure 1.12
Performance results
for our third Count
3s solution.

a modification of any part of a cache line is equivalent to a modification of the entire line, so this shared cache line bounces between the caches as `private_count[0]` and `private_count[1]` are repeatedly updated (see Figure 1.13). This phenomenon in which logically distinct data shares a physical cache line is known as *false sharing*. To eliminate false sharing, we can pad our array of private counters so that each resides on a distinct cache line (see Figure 1.14).

With this padding, the fourth solution removes both the overhead and contention of using mutexes, and we have largely achieved success, as shown in Figure 1.15. Our parallel solution running on one thread is almost as fast as the serial execution, the execution time of the parallel program is close to twice as fast when there are two threads, and it is almost four times as fast when there are four threads.

The only remaining problem with our solution is that with eight threads, the performance is no better than with four threads. There could be many possible reasons—related to the specifics of the hardware—for this behavior, but we conjecture that the L2 memory bandwidth is insufficient for such a large array. Figure 1.16 supports this conjecture by repeating the experiment on an array that does not contain any 3s. We see that even in this situation where there is no updating of shared variables, there is no performance improvement in moving from four to eight threads. While the Count 3s computation is unrealistic in the sense that it performs almost no work in relation to the amount of memory that it touches, this graph does point out one issue that will arise with future multi-core chips, namely, limited bandwidth to memory. Without changes in I/O technology, the bandwidth per core will shrink as increased transistor density supports a greater number of cores per chip without significantly increasing the chip perimeter on which I/O pins can be placed.

Figure 1.13
False Sharing. A cache line moves from RAM to the L3 cache, then to the L2 cache, and then to the L1 cache when a thread references its `private_count`. When the other thread references its `private_count`, the copy in the other L1 is invalidated, written back to the L2 cache, and then fetched into the other L1 cache. The line bounces between the L1 caches and the L2 cache, because although the references are to distinct memory locations, they use the same cache line.

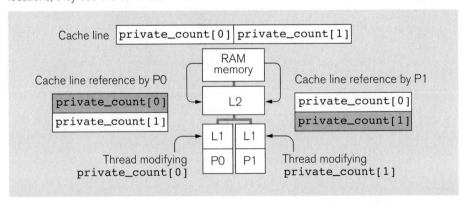

```
1    struct padded_int
2    {
3        int value;
4        char padding[60];
5    } private_count[MaxThreads];
6
7    void count3s_thread(int id)
8    {
9        /* Compute portion of the array this thread should
            work on */
10       int length_per_thread=length/t;
11       int start=id*length_per_thread;
12
13       for(i=start; i<start+length_per_thread; i++)
14       {
15           if(array[i] == 3)
16           {
17               private_count[id]++;
18           }
19       }
20       mutex_lock(m);
21       count+=private_count[id].value;
22       mutex_unlock(m);
23   }
```

Figure 1.14 The count3s_thread() for our fourth solution to the Count 3s computations; the private count elements are padded to force them to be allocated to different cache lines.

Figure 1.15

Results for our fourth solution to the Count 3s problem shows that one processor has performance that is close to the sequential solution, that performance is almost twice as good with two processors and four times as good with four processors, but that eight processors provide no additional performance advantage.

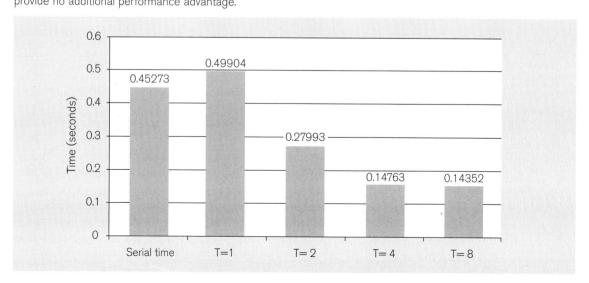

Figure 1.16
Performance for our fourth solution to the Count 3s problem on an array that does not contain any 3s suggests that memory bandwidth limitations are preventing performance gains for eight processors.

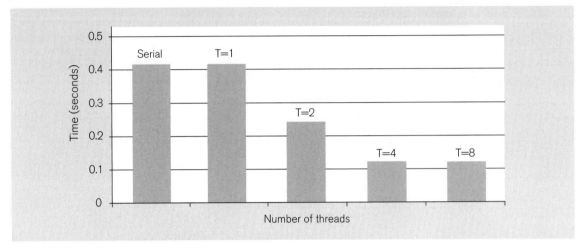

Note

Our Methodology. These results were obtained on an 8 processor Intel Xeon consisting of four 7100-series dual core microprocessor chips running at 2.60GHz. The system has three caches:

L3 cache:	4 MB, unified, 16-way associative
	64B cache line size
L2 cache:	1 MB (per core, total: 2 MB), unified, 8-way associative
L1 cache:	16 KB data and 16 KB instruction, 8-way associative

The program operates on a 50M entry array that is randomly populated with 30% 3s and reports the average of 1000 program runs (including thread creation and destruction) using a microsecond timer. The results were obtained using GNU/Linux 2.6.19-gentoo-r5 and gcc version 4.1.2 with −O2 optimizations turned on.

From this example, we can see that producing correct and efficient parallel programs can be considerably more difficult than writing correct and efficient serial programs. The use of mutexes illustrated the need to control the interaction among processors carefully. The use of private counters illustrated the need to reason about the granularity of parallelism—that is, the frequency with which processes interact with one another. The use of padding showed the importance of understanding machine details, as sometimes small details can have large performance implications. It is this collection of interacting considerations that often makes parallel performance tuning difficult. Finally, we have seen two examples where we can trade off a small amount of memory for increased parallelism and increased performance.

The Goals: Scalability and Performance Portability

The Count 3s program illustrates both that performance can be achieved through parallelism and that achieving it can be complicated. Having mastered some of the issues facing multi-core processors—race conditions, issues of granularity, and false sharing—it's tempting to think that parallel programming is concerned only with issues of correctness and performance. In fact, the goals of this book are broader. Our goal is to help you write good parallel programs, by which we mean parallel programs with four characteristics:

- They are correct
- They achieve good performance
- They are scalable to large numbers of processors
- They are portable across a wide variety of parallel platforms

The first goal does not require explanation, other than to notice that correctness can often be more difficult to achieve in a parallel program than in a sequential program. The second goal seems pretty clear, but as we will see in Chapter 3, defining what we mean by "good performance" is filled with subtleties.

The third and fourth goals, however, require some elaboration because they appear to be overly lofty and often unnecessary. For example, someone who programs a processor with a few cores has little interest in a parallel supercomputer with many thousands of processors. Indeed, there will always be some markets where the extreme desire for performance will dictate low-level non-portable solutions. But for the vast majority of programmers, scalability and portability are important because the landscape of parallel hardware is changing rapidly. For example, the first multi-core chips had only two cores per chip, but Intel has already discussed chips with 80 cores. Of course, as the number of cores increases, other micro-architectural features, such as the memory system, will have to change as well. Given this highly fluid hardware landscape, it's best not to be caught scrambling when new hardware arrives. The solution is to design for scalability and portability from the beginning, so that programs will enjoy a long lifetime, justifying the significant intellectual and economic investment in their creation.

Let's now briefly consider scalability and portability in more detail.

Scalability

To understand the issue of scalability, consider how our code is affected by increasing the number of processors. The Count 3s program was parameterized so that the number of threads could vary. This flexibility allows us to run the program on a sixteen-core chip with little modification. It would seem that we have produced a general solution that could scale to thousands simply be changing `maxThreads`. But we have not. It's true that the scan of the array, having been broken into segments, is independent, and therefore parallel for any number of threads. But the combining of the intermediate results is not, because all threads update one global sum. For a large number of threads, we would again encounter lock contention. Obviously, our pair-wise sum approach would fix this problem. Scalability requires scalable programming practices.

More generally, as the number of parallel processors increases, physical constraints force design changes that impact how programs perform. For example, communication latency—the delay encountered when transmitting information among processors—necessarily increases as the number of processors grows simply because of speed of light limitations. On a single chip, different issues apply, but they still affect communication latency when the number of cores grows large. For a small number of processors, proximity allows certain operations to be fast, but these operations do not remain fast as the size of the system grows. Exploiting these benefits makes sense when possible, but the program must avoid relying on them for its success. Well-written parallel programs can exploit the fast components and avoid over-using the slow components of a parallel computer.

Performance Portability

The problem just discussed—that physical constraints impact the characteristics of parallel computers as the number of processors increases—is not limited to slowing down certain operations. The problem is much more insidious.

Architects, grappling with physical constraints, have created scores of parallel computer designs. These machines can differ dramatically from each other. Unlike the sequential case, where a new computer usually requires only a recompilation of the source code to execute respectably well, a program running well on one parallel machine may have to be rewritten for a new one.

To give one example, parallel computers can mostly be divided into one of three classes: shared memory, typified by multi-core processors, shared address space, typified by various supercomputers, and separately addressed memories (shared nothing), typified by clusters. This distinction affects every memory reference in a program, so it has a tremendous impact on how the program should be written. Programs intended to port to all of these platforms must be robust to these differences in memory structure, and techniques for ensuring robustness will concern us throughout the book.

The classification by memory capability specifies the variety along one axis. There are many other differences among parallel processors. We could solve the portability problem by simply setting a high enough level of abstraction that none of these differences is visible; then, a compiler will map the high level specification to the platform. The strategy will make our programs insensitive to the parallel hardware, but it's not a good idea. Generally, though compilers can perform the mapping, they will usually introduce software layers to implement the abstractions; the added software hides the performance features of the hardware, making it difficult for program-mers to know how their code behaves. We cannot divorce ourselves entirely from the underlying hardware if we want high performance. So, we will use a different strategy, described in Chapter 2.

Our goal, then, is portability with performance, often called *performance portability*. It's not enough for the program to run on different parallel machines. It must run well on all of them.

Principles First

This book does not provide a step-by-step tutorial for writing good parallel pro-grams. Instead, it emphasizes the principles underlying parallel computation, explaining the various phenomena and explaining why they represent opportunities or barriers to successful parallel programming. Our reasons for this approach are twofold. First, by focusing on principles, we hope to provide enduring knowledge that will outlive the specifics of the latest hardware or software technology, which as we've pointed out, change rapidly. Second, and more importantly, the parallel pro-gramming community does not yet have all of the answers, so a step-by-step solu-tion is not available. Indeed, one of our goals is to inspire the next generation of researchers to understand the limitations of current technology so that they can build the better solutions of tomorrow.

After presenting these principles, we discuss some popular programming languages and tools used for programming contemporary parallel machines. Again, our goal is more concerned with the principles behind the approaches than with turning the reader into an expert in a specific language. Our treatments, therefore, are minimal, and readers should expect to consult reference manuals for more complete and detailed information.

Chapter Summary

The chapter began with the observation that parallelism—doing two or more things at once to achieve a single goal—is a familiar idea that we encounter in everyday life. Though familiar, parallelism has not been a significant aspect of programming in the past because sequential computer performance has increased steadily for decades. Such improvements have been due to a combination of technology improvements and the incorporation of parallelism into sequential processor design by computer architects (hidden parallelism). Because the architectural opportunities have largely been mined, the continued advancement of technology has made computers with multiple processors standard. This shift is having a pro-found effect on computer programming.

We noted that existing sequential programs generally cannot take advantage of a parallel computer. The primary reason is that existing programming languages and standard programming techniques strongly incorporate the sequential processing of the traditional von Neumann computer architecture. Parallel solutions, as illustrated by several simple computations—summation, parallel prefix and Count 3s—illustrated features of parallel computations. Though they might not have been the first solutions to come to mind, they were still quite intuitive. A change in thinking about computation will be required—we called it a shift in paradigm—before programmers instinctively devise parallel solutions to their computational problems.

In a quick and incomplete survey of parallel hardware, we noted platforms as diverse as chips with two processors to server centers with thousands of processors. Though dramatically different in scale and design, their parallel features rely on a small set of fundamental principles. We committed to focusing on those principles with the goal of empowering programmers to strive for parallel programs that achieve high performance, scalability, and performance-portability.

Historical Perspective

Parallelism has been applied in the design of sequential computers since the first commercial machines in the 1950s. A landmark parallel machine was the Illiac IV, built in the 1970s by a team at the University of Illinois, Urbana-Champaign. Though the Illiac IV was successfully programmed in low-level assembly-like code, the task of developing a compiler to translate sequential (Fortran) programs into a parallel form was begun by David Kuck and colleagues. Investigators throughout the community pursued the goal to the end of the century, resulting in an enormous literature on parallelizing compilers.

Exercises

1. Explain the meaning of the following vocabulary related to thread programming:
   a. Thread
   b. Race Condition
   c. Mutex
   d. Lock Contention
   e. Granularity
   f. False Sharing

2. Describe how the pair-wise summation computation can be changed to find the maximum element of an array.

3. Reformulate the pair-wise summation program to solve the Count 3s computation in log n time, assuming $P = n/2$.

4. Reformulate the pair-wise summation program to solve the Count 3s computation assuming that $n = 1024$, but $P = 8$.

5. Rewrite the iterative summation program using `forall`; don't forget about race conditions.

6. Locate the closest parallel computer—in your laptop, perhaps, or in a lab—and find out how many processors it has, how much memory each processor can access, and what languages and software are available to program it. Write a "hello world" program for this computer.

7. As presented, the tree summation algorithm was always illustrated with $n = 2^m$, causing the tree to be perfectly balanced. Revise the algorithm for the case when n is not a power of 2.

8. As presented, the tree summation algorithm requires $P = n/2$ processors, which allows it to achieve full parallelism. Revise the tree summation computation to work with fewer processors.

9. Write any sequence of 16 integers. Create a new sequence of "max prefixes" using the parallel prefix algorithm; build the tree structure (Figure 1.4) and construct the upward and downward value flows. What value "flows into the root" if the algorithm is to work with signed numbers?

10. Write the C code segments executed at the nodes in the parallel prefix algorithm for a) the upward flow, and b) the downward flow.

2

Understanding Parallel Computers

To write efficient parallel programs, it's important to have an understanding of parallel hardware. There is a huge amount of literature on this topic, because so many parallel architectures have been developed over the years. We will not attempt to discuss this subject comprehensively. Instead, our goal is to describe a representative set of contemporary machines to give programmers a good foundation for parallel programming.

Balancing Machine Specifics with Portability

As we discussed in Chapter 1, there is considerable diversity among parallel machines, from multi-core chips with a few processors to cluster computers with many thousands of processors. How much do we need to know about the hardware to write good parallel programs? At one extreme, intimate knowledge of a machine's details can sometimes yield significant performance improvements. However, because hardware typically has a fairly short lifetime, it is important that our programs not become too wedded to any particular machine, for then they will likely have to be rewritten when the next machine comes along. This goal of portability thus tempts us to ignore certain machine details.

The answer to the question, "How much do we need to know" likely will depend on the user. In some situations, programmers are willing to expend tremendous effort to improve performance. Examples include game developers, programmers of embedded systems, and hardware vendors. For many others, the desire for long-lived code will encourage an alternate view that places greater emphasis on portability.

The goals of this chapter, then, are first to illustrate the diversity of parallel computers and then to consider ways of abstracting away from the details to support performance portability. We will start by looking at six specific parallel computers to illustrate how varied these platforms can be. Then, we will abstract away from these machine details by considering two abstract models of parallel computers, the PRAM and the CTA. Finally, we will discuss the three major communication mechanisms that are presented to the programmer, namely, shared memory, one-sided communication, and message passing.

A Look at Six Parallel Computers

We now take a closer look at six parallel computers, which were chosen to reflect the diversity of current parallel hardware. Mostly, the details focus on those topics relevant to programmers, and because we will generalize over these and others, it is not necessary to study the specifics closely.

Chip Multiprocessors

The continuous improvement in silicon technology, popularly known as Moore's Law, has now allowed computer manufacturers to fabricate multiple instruction execution engines, popularly known as *cores*, on a single silicon chip. IBM was the first manufacturer with a multi-core design, announcing its PowerPC 970 in 2002; AMD introduced a Dual Core Opteron chip in May 2005, and Intel introduced its Core Duo Pentium in January 2006. We look first at the Core Duo, though all of these chips will make an appearance in this chapter.

Intel Core Duo. The following are features of the Intel Core Duo design:

- Two 32-bit Pentium processors on a single chip
- Each processor has its own 32K L1 data and instruction caches
- Shared 2MB or 4MB L2 cache
- Shared memory controller, I/O controller, and so on
- Fast on-chip communication between the two processors through shared memory

The Intel Core Duo design is based on the Pentium M architecture; it executes single-threaded code at the same speed as a comparable single processor Pentium M, so there is no penalty for programs that have not yet been parallelized. Figure 2.1 shows the logical organization of the Core Duo. The two processors have 32KB private level 1 caches for instructions (L1-I) and data (L1-D). These caches are supplied by the shared 2 MB (or 4 MB) level 2 cache (L2) capable of storing a mix of instructions and data. The bus controller mediates transfers between the L2 cache and the RAM via the Front Side Bus (FSB).

From the programmer's perspective, the key feature of the Core Duo architecture is that both processors see a consistent shared memory image. When a processor references a location in RAM, the cache line containing that location is transferred to

Figure 2.1
Logical organization
of the Intel Core
Duo. The bus con-
troller interfaces to
the Front Side Bus
that connects to the
RAM.

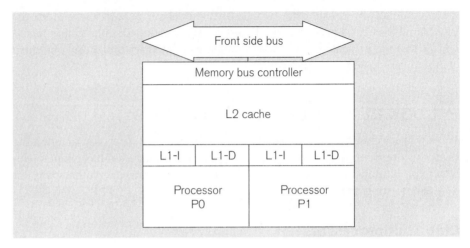

the L2 cache and from there to the L1 cache of the requesting processor. If the other processor also accesses that location, its presence in the L2 cache allows the line to be transferred immediately to that processor's L1 cache. Both processors then have fast access to their local copy of the location.

The complication comes when one of the processors wants to change the value in a location. If one processor changes its private L1 copy while the other processor continues to use its private L1 copy with the old value, then the values would be incoherent and the computation would be incorrect; the old value is said to be *stale*. This situation is avoided through the use of a cache coherency protocol. The protocol limits the interactions among the two L1 caches and the L2 cache to ensure that a processor only writes to a privately cached location when it has exclusive use of that line; subsequent use of that line by the other processor requires that its L1 cache be reloaded with the updated value. The specific protocol for the Core Duo, known as the MESI protocol—MESI is short for Modified, Exclusive, Shared and Invalid, the four possible states of a cache line—is complex, but effective. With it, separate threads can cooperate with the convenience of shared memory.

Though cache coherency may prevent one processor from trashing the other processor's work, there are other complications to connecting two cores on a chip. First, the protocol introduces overhead. That is, to make a modification to a shared cache line, the modifying processor must first obtain exclusive use of the line. For the simple case of sharing on a single chip, the Core Duo has an optimization to make the operation fast; generally, however, it is expensive because it potentially involves interaction among all processors of the system (see the section on Symmetric Multiprocessors Architectures). Second, when two processors are working on a problem, their memory bandwidth requirements can approach twice the bandwidth required of a single processor; the main savings come from sharing instructions. Intel has addressed this problem by doubling the average bandwidth available to the Core Duo.

It is instructive to compare the Intel Core Duo with the AMD Dual Core Opteron, a different 2-processor design of the same generation.

AMD Dual Core Opteron. The following are features of the AMD Dual Core Opteron design:

- Two AMD64 processors on a single chip
- Each processor has 64 K L1 data and instruction caches
- Separate 1 MB L2 cache per processor
- Direct Connect Architecture for shared memory access
- Fast on-chip communication between the two processors through the System Request Interface

AMD took a slightly different approach to the 2-processor architecture than did Intel. Figure 2.2 shows the logical organization of the Dual Core. The processors execute out of private 64 KB level 1 caches dedicated to instructions (L1-I) and data (L1-D). Each processor has a combined private L2 cache of 1 MB. The System Request Interface (SRI) handles the memory coherency responsibilities, ensuring that both processors see a single memory image. (Memory reference basically works as described above, but AMD uses the MOESI cache coherency protocol, which extends MESI by adding an "owned" state that allows cache values to be shared among processors even when the RAM copy is stale.) Requests to RAM (or to other processors) are implemented using the industry standard HyperTransport technology.

Comparison of Chip Multiprocessors. The main difference between the Dual Core and the Core Duo is the position of the L2 cache: In the AMD Dual Core it is private to a processor, and in the Intel Core Duo it is shared. The difference, though subtle, is important. By managing the coherence in the SRI at the "back" of

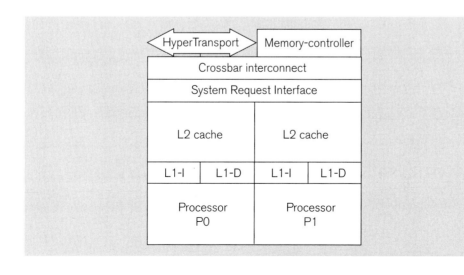

Figure 2.2
Logical Organization of the AMD Dual Core Opteron. The processors address a private L2 cache; memory consistency is provided by the System Request Interface; HyperTransport technology connects to RAM and, possibly, other Opteron chips.

the L2, the AMD design not only gives the processors more private memory but also allows coherence information to be easily combined with that of other processors, leading to a global architecture known as a symmetric multiprocessor (SMP). By contrast, by managing coherence at the "front" of the L2, the Intel design allows a processor to utilize more than its share of L2 cache when necessary, and it supports lower latency on-chip communication. A system using a single 2-processor chip may prefer the Intel design, but a system combining several 2-processor chips may prefer the AMD design. From the programmer's point of view, these two designs are largely indistinguishable. Both designs implement a coherent shared memory.

Symmetric Multiprocessor Architectures

Symmetric multiprocessors (SMPs) are parallel computers in which all processors access a single logical memory; a portion of the memory is sometimes physically near each processor, say, on the same board. To achieve a consistent memory view, the processors are connected at a common point, typically the memory bus, where each processor can *snoop* on the memory reference activity (see Figure 2.3). As an illustration of snooping—there are many protocols—imagine several processors needing to reference a memory block (or cache line) x. If processor P0 requests block x from memory, and processor P1 already has that block cached, then by snooping the bus, P1 notices P0's request and tags its copy of the block as "shared" to indicate that another processor also has a copy. If processor P2 issues a "request

Figure 2.3
Schematic diagram for a symmetric multiprocessor (SMP). Each processor's cache controller makes memory requests over the common memory bus. All cache controllers snoop the memory bus, noticing which addresses are referenced by other processors, and adjusting the tags on their cached values to ensure coherent cache usage.

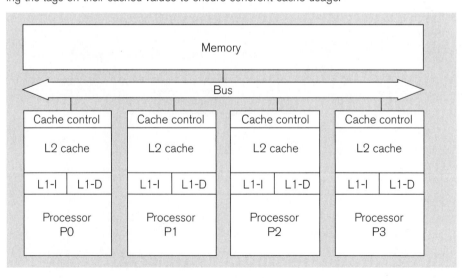

for writing" for block x, then both P0 and P1 see the request and invalidate their copies of x, ensuring that P2 has sole ownership of the block and ensuring that no other processor can use it while it is being changed; when P2 eventually makes the change, the memory will be updated and subsequent requests for block x will reflect the new value.

The common connection point, the bus, is a potential bottleneck, because one memory operation takes place at a time. The serial use of the bus limits the number of processors that can be connected in this way, which implies that SMPs are necessarily small, usually fewer than 20 connections. Notice that the bottleneck is measured in the number of memory requests per unit time, so ample L2 caching helps reduce congestion on the bus. Another implication is that replacing the processors with multiple cores doesn't help to create a larger machine, because the added cores will increase memory requests to the bus, making the bottleneck worse.

SMPs achieve high performance in two ways: first, by being small and necessarily clustered near the bus, they tend to be fast; second, by using sophisticated caching protocols, they tend to use the shared resource of the bus efficiently, reducing the likelihood that multiple communication operations will contend for the bus and possibly be delayed. The AMD Dual Core has an architecture well suited for constructing an SMP. Sun's Sun Fire E25, discussed next, is another example of an SMP.

Hardware Multithreading. Because processor speeds are so much faster than memory speeds, hardware multithreading has become increasingly common. The idea is analogous to context-switching in an operating system: Rather than waiting for long latency events to complete, the processor performs a context switch to some other process. Some multithreaded processors context switch on cache misses, while others, such as the Cray MTA1 (MTA stands for Multithreaded Architecture), context switch on every cycle. Hardware multithreading requires additional resources, so simultaneous multithreading (SMT), which shares hardware resources—bandwidth, cache, TLBs, and so on— among multiple processes, has become quite common. However, the move to simpler multi-core chips may reverse this SMT trend.

Note

Sun Fire E25K. The following are features of the Sun Fire E25K:

- Up to 72 processors, which are each capable of executing two hardware threads
- 150-MHz Sun Fireplane composed of three 18×18 crossbar interconnects for address, response and data, and 18 snoopy buses
- Access latency to shared memory is equal for all processors
- Shared memory of 1.15 TB

The Sun Fire E25K employs an aggressive shared memory design, as shown in Figure 2.4. Each of the 18 E25K boards contains four Ultra SPARC IV Cu processors; each processor can directly access up to 16 GB of memory, resulting in a total of 1.15 TB of shared memory for the system. The boards are connected by three

Figure 2.4
Sun Fire E25K.
Eighteen boards are
connected with
crossbars for
address, data and
response; each
board contains four
UltraSPARC IV Cu
processors; the
snoopy buses are
shown as dashed
lines.

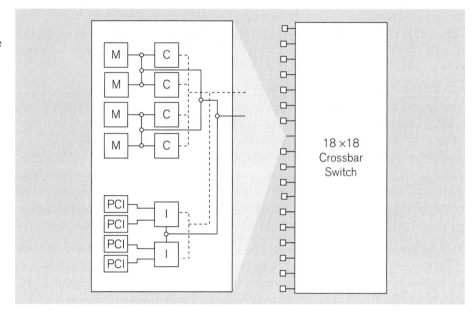

18×18 crossbars dedicated to addresses, data, and responses, which generally handle cache line transfers among processors. Furthermore, there are 18 snoopy buses (dashed lines in Figure 2.4) that enforce memory coherency. The architecture uses a *directory-based* cache coherency protocol among boards. In a directory-based protocol, memory requests are sent to a centralized directory that maintains the state of all cached memory blocks. In contrast to snooping protocols, directory-based protocols are more scalable but have longer latencies, as each memory operation consists of the original request to the directory, the forwarding of the operation to the appropriate cache, and the subsequent response to the requesting processor.

In the E25K design the crossbars provide a substantial amount of communication capability. Figure 2.5 shows a crossbar interconnect of four boards, indicating that there is a direct connection to each pair of boards. Crossbars grow in complexity as n^2 for n nodes, so they are only practical for small values of n, and the E25K's 18×18 approaches the limit. As noted, snooping is a potential source of congestion, but the snooped bus is limited only to a single board. The snooping logic communicates with the rest of the system via the crossbar. With a separate data transmission crossbar handling the movement of cache lines, the coherency traffic can take place in parallel.

Heterogeneous Chip Designs

An alternative to replicating a standard processor several times is to augment a standard processor with one or more specialized compute engines, which are called

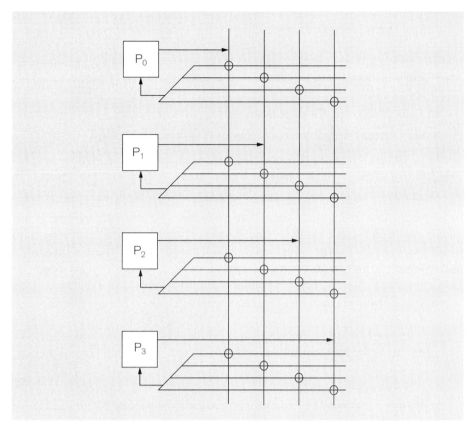

Figure 2.5
Crossbar switch con-
necting four nodes.
Notice the output
and input channels;
crossing wires do not
connect unless a
connection is shown.
Each pair of nodes is
directly connected by
setting one of the
open circles.

attached processors. The idea is that the standard processor performs the general, hard-to-parallelize portion of the computation that probably already executes fast enough, while the attached processors perform the compute-intensive portion of the computation. Among the familiar variations on this design are the following:

- Graphics Processing Units (GPUs)
- Field Programmable Gate Arrays (FPGAs)
- Cell processor, designed for video games

We discuss only the Cell architecture now and return to the topic of heterogeneous architecture in Chapter 10.

Cell. The Cell processor, targeting the video game market, is a joint development by Sony, IBM, and Toshiba. The Cell has a 64-bit PowerPC core and eight special-ized cores, called *synergistic processing elements (SPEs)*, supporting 32-bit vector operations. A key feature is the high communication bandwidth among processors that is made possible by the element interconnect bus (EIB) and the dual 12.8 GB/s memory buses connected to off chip RAM (see Figure 2.6). The following are features of the Cell processor:

- Dual-threaded 64-bit PowerPC processor
- Eight 32-bit Synergistic Processing Elements capable of executing vector instructions
- Each SPE has 256 KB on chip RAM
- High-speed Element Interconnect Bus (EIB) connecting the SPEs

Unlike the other chip multiprocessors that we have discussed, the Cell does not provide coherent memory for the synergistic processing elements, so the designers have chosen performance and hardware simplicity over programming convenience.

In keeping with a design philosophy that emphasizes performance over programmability, SPEs have 128-bit wide data paths that support *vector instructions*, in which one operation is performed on several data values in parallel: 8-bit integer operations on 16 values, 16-bit integer operations on 8 values, or 32-bit integer or (single precision) floating point operations on 4 values. The complication for pro-

Figure 2.6
Architecture of the Cell processor. The architecture is designed to move data: The high speed I/O controllers have a capacity of 76.8 GB/s; each of the two channels to RAM runs at 12.8 GB/s; the capacity of the EIB is theoretically capable of 204.8 GB/s.

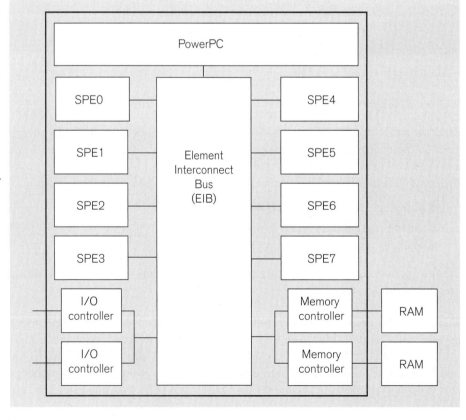

grammers is to carefully manage the movement of data to and from the SPEs so that the vector units can be kept busy. When successful, Cell processors can produce impressive throughput.

Vector Processors. The first successful parallel computers were known as *vector processors*. The Cray 1 is a well-known example. Vector processors augmented a fast sequential (RISC) processor with vector registers capable of containing, say, 64 words of memory. Vector instructions were available to load and store vectors (64-word blocks) from memory, perform basic integer and floating point arithmetic on corresponding elements in two registers, perform reductions (that is, combine the elements of a register), and so on. Though programmers could think of the vector operations as executing in parallel, they were deeply pipelined, allowing them to achieve outstanding performance.

Note

Clusters

Clusters are parallel computers made from commodity parts. The nodes are boards containing one or a few processors, RAM memory, and often times, disk storage. The nodes are connected by commodity interconnect, which is available in several forms, including Gigabit Ethernet, Myrinet, Quadrics, Infiniband, and Fiber Channel. By using commodity parts, clusters have a tremendous price/performance advantage over most other forms of high-end computing. The key property of clusters is that memory is not shared among the machines; a processor, which only accesses the memory on its board, communicates with other processors by passing messages.

Because of the commodity nature of clusters, instructions for assembling a cluster from commodity parts are widely available on the World Wide Web. A typical recipe produces a system with the following:

- Eight nodes each with an 8-way Power4 processor, 32 GB RAM and two disks
- One control processor
- Myrinet 16 port switch plus 8 PCI adapters on four boards
- Open Source software

The instructions both explain how to install the hardware and how to set up the software.

Of course, clusters can also be obtained pre-packaged from manufacturers under the name *blade server*. A blade is a board containing one or a few processor chips, RAM, disk, and communication ports, plus cooling fans. Blade servers vary widely in capability, and all can be programmed as parallel computers. One example is the HP Cluster Platform 6000 blade:

- Any (reasonable) number of blades, each with two dual core Itanium2 1.6 GHz processors with 3 MB cache
- 16 GB RAM per blade

- Double disks per blade, Fiber Channel interconnect
- Myricom Myrinet 2000 interconnect (3.2–2.6 µs NIC latency)

Supercomputers

Supercomputers, which are traditionally used by national labs and large companies, come in a variety of different architectures, including clusters, so it is difficult to speak generally about their designs. One noteworthy modern design is that of the BlueGene/L machine.

BlueGene/L. IBM continues to build large machines for the supercomputer market, the most recent of which is the BlueGene architecture. An interesting characteristic of BlueGene/L is that its processors run at a moderate 770 MHz speed, which is substantially slower than typical PC processor chips that run in the 2–3 GHz range. Nevertheless, because of its large number of processors, an instance of the BlueGene/L architecture jumped directly to the top of the Top 500 list of the world's most powerful supercomputers.

A BlueGene/L installation is configured as follows:

- 65,536 dual core nodes, where each node is a 440 PowerPC processor (see Figure 2.7)
- Each node has 32 K L1 instruction and data caches
- Each node has Double Hummer optimized floating point units that consist of two coupled standard floating-point units capable of four operations per cycle, that is, 2.8 GFLOPS

Figure 2.7
Logical organization of a BlueGene/L node.

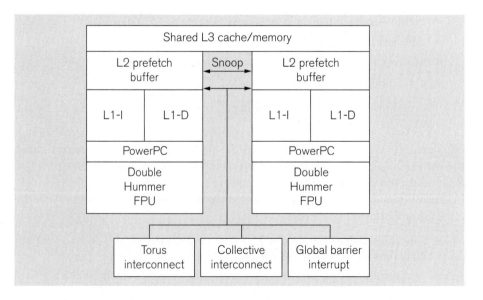

- Each node has a 4 MB sequentially consistent shared on-chip L3 cache and 512 MB of shared off-chip RAM
- Each node has six bidirectional ports to a 3-D torus interconnect
- Each node has three bidirectional ports to a collective network
- Each node has four ports to a barrier/interrupt network

The processor, though running at a moderate clock rate, has all of the usual high-performance processor features including dual issue, out-of-order execution, and single-cycle execution of most instructions, including multiply. The nominal processor rate is therefore 1.4 G operations/second.

The nodes are arranged in a 3 dimensional *torus network*, which is a mesh with its edges wrapped around (see Figure 2.8(a)). Each node is connected to its six nearest neighbor nodes, and the entire BlueGene/L expands to 64×32×32. Communication between processors that are not directly connected in the torus is routed along a path through the network. For example, data needed by the front, upper right node in Figure 2.8(a) that resides in the back, lower left node would be routed, perhaps

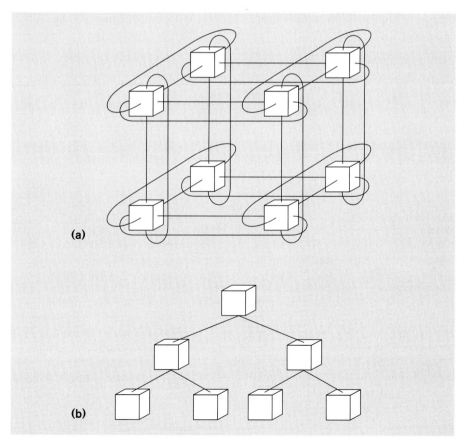

(a)

(b)

Figure 2.8
BlueGene/L communication networks;
(a) 3D torus for standard interprocessor data transfer;
(b) collective network for fast evaluation of reductions.

first in the horizontal direction, then in the vertical direction, then from back to front. Because the routers use a *cut through* routing technique, the data need not stop at each node. The worst case combined network latency, a transmission sent half way across each dimension, is 32 + 16 + 16 hops and takes 6.4 μs.

The *collective network* is a second, independent network connecting the nodes. The network chips have been augmented with arithmetic capabilities so that data flowing through the network can be combined to form, say, global sums (as illustrated in Chapter 1). Such global operations are common in parallel computations. BlueGene/L supports node operations of SUM, MIN, and MAX and bitwise OR, AND, and XOR. Equally important, the collective network supports broadcasts, simplifying one-to-all communication. The advantage of such hardware is tremendous: A global floating point add, which requires two passes through the network, one to find the maximum exponent and the other to sum the mantissas, requires about 10 μs total, which is little more than the worst case communication time to *reference* an arbitrary floating point value.

Finally, the *barrier network* provides a third type of global communication. In concept, the barrier network is a common wire connecting all nodes, which can be used for interrupts, barrier synchronization, and other simple, global communication; its implementation is quite different, of course. The network achieves a round trip latency of 1.5 μs.

When programmers write their code, they have access to 512 MB of RAM shared between the two cores. Since there is no other shared memory, the problem state of a large parallel computation will be divided among the processors' RAMs. Processors send messages back and forth through the torus network to communicate. To simplify programming, the memory structure allows one processor to be dedicated to communication and the other processor to be dedicated to computation. Of course, broadcasts are performed using the collective network, and synchronization is performed using the barrier network.

The Top 500 Supercomputer List. The Top 500 list (www.top500.org) is maintained jointly by the University of Mannheim, the University of Tennessee-Knoxville, and NSERC/LBNL. Computers are ranked by their performance on the LINPACK benchmark, a set of parallel linear algebra routines. Even given its bias toward scientific computations, several trends have become apparent that indicate that high-end parallel computing has diversified. Each year, a wider range of commercial sectors is involved, and these machines are being used by a broader range of companies running a broader range of applications. For example, in the table describing the applications the computers run, the highest reported areas in the November 2007 list were finance (72 entries), geophysics (43), research (38), service centers (28) and semiconductors (25). Another noteworthy trend is the increasing popularity of clusters, which now account for 406 entries on the list. By contrast, when the list was first started in 1993, it was dominated by custom-built supercomputers.

As we discuss later in this chapter, an important figure of merit for a computer architecture is the communication latency, λ, between a processor and any given byte of memory, measured in terms of instruction executions. For BlueGene/L the 1.4 G operations per second times the 6.4 μs network latency is $\lambda = 8960$, not including software overhead.

Observations from Our Six Parallel Computers

How are these six machines similar? How are they different? One difference is in the memory model. The Core Duo, Dual Core, and Sun Fire E25K implement a *shared address space* to a single coherent memory that all processors can access, while the HP cluster and the BlueGene/L implement a *distributed address space* in which each processor can only access a portion of the overall memory. (The Cell represents an attached processor model where the primary processor has global access to all memory and sets up the data streams for the SPEs; this case is considered further in Chapter 10.) With a distributed address space, processors that do not share memory communicate by passing messages to one another. Parallel computers that implement a distributed address space are frequently referred to as *distributed memory machines*.

The shared memory machines seem to be more convenient and natural to program, which raises the question, "Why build all these different types of machines? Why not build shared memory machines with relatively low memory latency and a large number of processors?" There are deep and fundamental reasons why large machines do not implement shared memory. One reason is that speed-of-light delays increase as the machine size increases. But the real challenge is not so much transmitting the information as it is keeping the memory coherent without dramatically increasing the effective memory-reference time. The technical challenges lie beyond the scope of this book, but they can at least be appreciated by observing the extreme differences between the architecture of the Sun Fire E25K and that of the multi-core chips: The Sun engineers had to combine many sophisticated ideas and apply aggressive engineering techniques to raise the number of processors to 72. Every additional increase is a greater challenge. There is little prospect, therefore, that a single, scalable, shared memory architecture will be invented, so parallel architectural diversity will be a fact in the foreseeable future.

Flynn's Taxonomy. In 1966 Michael J. Flynn suggested that computer architectures could be classified based on the number of instruction streams and data streams that they use.

	Single Instruction	Multiple Instructions
Single Data	SISD	MISD
Multiple Data	SIMD	MIMD

(continued)

SISD corresponds to our usual sequential computer, and MISD refers to multiple redundant computations, say for reliability. SIMD describes an instruction applied to many data values, as in Cell's SPE; and MIMD describes different instructions applied to many values, typical of most parallel machines today. Only the SIMD and MIMD terms are in general use.

Because our goal is performance portability, we ask "How can we write programs that perform well on such diverse machines?" The answer is to abstract away unimportant details. It is a proven and familiar approach.

An Abstraction of a Sequential Computer

Given the diversity of parallel machines and the undesirability of writing different programs for each type, it is essential that we have a single accurate model of parallel computers that can guide program development. To reason by analogy, notice that sequential computing has long benefited from such a model: The Random Access Machine (RAM) model, also known as the von Neumann model, after the computer pioneer who first described it. (RAM is the accepted acronym for both random access memory and random access machine; in this book we discuss both extensively, so to avoid confusion, we consistently refer to the latter as the *RAM model*.)

The RAM model abstracts a sequential computer as a device with an instruction execution unit and an unbounded memory. (Computers by definition require other parts, such as input and output, but the model ignores them.) The memory stores both program instructions and data, and any memory location can be referenced (read or written) in "unit" time without regard to its location. This unit time access is the random access feature that gives the RAM model its name. In the RAM model, the instruction execution unit fetches and executes one instruction every cycle, and unless directed otherwise by a branch, it proceeds to the next instruction in sequence on the next cycle. The instructions are primitive, operating on pairs of numeric values. This behavior models our familiar sequential computer.[1] It's so familiar, in fact, that we give it little thought, and we find it difficult to think about any other way to compute.

Before we attempt to use an analogous idea for the parallel case, let's first review how we benefit from the RAM model in sequential programming.

Applying the RAM Model

The simplicity of the RAM model is essential, because it allows programmers to estimate overall performance based on instruction counts within the model. For

---

[1]Today's computers depart in many ways from this idealization, though they continue to function *as if* they matched this description.

example, if we want to find an item (searchee) that might be in an array A of sorted items, we could use a sequential search or a binary search (see Figure 2.9). Given the RAM model, we know that the sequential search will take an average of $n/2$ iterations of the for loop to find the desired item, and we know that each iteration will typically require executing fewer than a dozen machine instructions. The binary search is a slightly more complex algorithm, but its expected performance is approximately $\log_2 n$ iterations of the while loop, which will take fewer than two dozen machine instructions. For small values of n, sequential search will be faster; binary search will be more efficient for larger values of n.

Evaluating the RAM Model

The realization of the RAM model in actual hardware is essential: The model describes how a program will run, and for the model to be useful the hardware has to perform as described. If this were not true, we would need a new model. A mismatch between model and artifact would force us to reevaluate our algorithms and their corresponding programs. Instead, this single long-lasting model has allowed algorithm design to proceed for many years without worrying about the myriad details of each particular computer. This feat is impressive considering that hardware has enjoyed 35 years of exponential performance improvement and 35 years of increased hardware complexity.

Of course, the RAM model is unrealistic. For example, the single cycle cost of fetching data is clearly a myth for current processors, as is the illusion of infinite memory, yet the RAM model works because for most purposes, these abstract costs capture those properties that are most important to sequential computers. While significant performance improvements can be obtained by customizing implementations of algorithms to machine details, the RAM model is successful because it effectively guides algorithm design in the general case.

Figure 2.9 Two searching computations: (a) linear search, (b) binary search.

```
(a) 1   location=-1;
    2   for(j=0; j<n; j++)
    3   {
    4       if(A[j]==searchee)
    5       {
    6           location=j;
    7           break;
    8       }
    9   }
```

```
(b) 1   location=-1;
    2   hi=n-1;
    3   lo=0;
    4   while(lo!=hi)
    5   {
    6       mid=lo+floor((hi-lo+1)/2);
    7       if(A[mid]==searchee)
    8           break;
    9       if(A[mid]>searchee)
    10          hi=mid;
    11      else
    12          lo=mid+1;
    13  }
```

Of course, the model does not apply to all hardware. In particular, vector processors, which can fetch long vectors of data in a single cycle, do not fit the RAM model, so conventional programs written with the RAM model in mind do not fare well on vector machines. It was not until programmers learned to develop a new vector model of programming that vector processors such as the Cray 1 realized their full potential.

The PRAM: A Parallel Computer Model

To translate the success of sequential programming to the parallel case, we need an idealized parallel computer that corresponds to the RAM model. Like the RAM model, it should be minimal and as universal as possible. The obvious extension of the RAM model is the PRAM, a parallel random access machine model. Though it may not be obvious, the generalization doesn't quite work, as we'll see in a moment.

The PRAM consists of an unspecified number of instruction execution units (like those found in the RAM model) connected to a single unbounded shared memory that contains both programs and data. The instruction execution units can follow their own program threads, but they execute instructions in lock step, making synchronization easier. All execution units reference the global memory, and all observe a single sequence of memory state changes, which we will call a *single memory image*. That is, if one instruction changes x[0] at the same time that another instruction changes x[1], then on the next instruction the values of both memory locations will have been updated. Thus, like the RAM model, memory access is in "unit time." One complication of the PRAM model occurs when multiple instructions access the same memory location at the same time. For reading, simultaneous access is often permitted. For writing, attempts to write different values to the same memory location are problematic, and different variations of the PRAM model specify different protocols. They range from outright prohibition to "simultaneous writes to the same memory location must all write the same value" to "distinct writes to the same memory location are allowed, but only one write—chosen arbitrarily—is successful." There is much literature on all of these variations.

Unlike the RAM model, the PRAM does not work well as a model for programmers. It fails by misrepresenting memory behavior, which is curious because simplifying the memory behavior is a key strength of the RAM model. The problem with the PRAM is that it is apparently impossible to realize the unit-time single memory image for scalable machines. That is, allowing all instruction execution units "to see" a single, consistent memory image and to reference memory at instruction execution rates in unit-time is possible only for small numbers of execution units. The multi-core and SMP architectures discussed above do this. But as the number of execution units increases, the delays required to keep the memory image consistent grow dramatically. Thus, the PRAM model's predictions are not observed in practice.

A crucial aspect of the mismatch is that it can lead algorithm designers astray, favoring algorithms that on actual hardware do not perform as well as other algorithms that the model predicts would be inferior. The problem is that by specifying unit time for all memory accesses, the PRAM completely ignores an important performance consideration for parallel computers, namely, communication cost. Because of this difficulty, we adopt a more realistic model of a parallel computer.

The CTA: A Practical Parallel Computer Model

To address the shortcomings of the PRAM, we need a model that accounts for communication costs. We now describe a model—known for historical reasons as the Candidate Type Architecture, or simply the CTA—that explicitly separates two types of memory references, namely, inexpensive local references and expensive non-local memory references.

Problems with the PRAM. The PRAM has been a valuable model for theoretically analyzing the limits of parallel algorithms, but its unit cost memory access time is not helpful for practical parallel programming. Specifically, the model, which would ideally guide programmers in selecting the best algorithm for a problem, directs them to the wrong solution. For example, consider the problem of finding the maximum of an array of elements. The best practical algorithm for finding the maximum is a tournament algorithm, a variation of the pair-wise summation algorithm given in Chapter 1; its performance for $n = P$ processors is proportional to log n. The best PRAM algorithm for finding the maximum is an ingenious idea known as Valiant's algorithm. It works in phases as follows: In the first phase, the n values are grouped into sets of three and processors are assigned to make all possible comparisons, discovering the largest of each set in one time step. Because three comparisons are required to find the largest of a three element set {a, b, c}, a:b, a:c, b:c, the $P/3$ sets will require $3*P/3$ processors, exactly P. This phase reduces the problem size by one-third; in subsequent phases, the sets are larger (seven for phase 2) but there are fewer of them, allowing all comparisons to be performed within the P processor budget. The solution completes in log log n phases, and since each phase is simply a constant number of instructions, the running time is proportional to log log n. As clever as the algorithm is, it's not practical, because, it cannot achieve the predicted running time—which was based on the unit time memory reference assumption—when it is run on actual hardware. Indeed, if we optimistically estimate a communication cost proportional to log P for a computer with P processors, then a phase will take time proportional to log P, implying that the PRAM algorithm would take log n (log log n), when $n = P$, which is somewhat worse than the practical tournament algorithm. So we see that the PRAM model does not guide programmers to the best practical solution.

Note

The CTA Model

A schematic of the CTA parallel computer model is shown in Figure 2.10. It is composed of P standard sequential computers, called *processors* or *processor elements*,

Figure 2.10
The CTA parallel computer model. (a) The schematic shows the CTA as composed of *P*
sequential computers connected by an interconnection network; the computer distinguished
by dashed lines is the controller and serves such clerical functions as initiating the processing. (b) Detail of a processor element. See the text for further details.

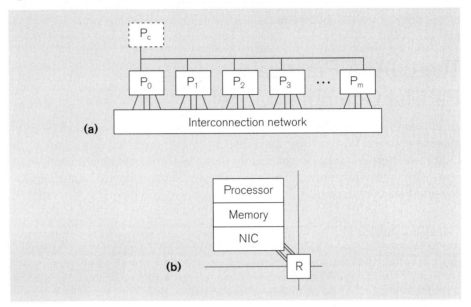

connected by an *interconnection network*, also called a *communication network*. The
processors, described by the RAM model, are composed of an execution engine and
a random access memory, which stores both programs and data. The $P + 1$st processor (denoted by dashed lines) is the *controller*, and its purpose is to assist with various operations such as initialization, synchronization, eurekas.[2] and so on. Many
parallel computers do not have an explicit controller, and in such cases processor P_0
serves that purpose.

The topology of the CTA's interconnection network is not specified. Figure 2.11
shows several common topologies used for interconnection networks. The best
topology for a parallel computer is a design decision made by architects based on a
variety of technological considerations. The topology is of no interest to programmers, so the details are not apparent in the CTA.

A *network interface chip* (NIC) mediates the processor/network connection (Figure
2.10(b)). The schematic in Figure 2.10(a) shows processors connected to the network by four wires, known as the *node degree*, but the actual number of connections

[2]A eureka is an interrupt from one processor to the others, used, for example, when performing a
search.

is a property of the topology and the network interface design; it could be as few as one (bidirectional) connection but typically no more than a half dozen. Data going to or coming from the network is stored in the memory and usually read or written by the direct memory access (DMA) mechanism.

Though the processors are capable of synchronizing and collectively stopping for barriers, they generally execute independently, running their own local programs. If the programs are the same in every processor, the computation is often referred to—recalling Flynn's classification—as *single program, multiple data*, or *SPMD* computation, though this term refers to software whereas Flynn's terms refer to hardware. The designation is of limited use, because even though the code is the same in all processors, the fact that they can each execute different parts of it—they each have a copy of the code and their own program counter—allows them complete autonomy.

Data references can be made to a processor's own *local memory*, which is supported by caches and performs analogously to standard sequential computers. Additionally, processors can reference non-local memory, that is, the memory of some other processor element. (The model has no global memory.) There are three widely used mechanisms to make non-local memory references: shared-memory, one-sided communication, which we abbreviate 1-sided, and message passing. The three mechanisms, described in the subsequent section on Memory Reference Mechanisms, place different burdens on programmers and hardware, but from the CTA machine model perspective, they are interchangeable.

Finally, note that the computers discussed at the beginning of this chapter are instances of the CTA. The BlueGene/L has 65,565 processor elements (dual processors) with local memory, a 3D torus interconnect (six connections to the network), and a controller-hardware (barrier/interconnect circuitry). At the other end of the spectrum, AMD's Dual Core has two processors, a direct connection (or crossbar depending on how the system is logically partitioned to register it with the CTA), and no controller. Other parallel computers can be similarly aligned with the CTA.

Communication Latency

A key aspect of parallel computers is that references to the local and the non-local memory require different amounts of time to complete. The delay required to make a memory reference is called *memory latency*. Memory latency cannot be specified in seconds, because the model generalizes over many different architectures, each built of different design elements from different technologies. Therefore, latency is specified relative to the processor's local memory latency, which is taken to be unit time. This convention implies that local memory latency roughly tracks processor rate, and we optimistically assume that local memory can be referenced at the rate of one word per instruction. Of course, local memory reference is influenced by cache behavior and many aspects of processor and algorithm design, making it quite variable. An exact value is not needed, however.

Figure 2.11
Common topologies used for interconnection networks;
(a) 2-D torus,
(b) binary 3-cube (see Exercise 8),
(c) fat tree,
(d) omega network.

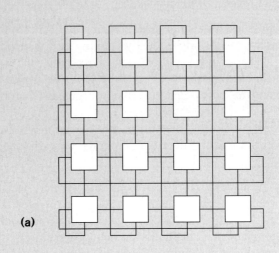

(a)

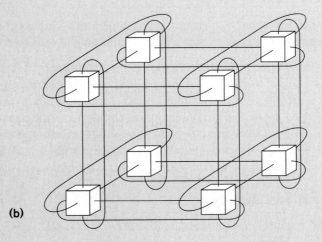

(b)

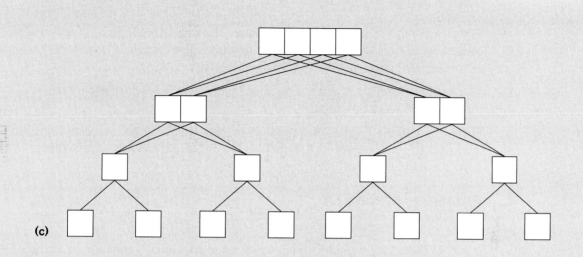

(c)

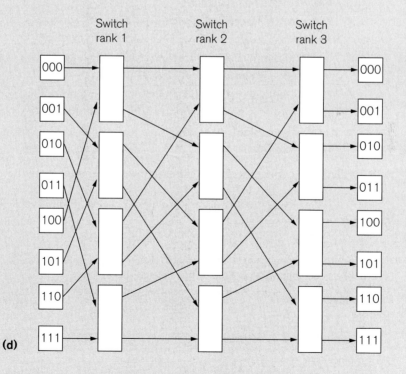

(d)

The non-local memory latency is designated in the CTA model by the Greek letter λ. Non-local memory references are much more expensive, having λ values 2–5 orders of magnitude larger than local memory reference times. As with local memory reference, the cost of non-local references is influenced by many factors, including technology, communication protocols, topology, node degree, network congestion, and the distance between communicating processors. But the numbers are so large that knowing them exactly is unnecessary.

To illustrate, Table 2.1 provides estimated values of λ for each type of machine introduced earlier in this chapter.

Finally, as with the RAM model, the CTA ignores external I/O. Obviously, I/O is important to performance, but it is even harder to generalize about I/O costs than it is the communication cost of the base architecture.

Properties of the CTA

The following summarizes the characteristics of our abstract machine:

- There are P processors, which are standard sequential computers executing local instructions
- Local memory access time is the usual memory access time of the sequential processor
- Non-local memory access time, $\lambda \gg 1$, can be between 2–5 orders of magnitude larger than local memory access time
- The low node degree implies that a processor cannot have more than a few (typically one or two) network transfers in flight at once
- A global controller assists with basic operations like initiation, synchronization, and so on

We will make further observations later in the chapter after a closer consideration of memory reference mechanisms.

Table 2.1 Estimates for λ for common architectures; speeds generally do not include congestion or other traffic delays.

Architecture Family	Computer	Lambda
Chip Multiprocessor*	AMD Opteron	100
Shared-memory Multiprocessor	Sun Fire E25K	400–660
Co-processor	Cell	N/A
Cluster	HP BL6000 w/GbE	4,160–5,120
Supercomputer	BlueGene/L	8960

*CMP's λ value measures a transfer between L1 data caches on chip.

The consequences of these properties for programming parallel computers can be encapsulated into a simple rule:

Locality Rule. *Fast programs tend to maximize the number of local memory references and minimize the number of non-local memory references.*

This guideline must remain foremost in every parallel programmer's thinking while designing algorithms.

> **Applying the Locality Rule.** To see how the Locality Rule can be applied, imagine a computation in which the threads running on the processors need a new random number *r* for each iteration of an algorithm. The obvious solution is to have one processor store the seed and generate *r* on each cycle, with the other processors referencing the random value. A better approach, consistent with the Locality Principle, is for each processor to store the seed locally and to generate *r* redundantly on each iteration. Though the second solution requires many more instructions to be executed, they are executed in parallel, so they do not take any more elapsed time than one processor generating *r* alone. More importantly, the second solution avoids non-local references, and since it's typically faster to compute a random number than to perform a single non-local memory reference, the overall computation is faster.

The CTA architecture mentions P processors, implying that the machine is intended to scale. Programmers will write code that is independent of the exact number of processors, and the actual value will be supplied at runtime. It is a fact that λ will increase as P increases, though probably not as fast; doubling the number of processors will usually not double λ in a well-engineered computer.

In summary, the CTA is a general purpose parallel computer model that abstracts the key features of all scalable (MIMD) parallel computers built in the last few decades. Though there are variations on the theme, the properties that the CTA exhibits should be expected of any parallel computer.

Memory Reference Mechanisms

The CTA model does not specify whether the memory referencing mechanism is by shared memory, 1-sided communication, or message passing. All three are commonly used and are described in the next sections.

Shared Memory

The shared memory mechanism is a natural extension of the flat memory of sequential computers. It is widely thought to be easier to use than the other mechanisms, but it has also been criticized for being difficult to program (race conditions are easy to create and difficult to find) and for encouraging the creation of inefficient programs by making it too easy to make non-local references. Shared memory, which presents a single coherent memory image to the multiple threads, generally requires some degree of hardware support to make it perform well.

While it is convenient to allow any thread to reference any memory location, the risk is that two or more threads will attempt to change the same location at the same time. Such race conditions occupied our attention in Chapter 1, though that example was particularly easy to handle. Generally, race conditions have a great potential for introducing difficult-to-find bugs, and they motivate programmers to scrupulously protect all shared memory references with some type of synchronization mechanism. See Chapter 6 for more information.

One-Sided Communication

One-sided (1-sided) communication, also known on Cray machines as *shmem* (for shared memory), is a relaxation of the shared memory concept as follows: It supports a single shared *address space*, that is, all threads can *reference* all memory locations, but it doesn't attempt to keep the memory coherent. This change simplifies the hardware by removing the need to implement a complex cache coherency protocol, but it places greater burdens on the programmer because different threads can see different values for the same variable.

With 1-sided communication, all addresses except those explicitly designated as *private* can be referenced by all processors. References to local memory use the standard load/store mechanism, but references to non-local memory use either a get() or put(). The get() operation takes a memory location argument and fetches the value from the non-local processor's memory. The put() operation takes both a memory location and a value and deposits the value in the non-local memory location. Both operations are performed without notifying the processor whose memory is referenced. Accordingly, like shared memory, 1-sided communication requires that programmers protect key program variables with some synchronization protocol to ensure that processors do not mistakenly use stale data.

The term "1-sided" derives from the property that a communication operation can be initiated by only one side of the transfer.

Message Passing

The message passing mechanism is the most primitive and requires the least hardware support. With no support for a shared address space, processors can only access local memory. To reference non-local data, messages are used, with the most basic operations being the send and receive operations, usually denoted send() and recv(). The send() operation transmits a message, which is some amount of data residing contiguously in memory, to some specified processor. The recv() operation accepts a message from some other processor, specifying the address of the local buffer in which to receive the message.

Thus, message passing is a two-sided mechanism, meaning that both the source and destination processors must collaborate to transfer data. Because message passing is initiated by the owner of the data values, a cumbersome protocol is required for some computing paradigms. For example, a processor cannot simply access a remote work queue. Instead, it must request work from the work queue manager. But to receive such a message, the manager must anticipate the request, typically by executing a polling loop that checks for any incoming messages.

Another complication is that programmers must reason about distributed data structures and use two distinct mechanisms for moving data: memory references are used to access local memory, and message passing is used to access non-local memory. On the other hand, message passing programs interact with one another in well-defined portions of their code, so it's been claimed that they are easier to debug than shared memory programs. This same claim would apply to 1-sided communication, which also explicitly identifies communication operations.

Memory Consistency Models

The notion of a memory consistency model has arisen because most modern microprocessors employ latency hiding techniques that improve performance but affect the semantics of parallel programs. Memory consistency models are relevant to parallel computers that implement a shared address space, whether it is through shared memory or one-sided communication.

The most intuitive model is *sequential consistency*, in which the result of any execution is the same as if (1) the operations of all the processors were executed in some sequential order, and (2) the operations of each individual processor appear in the order specified by its program. Unfortunately, sequential consistency limits multiprocessor performance by restricting the use of latency-hiding techniques such as buffering and pipelining.

A *relaxed consistency* model implements weaker ordering constraints than sequential consistency. To understand the motivation for such models, recall that over time, memory latency has been steadily increasing when measured in terms of processor cycles. (Fundamentally, it is difficult to build memory that is both large and fast, so improvements in memory latencies have not kept up with improvements in CPU clock speed.) To reduce the latency of write operations, modern microprocessors employ a *write buffer*, which resides on the same chip as the processor; when a processor issues a write command, the data is stored in the write buffer and the processor continues execution without waiting for the data to actually be written to main memory. Subsequent read operations to *other* addresses can then be serviced by DRAM without waiting for the buffered write operation to complete, thereby reducing their latency but violating sequential consistency. Various relaxed consistency models have been proposed, attempting to formalize the behavior of the memory system while permitting the hardware freedom to reduce the latency of memory operations. Unfortunately, the many different relaxed consistency models differ in subtle ways, and their complex semantics make parallel programming quite difficult.

To understand the difficulties of relaxed consistency, consider a simplified version of Dekker's classic algorithm for mutual exclusion between two processors, which assumes that flag1 and flag2 are both initially 0.

```
processor 1:                        processor 2:
flag1=1;                            flag2=1;
if(flag2==0)                        if(flag1==0)
{                                   {
/* critical section */              /* critical section */
}                                   }
flag1=0;                            flag2=0;
```

Under sequential consistency either flag1 or flag2 is set first, and all subsequent reads will recognize this fact, so we are guaranteed that at any time at most one of flag1 or flag2 will be 0 inside the critical section, ensuring that mutual exclusion is enforced in the critical section.

Under relaxed consistency, processor 1 can set flag1 and while the value is still in the write buffer, processor 2 can read flag1 and see the *old* value. Thus, the invariant that only one flag can ever be 0 is false, and the critical section is not protected.

To support selective sequential consistency, modern microprocessors implement special atomic operations that are guaranteed not to use the write buffer. For example, the following code uses a test_and_swap instruction that atomically tests the old value of a memory location and sets it to some new value.

```
/* critical section is empty when lock=0 */
do
{
   old = test_and_swap(&lock, 1);
} while(old != 0);
/* Enter critical section */
test_and_swap(&lock, 0);
/* Exit critical section: clear lock so others can enter */
```

Because the test_and_swap operation is atomic and does not use the write buffer, only one processor can both set the value to 1 and read an old value of 0, ensuring mutual exclusion to the critical section. Unlike Dekker's algorithm, the above code works for more than one processor.

To date, no one has been able to articulate a memory consistency model that is as practically usable as sequential consistency. Stepping back, one of the larger lessons from this discussion is the observation that parallel programming often breaks abstractions by preventing us from hiding certain low level details.

Programming Models

This section has discussed hardware communication mechanisms, with the implicit assumption that programmers will directly use the facilities provided. We note, of course, that we can always build software interfaces that do not match the underlying hardware interface. One obvious example is the Message Passing Interface—described in Chapter 7—which is almost universally implemented, even on hardware that implements shared memory. Others have also proposed Virtual Shared Memory, in which shared memory is implemented in software on underlying hardware that does not support shared memory, but such systems have typically not produced good performance. Chapter 8 presents a higher level programming language that can be built on top of machines that implement either shared memory, 1-sided communication, or message passing.

A Closer Look at Communication

The large non-local memory latency, λ, specified by the CTA model represents an extreme cost. To the extent that we can avoid it, our programs will run faster. Reducing its impact will be at the heart of nearly all of our programming efforts. This section addresses the question, "Can't something be done to reduce communication latency?" An affirmative answer would certainly simplify programming.

For P processors to communicate directly with each other, that is, for processor p_i to make, say, a direct memory access (DMA) reference to memory on processor element p_j requires that there be wires connecting p_i and p_j. A quick review of the topologies in Figure 2.11 indicates that not all pairs of processors are directly connected. Technically, no processor of the CTA is directly connected to any other; every processor is at least one hop from any other because it must enter the network. However, if in all cases pairs of processors could communicate in one hop we could count this as a "direct" connection, that is, not requiring *navigation* through the network. For the topologies of Figure 2.11, information must be switched through the network and is subject to switching delays, collisions, congestion, and so on. These phenomena delay the movement of the data.

For sound mathematical reasons, there are essentially two ways to make direct connections between all pairs of P processors: a bus and a crossbar.

- In the *bus* design (Figure 2.3) all processors connect to a common set of wires. When processor p_i communicates with processor p_j, it transmits data on the wires, so no other pair of processors can communicate at that time, because their signals would interfere with the $p_i - p_j$ communication. Thus, although there is a direct connection between any two processors, a bus can only be used for one communication operation at a time, implying that the communication operations are *serialized*.

- The *crossbar* design (Figure 2.4) overcomes the problem of serialized communication by connecting each processor to every other processor, which allows any set of distinct pairs of processors to communicate simultaneously. This design is ideal from a computational perspective, because it allows direct, conflict-free data transmission, but it is too expensive. The number of wires necessary to implement a crossbar grows as n^2, making it unrealistic except for very small computers, say $n = 32$ or fewer.

With just these two basic designs available, direct connection is possible only for a very small number of processors, either to reduce the likelihood that communication operations contend (in the case of a bus) or to reduce the cost of the device (in the case of a crossbar).

Because of the difficulties of direct connections, architects have invented many communication networks with varying topologies and protocols that allow parallel computers to scale. There is a large literature on the subject, and Figure 2.11 indicates only a few representatives. All of these interconnection networks implement less connectivity than the crossbar and use fewer resources, thereby incurring longer delays but at a lower cost. The greater delays force us to adopt the large λ value. Furthermore, the value of λ increases as the computer—and, therefore, the size of the communication network—scales, often not smoothly.

Applying the CTA Model

Recall that in Chapter 1 we solved the Count 3s problem assuming a shared memory interface. We began with a straightforward solution (Try 1), found that it had a race condition, which we then corrected (Try 2), found that the terrible performance was due to a common count variable, which led to excessive lock overhead that we then corrected (Try 3), and found that performance still suffered due to false sharing. The final program (Try 4) achieved reasonable performance, although in Chapter 4 we'll make one more improvement to it.

Would the CTA have been a good guide to solving the Count 3s problem? Yes. The CTA, being independent of the shared memory communication mechanism or caching, would not have introduced the problems fixed by Try 2 or Try 4. It would have directed us to avoid the mistake that was fixed with Try 3. The problem was the single global variable count and the lock contention caused by making updates to it. The model would have told us that using a single global variable means that many references would be non-local and therefore incur λ overhead just to update the count; we would know that a better scheme would be to form a local count to be combined later. Guided by the model, we would have written a better program in the first place.

Notice that the model predicted the problem (reliance on a single global variable) and the fix (local variables allocated per thread) but not the exact cause. The model worried about the high cost of referencing the global variable, while the actual problem was the high cost of many threads referencing a single global variable. The different explanations are not a problem as long as the model identifies the bad cases and directs us to the correct remedy, which it did. The CTA is not a real machine. It generalizes a huge family of machines, so it cannot possibly match the implementation of each one. But to give enough information for writing quality programs, it provides general guidance about the operation of a parallel computer, capturing its essential features while ignoring the details. Thus, some implementations do have a memory latency problem referencing the global variable; some don't, but they have other problems, like contention or even stranger problems. Different implementations will manifest the fundamental behaviors of parallel computation in different ways.

Chapter Summary

Parallel computers are quite diverse, as the six computer profiles indicate. It would be impossible to know the hardware details of all parallel machines and to write portable programs capable of running well on any platform. To solve the problem, we adopted the CTA, an abstract parallel machine, as the basis for our programming activities. By designing programs for the abstract machine—in the same way that we design sequential algorithms for the RAM model—we can design programs that can run on all machines modeled by the CTA, which represents virtually all multiprocessor computers.

Historical Perspective

There is an enormous literature on the topics of this chapter. Beginning with Flynn's taxonomy and continuing through present-day processor design, parallel hardware has attracted extensive research. In the theoretical community, the PRAM has been the basis for extensive analysis aimed at identifying the limits to parallelism, as well as the basis for a great many parallel algorithms, including Valiant's algorithm for computing the maximum, which appeared in 1975. The CTA model was introduced in 1986 as a means of unifying parallel computers. Of the three principal methods of interprocessor communication, shared memory and message passing have spawned a huge literature.

Exercises

1. What is the communication cost predicted by the CTA (expressed in terms of λ) for four threads adding 1,024 numbers assuming a single variable, sum, allocated to one processor's memory (Try 2 from Chapter 1)? Assume the data is evenly split among the four processors.

2. Repeat Exercise 1, but revise the algorithm so that each thread keeps a local copy of the count (Try 4).

3. How is a Sunfire E25K modeled by the CTA?

4. How are cluster computers, specifically the HP Cluster Blade Platform 6000 modeled by the CTA?

5. The interconnection network of the CTA specifies simultaneous communication by multiple processors, implying parallel data transmission, but a bus is serialized. Why is it reasonable to use the CTA to model an SMP?

6. Assume the BlueGene/L has one number in each processor, that is, two per node; estimate how long it will take to compute the global sum of those numbers and broadcast the value back to each processor.

7. Using the WWW locate a description of another "blade cluster" configuration and estimate its λ value.

8. A single processor is a 0-cube, two processors connected are a 1-cube; given two n-cubes, connecting corresponding elements produces an $(n + 1)$-cube. In an n-cube, what is the length of the path required to connect two arbitrary nodes?

9. If a "hop" refers to a packet being sent from a node to one of its six neighbors in the 3D Torus of the BlueGene/L machine, how many hops does a packet travel to go from node (1,2,3) to node (4,5,6)?

10. If the BlueGene/L didn't have a combining circuit for global +-reductions, processors would have to implement a tree arrangement as shown in Figure 1.3; how deep—that is, how many levels—would this tree be?

Reasoning about Performance

Performance is perhaps the most important goal of parallel computing, and we saw in Chapter 1 how performance can be difficult to achieve. In this chapter, we introduce concepts that will help us reason about parallel performance. We start by distinguishing between parallelism and performance, and by defining basic terms. After identifying the various factors that limit parallel performance, we explain how we can frame our thinking in terms of dependences, locality, and granularity. We then discuss in more detail the many trade-offs that must be considered to produce efficient parallel programs. Finally, we discuss ways to measure performance—it's not as easy as it might seem—and we use these techniques to show why scalable performance is hard to achieve.

Motivation and Basic Concepts

As the add-a-vector-of-numbers example of Chapter 1 indicates, programs can embody different amounts of parallelism despite requiring the same amount of work; in that case each program had the same number of additions. The naive summation loop produced a sequential specification, which if executed as specified, requires $O(n)$ time because no provision was made for other processes to contribute to the solution. The tree summation was described in a way that allows subcomputations to be performed simultaneously, which with sufficient processing capacity leads to an $O(\log_2 n)$ time execution. Is this the best solution available? What limitations might prevent the best performance? Are there opportunities that are not being exploited? We discuss such issues in this chapter.

Parallelism versus Performance

Ideally, a problem that takes T time to execute on a single processor can execute in T/P time on P processors. Of course, there are several reasons why this ideal is rarely met. First, there is the need to identify at least P-fold parallelism. Second, as we saw in the Count 3s solution in Chapter 1, the parallel computation typically introduces overhead that is not present in the sequential computation. Third, even for well-designed parallel programs, the challenge of meeting the T/P goal becomes more difficult as P increases, because, for example, the marginal advantage of parallelism decreases compared to the overhead costs. But to further complicate matters, there are certain cases where the P processors can produce shorter execution time than predicted by the T/P estimate! Thus, parallelism and performance are related, but they are not the same.

The remainder of this section defines the terms we need to explore these points in detail.

Threads and Processes

There are two common abstractions for describing parallelism: threads and processes.

A *thread* refers to a thread of control, logically consisting of program code, a program counter, a call stack, and some modest amount of thread-specific data, including a set of general purpose registers. Threads share access to memory, so threads can communicate with other threads by reading from or writing to memory that is visible to them all. (Threads also share access to the file system.) Programming with threads is known as *thread-based parallel programming* or *shared memory parallel programming*.

A *process* is a thread that also has its own private address space. Processes communicate with one another by passing messages (or more rarely via the file system). Parallel programming with processes is often referred to as *message passing parallel programming* or *non-shared memory parallel programming*.

Because processes have much more associated state than threads, there is a larger cost to creating and destroying them than there is for creating and destroying threads. Thus, processes tend to be long-lived, while threads are sometimes dynamically spawned and destroyed as a computation proceeds.

Latency and Throughput

Before we begin our discussion of performance issues, we must agree upon the meaning of performance. Though it is common to speak of speeding up a computation, there are two possible aspects of "better speed": latency and throughput. Each represents different issues with different solutions.

> *Latency.* Latency refers to the amount of time it takes to complete a given unit of work.
>
> *Throughput.* Throughput refers to the amount of work that can be completed per unit time.

Parallelism can often be exploited to improve throughput. For example, a pipelined microprocessor executes more instructions per second by dividing the execution of an instruction into multiple stages and then pipelining the execution of multiple instructions, as shown in Figure 3.1. In this example, the time to complete a single instruction is not reduced—in fact, it's typically increased slightly—but a larger number of instructions can complete per second. With the possibility of five instructions executing at once, there is a potential for a five-fold increase in throughput, which translates to a reduced program execution time.

We can sometimes exploit parallelism to hide latency. The idea has been used in operating systems since the Multics system of the 1960s: Instead of waiting for a long latency operation, the processor switches contexts and executes on behalf of another process. The principle—rather than remain idle, try to make progress on some other part of the computation—frequently applies. Such latency hiding techniques do not actually reduce latency; they merely hide the cost of the latency, that is, the lost execution time due to waiting. Note also that such techniques rely on the availability of sufficient parallelism—independent tasks—to keep the processor busy while waiting for the long-latency event. The amount of parallelism needed typically increases as the latency we're trying to hide increases.

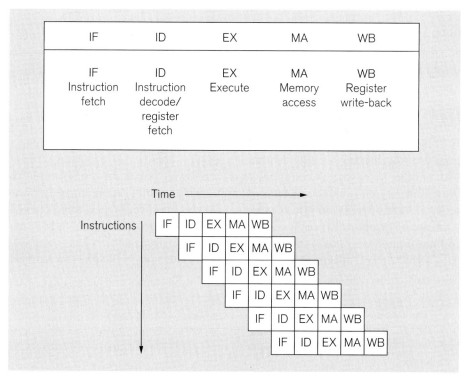

Figure 3.1
Simplified processor pipeline. By dividing instruction execution into five equal-size parts, five instructions can ideally be executing simultaneously, giving (ideally) a five-fold improvement over executing each individual instruction to completion.

Not surprisingly, there are also many hardware techniques for using parallelism to actually reduce latency, such as the use of caches and memory prefetching.

Sources of Performance Loss

While we ideally would hope that P processors could speed up a computation by a factor of P, there are four basic reasons this might not be the case. These causes, which sometimes overlap, are:

1. Overhead, which the sequential computation does not need to pay

2. Non-parallelizable computation

3. Idle processors

4. Contention for resources

All other sources are special cases of these four.

Overhead

Any cost that is incurred in the parallel solution but not in the serial solution is considered *overhead*. There is overhead in setting up threads and processes to execute concurrently and also some for tearing them down, as the schematic in Figure 3.2 indicates.

Because memory allocation and its initialization are expensive, processes incur greater setup overhead than threads. After the first process is set up, all subsequent thread and process setups incur overhead not present in a sequential computation. These costs represent overheads of parallelism.

In general, we recognize four sources of parallel overhead.

Communication. Communication among threads and processes is a major component of overhead. Since a sequential computation does not have to communicate with another processor, all communication is a form of overhead. For example, in the Count 3's solution, false sharing was a form of communication among processors—albeit unwanted communication—as cache lines were repeatedly bounced back and forth among the caches of different processors. In that computation, some communication overhead—for communicating the shared counter—was unavoidable, while other communication—due to false sharing—could be avoided by expending other resources, namely, extra memory.

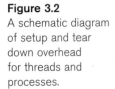

Figure 3.2
A schematic diagram of setup and tear down overhead for threads and processes.

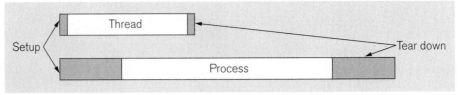

The specific costs of communication will depend on the details of the hardware. Table 3.1 shows the various components of hardware communication costs for different hardware communication mechanisms.

Synchronization. Synchronization is a form of overhead that arises when one thread or process must wait for an event on another thread or process. For example, a thread might wait for some other thread to compute a value or free a resource. For instance, in the Count 3's example, the need for the threaded code to acquire and release locks was synchronization overhead that the sequential code did not have to perform. We saw in that example how such overhead could be significant if the number of lock acquisitions were too numerous. Synchronization is implicit in many forms of message passing, while synchronization is often explicit when programming with threads.

Computation. Parallel computations almost always perform extra computations that are not needed in the sequential solution. An example would be figuring out what part of a computation a thread is responsible for. In the Count 3s example, this overhead was minimal. Another example is computation that appears in the sequential program as well as in *each* of the threads; initializations are an example because t threads execute the code t times, not once. These redundant computations represent a special case of non-parallelizable code, which we will discuss in more detail shortly.

Memory. Parallel computations often incur a memory overhead. While such overheads do not always hurt performance—in the case of the Count 3's example the extra padding, which is memory overhead, actually improves performance—they can be significant for parallel computations whose size is limited by memory constraints.

Non-Parallelizable Code

Of course, if a computation is *inherently sequential*—meaning it cannot be parallelized— then using more processors will not improve its performance. Sometimes such code is expressed in a parallel computation as redundant computation. For example, if both the sequential and parallel computation loop k times, then the loop overhead—such as incrementing the induction variable and testing for termination—is not sped up by parallelism. In other cases, a single thread or process will

Table 3.1 Sources of communication overhead by communication mechanism.

Mechanism	Components of Communication Cost
Shared Memory	Transmission delay, coherency operations, mutual exclusion, contention
1-sided	Transmission delay, mutual exclusion, contention
Message Passing	Transmission delay, data marshalling, message formation, demarshalling, contention

perform the computation while the others sit idle. An example might be disk I/O, where some processors are not attached to the network and must remain idle while I/O is being performed.

Amdahl's Law. The existence of non-parallelizable computations is important because it limits the potential benefit from parallelization. *Amdahl's Law* observes that if $1/S$ of a computation is inherently sequential, then the maximum performance improvement is limited to a factor of S. The reasoning is that the execution time, T_p, of a parallel computation will be the sum of the time for its sequential component and its parallelizable component. If the computation takes T_S time to execute sequentially, then for P processors we have

$$T_p = 1/S \cdot T_S + (1 - 1/S) \cdot T_S / P$$

Imagining a value of P so large that the parallelizable portion takes negligible time, the maximum performance improvement is a factor of S. That is, the proportion of sequentially executed code in a computation determines its potential for improvement using parallelism.

> **Note**
>
> **Amdahl's Law.** Amdahl's Law was enunciated in a 1967 paper by Gene Amdahl, an IBM computer architect. It is a law in the same sense that the Law of Supply and Demand is a law: It describes a relationship between two components of program execution time, as expressed by the equation given in the text. Both laws are powerful tools to explain the behavior of important phenomena, and both laws assume as constant other quantities that affect the behavior. In particular, Amdahl's Law applies to a single program instance.

The situation is actually somewhat worse than Amdahl's Law implies. One obvious problem is that the parallelizable portion of the computation might not be improved to an unlimited extent—that is, there is probably an upper limit on the number of processors that can be usefully employed and still improve the performance—so the parallel execution time is unlikely to vanish. Furthermore, as mentioned in the last section, a parallel implementation often executes more total instructions than the sequential solution, making the $(1 - 1/S) \cdot T_S$ an underestimate.

Many, including Amdahl, have interpreted the law as proof that applying large numbers of processors to a problem will have limited success, but this seems to contradict reports in which huge parallel computers improve computations by huge factors. What gives?

Amdahl's law describes a key fact that applies to an *instance* of a computation. Portions of a computation that are sequential will, as parallelism is applied, dominate the execution time. The law fixes an *instance* and considers the effect of increasing parallelism. Most parallel computations fix the parallelism and expand the size of the instances. In such cases, the proportion of sequential code often diminishes as larger instances are considered. Therefore, doubling the problem size may increase the sequential portion negligibly, making a greater fraction of the problem available for parallel execution.

In summary, Amdahl's law does not deny the value of parallel computing. Rather, it reminds us that to achieve parallel performance we must be concerned with the entire program.

Contention

Contention is the degradation of system performance caused by competition for a shared resource. We could consider contention a special case of overhead, but contention deserves special attention because its effects can often lead to slowdown, that is, worse performance than we'd get with a single processor. For example, we saw in Chapter 1 how lock contention can reduce performance by creating excessive load on the memory. In particular, if the lock is implemented as a *spin lock*, in which a waiting thread repeatedly checks for the availability of a lock, the waiting lock will increase bus traffic. Such contention is particularly harmful because it affects all threads that attempt to access the shared bus, even those that are not contending for the same lock. Chapter 1 also illustrated a second form of contention, when false sharing degraded performance by causing data values to bounce back and forth among different caches. In that case, two local caches were contending for the same cache line, but the effects were seen by all processors in the form of increased bus traffic.

Idle Time

Ideally, all processors are working all of the time, but this might not be the case. A process or thread might not be able to proceed due to a lack of work or because it is waiting for some external event, such as the arrival of data from some other process. Thus, idle time is often a consequence of synchronization and communication. As the next section on dependences demonstrates, idle time manifests itself in many ways.

Load Imbalance. One common source of idle time is an uneven distribution of work to processors, which is known as *load imbalance*. The extreme example occurs when a sequential computation runs on one processor of a parallel machine, while the other processes remain idle. In other cases, there is work that can be executed in parallel, but the workload is unevenly assigned.

For example, in the tree-based parallel summation in Chapter 1, the first set of pair-wise sums to be computed required $n/2$ processors, the next set of pair-wise sums required $n/4$ processors, and so on. Thus, after the first step of the computation, half of the processors were idle while the summation was performed. In Chapter 4, we will see a clever way to reduce the impact of such imbalances.

Memory-Bound Computations. A processor may also stall if it is waiting for a memory operation, such as a read from DRAM. There are two aspects of memory system performance—bandwidth and latency. DRAM latencies have historically improved at a slower rate than processor speeds, so the distance to DRAM in terms of CPU cycles continues to increase. When data can be kept in caches, these latencies can be avoided, but computations that exhibit poor locality or that access large amounts of data must often access the slower DRAM. DRAM bandwidth is important for two reasons. First, many latency-hiding techniques, such as prefetching and hardware multithreading, introduce extra memory traffic in an attempt to reduce memory latency. Second, even computations whose working sets can reside in cache must consume memory bandwidth as they load these caches.

Bandwidth Constrained Multi-Core Chips. Memory bandwidth constraints are particularly problematic for multi-core chips because while the number of cores can increase in proportion to the exponentially increasing transistor density, memory-bandwidth and I/O-bandwidth are limited by the number of pins on a chip, which are currently restricted to the edges of the chip. New process technologies may address this bandwidth issue, but the solutions are not yet commercially available.

Parallel Structure

Having seen how various factors can degrade parallel performance, we now turn to three closely related concepts that can help us avoid such problems. The notion of dependences provides a way to reason about sources of inefficiency; the concept of granularity helps us match a computation to the underlying hardware's resources; and the goal of locality guides us to think about solutions that will naturally have suitable granularity and few dependences.

Dependences

A *dependence* is an ordering relationship between two computations. Dependences can arise in different ways in different contexts. For example, a dependence can occur between two processes when one process waits for a message to arrive from another process. Dependences can also be defined in terms of *read* and *write* operations, which for threaded computations correspond to memory loads and stores. Consider a program that requires a particular memory location to be read (loaded) after it is written (stored).

For the correct result to be produced, there is a dependence between the write operation and the read operation; see Figure 3.3. If the order of the two operations is skewed in time so that the Thread 2 read precedes the Thread 1 write, the dependence would be violated and the semantics of the program would be altered (see Figure 1.8 for an example of this situation). Any ordering of the execution that obeys all dependences will produce the same result as the originally specified pro-

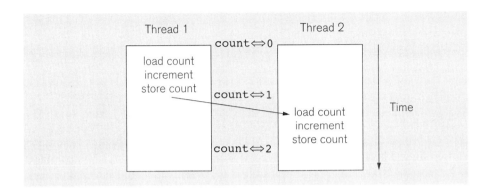

Figure 3.3
A dependence
between a memory
write (store) opera-
tion of one thread
and the memory read
(load) of another
thread.

gram. Thus, the notion of dependences allows us to describe and to distinguish those execution orderings that are necessary for preserving program correctness and those that are not.

Dependences provide a general way to describe limits to parallelism, so they are not only useful for reasoning about correctness, but also they provide a way to reason about potential sources of performance loss. For example, a data dependence that crosses a thread or process boundary creates a need to synchronize or communicate between the two threads or processes. By knowing that the data dependence exists, we can understand the consequences for parallelism even if we don't know what aspect of the computation caused the ordering relationship in the first place. To make this point more concrete, let's consider a specific type of dependence, known as data dependences.

Data Dependence. A data dependence is an ordering on a pair of memory operations that must be preserved to maintain correctness. There are three kinds of data dependences:

- *Flow dependence*: read after write
- *Anti dependence*: write after read
- *Output dependence*: write after write

Flow dependences—the type just described—are also called *true dependences* because they represent fundamental orderings of memory operations. By contrast, anti and output dependences are referred to as *false dependences* because they arise from the reuse of memory rather than from a fundamental ordering of the operations; although they may be called "false," they still matter to us, because we often wish to reuse memory. For completeness, it's sometimes useful to consider a fourth type of dependence, *input dependences* (read after read), which do not impose any ordering constraints, but which can sometimes be useful for reasoning about temporal locality.

To understand the difference between true and false dependences, consider the following code fragment:

```
1   sum=a+1;
2   first_term=sum*scale1;
3   sum=b+1;
4   second_term=sum*scale2;
```

There is a flow dependence (via `sum`) relating lines 1 and 2, and similarly, there is a flow dependence relating lines 3 and 4. Further, there is an anti dependence on `sum` between lines 2 and 3. This anti dependence prevents the first pair of statements from executing concurrently with the second pair. But we see that by renaming the `sum` in the first pair of statements to be `first_sum` and by renaming the `sum` in the second pair of statements to be `second_sum`, the pairs can execute concurrently, as follows:

```
1   first_sum=a+1;
2   first_term=first_sum*scale1;
3   second_sum=b+1;
4   second_term=second_sum*scale2;
```

Thus, at the cost of increasing the memory usage, we have increased the program's concurrency.

By contrast, flow dependences cannot be removed by renaming variables. It may appear that the flow dependences can be removed simply by substituting for `sum` in lines 2 and 4 as follows:

```
1   first_term=(a+1)*scale1;
2   second_term=(b+1)*scale2;
```

but this doesn't eliminate the dependence, because no matter how it is expressed the addition must precede the multiplication for both terms. The flow of data—the write of the sum (possibly to an internal register) to the read of the sum as an operand (possibly from an internal register)—remains.

Dependences Limit Parallelism

To understand how dependences limit parallelism, recall the example from Chapter 1 of computing the sum of *n* numbers. We described the following code fragment as sequential:

```
sum=0;
for(i=0; i<n; i++)
{
    sum+=x[i];
}
```

And we claimed that the following code admitted more parallelism, even though both code fragments were expressed in a sequential language:

```
((x[0]+x[1])+(x[2]+x[3]))+((x[4]+x[5])+(x[6]+x[7]))
```

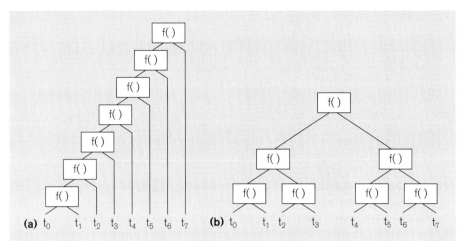

Figure 3.4
Schematic diagram of sequential and tree-based addition algorithms; edges not connected to a leaf represent flow dependences.

Figure 3.4 graphically depicts the two code fragments; an edge not involving a leaf represents a flow dependence because the computation of the lower function will write to memory, and the upper function will read from the same memory location. The key difference between the two pieces of code is now evident. In Figure 3.4(a) the sequential solution defines a sequence of flow dependences whose ordering must be respected. By contrast, Figure 3.4(b) specifies shorter chains of flow dependences, imposing fewer ordering constraints and permitting more concurrency. In effect, when we gave the C specification for adding the numbers, we were specifying more than just which numbers to add; we were implicitly specifying ordering constraints. (We need to recognize that the operation (addition) is associative to know that the two solutions produce the same result.)

The point is that when creating a parallel program, we must be careful to avoid introducing dependences that do not matter to the computation, because such dependences will unnecessarily limit parallelism. (Knowing that $f()$ is addition can enable powerful compiler techniques that might transform this code into a more parallel form, but such technology has a limited scope of application; it's best to avoid the dependences in the first place.)

Embarrassingly Parallel Computations. Some computations are easy to parallelize because they consist of a large number of threads that clearly have no dependences among them. Such computations are said to be *embarrassingly parallel*. One such example is the Mandelbrot set, a fractal computation in which each point on a complex plane can be computed independently of any other. *Ray tracing*, a graphics rendering technique that models the transport of light to produce realistic images, is also embarrassingly parallel, as it traces multiple independent rays to render an image. (While the traditional recursive ray tracing algorithm is embarrassingly parallel, the algorithm may not perform well on a bandwidth-constrained multi-core chip because it makes inefficient use of the memory hierarchy.)

Note

Granularity

A key concept for managing the constraints imposed by dependences is the notion of granularity, which is typically described using the terms *coarse* and *fine*, although *large* and *small* are also used.

Granularity of Parallelism. The granularity of parallelism is determined by the frequency of interactions among threads or processes, that is, the frequency with which dependences cross thread or process boundaries. Here, frequency is measured in the number of instructions between interactions. Thus, coarse grain refers to threads and processes that only infrequently depend on data or events in other threads or processes, while fine grain computations are those that interact frequently. This notion of granularity is important because each interaction introduces communication or synchronization along with their associated overheads.

Hardware platforms that implement low-latency communication, such as multi-core chips, support finer-grained computations. For platforms that implement higher-latency communication, larger granularities are better because the overhead of interaction is higher. Message passing programs typically work best when phrased as coarse-grained computations, even on low-latency communication substrates, because the software overhead of message passing is typically large. As we discuss later in this chapter, there are many techniques for creating coarse-grained computations, and these typically trade off memory or computation either to reduce the frequency of interactions or to hide the latency of such interactions.

Applying Granularity Concepts. An important observation is that no fixed granularity is best for all situations. Instead, it is important to match the granularity of the computation with both the underlying hardware's available resources and the solution's particular needs. For example, the original prefix summation described in Chapter 1 was a fine grain computation involving a small amount of work and fine grain interactions with the adjacent threads.

In the limit, the coarsest computations involve huge amounts of computation and no interaction. BOINC, the Berkeley Open Infrastructure for Network Computing, supports such computations by allowing subproblems to be distributed to personal computers and solved entirely locally; the only communication comes at the end to report the results to the problem dispenser. In this setting the parallel computer can be an Internet-connected collection of PCs. Such super-coarse grain is essential because of the huge latencies of communication.

At the other end of the spectrum are threads running on multi-core chips that implement low-latency communication among processors residing on the same chip, making it practical to use fine grain threads with hundreds of instructions between interactions.

Locality

A concept that is closely related to granularity is that of locality. Computations can exhibit both temporal locality—memory references that are clustered in time—and spatial locality—memory references that are clustered by address. Recall that locality is an important phenomenon in computing, being the reason why caches work. Of course, the processors of parallel machines also use caches, so all of the benefits of temporal and spatial locality are available, provided the references remain local so that they can stay in the cache. Indeed, algorithms that operate on blocks of data rather than single items almost always exploit spatial locality, so they are generally preferred.

In the parallel context, locality has the added benefit of minimizing dependences among threads or processes, thereby reducing overhead and contention. As outlined above, non-local references imply some form of communication, which is pure overhead that limits parallel performance. Furthermore, by making non-local references, threads or processes will often contend for resources, either in the interconnection network or the memory system.

To make the advantages of locality concrete, consider the final solution (Try 4) to the Count 3s problem. By working on a contiguous block of memory, each thread exploits spatial locality; by accumulating intermediate sums in a local variable, each thread exploits temporal locality; by each thread updating the shared sum only once, the code minimizes communication, which improves locality and reduces overhead and communication. Note that the use of a local accumulation variable is another example where the use of a small amount of extra memory can break false dependences.

Performance Trade-Offs

The previous sections have explained how dependences limit parallelism and why it's important to think about locality and the appropriate granularity. We now explain why it can be difficult to produce efficient parallel programs. We start by contrasting the situation with sequential performance analysis, and then we discuss the many possible trade-offs that can be made.

Typically, it is fairly straightforward to reason about the performance of sequential computations. For most programs, it suffices to count the number of instructions that are executed. In some cases, we realize that memory system performance is the bottleneck, so we find ways to reduce memory usage or to otherwise improve memory system performance. In such a setting, programmers are generally encouraged to avoid premature optimization by remembering the 90/10 rule, which states that 90 percent of the time is spent in 10 percent of the code. Thus, a prudent strategy is to write a program in a clean manner, and if its performance needs improving, to identify the 10 percent of the code that dominates the execution time. This 10 percent can then be rewritten, perhaps even rewritten in some alternative language that offers greater control, such as C or assembly language.

Unfortunately, the situation is much more complex with parallel programs. If nothing else, Amdahl's Law tells us that not parallelizing 10 percent of the computation will limit our maximum improvement from parallelization to at most a factor of 10, which may be insufficient in many situations. Moreover, the factors that determine performance are not just instruction counts, but also communication time, waiting time, dependences, and so on. Dynamic effects, such as contention, are time-dependent and vary from problem to problem and from machine to machine. Thus, it is much more complicated to control costs and identify bottlenecks than in the sequential case.

We have seen that communication costs, idle time, wait time, and many other quantities can affect the performance of a parallel computation. The complicating factor is that attempts to lower one cost can increase others. It is important to understand these trade-offs, because different algorithms and computing platforms will favor different trade-offs. This section now considers such issues.

Communication versus Computation

Communication costs are often a significant source of overhead. Fortunately, it is often possible to reduce communication by performing additional computations.

Overlapping Communication and Computation. One way to reduce communication costs is to overlap communication with computation. The key is to identify computation that is independent of the communication. By executing both the computation and communication concurrently, the latency of the communication can be partially or wholly hidden. We show concrete examples of this technique in Chapters 6 and 7. From a performance perspective, the overlapping of communication and computation is generally a win without costs. From a programming perspective, the overlapping of communication and computation can complicate a program's structure, sometimes in non-trivial ways.

Redundant Computation. Another way to reduce communication costs is to perform redundant computations, that is, to recompute a value locally rather than wait for it to be transmitted. We observed in Chapter 2, for example, that the local generation of a random number, r, by all processes was superior to generating the value in one thread and then sharing it with all other threads. Unlike the overlapping of communication and computation, redundant computation incurs a cost because all processes must execute the random number generator code. Stated another way, we have increased the total number of instructions to be executed in order to remove the communication cost. Whenever the cost of the redundant computation is less than the communication cost—as it often is for simple computations like generating random numbers—redundant computation is a win.

Notice that this redundant computation *also removes dependences* between the generating process and the processes that will need the value. Because such dependences often lead to synchronization costs, it can be useful to remove dependences even if the cost of the added computation exactly matches the communication cost. In the case of the random number generation, redundant computation removes the possibility that a client process will have to wait for the server process to produce it. Such considerations complicate the assessment of this trade-off.

Memory versus Parallelism

Parallelism can often be increased at the expense of increased memory usage. In some situations a small amount of extra memory can significantly improve performance. (Of course, we have to be careful, since there are cases where the primary benefit of parallel computing is the larger amount of available memory, so we don't want to throw away this benefit.)

Privatization. Parallelism can be increased by using additional memory to break false dependences. For example, in the Count 3s program, the use of `private_count` variables removed the need for threads to interact each time they encountered a 3. The effect was to increase the number of count variables from 1 to `t`, the number of threads. It was a tiny memory cost for a substantial savings in reduced dependences.

Padding. Parallelism can also be increased by padding, allocating extra memory to force variables to reside on their own cache line. We saw in the Count 3s example how padding can eliminate false sharing, which occurs when references to independent variables become dependent because they are allocated to the same cache line. We can view false sharing as a special type of false dependence, so the removal of false sharing can significantly improve performance by reducing the frequency of interactions among threads.

Overhead versus Parallelism

Parallelism and overhead are often at odds. At one extreme, all parallel overhead, such as lock contention, can be avoided by using just one thread. As we increase the number of threads, the parallelism likely increases but so does overhead and contention. If the problem size remains fixed as we increase the number of threads, then each thread has less work to perform between synchronizations, causing synchronization to become a larger portion of the overall computation. A smaller problem size per thread also implies that there is less computation available to overlap with communication, which can increase the wait times for data.

It is the overhead of parallelism that usually prevents the number of processors, P, from profitably increasing without bound. Indeed, even computations that could conceptually be solved with one processor devoted to each data point are typically buried by overhead before $P = n$. Thus, for a given input size, we find that most programs have an upper limit at which the marginal value of an additional processor approaches 0, that is, there is no benefit to adding more processors. Consider the following three trade-offs between overhead and parallelism.

Parallelize Overhead. In the Count 3s example, the threads initially used a single global variable to accumulate each thread's `priv_count`; if the number of threads is extremely large, this final accumulation could become a performance bottleneck. A simple solution would be to use the tree summation approach, in which threads combine their `priv_count` values in pairs. In essence, the threads divide the task of accumulating intermediate values into several independent parallel activities, thereby parallelizing some of the overhead and reducing its cost.

Load Balance versus Overhead. Increased parallelism can also improve load balance, as it's often easier to distribute evenly a large number of fine-grained units of work than a smaller number of coarse-grained units of work. This idea of over-decomposing a problem is particularly useful for computations in which the amount of work is irregular or dynamically variable. In such cases, it can be difficult to determine exactly how much work to assign to each processor, so by over-decomposing the problem, there's a greater likelihood that all processors can be kept busy. Of course, the disadvantage of over-decomposition is an increase in overhead and typically an increase in communication or synchronization.

Granularity Trade-Offs. Many of the above trade-offs are related to the granularity of parallelism. One way to reduce the number of dependences is to increase the granularity of interaction. *Batching* is a programming technique in which work is performed as a group. For example, rather than transmitting individual elements of an array, it's typically more efficient to send a whole row or column of the array; instead of grabbing one task from the task queue, there will be less contention if threads grab several tasks at once. Batching increases the granularity of interactions to reduce their frequency of interactions.

Naturally, there is a limit to how much the granularity can be profitably increased. The best granularity often depends on both algorithmic characteristics and hardware characteristics. We've already seen the advantage of matching the granularity of a data structure to that of the underlying hardware, when we padded the `priv_count` array to avoid false sharing. In that case, the solution didn't reduce parallelism, but reduced parallelism is a common result of increased granularity. In general, for systems with high communication and synchronization latency, it pays to create a coarse-grained computation that avoids as many interactions as possible while fully exploiting available parallelism.

> **Note**
>
> **Parallelizing Functional Programs.** Because purely functional languages provide *referential transparency*—that is, the value of an expression does not change over time—an expression's sub-expressions can be evaluated in any order without affecting its result, so functional programs provide an ample source of parallelism. Indeed, there is a

long history of research in the area of parallelizing functional programs. In this chapter, however, we have argued that there is considerably more to obtaining good parallel performance than simply identifying parallelism: We must carefully manage data movement and interaction among threads, and we must carefully choose an appropriate granularity of parallelism. So, although functional languages make it trivial to identify substantial amounts of fine-grained parallelism, they provide no mechanism for controlling locality, granularity, and cross-thread dependences. With respect to locality, functional languages abstract away the notion of a memory location, making it difficult for either the programmer or the compiler to reason about locality. With respect to granularity, it is possible to spawn a new thread for each function's sub-expressions, but it may do little work before it must synchronize with another thread; in such cases, the overhead of the extra thread may outweigh any performance gain from parallelization. Unfortunately, it is difficult to know which expressions to combine to create coarser-grained threads. Finally, without the ability to reason about either locality or granularity, it is difficult to reason about cross-thread dependences.

Measuring Performance

As we have just seen, when it comes to parallel computing, the notion of performance is complex because there are multiple aspects to consider, including memory usage, processing time, and overhead. It is not surprising then, that the fair use of performance metrics involves many subtleties. We now consider several performance metrics, with a focus on understanding their strengths and weaknesses.

Execution Time

Perhaps the most intuitive metric is *execution time*, also called latency. A simple definition, which we return to in Chapter 11 where we discover that it's more complicated than it appears, is the time elapsed from the point at which the first processor begins executing the program to the time the last processor completes execution.

Another common metric is FLOPS, short for *floating-point operations per second*. FLOPS is commonly used as a figure of merit in scientific computations and is reported for either single or double precision. An obvious downside to using FLOPS is that it ignores other costs such as integer computations, which may also be a significant component of computation time. Perhaps more significant is that FLOPS rates can often be affected by extremely low-level program modifications that allow the programs to exploit a special feature of the hardware, for example, a combined multiply/add operation. Such "improvements" typically have little generality, either to other computations or to other computers for the same computation.

A limitation of both of the above metrics is that they distill all performance into a single number without giving any indication of the parallel behavior of the computation. Instead, we often wish to understand how the performance of the program scales as we change the available parallelism.

Speedup

Speedup is defined as the execution time of a sequential program divided by the execution time of a parallel program that computes the same result. In particular, *Speedup* = T_S / T_P, where T_S is the sequential time and T_P is the parallel time running on P processors. Speedup is often plotted on the *y*-axis with the number of processors on the *x*-axis, as shown in Figure 3.5.

This speedup graph shows a feature typical of many parallel programs, namely, that the speedup curves level off as we increase the number of processors. This feature is the result of keeping the problem size constant while increasing the number of processors, which causes the amount of work per processor to decrease; with less work per processor, costs such as overhead become more significant, causing the total execution time not to improve linearly.

Superlinear Speedup

A curious phenomenon sometimes occurs in which a parallel program runs more than a factor of P times faster than its sequential counterpart, yielding what is known as *superlinear speedup*. For example, the curve for Program 1 in the graph of Figure 3.5 indicates superlinear speedup when eight processors are used.

Superlinear speedup seems counter intuitive, since a sequential program, which is the basis for the speedup comparison, could simply simulate the P processes of the parallel program to achieve an execution time that is no more than P times the parallel execution time. How is superlinear speedup possible? The basic explanation is

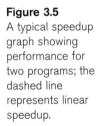

Figure 3.5
A typical speedup graph showing performance for two programs; the dashed line represents linear speedup.

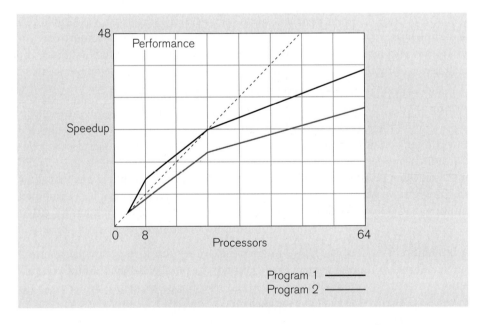

that the parallel program does less work. The most common situation occurs when the parallel execution is able to access data that fits in each processor's cache, while the sequential execution must access the slower parts of the memory system because the data does not fit in a single cache. Of course, superlinear speedup is still somewhat rare, because the more efficient use of the memory system must overcome all parallel overheads.

A second case of superlinear speedup occurs when performing a search that is terminated as soon as the desired element is found. When performed in parallel, the search is effectively performed in a different order, implying that the total amount of data searched can actually be less than in the sequential case. Thus, the parallel execution performs less work.

Efficiency

Efficiency is a normalized measure of speedup that indicates how effectively each processor is used: *Efficiency = Speedup/P*. An ideal efficiency of 1 indicates linear speedup and that all processors are being used at full capacity. Because of various sources of performance loss, efficiency is more typically less than 1 and diminishes as the number of processors is increased. Efficiency is greater than 1 in the case of superlinear speedup.

Concerns with Speedup

Since speedup is a ratio of two execution times, it is a unitless metric that would seem to factor out technological details such as processor speed. Instead, such details subtly affect speedup, so we must be careful in interpreting speedup figures. There are several concerns.

Hardware Generations. First, recognize that it is difficult to compare speedup from machines of different generations, even if they have the same architecture. The problem is that different components of a parallel machine are generally improved by different amounts, changing their relative importance. So, for example, processor performance has increased over time, but communication latency has not kept pace. Thus, on a new computer, the time spent communicating will not have diminished as much as the time spent computing. As a result, speedup values have generally decreased over time, because the communication components of a computation have become relatively more expensive compared to the processing components.

Sequential Time. The next issue concerns T_S, speedup's numerator, which should be the time for the fastest sequential solution for the given processor and problem size. If T_S is artificially inflated, speedup will be greater. A subtle way to increase T_S is to turn off scalar compiler optimizations for both the sequential and parallel programs. This might seem fair because it applies to the compiler used for both programs. However, the change effectively slows the processors, improving—

relatively speaking—communication latency. When reporting speedup, the sequential program should be stated and the compiler optimization settings detailed.

Relative Speedup. Another common way to unfairly increase speedup is to use as T_S the one-processor performance of the *parallel* program. Speedup computed on the basis of T_1 is called *relative speedup* and should be reported as such. True speedup includes the likely possibility that the sequential algorithm is different from the parallel algorithm. Relative speedup, which simply compares different runs of the same algorithm, takes as the base case an algorithm optimized for concurrent execution but with no parallelism; it will likely run slower because of parallel overheads, causing the speedup to look better. Notice that a well-written parallel program on one processor can sometimes be *faster* than any known sequential program, making it the best sequential program, too. In such cases we have true speedup, not relative speedup, and the situation should be explicitly identified.

Relative speedup cannot always be avoided. For example, for large computations it may be impossible to measure a sequential program on a given problem size because the data structures do not fit in memory. In such cases, relative speedup is all that can be reported. The base case will be a parallel computation on a small number of processors, and the y-axis of the speedup plot should be scaled by that amount. So, for example, if the smallest possible run has $P = 4$, then dividing by the runtime for $P = 64$, will show perfect speedup at $y = 16$.

Cold Starts. Cold starts are another way to inadvertently affect T_S. An easy way to accidentally get a large T_S value is to run the sequential program once and include all of the paging behavior and compulsory cache misses in its timing. It is good practice to run a computation a few times, measuring only the later runs. This allows the caches to "warm up," so that compulsory cache miss times are not unnecessarily included in the performance measure and do not complicate our understanding of the program's speedup. (Of course, if the program has conflict misses, they should and will be counted.) Though easily overlooked, cold starts are also easily corrected.

Peripheral Charges. More worrisome are computations that involve considerable off-processor activity—for example, disk I/O. One-time I/O bursts, say to read in problem data, are fine because timing measurements can bypass them; the problem is continual off-processor operations. Not only are they slow relative to the processors, but also they greatly complicate the speedup analysis of a computation. For example, if both the sequential and parallel solutions have to perform the same off-processor operations from a single source, huge times for these operations can completely obscure the parallelism because they will dominate the measurements. In such cases, it is not necessary to parallelize the program at all. If processors can independently perform the off-processor operations, then this parallelism alone dominates the speedup computation, which will likely look perfect. Any measurements of a computation involving off-processor charges must control their effects carefully.

Scaled Speedup versus Fixed-Size Speedup

Choosing a problem size can be difficult. Speedup curves are typically most intuitive when the problem size is fixed across all numbers of processors. However, this fixed-size speedup is problematic when the range of processors is large because a problem size that is small enough to fit into the memory of one processor can easily be unreasonably small when hundreds or thousands of processors are used. The general problem is that the efficiency of a parallel computation typically depends on the problem size, so a fixed-size problem is likely to bias toward some particular number of processors.

The obvious solution is instead to scale the problem size with the number of processors, so that a four-processor system operates on a problem that is twice as large as a two-processor system. Even here, it's not always clear what "twice as large" really means, since the asymptotic complexity of most computations does not grow linearly. Moreover, the memory and communication requirements do not always grow at the same rate as the computational requirements, so almost any change that we make to the problem size will likely change the relative importance of the memory sub-system, the computational power, or the communication infrastructure.

Scalable Performance

Naively, we would like to assume that having more processors improves performance. This perspective might mistakenly be reinforced by the observation that as parallel computers grow in terms of number of processors, they tend to have simpler, less powerful processors, implying that the number of processors is more important than their individual power. Indeed, there are predictions that future multi-core computers will employ significantly simpler CPUs than are used today. This section examines the cause of these hardware trends as we consider several issues related to scalable performance.

Scalable Performance Is Difficult to Achieve

We start by demonstrating that scalable performance is difficult to achieve, because as we increase P, it becomes more difficult to achieve good parallel efficiency. To illustrate, imagine an algorithm, say a parallel alphabetizing algorithm, in which a process is responsible for ordering all words starting with the same letter as follows: The process

  a. removes from the initial data structure all words starting with the given letter,
  b. orders them locally, and
  c. returns them to their proper location in the overall ordering.

If fewer than 26 processors are available, each process handles multiple letters. (We will see the details of such a computation in Chapter 4.) Parts a and c are parallel overhead, because b is sufficient to solve the problem sequentially. Assume optimistically (and unrealistically) that the amount of overhead remains constant as we increase the number of processors and that the overhead is 20 percent when executed on one processor.

Assume that the sequential computation time for the local alphabetization (b) is T_S. Because the 20 percent overhead is not parallelizable, the parallel solution on two processors will take time T_2:

$$T_2 = \frac{T_S}{2} + 0.2T_S$$

$$= 7\frac{T_S}{10}$$

Our efficiency on two processors is

$$E_2 = \frac{\dfrac{T_2}{T_S}}{2} = \frac{\dfrac{10}{7}}{2} = \frac{5}{7} = .71$$

On 10 processors, execution time is

$$T_{10} = \frac{T_S}{10} + 0.2T_S = \frac{3T_S}{10}$$

So, efficiency on 10 processors is

$$E_{10} = \frac{\dfrac{10}{3}}{10} = .33$$

For 100 processors we have

$$T_{100} = \frac{T_S}{100} + 0.2T_S = \frac{21T_S}{100}$$

$$E_{100} = \frac{\dfrac{100}{21}}{100} = \frac{1}{21} = .047$$

Thus, for 100 processors, each is performing useful work only 4.7 percent of the time! This extremely low efficiency shows that the marginal benefit of adding more processors decreases as the number of processors increases. This highlights the importance of minimizing overhead as we move to large parallel systems.

Implications for Hardware

The above example explains why we can afford to use less powerful processors as we increase the number of processors: As the number of processors increases, the marginal benefit of improving each processor's CPU speed is minimal. Said another way, with slower cores a smaller fraction of the original computation is non-parallelizable, so Amdahl's Law suggests that we can get better speedup and efficiency by using slower cores. It makes sense then that BlueGene/L, with $P = 64K$, has relatively slow processors compared to other machines described in Chapter 2.

Implications for Software

As we mentioned earlier, one common method of reducing overhead is to perform batching, which tends to increase granularity by increasing the amount of local work per process while decreasing the proportion of time spent interacting with other processes. Batching is beneficial for algorithms with a good "surface area to volume ratio." For example, an algorithm that computes locally on an $m \times m$ array of data and interacts with other threads or processes along the edges of this 2D array has communication costs that grow linearly with m but computation costs that grow quadratically with m. Moreover, as the value of m increases, there are more opportunities to perform latency-hiding techniques, such as overlapping communication with computation.

The need to reduce overhead suggests that the need to tune for machine-specific characteristics is particularly important for parallel computers with many processors. Consider, for example, the idea of parallelizing the accumulation of private sums, as outlined in the previous section on Overhead versus Parallelism. As the number of processors grows, there is a trade-off between communication costs and computation costs: A combining tree with a low degree of fanout will be taller and will incur greater communication latency, while a combining tree with a large degree of fanout will need to perform greater amounts of computation at each node of the tree. These trade-offs probably don't become significant until the number of processors is quite large.

The notion that larger problem sizes yield better parallel performance is implicit in the *half performance metric*, denoted as $n_{1/2}$, which measures for a given program and machine, the input size needed to obtain an efficiency of one-half.

Scaling the Problem Size

Our analysis of efficiency assumed that the problem size remained constant as we increased the number of processors. However, we typically wish to increase the problem size as we move to more powerful machines with more processors. So ignoring memory constraints and assuming perfect speedup, consider how parallelism affects problem size.

For a sequential algorithm whose running time is $O(n^x)$, we have

$$T = cn^x.$$

If we assume that P processors can increase the problem size by a factor of m, then for the same execution time, T, we get

$$T = \frac{c(mn)^x}{P} = cn^x$$

Solving for m yields

$$(mn)^x = Pn^x$$

$$m^x n^x = Pn^x$$

$$m = P^{(1/x)}$$

Thus, to increase the problem size by a factor of 100 for a problem whose asymptotic complexity is $O(n^4)$, we need 100,000,000 processors! By contrast, to increase by a factor of 100 a problem whose asymptotic complexity is $O(n^2)$, we need 10,000 processors; if the complexity is linear only 100 for processors are needed. The lesson here is that the basic algorithm needs to be as scalable as possible, and simply adding more processors does not change this fact—it exacerbates it. This argument has been called *the corollary of modest potential*.

The Challenge Facing Many-Core. Current chip multiprocessors contain a handful of cores, but architects are already talking about many-core machines with dozens or hundreds of processors. In combining what we have learned in this section and in Chapter 2, we can see that this idea of many-core faces many problems. First, as the number of cores grows, the communication latency among cores will grow. As latency grows, we'd like to employ larger-grained parallelism. Thus, on a many-core chip, we'd ideally like to execute many independent processes, but this will be difficult because of limited aggregate bandwidth between RAM and the chip. If, on the other hand, the cores cooperate on a smaller number of parallel tasks, we see that efficiency becomes a problem unless we can scale the problem size. In either case, the best way to make effective use of a large number of cores requires a large amount of memory bandwidth, which will be limited by the physical dimensions of a many-core chip.

Chapter Summary

In this chapter we have seen that increased parallelism by itself does not translate to increased performance, by which we can mean either reduced latency or increased throughput. We have also seen that the concept of parallel performance is complex because there are many interacting facets of performance: memory consumption, processor utilization, and synchronization and communication costs. Therefore, to improve performance, we can often make different trade-offs among these facets to achieve our general goals of increasing locality, reducing cross-thread dependences, and controlling granularity. Finally, given the complexity of parallel performance, we have seen that there are many nuances to be aware of when evaluating performance and choosing performance metrics.

Historical Perspective

The topics of this chapter have dominated parallel computation research throughout its history, and the vocabulary and ideas introduced here appear in virtually every paper. Amdahl's Law was explicated in Amdahl's 1967 paper; there is a large descendant literature on his idea. The $n_{1/2}$ performance metric was originally introduced by Roger W. Hockney in 1977 to assess performance of vector computers; see Hockney and Jessoup [1988] for a nice treatment. The corollary of modest potential is described by Snyder [1986].

Exercises

1. In transactional memory systems, a thread optimistically assumes that it makes no references to shared data that conflict with other accesses by other threads. The transaction either *commits* successfully if there was no access violation detected, or the transaction *rolls back* if there was. Identify the sources of performance loss in a transactional memory system, classifying each as overhead, contention, or idle time.

2. Should contention be considered a special case of overhead? Can there be contention in a single-threaded program? Explain.

3. Should idle time be considered a special case of overhead? Can there be idle time in a single-threaded program? Explain.

4. Amdahl's Law states that the proportion of sequential code in a computation determines its potential for parallel speedup. Does the possibility of super-linear speedup contradict this conclusion? Explain.

5. Describe a parallel computation whose speedup does not increase with increasing problem size.

6. Assuming a 5 percent overhead for a parallel computation, compute the efficiency of applying 128 processors to it, assuming that the overhead remains constant as processors are added.

7. Most parallel dense matrix multiplication programs use algorithms that perform n^3 arithmetic operations. Using the reasoning of the section on Scaling the Problem Size, how many processors will be required to make a 10-fold improvement in matrix multiplication?

8. What kind of dependence is illustrated in Figure 3.3?

9. In the section on Overhead versus Parallelism, it was asserted: "...most programs have an upper limit [for each data size] at which the marginal value of an additional processor approaches zero... ." Describe the speedup curve for such computations at the upper limit.

10. The section on Overhead versus Parallelism introduced the idea of revising the Count 3s program by accumulating the `priv_counts` using a tree. Postulate a new program, Count 3s plus Find Min & Max that also uses the tree accumulate. Show how to use the idea of batching in this new program to avoid performing three consecutive tree-based accumulations.

part

2

Parallel Abstractions

With the foundations well established in Part 1, we now consider ways to create efficient parallel algorithms whose degrees of parallelism can scale as more processors become available. We present successful algorithms, as well as outline principles that promote concurrency for a variety of computational situations.

To be precise in our presentation of algorithmic techniques, we introduce a pseudocode for writing parallel programs. Pseudocodes—simplified and informal notations for presenting algorithms—are common in algorithms textbooks. They allow the display, discussion, and analysis of algorithms without biasing toward a particular programming language and without the distractions of unimportant details. An algorithm presented in pseudocode is a conceptually complete program for humans, though not for computers. Once an algorithm is understood, however, it is straightforward to implement it in a full-featured programming language, which a computer can understand. In Part 2 we strive to build the reader's intuition about strategies for parallelizing computations. The development of a parallel program often requires judgment about when to exploit parallelism and when to ignore it because the overhead incurred to exploit it is too high compared to the potential performance gain. We nurture the intuition by presenting well-tested techniques for data allocation, work allocation, data structure design, and algorithms. Such wisdom is an ideal resource for the actual programming, which is treated in later chapters.

4

First Steps Toward Parallel Programming

To become effective parallel programmers, we must learn to express basic parallel concepts such as algorithms and data structures. We must also learn how to analyze programs to determine their runtime and memory usage, which is a topic discussed in Chapter 11. For now, it's perhaps most important that we acquire the ability to think in a way that produces algorithms that are good matches for the languages and computers available to us. We start by introducing two broad classes of parallel computations. We then introduce a notation for describing parallel algorithms, and we use this notation to explore three ways of formulating parallel computations: Unlimited Parallelism, Fixed Parallelism, and Scalable Parallelism. Then we use an alphabetizing example to compare the effectiveness of these approaches.

Data and Task Parallelism

Parallel computations can generally be divided into two broad classes: data parallel and task parallel. These terms guide our thinking in parallel algorithm design.

Definitions

Many definitions have been proposed for data and task parallelism, but we adopt the following because they distinguish two ways of thinking about the parallelization, namely, do we parallelize the data or the code?

- A *data parallel* computation is one in which parallelism is applied by performing the same operation to different items of data at the same time; the amount of parallelism grows with the size of the data.

- A *task parallel* computation is one in which parallelism is applied by performing distinct computations—or tasks—at the same time. Since the number of tasks is fixed, the parallelism is not scalable.

As with most taxonomic efforts, classifying computations is not always clear-cut. Many computations are hybrids, being composed, say, of a fixed number of tasks, some of which can be data parallel. Even when computations don't fall neatly into one of the two classes, the terminology gives us the tools to understand their constituent parts.

Illustrating Data and Task Parallelism

To emphasize the distinction between the two types of parallelism, consider the job of preparing a banquet.

The data parallel approach views each meal as a unit of parallelism, so it uses P chefs to create N meals, with each chef producing N/P complete meals. As the value of N increases, we can increase P if we have sufficient resources, such as stoves, refrigerators, cutting boards, and so on.

The task parallel approach recognizes that meal preparation consists of tasks, such as preparing the appetizer, salad, main course, and dessert. With this approach, we could enlist four separate chefs who would each focus on one of these tasks. Of course, additional parallelism could be exploited by refining the tasks. For example, the salad preparation can be further divided into the subtasks of washing, dicing, and assembling. There are dependences among the subtasks, because we want to wash the vegetables before dicing them, and we need to dice them before we can assemble a salad. The result is a greater amount of parallelism, because once salad preparation is in full operation, washing, dicing, and assembling are performed simultaneously.

Our salad preparation example illustrates an important type of task parallelism known as pipelining. In pipelining, a series of tasks is solved in sequence; at any point, each task operates on a different instance of the problem, and when a task is done, it passes its instance to the next task in the series. In the section on Latency and Throughput in Chapter 3, we saw how processors use pipelined execution to improve instruction throughput, and the idea applies generally to a sequence of operations that must process many instances.

Hybrid solutions that combine both data and task parallelism also exist. In our example, we could first partition the banquet preparation into a number of tasks, and we could then apply data parallelism to each of the tasks. For example, multiple cooks could dice vegetables for the salad, yielding data parallelism within the dicing task.

The Peril-L Notation

Sequential algorithms are typically presented using some sort of pseudocode because it allows core ideas to be presented without having to specify every detail. We'd like something similar for parallel algorithms, so we now define a pidgin programming language—which we call *Peril-L*—that can be used to develop and analyze parallel algorithms.[1] This language has the following goals:

- It should be minimal so that it's easy to learn.
- It should be universal so that it does not bias toward any one language, parallel computer, or algorithmic approach.
- It should allow us to reason about performance.

As a result, Peril-L will be neutral to many of the issues raised in Chapter 2 as long as we imagine that the computations execute on the CTA. Accordingly, Peril-L will be aware of the differences between local and global memory reference times, λ. Because parallel programming is more involved than sequential programming, we will need to introduce additional concepts not used by the typical sequential pseudocode language.

Extending C

To reduce the number of concepts to be learned, Peril-L will extend the basic computational facilities of the C programming language, which we choose because it is stable and familiar. It is also sufficiently primitive to allow standard bit manipulation operations, which are occasionally needed in our algorithms, while being high level enough that simple examples are short.

Parallel Threads

The computational world of Peril-L begins as a sequential thread. Multiple threads are introduced by the `forall` statement, which we mentioned in Chapter 1. The statement has the following form, where the *<integer variable>* is an implicit declaration of an integer variable:

```
forall(<integer variable> in(<index range specification>))
{
   <body>
}
```

The statement has the following semantics: The index range specification is evaluated, resulting in a set *S* of indices. The *S* indices are the names for |*S*| logical threads. Each thread *s* in *S* executes a copy of the code given in *<body>*, such that the value of *<integer variable>* within that thread is *s*. Finally, each thread terminates when it reaches the closing brace. Except for the parallelism indicated by a `forall` statement, there is a single thread of control, so one statement does not begin executing until the previous statement has completed. In particular, a `forall` statement is not considered to have completed until all of its threads have terminated. Notice that `forall` statements can be nested by placing a `forall` statement in the *<body>* of another `forall` statement.

[1] The name is chosen to be homophonic with "parallel," not to imply that there is anything dangerous about it.

As an example of the `forall` statement, the following code prints a dozen lines, in some unknown order:

```
forall(index in(1..12))
{
  printf("Hello, World, from thread %i\n", index);
}
```

In this example, the output from the different threads is unpredictable because logically all of the threads execute simultaneously, though not in lock step. Indeed, the execution of the threads might be interleaved, or some may be executed to completion before others are started. Even a sequential execution of the statements in order is possible. As a result there is no way to predict what the output will be without some form of synchronization.

Synchronization and Coordination

As we saw in the previous Hello World example, it is sometimes useful to order operations among threads. In Peril-L, the *exclusive block* provides mutual exclusion. Its syntax is as follows:

```
exclusive { <body> }
```

Its semantics ensure that only one thread can execute the *<body>* at a time. If one thread is executing the *<body>*, other threads attempting to execute the *<body>* must wait. When one thread finishes executing *<body>*, waiting threads proceed in an unspecified order. We can use this construct to improve the quality of our Hello World example as follows:

```
forall(index in(1..12))
{
  exclusive
  {
    printf("Hello, World, from thread %i\n", index);
  }
}
```

With the use of the `exclusive` block, the above code will print each of the 12 lines in its entirety, with the 12 lines appearing in some unspecified order. Alternatively, we could achieve the same effect by putting the `exclusive` block in the *implementation* of the `printf()` routine.

A second tool is the barrier synchronization,

```
barrier
```

which has meaning only inside of a `forall`. The `barrier` statement forces threads to stop and wait until all threads have arrived at the `barrier`, at which point they can proceed. For example, the following code uses a `barrier` to ensure that all of the "tweedle dees" appear before any of the "tweedle dums."

```
forall(index in(1..12))
{
  printf("tweedle dee\n");
  barrier;                          Wait for the last of the tweedle dees
  printf("tweedle dum\n");
}
```

Peril-L also provides a method for performing fine-grained synchronization, but before discussing that mechanism, we first explain Peril-L's memory model.

Memory Model

To avoid any bias toward either shared memory or non-shared memory, the Peril-L language provides two address spaces: a global address space and a local address space. Variables in the global space are visible to all threads, while variables in the local space are each visible to only one thread. By declaring a variable within a `forall` statement, a local copy is created for each thread, while a variable that is declared outside of a `forall` statement is a global variable and visible to all threads created by the `forall` statement.

In keeping with the CTA model, global variables are assumed to have a latency of λ time, while local variables can be accessed in unit time. Accordingly, Peril-L uses the following convention to visually distinguish global variables from local variables:

Peril-L Naming Convention. Global variables are distinguished by being underlined; local variables are not underlined.

Definition

To illustrate, consider a program that computes the absolute value an array <u>data</u> of <u>n</u> numeric values:

```
int data[n];
forall(index in(0..n-1))
{
  if(data[index]<0)
  {
    data[index]=-data[index];
  }
}
```

Notice that the Peril-L memory model is defined in terms of logical threads, so if multiple threads are assigned to the same processor, their local variables remain distinct.

Reading and Writing Global Memory. In Peril-L's memory model, multiple threads can simultaneously *read* the same global location, performing what are known as *concurrent reads*. However, only one thread can change a global location at a time. If two threads write the same location, then the value stored in the location is defined to be the last value written, but because the timing is unknown, the final result is unknown. It is generally difficult to analyze the correctness of a program when the values of variables are unknown, so we recommend that threads not perform simultaneous writes to the same global variable without some protection, such as the `exclusive` statement.

In the above example, threads read and write the global data array, `data`, at the same time, but because each thread references only the item corresponding to its value of `index`, concurrent reads and concurrent writes will never occur.

Notice that depending on the hardware, the use of simultaneous global memory references can have performance implications beyond the standard λ cost, because in some hardware they need to be serialized.

Connecting Global and Local Memory. Because the CTA model does not have a global memory, global data structures are distributed throughout the local memories of the processors; global addressing is implemented by translating global addresses into the appropriate local addresses of specific processors.

We often wish to design algorithms that operate on the part of the global data structure that has been assigned locally to a given thread, so we need a way to refer to the globally named data with a local name. In Peril-L, the `localize()` function serves this purpose, and we use it to initialize the local data structure. For example,

```
int allData[n];                 Declare global data structure
forall(threadID in(0..P-1))     Spawn threads
{
   int size=n/P;                Compute size of the local allocation
   int locData[size]=localize(allData[]);
                                Map globals to this thread's locals

   ...

}
```

The `localize()` function returns a reference to the portion of the global data structure that is allocated to the processor on which the thread executes; thereafter, all modifications of the local data structure using the local name are equivalent to modifications of the global data structure but without the λ-penalty.

The `localize()` function is useful because it allows us to create algorithms without knowing the details of how the global data is distributed across processors. At the same time, it allows us to write algorithms that operate on the local data.

There are three important issues regarding the localization of global memory:

1. Arrays containing localized data use local indexes; so regardless of the values of their global indices, the first item of the local array is index 0.
2. If multiple threads are assigned to a processor, the `localize()` function apportions global data structures among each of them; that is, each thread operates on only its part of the global data structure.
3. There is no local copy—both global and local references are to the same memory location.

In light of the third point, it is generally wise to not mix global and local references to a data structure without establishing some sort of synchronization. For example, threads might make protected global references and the call to `localize` to make local references. Such precautions promote a consistent memory image.

> **Owner Computes Rule.** The `localize()` function enables a data parallel programming style known as *owner computes*. The idea is to assign to a process the computations that apply to the portion of the global data structure allocated to it—the data that it "owns." Such a rule, widely used by compilers for parallel languages, tends to maximize the number of local data references.

Two other routines are also useful. The `mySize(global, i)` function returns the size of the `ith` dimension of the localized portion of the `global` array. Thus, although the above example assumed that `P` divides `n` exactly, a better solution would be to compute `size` as follows:

    size = mySize(allData[], 0); *Size of first dimension of local allocation*

Finally, the `localToGlobal(locData, i, j)` returns the global index that corresponds to the `ith` index of the `jth` dimension of the local allocation, `locData`.

> **Global versus Local Views.** Our use of the `localized()` function should not imply a value judgment about whether programming languages should adopt global or local indices. In Chapter 9 we define the terms *Global View language* and *Local View language*, and we argue that Global View languages provide programming conveniences that Local View languages do not. But because the goal of Peril-L is to allow programmers to express algorithms for any programming model, we need to provide access to both global and local views of the data. Moreover, there are times when Peril-L code is used to describe the uses of reductions, for which a global view of data might be useful, and there are times when we use Peril-L to describe the implementation of the reduce operation, for which the local view is needed.

Synchronized Memory

In Peril-L we recognize one other kind of memory, referred to as *full/empty variables*, which are global variables that enable fine-grained synchronization. A full/empty variable—or more succinctly *FE variable*—works like its name suggests. When it is declared it is *empty*, that is, it contains nothing. Any empty FE variable can be assigned a value, at which point it becomes *filled*. We say that a filled FE variable is *full*. Any full FE variable can be referenced (read), which empties it, that is, returns it to the empty state. The two other possibilities—trying to fill a full FE variable or trying to reference an empty FE variable—cause the computation to stall until the variable is emptied or filled, respectively. These states are summarized in Table 4.1. One way to think of FE variables is that they treat information like matter: In order to put it somewhere, the place must be empty, and when it's taken away, it's gone.

Table 4.1 Semantics of full/empty variables.

State of FE Variable	Variable Reference (read)	Variable Assignment (write)
Empty	Stall	Fill with value, leave full
Full	Take value, leave empty	Stall

We syntactically distinguish full/empty variables by placing an ' at the end of the variable name. For example, we can declare a FE variable as follows:

    `int t'=0;`   *Declare* `t'` *and fill it*

Because they are visible to all threads, full/empty variables are global, so they incur the same costs that standard global memory references incur. There is also some additional overhead incurred by the synchronization mechanism even when the thread does not stall.

Reduce and Scan

Recall that in Chapter 1 we introduced the global sum (+-reduce) and the parallel prefix summation (+-scan). To generalize these collective operations, we permit reduce and scan to apply to any associative and commutative primitive operation in the language, including +, *, &&, ||, max and min. The operations are written using a slash (/) for reduce and a backslash (\ ) for scan between the operator and the operand, as follows:

    `+/count`   *Reduce, that is, add the elements of* `count`
    `min\items`   *Scan, that is, find the smallest of* `items`*' prefixes*

We permit the operand values to be entire `structs` provided the operation applies to the components.

> **Curious Notation for Reduce and Scan.** Peril-L's use of the slash or backslash separating an operator and an operand may be foreign to most programmers. Many languages choose notation like `plus-reduce(count)` or `min-scan(items)`. But such notation, indistinguishable from the program's routine function calls, obscures the importance of these powerful abstractions and devalues their role. We purposely adopt the slashes—respecting their origin in the APL language—to emphasize the significance of reduce and scan. *Note*

Global and Local Operands. Reduce and scan can apply to global values to produce locally available results as in the following:

    `least=min/dataArray;`

which results in a scalar that is stored in the local variable `least` of each thread. But reduce and scan can also combine values across multiple threads. The operands, that is, the values to be combined, can also be local variables, and the result can be assigned to either a local or a global variable. Thus, in the statement

```
total=+/count;
```

the local `count` variables, one in each thread, are combined, and the single result is stored in the local variable, `total`. That is, each thread receives a copy of the result.

When scan applies to local values across multiple threads, as in the statement

```
beforeMe=+\count;
```

the `count` variables are accumulated (in the order of the threads' index values); so the ith thread has its `beforeMe` variable assigned the sum of the first i `count` values.

Reduce and Scan Synchronization. Notice that because reduce and scan can operate across multiple threads, they have implied synchronization *when they reference and assign only to local variables*. Specifically, in

```
largest=max/localTotal;
```

the `localTotal` values of each thread are combined and assigned to `largest`. All threads must arrive at this statement to perform the summation, and no thread can proceed until the assignment has been completed. Therefore, an assignment of either a reduced or scanned local value to a local has the effect of a barrier synchronization. If the result is stored in a global, then once a thread contributes its value and performs its role in the tree operations, it continues executing.

The Reduce Abstraction

Finally, as an important programming guideline, we recommend that when values are to be combined from multiple threads, a reduce operation be used instead of code that programs the computation explicitly. It is easy enough in Peril-L to program a global accumulation directly, as in

```
exclusive { total+=priv_count; }                              (1)
```

but it is even easier to use reduce, as in

```
total=+/priv_count;                                           (2)
```

But the issue is not ease of programming. Rather, it is the importance of stating that a global accumulation is being performed so that scalable code can be created for the operation.

To see the issue, imagine that $P = 10,000$. In performing the explicit summation using an `exclusive` block (1), the processes must serialize; there can be no parallelism in the execution, so performance will be significantly limited. By contrast, the reduce (2) will be implemented by a tree, as described in the earlier chapters, or perhaps by special-purpose hardware as is available on machines such as BlueGene/L (see Chapter 2). The tree implementation will realize parallelism and avoid serialization. In simplistic terms it will convert an operation from $O(P)$ to $O(\log P)$. Could a compiler recognize that statement (1) is an instance of a +-reduce? Perhaps, but why gamble? Stating it explicitly helps compilers *and* humans, as well as improving worst-case performance bounds.

Count 3s Example

Chapter 1 presented several versions of the Count 3s computation. We can use Peril-L to specify all of them. For example, a Peril-L program that corresponds to Try 3 is shown in Figure 4.1. Notice that to match the original Try 3 logic we have—just this once—violated our rule of always using reduction to perform a global sum. In all subsequent cases we will use reduction.

Formulating Parallelism

How should we formulate a parallel computation? Before presenting our answer, consider two obvious approaches that lead to unsatisfactory results.

Fixed Parallelism

Because we often know (initially, at least) which computer will be running the program—a *k* processor multi-core chip, for example—it's natural to formulate a solution that applies exactly that amount of parallelism—in this case, a *k*-way parallel algorithm. Though perhaps convenient heuristically as an aid to our thinking while programming, fixing a specific degree of parallelism will produce a program that does not scale. An improved multi-core chip with 2*k* processors will realize no improvement.

Figure 4.1
The Count 3s computation (Try 3) written in the Peril-L notation.

```
1   int array[length];                                  The data is global
2   int t;                                              Number of desired threads
3   int total=0;                                        Result of computation, grand total
4   int lengthPer=ceil(length/t);
5   forall(index in(0..t-1))
6   {
7     int priv_count=0;                                 Local accumulation
8     int i, myBase=index*lengthPer;
9     for(i=myBase; i<min(myBase+lengthPer, length); i++)
10    {
11      if(array[i]==3)                                 There's no concurrent read since
12      {                                               Array has been partitioned
13        priv_count++;
14      }
15    }
16    exclusive { total+=priv_count; }                  Compute grand total
17  }
```

The Count 3s program, though quite simple, has a Fixed Parallelism version, say for four processors. Shown in Figure 4.2, it is basically the Figure 4.1 solution instantiated for t=4. Good programming practice would motivate us to generalize this solution to *t* threads anyway, but for more complex computations, the constrained version typically embeds the processor count into the computation much more fundamentally.

A related problem is to notice that the computer of interest scales by a rule with some mathematical property—P is a power of 2, P is a perfect square, and so on—and to embed this assumption into the parallelism of the program. The program can apply increasing parallelism, so adopting the assumption is not devastating. But many architectures don't scale by such rules, so porting to those machines may waste considerable computing power. Generally, it's wise to avoid hard coding any specific degree of concurrency.

Unlimited Parallelism

A natural alternative to the above approach is to assume that the underlying hardware provides unlimited parallelism and therefore to expose all possible parallelism; when necessary, the concurrency in the algorithm can be aggregated into sequential code to match the available parallelism implemented in the hardware.

With this view, we could solve the Count 3s problem by exposing maximum parallelism:

```
1   int count=0;                              Performed by, say, p_0
2   forall(i in(0..n-1))
3   {                                         Performed by p_i
4       count =+/(array[i]==3?1:0);
5   }
```

Figure 4.2
Fixed Parallelism solution to Count 3s (t=4).

```
1   int array[length]; total;                 The data is global
2   int seg=ceil(length/4);
3   forall(j in(0..3))
4   {
5       int priv_count=0;                      Local accumulation
6       for(i=u*seg; i<min(length, j*(seg+1)); i++)
7       {
8           if(array[i]==3)                    Check local segment
9           {
10              priv_count++;
11          }
12      }
13      total =+/priv_count;                   Compute grand total
14  }
```

This elegant piece of code, which tests the items and uses +-reduce to accumulate the total number of elements matching 3, is somewhat deceptive. Assuming that the +-reduce is implemented using the tree algorithm, the computation appears to require $O(\lambda \log n)$, because there is a constant amount of overhead to set up the thread, a constant amount of computation to make the equality test, and the logarithmic cost of combining. (We include λ in the time analysis because, although we think of it as a constant, it does grow as P increases.) But in fact, the computation should be charged as taking $O(\lambda \log P + n/P)$, because when $P << n$, a balanced allocation allocates n/P elements per process that must be tested sequentially. The computation to perform the local test—lines 5–14 in the Fixed Parallelism solution shown in Figure 4.2—is not visible but will be required when, for example, $P = 4$. Such considerations are relevant, because P is effectively never equal to n, at least not for data parallel computations.

But the problem is actually worse than simply hiding relevant costs—we could, after all, train ourselves to do such analysis. The main problem is that serializing programs based on unlimited parallelism is expensive. When $P < n$ the compiler has two choices: It can simulate the nonexistent processes working on the code, which is what the program semantics actually say; or it can somehow generate scalable code to implement what the programmer writes, which means, basically, to invent the code on lines 7–16 of Figure 4.1. The former is inefficient and the latter is very difficult for compilers (though possibly not in our trivial Count 3s case here). The universal but expensive solution is to simulate the nonexistent processes.

The important point is that identifying parallelism is usually *not* the difficult part of parallel programming. Instead, the difficulties lie in structuring the parallelism to manage and reduce interactions among threads, because these interactions typically lead to performance loss.

Scalable Parallelism

A third approach is one that respects the Locality Principle from Chapter 2 and formulates a parallel solution as follows: After determining how the components of the problem—data structures, work load, and so on—grow as the computation's size, n, grows, we formulate a set S of *substantial* subproblems in which *natural* units of the solution, of size s, are assigned to each subproblem and solved as *independently* as possible.

- The emphasis on "substantial" subproblems ensures that there is sufficient local work in a thread to amortize the parallel overheads, such as communication, and to justify distributing the problem data, which will be our plan. By contrast, the Unlimited Parallelism solution to the Count 3s problem had threads with trivial amounts of work.

- The emphasis on "natural" subproblems respects the fact that computation is not always as smoothly partitionable as our Count 3s problem; for example, array computations might best be defined in terms of whole rows or columns. Because the subproblem size, s, determines the amount of parallelism, $S = n/s$, s will be adjusted at execution time so that $S = P$.

■ The emphasis on "independent" subproblems respects the fact that reducing the interactions among the subproblems leads to less idle time, communication, and so on. By incrementing the global count, the Unlimited Parallelism approach failed in this respect as well.

These qualitative terms mutually interact. For example, there will be a limit to how small a subproblem can be and still effectively amortize overhead, implying, for a given n, a lower limit on s and an upper limit on P.

Because problems are not always smoothly partitionable, it may be difficult in some cases to create for a given n, subproblems of suitable size s so that $n/s = S = P$. Clearly, if $S \geq P$, then multiple subproblems are assigned to a process, which is the usual case. If $S < P$, then fewer processes can be used with the given solution.

The Count 3s program shown in Figure 4.3 is a scalable version. Notice that it follows the Locality Principle by localizing the data and applying the owner computes rule. There is no interaction among the threads until the reduce at the end of the computation, so the program is very efficient.

Alphabetizing Example

The Count 3s example allowed us to illustrate the ideas of Fixed, Unlimited, and Scalable parallel solutions. But the Count 3s problem is so simple that the differ-

Figure 4.3
Scalable Parallelism solution to Count 3s. Notice that the array segment has been localized.

```
1   int array[length];                        The data is global
2   int t;                                     Number of desired threads
3   int total;                                 Result of computation, grand total
4   forall(j in(0..t-1))
5   {
6      int size=mySize(array,0);               Figure size of local part of global data
7      int myData[size]=localize(array[]);
                                               Associate my part of global data with
                                               local variable
8      int i, priv_count=0;                    Local accumulation
9      for(i=0; i<size; i++)
10     {
11        if(myData[i]==3)
12        {
13           priv_count++;
14        }
15     }
16     total =+/priv_count;                    ompute grand total
17  }
```

ences in approaches might seem relatively minor. To emphasize the distinctions among the three approaches and to illustrate Peril-L in action, consider the problem of alphabetizing a sequence of *L* records on some field, *x*.

Alphabetizing is a common sorting computation applied to data both small (file names in a directory) and large (databases). In our examples we assume that records of type rec (C structs) are stored in the global memory of the parallel machine as a linear array; if the data were on disk, similar techniques apply, but the time analysis may be dominated by disk-to-processor transfers, which are much more expensive than λ.

A few helper functions, used in the alphabetize programs, are listed in Table 4.2.

We now describe solutions produced by the three approaches, which will be followed by a comparison of the three resulting algorithms.

Unlimited Parallelism

In the spirit of the Unlimited Parallelism approach, we might notice that the maximum number of comparisons that we could simultaneously perform is to compare half of the records with the other half of the records. This solution is known as the Odd/Even Interchange Sort (see Figure 4.4). In a sequence of steps, consecutive odd/even pairs of values are checked in parallel, and they are interchanged if they are out of order; this half step is followed by a similar operation on even/odd pairs. The alternating pairs of tests—odd indices then even—are executed in sequence until no more interchanges are possible.

This program uses two global variables—L and continue; all other variables—i, done, temp—are local to the threads. In each forall loop, each element of L is only accessed by a single thread, so there are no race conditions in referencing L. The global Boolean variable continue is used to stop the computation when the alphabetization is complete. In particular, at the end of the second forall loop all of the local done variables are combined using an &&-reduce, which computes continue, a summary of whether work remains.

Though there is plenty of concurrency, there is also plenty of copying. For example, a list with the smallest element at the end will move through every position in the file.

Table 4.2 Helper functions.

Helper Function	Description
strcmp(str1, str2)	Compares null-terminated strings str1 and str2 returning a value less than, equal to, or greater than zero; as found in string.h
charAt(str, pos)	Returns the character in the pos position (0-origin); as in JavaScript
letRank(chr)	Returns the rank (0-origin) of its argument letter
alphabetizeInPlace()	Reorders the argument array of records to be alphabetical

Figure 4.4
Odd/Even Interchange to alphabetize a list L of records on field x.

```
 1  bool continue=true;
 2  rec L[n];                                    The data is global
 3  while(continue) do
 4  {
 5    forall(i in(1:n-2:2))                      Stride by 2
 6    {
 7      rec temp;
 8      if(strcmp(L[i].x,L[i+1].x)>0)            Is odd/even pair misordered?
 9      {
10        temp=L[i];                             Yes, fix
11        L[i]=L[i+1];
12        L[i+1]=temp;
13      }
14    }
15    forall(i in(0:n-2:2))                      Stride by 2
16    {
17      rec temp;
18      bool done = true;                        Set up for termination test
19      if(strcmp(L[i].x,L[i+1].x)>0)  Is even/odd pair misordered?
20      {
21        temp=L[i];                             Yes, interchange
22        L[i]=L[i+1];
23        L[i+1]=temp;
24        done=false;                            Not done yet
25      }
26      continue=!(&&/done);                     Were any changes made?
27    }
28  }
```

Fixed Parallelism

Because there are only 26 letters in the English alphabet, we can imagine a 26-thread parallel solution in which each thread is responsible for one letter; we call this solution *alphabetic batches*. After localizing the global data—that is, setting up work only on that portion of the L array assigned to it—each thread counts the number of records that it has that begin with each letter. A +-reduce over these local counts determines, globally, the number of records that start with each letter, that is, the batch size. Each thread, knowing it is responsible for myLet size batches, allocates sufficient local memory, grabs its records from the global array, and sorts them locally. Finally, after a +-scan of myLet, each thread knows how many records precede its letter in the final arrangement, so it returns its batch to the original global array. The solution is obviously not scalable beyond 26 threads, but each item incurs only 2λ *communication* cost—to move from its original location to the local memory, and then back to its final position. Figure 4.5 shows the details of this solution, which was referred to in the Scalable Parallelism section of Chapter 3.

Figure 4.5
Fixed 26-way parallel solution to alphabetizing. The function `letRank(x)`
returns the 0-origin rank of the Latin letter **x**.

```
1   rec L[n];                                    The data is global
2   forall(j in(0..25))                          A thread for each letter
3   {
4      int myAllo=mySize(L, 0);                  Number of local items
5      rec LocL[]=localize(L[]);                 Make data locally referenceable
6      int counts[26]=0;                         Count number of each letter
7      int i, j, startPt, myLet;
8      for(i=0; i<myAllo; i++)                   First, count number w/each letter; need this
9      {
10        counts[letRank(charAt(LocL[i].x,0))]++;
11     }
12     counts[index]=+/counts[index];            Figure how many of each letter
13     myLet=counts[index];                      Number of records of my letter
14     rec Temp[myLet];                          Allocate local storage for records
15     j=0;                                      Index for local array
16     for(i=0; i<n; i++)                        Move records locally for local alphabetize
17     {
18        if(index==letRank(charAt(L[i].x,0)))
19        {
20           Temp[j++]= L[i];                     Save record locally
21        }
22     }
23     alphabetizeInPlace(Temp[]);               Alphabetize within this letter locally
24     startPt=+\myLet;                          Scan counts # records ahead of these; scan
                                                 synchs, so okay to overwrite L, once sorted
25     j=startPt-myLet;                          Find my starting index in global array
26     for(i=0; i<count; i++)                    Return records to original global memory
27     {
28        L[j++]=Temp[i];
29     }
30  }
```

Reduce and scan play important roles in this solution. To start, each thread determines the number of its locally-stored records that begin with each letter; a +-reduce over these counts[] then determines how many it is responsible for globally (see line 12). The threads can then grab their records and sort them locally. Finally, the +-scan (line 23) tells each thread the number of records that will precede its batch in the final output, which allows each thread to begin returning the elements to the original array.

Notice that alphabetized batches cannot be returned to the global array until all threads have removed their batch from it. The solution in Figure 4.5 doesn't have explicit synchronization for this; rather, the synchronization required to perform the +-scan ensures that all the data has been moved out of the way.

This Fixed Parallelism solution is better than the Unlimited Parallelism solution, but as noted, it does not scale.

Scalable Parallelism

The third and final solution uses the Scalable Parallelism approach to produce an algorithm, Batcher's Bitonic Sort, that is both scalable and the parallel version of the familiar sequential mergesort algorithm. Batcher developed the algorithm for hard-wired sorting networks, and, of course, our interest is in its parallel version.

Preliminaries. The overall idea is that each thread (they must be a power of 2) will contain some number of local records, which it sorts initially in either ascending or descending order depending on the thread's index and the progress of the computation. Then, pairs of threads merge their sequences in an elegant protocol that creates longer sorted sequences until the whole array is alphabetized. In the remainder of this discussion, refer to Figure 4.6, which shows a sequence of $n = 24$ values being sorted by $t = 8$ threads.

The figure shows pairs of threads merging according to a protocol specified by two parameters, (p, d); p indicates which pairs of threads will merge values, and d indicates the direction of the ordering.

The parameter p is guided by the binary representation of a thread's index. Threads differing only in bit position p are paired for merging. (The binary representation $b_r...b_0$ of the thread index is shown at the top of the figure.) For example, in the first phase $(0,1)$ thread 0, whose binary encoding is 0000, and thread 1, whose binary encoding is 0001, perform a merge because they differ in bit position b_0, similarly for the other adjacent pairs. On the next phase $(1,2)$ thread 0 merges with thread 2, whose binary representation is 0010 because they differ in bit position b_1. And so forth.

The direction of the ordering is controlled by parameter d, the dth bit of the thread index b_d. When $b_d = 0$ the sort is ascending, and when $b_d = 1$ the sort is descending. Notice that p is never equal to d; the value of p starts a phase at $d - 1$ and decreases on successive sub-phases. So the two merging threads, which differ only in the b_p position, necessarily agree on the direction of the sort given by the b_d position.

The first merge of a phase begins by merging two *sorted* sequences. A sorted sequence is *monotonic increasing* or *monotonic decreasing*. (Technically, because Batcher's sort works fine when there are repeated values, the proper terms are non-decreasing or non-increasing, respectively, but we simplify for readability.) Merging will produce two *bitonic sequences*, that is, sequences with an increasing and a decreasing subsequence, making them appear schematically as a $\vee$ or a $\wedge$. A merge compares corresponding elements, moving the smaller values (those closer to the front of the alphabet) to one half, which we call the *lower* bitonic half. Schematically, the merge is described in the following illustration:

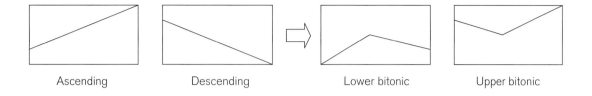

Ascending   Descending   Lower bitonic   Upper bitonic

Figure 4.6
Ordering $n = 24$ numbers using $P = 8$ threads running Batcher's sort. (A threads index is expressed in binary as $b_3b_2b_1b_0$.) Arrows show the direction of increasing order, that is, a right arrow is ascending. Step (-,0) is an initial local sort; thereafter processes perform a merge step in which threads differing only in bit position b_p merge to produce an ascending ($b_d = 0$) or descending ($b_d = 1$) sequence.

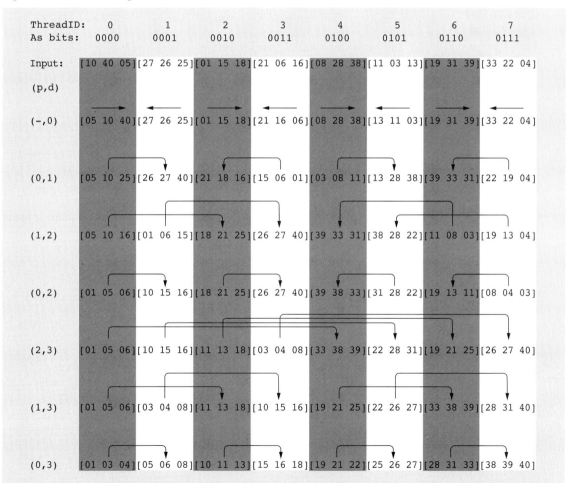

Clearly, if these two halves are then sorted—a recursion that is implemented by the remaining sub-phases—the combined sequence is sorted. Though the algorithm has a satisfying recursive elegance, our Peril-L solution focuses on the fast, direct bottom-up approach.

Peril-L Solution. Initially, each thread is assigned a sequence of records by means of the `localize()` function. Then each thread compresses the records into a new data structure, K, containing for each record only its key field x and its global index, using the `key()` function:

```
struct key(char[32] x, int home);
```

This compression avoids unneeded data transfer, speeding up the solution. (This compression could have been performed on the Fixed and Unlimited algorithms too, but it would not have been of significant value.) Each thread starts the alphabetization by locally sorting the compressed file (up or down, as needed based on b_0) and then enters the phase structure of the algorithm with $p = 0$ and $d = 1$.

The inner loop of the Batcher parallel sort is a merge of two bitonic sequences, called a *bitonic merge*, in which corresponding positions in each sequence are compared and swapped if the larger item is in the lower half; the result is another bitonic sequence. Bitonic merge of bitonic sequences produces bitonic sequences, which is the basis of the proof that this algorithm actually produces an ordered sequence.[2]

To implement both ascending and descending sorts, there are two merge operations, `mergeUp()` and `mergeDown()`. The difference is whether the lower half is in the smaller thread index (up) or the larger thread index (down), because the terms ascending and descending are relative to increasing thread index. We see in in Table 4.3 that a thread $b_r...b_0$ can operate in one of four capacities. The code to handle these four cases makes up the inner loop of the algorithm (see Figure 4.7, lines 32–71).

The data movement of the algorithm works as follows. The two threads exchange their data at the beginning of a sub-phase and then locally store the lower or upper half of the merge in the inner loop, depending on their role as indicated by Table

Table 4.3 Merge operations.

Operation	How Index Is Related to Other of Pair	What to Keep from Merge
Merge Up	Smaller Index, $b_r...b_{p+1}0b_{p-1}...b_0$	Keep Lower Half
	Larger Index, $b_r...b_{p+1}1b_{p-1}...b_0$	Keep Upper Half
Merge Down	Smaller Index, $b_r...b_{p+1}0b_{p-1}...b_0$	Keep Upper Half
	Larger Index, $b_r...b_{p+1}1b_{p-1}...b_0$	Keep Lower Half

[2]See Kunth, vol. III.

Figure 4.7

Peril-L program using Batcher's sort to alphabetize records in L.

1	`int t;`	*Thread count, must be 2^m*
2	`int m=log2(t);`	*Exponent of thread count*
3	`rec L[n];`	*Records to be alphabetized*
4	`int size=n/t;`	*Local portion; assume divisibility*
5	`key BufK[m][size];`	*Buffer to pass keys through*
6	`bool free'[m] = false; ready'[m];`	*Full/empty variable to manage buffers*
7	`forall(index in(0..t-1))`	*Start threaded section*
8	`{`	
9	`  int i, d, p; bool stall;`	
10	`  rec LocL[size]=localize(L[]);`	*Map global to local*
11	`  rec inputCopy[size];`	*Local copy of values simplifying synch*
12	`  key Kn[size]=localize(BufK[]);`	*Map global buffer to local for fast access*
13	`  key K[size];`	*Working sequence array*
14	`  for(i=0; i<size; i++)`	*Compress just to keys*
15	`  {`	
16	`    K[i].x=LocL[i].x;`	*Save letter string*
17	`    K[i].home=localToGlobal(LocL,i,0);`	*Remember global index*
18	`  }`	
19		
20	`  alphabetizeInPlace(K[],bit(index,0));`	*Locally sort, up or down based on bit 0*
21	`  for(d=1; d<=m; d++)`	*Main loop, m phases*
22	`  {`	
23	`    for(p=d-1; p<0; p--)`	*Define p for each sub-phase*
24	`    {`	
25	`      stall=free'[neigh(index,p)];`	*Stall till I can give data*
26	`      for(i=0; i<size; i++)`	*Send my data to my neighbor for this step*
27	`      {`	
28	`        BufK[neigh(index,p)][i]=K[i];`	*Send mine to neighbor*
29	`      }`	
30	`      ready'[neigh(index,p)]=true;`	*Release neighbor to compute*
31	`      stall=ready'[index];`	*Stall till my data is available*
32	`      if(bit(index,d)==0)`	*What direction to sort?*
33	`      {`	
34	`        for(i=0; i<size; i++)`	*Merge Up: move earlier data to the lower*
35	`        {`	*index thread*
36	`          if(bit(index,p)==0)`	*Lower thread of pair*
37	`          {`	
38	`            if(strcmp(Kn[index][i].x, K[i].x)>0)`	
39	`            {`	
40	`              K[i]=Kn[i];`	
41	`            }`	
42	`          }`	
43	`          else`	*Upper thread of pair*
44	`          {`	
45	`            if(strcmp(Kn[index][i].x, K[i].x)<0)`	

(continued)

Figure 4.7 (*continued*)
Peril-L program using Batcher's sort to alphabetize records in L.

```
46                  {
47                          K[i]=Kn[i];
48                  }
49              }
50          }
51      }
52      else
53      {
54          for(i=0; i<size; i++)              Merge Down: move earlier
55          {                                  data to higher index thread
56              if(bit(index,p)==1)            Lower thread of pair
57              {
58                  if(strcmp(Kn[index][i].x, K[i].x)>0)
59                  {
60                      K[i] = Kn[i];
61                  }
62              }
63              else                           Upper thread of pair
64              {
65                  if(strcmp(Kn[index][i].x, K[i].x)<0)
66                  {
67                      K[i]=Kn[i];
68                  }
69              }
70          }
71      }
72      alphabetizeInPlace(K[],bit(index,p));    Locally sort, up/dn based on bit p
73      free'[index]=true;                       Finished w/ buffer, enable
74      }                                        End of sub-phase loop
75  }                                            End of phase loop
76  for(i=0; i<size; i++)                        Grab records belonging with this thread
77  {
78      inputCopy[i]=L[K[i].home];               Get record and save locally
79  }
80  barrier;                                     Wait until everyone is done
81  for(i=0; i<size; i++)1                       Make output available
82  {
83      LocL[i]=inputCopy[i];                    Make records globally available
84  }
85  }
```

4.3. Though both make the same set of comparisons, this solution increases the granularity of the computation, allowing the sequences to be pipelined in a single transmission. To serve as a buffer for transmitting data, a global variable BufK is declared for each index into which the data is stored; it is localized for fast reference.

Synchronization is required to ensure that no data is stored in the buffer until it is free. One solution would be to declare `BufK` to contain full/empty variables, but a single full/empty variable is sufficient to refer to the whole buffer. We use two such full/empty variables, `free'` and `ready'`, to control the interaction of a pair of threads. When `free'` is full, which is how it is initialized, the buffer is available to be filled by the other thread of the pair; when `ready'` is full, the data has been sent to the receiving thread and the merge can begin.

The synchronization policy is as follows: A thread stalls until its neighbor's buffer control variable `free'` is full; it puts the data into its neighbor's buffer (`BufK`) and then tells the neighbor to proceed by filling `ready'`; it then stalls until its own buffer has been loaded by its neighbor and it has been told to proceed; at completion, it sets its `free'` variable to full again, indicating that it is ready for the next sub-phase.

To summarize, the (p,d) policy controls the overall activity of the algorithm, which consists primarily of merge operations, and the two threads of a pair manage their interactions with two synchronization variables, which they either set for their neighbor (`ready'`) or themselves (`free'`).

Comparing the Three Solutions

The three solutions are quite different, and it is not possible to view one as a variation of another. The Fixed and Unlimited solutions are somewhat easier to create, perhaps, than the Scalable solution. Further the Scalable solution used the features of Peril-L much more completely, implying that its parallel structure is more sophisticated. Which is most efficient?

"Efficient" has many meanings. We observe that the odd/even solution is inefficient by any definition because it shifts the data from one position to an adjacent position, a ponderous way to order items. The alphabetic bins solution has the minimum amount of data movement—a maximum of two transfers for any record—but it uses excessive global communication to compute the positions of the letters. That is, to identify the records "belonging" to a given letter, each thread reads all of the data, which requires the x field to be moved twice from wherever the record is stored to each of the processes. Thus, although data motion is minimized, data reference is not. The Scalable solution requires significant movement of the descriptors of the data, but unlike the Unlimited solution it moves them in streams that can be pipelined. Unlike the Fixed solution, it moves them to fixed, predictable destinations. The actual records are moved only once, at the end when they are put in order. Also, all of the computation of the Scalable solution is local, except for the passing data to the other thread of a pair.

But the main difference in the solutions—as was to be demonstrated—is in their generality with respect to the number of processes. When $n > P$, the Unlimited solution must simulate the nonexistent processes via multithreading. The Fixed solution cannot use more than 26 processes, though when $P < 26$, it is easy enough for one process to double up on multiple letters with simple multithreading. The Scalable solution works for any number of processes up to $P = n$, though P must be a power of 2, and when it is not, processes are wasted. The effort of programming the Scalable solution is justified because it is efficient and can be used in a wide range of circumstances.

Chapter Summary

In this chapter we introduced Peril-L, a notation for describing parallel algorithms. Using this notation, we described three different approaches to formulating parallel algorithms.

We argued that the Fixed Parallelism approach is too limiting, as it cannot adapt to increasing numbers of processors. We showed that the Unlimited Parallelism approach produces a solution that is directly applicable only in the unrealistic case that $n = P$ and that it introduces significant complications when $n > P$. Finally, we argued that the Scalable Parallelism approach is best, as it is capable of using many processors while limiting communication and thread interaction. Chapter 5 continues this discussion by introducing abstractions that support the goals of scalable parallelism.

Historical Perspective

Pidgin languages, developed for the purposes of illustrating algorithms, are a long-standing tradition in computer science, dating back to Knuth's invention of MIX, as described in his *Fundamental Algorithms* [1997]. The idea overlaying a global address space on local memories of independent processors has regularly been used in computer architectures since the Cray T3D; software variations of the overlay concept arise in partitioned global address-space (PGAS) languages. Reduce and scan (in the form used here) first appeared in Iverson's *A Programming Language* [1962]. Full/empty bit tagged memory was first used in the HEP computer, and is described in Smith [1978]. Knuth's *The Art of Computer Programming, Volume III Sorting and Searching* [1998] contains a proof that Batcher's sort produces a sorted order.

Exercises

1. Does quicksort provide data parallelism or task parallelism? Explain.

2. Does a chess program provide data parallelism or task parallelism? Explain.

3. Revise the Odd/Even Interchange sorting program to work with fewer than $P = n$ processors. That is, each processor is responsible for $s = n/P$ items.

Consider two cases:

a. The s items are consecutive elements of L.

b. The s elements that are the responsibility of processor `index` in
   `[0..n-1]` are at `index`, `index+P`, `index+2P`, ...

4. Using solution 3(b) and assuming that all of the communication required to perform each interchange (odd/even or even/odd) can be completed in λ time, estimate the execution time in terms of λ for a 1,000,000 record file on a 1024 processor.

5. Using the problem size from Question 4, estimate execution time for the alphabetic bins solution.

6. Calculate the number of sub-phases that are required for Batcher's sort for 2^{20} inputs on 2^5 processors.

7. For the conditions of Question 6 and the assumption that each record in L is 256 bytes long, compute how much is saved in data transmission for each sub-phase by building K.

8. Give the sequence of values for `free'[0]`, `free'[1]`, `ready'[0]`, and `ready'[1]` in the first two phases of the Batcher sort.

9. Explain the role of `inputCopy` in the Batcher sort.

10. The Red/Blue computation simulates two interactive flows: an $n \times n$ board is initialized so cells have one of three colors: red, white, and blue, where white is empty, red moves right, and blue moves down. Colors wrap around to the opposite side when reaching the edge. In the first half step of an iteration, any red color can move right one cell if the cell to the right is unoccupied (white); on the second half step, any blue color can move down one cell if the cell below it is unoccupied; the case where red vacates a cell (first half) and blue moves into it (second half) is okay. Viewing the board as overlaid with $t \times t$ tiles (t divides n), the computation terminates if any tile's colored squares are more than $c\%$ one color. Use Peril-L to write a solution to the Red/Blue computation.

5

Scalable Algorithmic Techniques

Armed with a notation for describing parallel algorithms, we're now ready to discuss methods of producing scalable parallel programs. Here, the emphasis is on obtaining good parallel efficiency as the number of processes, P, increases. Often, this efficiency can be increased by increasing the problem size. Thus, this chapter focuses on data parallel computations, because in general task parallelism does not scale significantly with P. Of course, because many task parallel computations can exploit data parallelism within a task, the ideas discussed in this chapter are broadly applicable.

This chapter starts by briefly discussing the ideal data parallel computation—one that can be executed at an Internet scale because it has a structure with many large blocks of independent computation. We then apply this structure to produce a scalable technique for combining values across multiple processes. We also describe a generalized implementation of reduces and scans—scalable abstractions with many uses—based on the same structure. The chapter concludes by connecting the goal of scalable parallelism to the issue of allocating data across processes, first by considering static allocations and then by considering dynamic allocations.

Blocks of Independent Computation

The ideal parallel computation is one composed of large blocks of independent computation with no interactions among blocks. Such computations, though relatively rare, exist and can be solved over the Internet by harnessing unused PC computing cycles. The BOINC project at Berkeley coordinates a list of such projects. Typically, independent computational tasks are downloaded to a participant's idle PC, computed, and the results returned to the server, which aggregates them. Such problems may be ideal, but they are not typical; instead, nearly all parallel computations require that threads interact, and the amount of interaction affects the ease with which we can achieve good performance.

Other parallel computations, though more complicated, still benefit whenever they can exploit the blocks-of-independent-computation strategy. Our Count 3s solution from Chapter 4 used this approach. As shown in Figure 4.1, each thread is responsible for a block of `lengthPer` items. This solution is one example of many that illustrates the following important principle:

> Parallel programs are more scalable when they emphasize blocks of computation—typically the larger the block the better—that minimize the inter-thread dependences.

The use of large blocks is important because if we assume a fixed problem size, then each process will operate on a smaller block as the number of processes increases. As mentioned in Chapter 3, there is generally a lower limit to the size of an effective block, but until that point is reached, continued scaling is possible. Such limit points should be determined during a tuning phase late in the programming process or when the program is ported to new hardware (see Chapter 11).

Schwartz' Algorithm

Our guiding principle can be seen in the algorithm that Jacob "Jack" Schwartz, an NYU computer scientist, proposed for tree operations, such as +-reduce. His main observation is that the tree structure should be used to connect the processes rather than to connect all of the items. For a fixed number of processes P and some number of values n, $P < n$, there are two approaches for computing +-reduce: (1) Introduce logical threads that implement a combining tree that literally encodes the solution in Figure 1.3 with $n/2$ logical concurrency, or (2) have each process add n/P of the items locally, and then combine the P intermediate sums with a P-leaf tree that connects the processes. Schwartz argued that the latter solution is better because it is faster to add numbers in a tight loop than to multiplex threads. Essentially, Schwartz' algorithm solution has all processes working directly on the problem, and there is no improving on that fact. Schwartz' algorithm illustrates the point made in Chapter 4 that the Unlimited Parallelism approach is inferior to the Scalable Parallelism approach: The first solution provides greater logical concurrency, but there is never more than P-fold actual parallelism, and the extra logical concurrency generally leads to extra work that is not needed in the local solution. (Schwartz provides a more subtle analysis, but the point is clear.)

Figure 5.1 shows a schematic of Schwartz' algorithm. We see that all processes operate locally before using a tree to combine their results. In this tree combination phase the parallelism is uneven, as process 0 is involved in every level of the tree while others participate only to the extent that they send their values to the adjacent process.

The combining tree for Schwartz' algorithm can be elegantly formulated in our Peril-L pidgin language. Shown in Figure 5.2, the program relies on the use of full/empty variables. Recall that the semantics of such variables are described in

Figure 5.1
Process-induced
tree. Each process
computes locally on
a sequence of values
(heavy lines), and
then combines the
results pair-wise,
inducing a tree;
notice that process 0
participates at each
level in the tree.

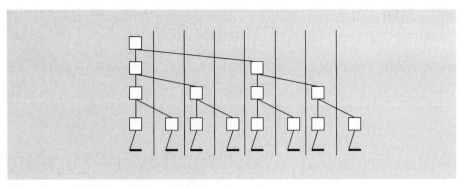

Figure 5.2
Schwartz algorithm inducing the tree of Figure 5.1. Line 8 loads the locally computed value
into the tree; line 14 performs the summation when both operands are available. Threads
exit when they have nothing left to do.

```
1    int nodeval'[P];                              Global full/empty variables for
2                                                  saving the value from right child
3    forall(index in(0..P-1))
4    {
5       int tally;
6       stride=1;
7       ...                                        COMPUTE tally HERE
8
9       while(stride<P)                            Begin logic for tree
10      {
11        if(index%(2*stride)==0)
12        {
13           tally=tally+nodeval'[index+stride];
14           stride=2*stride;
15        }
16        else
17        {
18           nodeval'[index]=tally;                Send initially to tree node
19           break;                                Exit, if no longer a parent
20        }
21      }
22
23   }
```

Table 4.1. They begin empty, and a reference to empty location stalls; an assignment
fills an empty location, and a reference to a filled location removes the item; finally,
assignments to filled locations stall until the occupying item is removed. The synchronization available with full/empty variables allows the code to execute in an

adaptive and particularly elegant way. When a thread discovers that its height is even, it combines its two children, the left of which has the same value (`index`) as the thread and the right of which is `stride` units away (`index+stride`). As the operands are referenced, their memory locations are emptied by the semantics of full/empty variables, which allows the resulting value to be stored back into the parent's node. After each iteration of the `while` loop, half of the threads complete.

In accordance with Schwartz' insight, we will view reduce, scan, and other tree-based algorithms as being a combination of local operations and a *P*-leaf global combining tree. When we use such operations in programming, as in

    total = +/ data;

we expect the compilers to emit code that uses Schwartz' local/global approach.

Higher-Degree Trees. We have used *binary* trees in our examples, but the binary characteristic should not be taken as gospel. Trees with higher degree nodes present a trade-off: a higher degree leads to a shallower tree, which decreases the latency of communicating from the root to a leaf, but a higher degree also reduces the amount of available parallelism and increases contention as multiple children attempt to communicate with the same parent.

The Reduce and Scan Abstractions

We have discussed the value of the tree communication structure. In Chapter 1, we first used a tree to remove sequentiality from the summation of an array of values. We later used a Schwartz-style tree to remove contention in a version of the Count 3s computation when otherwise many processes would contend for the same shared location. A tree structure was also used to describe the reduce and scan operations, which were defined with operations such as +, *, and, or, min, and max. In this section we argue that these abstractions are much more powerful than suggested by this limited set of operations, and we develop generalized reduce and scan functions that can be customized to perform a great many operations.

Why are reduce and scan important abstractions? Let's look at each in turn:

- **Reduce**, which combines a set of values to produce a single value, is almost always needed because in a parallel computation it is almost always necessary at some point to compare or combine results produced by different threads, either to summarize the computation or to control its execution.

- **Scan**, the parallel prefix computation, embodies the logic that performs a sequential operation in parts and carries along the intermediate results. Loop iterations often appear to be sequential because they accumulate information in order as they iterate, but on closer inspection, they can often be solved using a scan, which admits more parallelism.

We advocate the use of reduce and scan to the maximum extent possible. Even when the operations are not available in the programming language, they should be abstracted as functions, rather than hard-coded into the program. First, they are high level, and their use conveys valuable information about the program logic. Second, the use of the abstraction allows the implementation to be customized to the target machine. Some parallel computers even provide hardware support to perform global sums; for example, BlueGene/L, described in Chapter 2 has a combining network, as shown in Figure 2.10(b). Finally, there are often significant opportunities for optimizations. For example, to compute the bounding box of an array Pt of n Euclidean points, each with an x coordinate and a y coordinate field, we might write the following:

topEdge	= max/Pt.x;	*Find largest x field of the Pt array*
botEdge	= min/Pt.y;	*Find smallest x field of the Pt array*
rightEdge	= max/Pt.x;	*Find largest y field of the Pt array*
leftEdge	= min/Pt.y;	*Find smallest y field of the Pt array*

This code can be combined (by certain compilers or manually by programmers) into a single pass across the data. Such optimizations are not so obvious when looking at the specific details of the implementation.

To maximize the use of these powerful ideas, it's important to support generalized reduces and scans, which is the topic of the next section.

Two Kinds of Scan. Be aware that scans can differ depending on whether the accumulation of the *ith* element *includes* the *ith* value, called *inclusive scan*, or *excludes* the *ith* value, called *exclusive scan*. For the sequence A={ 2, 4, 6}, the inclusive scan produces +\$\backslash_{in}$ A={2, 6, 12}; the exclusive scan produces +\$\backslash_{ex}$ A={0, 2, 4}. For exclusive scan, the first entry is usually the identity for the function, or some other placeholder. Because of the identity

A <op>(<op>\$\backslash_{ex}$ A)≡<op>\$\backslash_{in}$ A

it makes little difference which is implemented; Peril-L uses the more common inclusive scan.

Example of Generalized Reduces and Scans

To understand the power of reduces and scans, consider the following problems, along with a description of their solution. Here, *we describe each solution sequentially, but each can be solved in parallel using customized reduce operations*:

- **Second smallest array element**—Identify the second smallest element in an array, which might be useful, for example, to identify the smallest positive number in an array that also contains 0s. The solution is to keep two variables, smallest and next-smallest—each initialized to +-infinity—and to compare their values against each element of the array: If the array's value is smaller than the value of smallest, then both smallest and next-smallest are updated accordingly; otherwise, if the array's value is smaller than next-smallest value, then the value of next-smallest is updated.

- **Histogram (k-way)**—Given an array of values, a, compute a histogram with k intervals. The solution assumes that min and max reduces have been used to compute the smallest and largest values in the range. Once these values are known, we can initialize a k-element array, hist, to 0s. We can then iterate through the a array, computing the interval to which each element belongs and then incrementing the corresponding element of the hist array.

- **Length of longest run of 1s**—Given an array of values, v, compute the longest run of consecutive 1s. This problem can be solved by using two variables, current and longest, which are initialized to 0s. The current variable will hold the length of the current run of 1s, and the longest variable will store the length of the longest run of 1s seen so far. We then iterate over the array v: if the value of v is a 1, we increment the value of current; if the value of v is not 1, we set the value of longest to be max(current, longest) and reset the value of current to 0. When we're done, the answer will be max(current, longest).

- **Index of first occurrence of** x—Given an array of symbols, s, return the position of the first occurrence of x. The solution is to initialize a 2-element temp array to x and +-infinity, then iterate through the data structure looking for x, and when found, keep the smaller of the saved index and the found index.

Though these computations can be programmed in Peril-L or another language easily enough, they will ultimately require that intermediate results be combined, probably with a conventional reduce. It's probably wiser to invoke a more abstract solution for the whole computation.

Notice that in all of the above examples, the solution utilizes a constant amount of extra memory to accumulate intermediate results. For example, in the *second smallest* computation, we remember the smallest and next smallest values; in computing the *histogram,* we remember the k values of the hist array; and in identifying the *longest run of 1s,* we remember the current length and the longest length. When we develop our generalized reduce solution, we will exploit this commonality by holding these intermediate values in a small array that we refer to as the *tally.*

Like the reduce abstraction, the scan abstraction is quite powerful because it can compute in parallel computations that are seemingly inherently sequential. Consider the following examples. As before, we specify our examples sequentially here, but we solve them in parallel later.

- **Team Standings**—Given an array, results, that represents a series of n games among k teams, produce as output the ID of the team with the most wins through each round of games (if multiple teams are tied for the most wins, represent the tie by outputting a 0). Assume that the *ith* entry of the results array holds the ID of the team that won the *ith* game. The solution maintains a k-element array, times-won, which is initialized to all 0s; the solution then iterates over the `results` array, incrementing the winner's entry in the `times-won` array and outputting the number of the team that is ahead at that point.

■ **Keep the longest sequence of 1s**—Given a binary array, remove all 1s that are not a part of the longest contiguous subsequence of 1s. Similar to the reduce that finds the length of the longest run of 1s, this solution keeps for each location the number of 1s in the run to which it belongs and the length of the longest subsequence seen so far; when the global answer is known, the solution iterates through the array in reverse order looking for the sequence and zeroing any cells that are not part of it.

■ **Index of Last Occurrence**—Given an array of values chosen from $(1..k)$, output for index i the index of the most recent occurrence of the element of the value stored at index i; output 0 if it is the first occurrence.

There are many other examples, but these illustrate the idea. As with the reduce operations, each scan relies on a constant amount of extra space that we refer to as the tally.

The Basic Structure

There is a basic structure that is common to all reduce and scan operations. Because we seek a scalable solution, we assume that the data structure upon which the reduce or scan operates has been allocated in pieces to an unknown number of processes. Since we are combining values globally, we will use a Schwartz-like algorithm that computes locally and then uses a tree to complete the computation. We will also assume the existence of a local variable in each process, called `tally`, which corresponds to the extra memory referred to in the motivating examples, and which is used to store intermediate results of the reduce and scan operations. With these assumptions, all reduce and scan operations can be implemented by defining variations of the following functions:

■ The `init()` function initializes the tally in preparation for the local computation.

■ The `accum()` function performs a local accumulation of an operand element into the tally.

■ The `combine()` function composes the intermediate tally results from its two sub-trees and passes the result to its parent.

■ The x-`gen()` function takes the global result and generates the final answer. There are separate forms of the x-`gen()` function for reduce and scan.

As an illustration, we define the functions that implement the standard +-reduce, that is, `+/ A`.

■ The `init()` function sets up an integer temporary, `tally`, and initializes it to 0.

- The accum(tally, val) function adds val, which will be A[i] for some i, to tally, and assigns the result to tally.
- The combine(left, right) function adds left and right tally values and passes the result to its parent.
- The reduce-gen(root) function is a no-op for this simple operation, and it returns its argument as the global result.

At the end of the local accumulation operation, each process sends its value to its parent. Figure 5.3 illustrates this logic, and Figure 5.4 gives Peril-L code to implement the logic.

Structure for Generalized Reduce

For the simple operation of +/ A, the four-component formulation is excessively general, but this structure is essential in more complex (and more powerful) cases. Our goal is to think about reduces in this more abstract way. To illustrate, we give

Figure 5.3
Schematic diagram of the generalized reduce logic for implementing +/ A. The large box at the bottom summarizes the local computation, beginning with init() and applying accum() to each of the A values; when local accumulation is complete, the tally is passed to the parent; the nodes of the tree apply combine() to the tally values from their children; and the root finally extracts the result using reduceGen().

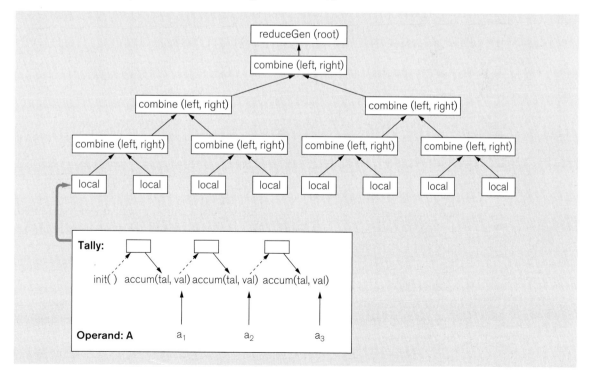

Figure 5.4
Peril-L code for the generalized reduce logic. Notice the sites for the four component functions. The tree combining relies on the use of full/empty memory, which drives the tree accumulation. As threads complete their roles in the combining tree, they terminate.

```
1   int nodeval'[P];                                    Global full/empty variables
2   int result;
3   forall(index in(0..P-1))
4   {
5     int myData[size]=localize(dataarray[]);           Local portion of global data values
6     int tally;
7     int stride=1;
8     tally=init ()                                      Initialize tally
9     for(i=0; i<size; i++)
10    {
11      tally=accum (tally, myData[i]);                  Local accumulation
12    }
13    nodeval'[index]=tally;                             Send initially to parent
14    while(stride < P)                                  Begin logic for tree
15    {
16      if(index%(2*stride)==0)
17      {                                                Combine values globally
18        nodeval'[index]=combine(nodeval'[index],
19                                nodeval'[index+stride]);
20        stride=2*stride;
21      }
22      else
23      {
24        break;
25      }
26    }
27    if(index==0)
28    {
29      result=reduceGen (nodeval'[0]);                  Generate reduced value
30    }
31  }
```

code that shows how secondMin/ A, the second smallest magnitude, is computed. Figure 5.5 gives the declaration for the tally item and the four functions that implement the reduce.

It should be obvious that with minor adjustments the four functions of Figure 5.5 could replace the corresponding functions in Figure 5.4 to produce a highly parallel, scalable implementation of secondMin/ A. The Schwartz template provided the structure, and we only had to decide what operations to perform at various points in the process.

Figure 5.5

The four generalized reduce functions implementing `secondMin` reduce. The tally is a two-element `struct`.

```
1   struct tally
2   {
3     float smallest1;                              Smallest element
4     float smallest2;                              Second smallest
5   };
6
7   tally init()                                    Initialize tally
8   {
9     tally t;
10    t.smallest1=MAX_FLOAT;
11    t.smallest2=MAX_FLOAT;
12    return t;
13  }
14
15  tally accum(tally t, float elem)                Local accumulation
16  {
17    if(t.small1>elem)                             Is this a new smallest?
18    {
19      t.smallest2=t.smallest1;
20      t.smallest1=elem;
21    }
22    else
23    {
24      if(t.smallest2>elem)                        Is it a new second smallest?
25      {
26        t.smallest2=elem;
27      }
28      return t;
29    }
30  }
31
32  tally combine(tally left, tally right)          Combine into "left" by
33  {                                               accumulating right values
34    tally t;
35    t=accum(left, right.smallest1);
36    t=accum(t, right.smallest2);
37    return t;
38  }
39
40  float reduceGen(tally t)
41  {
42    return t.smallest2;
43  }
```

Example of Components of a Generalized Scan

The generalized scan applies the same concepts as the generalized reduce. The primary difference is that after the combining is complete the intermediate results must be passed back down the combining tree. That is, in order to complete the prefix computation on the local values, an intermediate value from the combining tree will be needed by each process. (Refer to the parallel prefix discussion in Chapter 1, with particular attention to Figure 1.4.)

The generalized scan begins like the generalized reduce, and the two algorithms are conceptually identical in the init (), accum (), and combine () functions. However, to propagate intermediate values to all processes, tally values are propagated down the tree subject to the following constraint:

> *The value that each process receives from its parent is the tally for the values that are left of the parent's leftmost leaf.*

Because we are computing on blocks, the tally received from the parent is the combined values of the items left of the first item in the leftmost leaf's block. Because the root has no parent, init() must be modified to create the value as the input for the logical parent of the root. Each node receives a value from its parent and relays it to its left child; for its right child, it combines the value received from its left child on the upsweep with the value received from its parent, and then it sends the result to its right child.

When the tally value is received at a leaf, it must be combined with the values stored in the operand array to compute the prefix totals, which are the result. In Figure 5.6 these operands are shown schematically in the box at the bottom. Thus, the scanGen() procedure produces the final result.

Figure 5.7 shows the logic of a generalized scan. Comparing with the logic of Figure 5.5, we notice several points:

- Global storage (ltally) is allocated to save the left child value during the up sweep (see line 19).
- The reduce and scan match through line 28, except for the saving of the left child values.
- The init()function is called (line 33) to provide the parent value to the root.
- All threads enter the down sweep while loop (lines 35–41), but only those having received a parent value can proceed. They save the parent tally (line 37) and send it to the left child (line 38), combine it with the saved left child tally, and send the result to the right child (line 39).
- The down sweep delivers a ptally to every thread, which is used in scanGen() to compute the final result (line 44).

Notice that init() and combine() are used in two different ways for the scan.

Figure 5.6

Schematic of the scan operation. The first part of the algortihm is simply the generalized reduce, shown in Figure 5.3. Once the global tally is found, prefixes are propagated down the tree according to the rule: Parent values are sent to the left child (dashed arrows), combine (left, parent) is sent to right child. When a prefix arrives at a leaf, the local operation applies the **scanGen()** function and stores the result in the operand element.

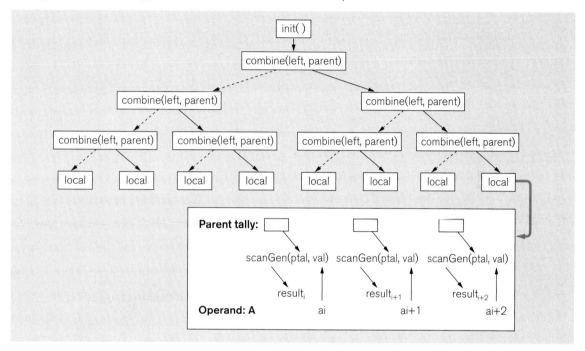

Figure 5.7

Generalized scan program. The down sweep of the tally values, beginning on line 35, distributes intermediate results to all threads to compute the final result (line 44).

1 `int nodeval'[P];`	*Global full/empty memory*
2 `int ltally[P];`	*Store left operand of combine*
3 `forall(index in(0..P-1))`	
4 `{`	
5 `  int myData[size]=localize(operandArray[]);`	*Local data values*
6 `  int tally;`	***Tally***
7 `  int ptally;`	*Tally from parent*
8 `  int stride=1;`	
9 `  tally=init ();`	***Initialize***
10 `  for(i=0; i<size; i++)`	
11 `  {`	
12 `    tally=accum (tally, myData[i]);`	***Accumulate***
13 `  }`	
14 `  nodeval'[index]=tally;`	*Send initially to parent*
15 `  while(stride<P)`	*Begin logic for tree*

(continued)

Figure 5.7 (*continued*)
Generalized scan program. The down sweep of the tally values, beginning on line 35, distributes intermediate results to all threads to compute the final result (line 44).

```
16   {
17     if(index%(2*stride)==0)
18     {                                           Combine
19       ltally[index+stride]=nodeval'[index];
20       nodeval'[index]=combine (ltally[index+stride],
21                                 nodeval'[index+stride]);
22       stride=2*stride;
23     }
24     else
25     {
26       break;
27     }
28   }
29   stride=P/2;
30   if(index==0)
31   {
32     ptally=nodeval'[0];                         Clear existing up sweep value
33     nodeval'[0]=init ();                        Set init() as parent input
34   }
35   while(stride>1)                               Begin logic for tree descent
36   {
37     ptally=nodeval'[index];                     Grab parent value
38     nodeval'[index]=ptally;                     Send it down to left
39     nodeval'[index+stride]=                     Send parent + left child right
         combine (ptally, ltally[index+stride]);
40     stride=stride/2;                            Go down to next level
41   }
42   for(i=0; i<size; i++)
43   {
44     myResult[i]=scanGen (ptally, myData[i]);    Generate Scan
45   }
46 }
```

Applying the Generalized Scan

To illustrate the operation of the generalized scan, imagine an array A of integers from the sequence $1, ..., k$. The scan

```
lastOccurrence\ A
```

returns in index position i the index of the most recent occurrence of A[i] or it returns 0 if this is the first occurrence. We use as a tally an array of k elements, which is initialized to 0s; if A[i] is j, the accum() function stores i in tally[j] as the last occurrence; the combine() function takes the maximum of each element of the two arrays; and the scan generator reprocesses the block of data, using the ptally as its initial value. Figure 5.8 shows the functions that produce this result. (Notice that the tally array at the end is a histogram for the array.)

Figure 5.8
Customized scan functions to return the index of the last occurrence of the element in the *ith* operand position; the tally is a globally allocated array of *k* elements.

```
tally init(tally t)                              Setup globally allocated array
{
   for(i=0; i<k; i++)
   {
      t[i]=0;
   }
   return t;
}
tally accum(int elem, tally t, int i)            Local accumulation, array index
{                                                needed
   t[elem-1]=i;
   return t;
}
tally combine(tally left, tally right)           Combine into "left"
{
   for(i=0; i<k; i++)
   {
      left[i]=max(left[i],right[i]);
      return left;
   }
}
int scanGen(int elem, tally t, int i)            Finalizing scan
{
   t[elem-1]=i;                                  Accum w/parent tally
   return t[elem-1];                             Store running count
}
```

Generalized Vector Operations

We have generalized reduce and scan operations considerably. Though we have used small examples that are easy to program and explain, it should be clear that a substantial amount of computation can be packaged into this form. Indeed, one way to view many data parallel computations is as a sequence of local operations, with scans and reduces interspersed when more global information is required. In this view, the contributing reduces and scans lose their identity and the computation can be thought of as a general vector operation. In this view both the local and global computation are efficiently computed. It's a programming approach to keep in mind.

Assigning Work to Processes Statically

Implicit in our discussion of reduce and scans was the notion that items of our data structure were allocated in groups to different processes. We now explore in more detail this issue of allocating data and work to processes. This section discusses methods of statically allocating work to processes, and the next section will consider the need for dynamically allocating work to processes.

In keeping with the Scalable Parallelism approach introduced in Chapter 4, we will think in terms of an allocation to some logical set of processes, so that the resulting program is not tied to any specific number of processors. For example, a 2-dimensional array A might be allocated such that blocks of size $u \times v$ are assigned to each thread. At a later date the configuration can be adjusted to use different values of u and v as appropriate.

We start by considering the case of statically allocated arrays. Our basic approach is to statically allocate data to threads and then to give each thread the responsibility of computing on the data that it "owns." In a shared memory system, the allocation of data to threads may be implicit, that is, the data structures are allocated globally and each thread computes on only one portion of the structure, which naturally migrates to its portion of the cache hierarchy. In a distributed memory system, each process will allocate its own portion of the data. Regardless of the memory model, the concepts in this section apply.

Block Allocations

If our goal is to exploit locality, it follows that for most computations contiguous portions of a data structure should be allocated together on the same process. This is the familiar spatial and temporal locality that caches exploit. Thus, 1-dimensional arrays are assigned to processes in blocks of consecutive indices. For 2-dimensional arrays, allocating by 2-dimensional blocks (that is, consecutive indices in both dimensions) generally leads to efficient solutions. Furthermore, 2-dimensional blocks tend to make more sense than allocating, say, whole rows, because block allocations can often reduce communication. For example, for computations that rely on neighboring values, the so-called *stencil computations*, such as

```
B[i, j]=(A[i-1, j]+A[i, j+1]+A[i+1, j]+A[i, j-1])/4.0;
```

blocks are preferable to rows, as can be seen in Figure 5.9. A square-like block of array values has the property that the elements that must be referenced by other processes for the stencil computation are on the edge, and as the size of the block increases, the number of edge elements grows much more slowly, reducing communication costs. We say that blocks have a *surface area to volume advantage*, because as the size (volume) grows the number of edge elements (surface area) grows more slowly, which implies that less data is sent among threads or processes. The small 4 × 4 example shown in Figure 5.9 must receive $4 \times 4 = 16$ elements from its neighbors compared to the row allocation that requires $2 \times 16 = 32$ elements from its neighbors. On a larger problem, say a 1024×1024 array with $P = 256$, a 2D blocked layout has 64×64 elements allocated to each process, while a 1D layout would have 4×1024 elements allocated as whole rows; the block allocation requires $4 \times 64 = 256$ elements from neighbors, while the row allocation requires $2 \times 1024 = 2048$ elements from neighbors.

Figure 5.9

Two allocations of a 16 × 16 array to 16 processes: (a) 2-dimensional blocks and (b) rows. For a computation in which each element depends on its four nearest neighbors, the process with the gray values must communicate with its neighboring processes to receive the dark values. The row allocation requires twice as many values to be transmitted, and because of the surface area to volume advantage, the advantage of the block allocation increases as the number of local items increases. One complicating issue is the fact that the row allocation sends fewer messages per process. Chapter 7 discusses why it's often the *number* of messages sent and not the size of the message sent that is important, because the software overhead of sending a message is typically quite large and the actual data transmission is usually efficiently pipelined. Note, however, that the advantage of the row allocation is a fixed one, whereas the advantage of the 2-dimensional block allocation scales with the size of the arrays.

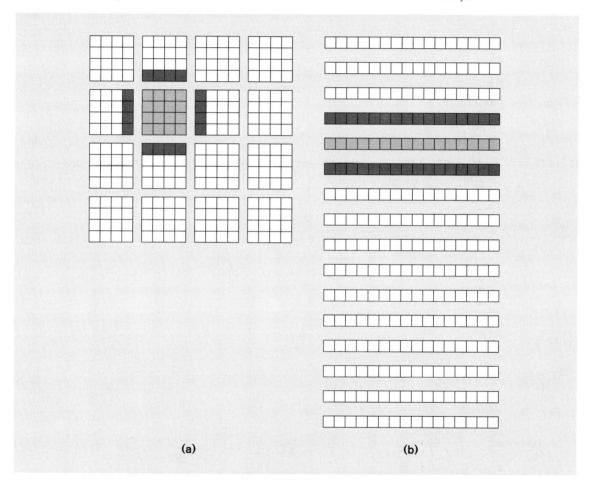

(a)   (b)

For higher *d*-dimensional arrays, allocating as *d*-dimensional blocks is frequently used for its surface area to volume advantage. But allocating only two of the dimensions and keeping the other dimension(s) allocated locally is almost as common. The latter choice is usually motivated by an insufficient number of processes for a *d*-dimensional allocation or by extreme aspect ratios.

Overlap Regions

Our principle of operating on large blocks of computation leads to the concept of an *overlap region*, which is a type of software cache. For example, in many array-based computations, the value of each element is computed by referencing a fixed set of neighboring array values, producing what are known as *stencil computations* because their memory reference pattern (and induced communication pattern) is a stencil that applies at each point in the array. These computations reference values owned by neighboring processes. For example, the 4-point nearest neighbor stencil

```
B[i, j]=(A[i-1, j]+A[i, j+1]+A[i+1, j]+A[i, j-1])/4.0;
```

references values stored on each process' four neighbors. For block allocations, Figure 5.9(a) shows that for the top row of the allocation, references to A[i-1,j] reside in the process above it, and similarly for the other edge elements of the block. Such neighbor values are best referenced as follows:

■ When allocating storage for the local portion of a distributed array, allocate extra space to hold the non-local values that will be referenced. This extra storage, known as an *overlap* region, is allocated so as to be contiguous with the local portion of the array, as if the process also owned those non-local portions of the array.

■ Obtain the necessary non-local values from the other processes, storing them in the overlap regions.

■ Perform the computation on what are now entirely local data values. These cached non-local values can be accessed until the owning process modifies their value, at which point new values will need to be obtained.

See Figure 5.10.

Figure 5.10
The overlap region (gray) for an array block showing the non-local values on adjacent processes that must be moved to fill the overlap region; once the overlap region is filled, the stencil computation is entirely local. (The "missing corners" are not used, but they are allocated to simplify array index calculations.)

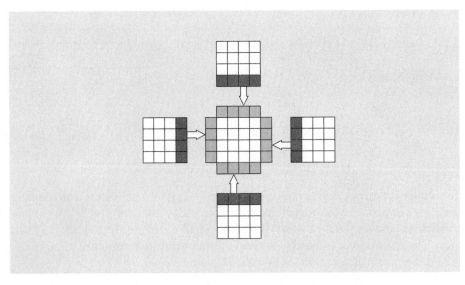

Several advantages recommend this approach. First, once the overlap region is filled, all references in the computation are local, yielding large blocks of independent computation. Second, the computation uses the same index calculations for all references to the array, so it can be performed in a single loop nest with no special edge exceptions. Third, by batching communication, we effectively merge multiple cross-process dependences into b dependences, where the computation references data from b neighboring processes. Finally, by batching communication, we typically reduce communication costs. For distributed memory programming models, data transmission takes $t_o + dt_b$ seconds to transmit d bytes, where t_o is (setup) overhead and t_b is the time per byte. The batched communication amortizes the overhead across a larger message size. For shared memory machines, this approach reduces communication costs by moving entire cache lines, as opposed to making redundant memory requests for individual array elements; the use of overlap regions also reduces false sharing.

Cyclic and Block Cyclic Allocations

In algorithms in which the amount of work is not proportional to the amount of data, block allocations may suffer from poor load balance. For example, consider LU decomposition, a linear algebra computation that decomposes a matrix into the product of two matrices as a way to solve a system of linear equations. This computation iterates over a matrix and at each iteration solves one row and one column of the result, so the amount of work decreases after each iteration. Figure 5.11 shows that the distribution of the remaining work is uneven. Figure 5.11(a) shows in white

Figure 5.11
Schematic diagram of (a) the LU Decomposition algorithm, (b) sixteen processes arranged in a logical grid, and (c) the allocation of the array elements to the processes. For example, process P_0 is assigned that part of the array in the upper left three columns and rows that are complete.

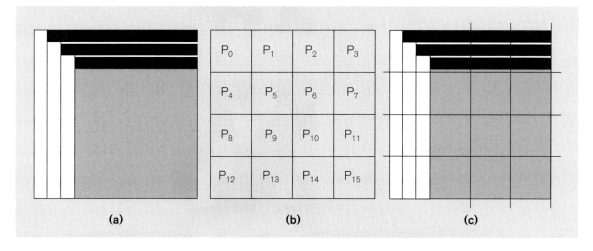

(a)   (b)   (c)

and black the columns and rows whose results have been completed, respectively. Figure 5.11(b) shows sixteen processes logically arranged as a grid, and Figure 5.11(c) shows how the matrix might be allocated to the processes using a block allocation. We see that as the algorithm proceeds, the processes that own the black and white portions of the matrix have decreasing work to do. For example, after the first 25 percent of the rows have been added to the result arrays, there is no more work to do for the seven processes on the left and top sides of the array (44 percent). Therefore, nearly half of the processes will be idle after one quarter of the rows have been processed. Indeed, the last 25 percent of the rows is computed sequentially by process P_{15}.

One way to address this load imbalance is to use a cyclic distribution, which allocates individual elements to different processes in a round-robin fashion in much the way that cards are dealt in a Poker game (see Figure 5.12). Cyclic allocations balance the load because they tend to distribute the hot spots across multiple processes. However, a cyclic distribution can increase communication costs by increasing the number of cross-process dependences; a cyclic allocation is essentially the antithesis of the "large block of computation" approach.

To provide a balance between locality and load balance, it's common to use a block-cyclic allocation, in which blocks of elements are distributed cyclically. Figure 5.13 shows a block-cyclic allocation in which consecutive blocks of the matrix are

Figure 5.12
Illustration of a cyclic distribution of an 8 × 8 array onto five processes.

Figure 5.13
Block-cyclic allocation of 3 × 2 blocks to a 14 × 14 array distributed to four processes (colors).

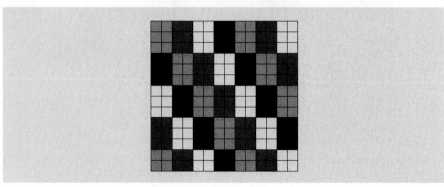

assigned cyclically to different processes. The figure shows several features of block-cyclic allocations. First, a block's dimension does not have to divide the matrix's dimension; the block is simply truncated where necessary. Second, each process receives blocks from throughout the matrix, so as the computation proceeds, completed portions will be resident on each process, as will the incomplete portions. Figure 5.14 shows the allocation of Figure 5.13 as it would appear midway through an LU computation. Notice how well the remaining work is balanced across the processes.

The particular allocation shown in Figure 5.13 uses 3×2 blocks, and we see that every element is adjacent to an element that is allocated to a different process, so this small block size is likely to incur considerable overhead if nearest neighbors must be referenced for some other part of the computation. First, there is considerable communication among blocks. Second, the overlap region for each 3×2 block requires more memory than the block itself. Third, the tiny blocks do not exploit locality well. The use of larger blocks, say 64×64, can reduce the amount of communication and amortize some of the overhead per block. But if the blocks become too large, the chance of load imbalance increases again. In general, balancing the competing goals of a block-cyclic allocation is a delicate matter.

Example: Load Balancing with Cyclic Allocation. Julia sets, which are based on Mandelbrot sets, are defined by an iterated function

$$z_{n+1} = z_n^2 + c$$

where z_n is the value of the nth iteration of the function, c represents a complex coefficient that determines the shape of the Julia set on the complex plane, and the first iteration of the function is defined as $z_0 = a_0$ for some constant value a_0. To generate a set for a given coefficient, c, each point on the complex plane (based on some specified resolution) is iterated upon until the absolute value of the result passes 2.0 or until some upper limit on the number of iterations is reached. The number of iterations that each point on the plane iterates through determines the color of that point.

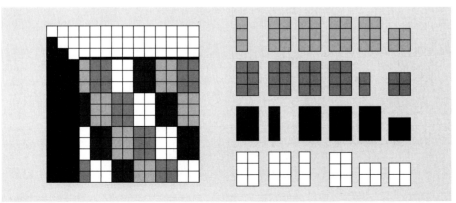

Figure 5.14
The block-cyclic allocation of Figure 5.13 midway through the computation; the blocks to the right summarize the active values for each process.

We use the creation of Julia sets as an example of a parallel computation that requires load balancing (see Figure 5.15). Though the computation is embarrassingly parallel—every position can be computed independently—the number of iterations required to converge is highly variable. If we assign work to processes spatially based on a point's position in the figure, then some processes will finish long before others. Indeed, most allocations based on neighborhoods lead to poor allocations.

The obvious solution is to allocate pixels to processes in a cyclic fashion. Thus, pixel $(0, 0)$ is assigned process P_0, pixel $(0, 1)$ is assigned to process P_1, and in general if the image is $x \times y$, then pixel (r, s) is allocated to process $P_{(ry+s) \bmod P}$. If P doesn't divide y, this allocation ensures that the tasks are sampled regularly over the image giving a roughly even allocation of easy and hard pixels. When P divides y, the allocation results in vertical lines of pixels, which may still be okay. But if not, we can avoid the problem by assigning work based on a small $k \times k$ region of pixels such that k is relatively prime to the row size.

Irregular Allocations

Of course, there are many algorithms that use data structures other than arrays. For example, unstructured grids, irregularly shaped grids typically made up of triangles, are commonly used in finite element computations to simulate things such as the

Figure 5.15
Julia set generated from the site http://aleph0.clarku.edu/~djoyce.

fluid dynamics of an airplane wing (see Figure 5.16). Despite the more complex data structure, the same principles apply. Assuming that interactions occur across grid boundaries, communication among processes is minimized by identifying large portions of the grid that have a large surface area to volume ratio. The techniques for such partitioning generally fall into two categories, those based on geometric partitioning and those based on graph-theoretic partitioning. The literature of partitioning is generally accessed through terms such as "mesh partitioning."

Because the data references are irregular—and often not known until runtime—it can be a very inefficient process to fetch the non-local values: Discover that a reference is non-local, fetch it, discover the next non-local reference, fetch it, and so on. To avoid this fine-grained, serial solution—and hopefully to apply sound parallel concepts—a technique called *inspector/executor* has been developed. Prior to executing an iteration or other large segment of code, the data references for its irregular data structures are "inspected," that is, analyzed to identify those that are non-local and the process to which they are assigned. All references to a non-local process are batched and then fetched. Then, with the data local, the executor performs the computation. Notice that this is the same idea as using overlap regions to cache non-local data for array allocations.

The inspector/executor is one example of a dynamic allocation technique. We now look at other dynamic allocation techniques.

Figure 5.16
Example of an unstructured grid representing the pressure distribution on two airfoils. Image from http://fun3d.larc.nasa.gov/example-24.html.

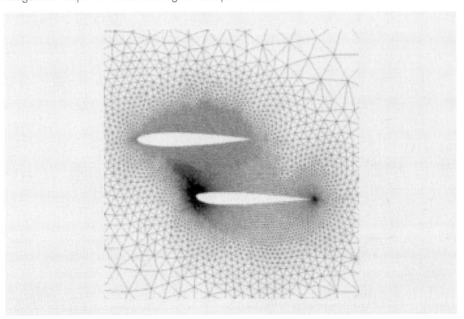

Assigning Work to Processes Dynamically

In many cases, it's impossible to adopt a fixed work assignment because new work is dynamically created during the computation. Examples include a server that processes client requests, an *adaptive algorithm* that creates new work to apply additional computing power where the solution needs the greatest effort, and many graph algorithms. In other cases, the amount of computational effort is not proportional to the amount of data, so a static allocation leads to poor load balance; in such situations dynamic work allocation can balance the load, as otherwise idle processes can be assigned additional work. This section describes work queues as a strategy for dynamically assigning work to processes. Our discussion will focus on the interactions of the processes with the work queue, but it's important to remember that the tasks on the work queue may interact with each other directly, and the development of a parallel algorithm needs to consider those interactions as well.

Work Queues

A work queue is a data structure for dynamically assigning work to threads or processes. Work queues have uses in many sequential algorithms, particularly when work is dynamically generated during the course of the computation, and the generalization to multiple processes is a natural one. The simplest work queue is a first-in first-out (FIFO) list of task descriptors, where newly created tasks are added to one end of the queue, and tasks to be processed are removed from the other end of the queue. For example, the common *producer/consumer* paradigm uses a FIFO list to communicate work between a producing process and a consuming process.

As an example of a trivial task that can be expressed in work queue form, consider the $3n + 1$ conjecture (or Collatz Conjecture), which proposes an affirmative answer to the question "For any positive integer a_0, does the process defined by

$$a_i = \begin{cases} 3a_{i-1} + 1 & a_{i-1} \text{ odd} \\ a_{i-1}/2 & a_{i-1} \text{ even} \end{cases}$$

converge to 1?" (See http://mathworld.wolfram.com/CollatzProblem.html.) For example, we have for $a_0 = 15$, 16, and 17, the sequence of a_is is

15, 46, 23, 70, 35, 106, 53, 160, 80, 40, 20, 10, 5, 16, 8, 4, 2, 1
16, 8, 4, 2, 1
17, 52, 26, 13, 40, 20, 10, 5, 16, 8, 4, 2, 1

The conjecture is known, by computer search, to be true for all integers less than $3 \cdot 2^{53}$, but the problem we're interested in is "What is the *largest factor of expansion*, defined to be $max(a_i)/a_0$?" That is, how large is the largest intermediate result relative to the starting value? For 15, the expansion factor is $160/15 = 10.67$, while for 16 it's 1, and for 17 the expansion factor is $52/17 = 3.06$. (It is not known if the expansion factor is bounded, or indeed, even important.) We will implement a search for the largest expansion factor as an example, because it is a simple illustration of several aspects of work queues.

Our solution postulates a work queue containing the next integers to test. For P processes, we initialize the queue to the first P positive integers:

```
int i;
for(i=0; i<P; i++)
{
   q[i]=i+1;
}
```

The integers are our task descriptors. As a general principle, it is wise to make the task descriptors as small as possible, while making them self-contained. In this case, integers suffice because they are the numbers to be tested.

Each thread will play the role of both producer and consumer. As a consumer, it removes the first item from the queue; as a producer the thread adds P to the value that it just removed and then appends the new value to the end of the queue. The rationale for adding P is that P threads will be checking integers at once, so advancing by P will skip those values that will be processed by other threads. The thread has the logic shown in Figure 5.17.

Figure 5.17
Code for computing the expansion factor for the Collatz Conjecture.

```
1    float ef=1.0;                        Best expansion factor
2    int bestA=1;                         Record which a_i had best expansion
3    int head=0;                          Next item on Q to process
4    forall(index in(0 .. P-1))          Define P threads to perform test
5    {
6       int a=1;                          Test number
7       float myEF=1.0;                   Local Expansion Factor
8       int big, atest=1;                 Locals to compute expansion factor
9
10      while(a<runSize)                  Limit to 2 billion or expand single precision
11      {
12         exclusive                      Get a from Q and leave a + P
13         {
14            a=q[head];
15            q[head]=a+P;
16            head=(head+1)%P;
17         }                              End of single thread section
18         atest=a;                       Set up for a test
19         big=a;                         The start could be the largest value we see
20         while(atest!=1)
21         {
```

(continued)

Figure 5.17 (*continued*)
Code for computing the expansion factor for the Collatz Conjecture (*continued*).

```
22          if(even(atest))
23          {
24              atest=atest/2;
25          }
26          else
27          {
28              atest=3*atest+1;
29              big=max(big, atest);
30          }
31      }
32      myEF=big/a;                    Compute expansion for this a
33      exclusive                       Get a from Q and leave a + P
34      {
35          if(myEF>ef)                Record any progress (after 1st time)
36          {
37              ef=myEF;
38              bestA=a;
39          }
40      }
41   }
42 }
```

After declaring variables and creating threads, the computation enters a `while` loop to process a set of integers. The first step in this process is to enter a single threaded region to allow the thread to manipulate, race-free, the global queue. The next number is removed from the queue, the queue is updated with a new number, and the head of the queue is advanced.

In the body of the computation, the thread sets up two values (`big`, `atest`) and then enters a `while` loop that defines the a-sequence. With each $3 \times a + 1$ change, the new a is tested to see if it is larger than those seen previously; if so, it is saved. When `a==1`, the loop completes. At the conclusion, the `exclusive` region is entered again to check whether the last expansion factor was a new high; if so, it is recorded along with the a_i that caused it.

Now consider the behavior of the work queue. First, notice that in effect P subsequences are being checked simultaneously, but they will not remain in lock step because the amount of work required of each check is different. For example, with four processes the queue might at the beginning transition through the following states, where the most recent assignment is shown in bold:

Work Queue	Active Processes
1, 2, 3, 4	—
2, 3, 4, 5	$p_0[\mathbf{1}]$

3, 4, 5, 6	$p_0[2]$
4, 5, 6, 7	$p_0[2], p_1[3]$
5, 6, 7, 8	$p_0[2], p_1[3], p_2[4]$
6, 7, 8, 9	$p_0[5], p_1[3], p_2[4]$
7, 8, 9, 10	$p_0[5], p_1[3], p_2[4], p_3[6]$

We see that because the processing of 1 is trivial, p_0 might return to the queue to get the next value, 2, before any of the other processes even start; the processing of 2 is also easy, so p_0 returns again quickly. Notice also that workers do not necessarily process a similarly spaced subsequence. Indeed, if the timing works out, all of the processes could be working on the same subsequence at once. Summarizing, although our work queue is regimented, its dynamic nature allows it to accommodate many different timing characteristics.

Variations of Work Queues

There are many variations of work queues. Algorithmically, the elements of the queue do not have to be processed in FIFO order but could be in last-in first-out (LIFO), randomized, or priority order, each with their own obvious uses.

Specific uses of work queues can also vary based on the granularity of work. In our example we have assumed that the unit of work is a single task descriptor, which is as small as possible for the Collatz Conjecture problem. However, as mentioned in Chapter 3, the granularity of work presents a trade-off. A small-grain size increases queue manipulation overhead and increases the likelihood of contention; a large-grain size increases the chance of suffering from load imbalance.

One strategy that attempts to strike a balance between overhead and load imbalance is to use a *variable grain size* that is proportional to the number of elements in the queue. When the queue is full, threads or processes grab large chunks of work, assuming there is enough to keep all processes busy. As the number of elements in the queue shrinks, the grain size also shrinks.

Until now we have considered a single work queue, which of course is not scalable. A more scalable strategy is to use multiple queues, with each thread or process assigned to a different queue or set of queues. This approach reduces contention but can increase latency if a thread needs to inspect multiple queues before it can find a non-empty queue. The use of multiple queues also introduces a load balancing issue. What happens if one queue is empty while others are not? One solution is to let threads retrieve work from queues to which it was not assigned, an act which is often referred to as *work stealing*.

Case Study: Concurrent Memory Allocation

Consider the problem of implementing a memory allocator for a symmetric multiprocessor. A memory allocator takes requests for memory and returns an address to a block of memory of the requested size. A good allocator will scale with the number of processors, will avoid false sharing, and will use virtual memory efficiently. Other goals such as low fragmentation—the free memory should not be fragmented into many small pieces—are also important, but for simplicity we will ignore such issues in this discussion.

Before explaining one particularly nice solution, we first explain some previous solutions and their problems.

- The simplest solution is to use a *single heap* that satisfies all requests. However, with multiple processors accessing this heap, contention for the heap and its mutex will become a bottleneck as the number of processors grows.

- A second common solution is to use one *private heap* per processor, in which case there is no need for locking because there is no sharing. However, this scheme can suffer from unbounded memory allocation—even for situations that use a bounded amount of memory—which will eventually crash the program. To see this, consider a producer-consumer relationship between two processors, p and c. Processor p will allocate memory that is consumed by c, and when c is done with this memory it will free it, returning it to c's private heap. Because p never gets access to the freed memory, it must continue to allocate memory to satisfy each of p's requests, leading to unbounded memory allocation.

- A third solution avoids unbounded growth by using a *private heap with ownership*, meaning that each piece of memory is owned by the allocating processor, so when it is freed, it is returned to the owning processor's heap. Thus, in our producer-consumer scenario, c will return the memory to p's heap, and we will no longer see unbounded growth as p can reuse memory that it previously allocated. The problem here is that there is no sharing of free memory, so when one processor allocates memory, no other processor can benefit from it. Thus, this scheme can suffer from P-fold increase in memory allocation. Consider the case where P processors form a chain of producer-consumer relationships, so that processor $i \bmod P$ allocates a block, and processor $(i+1) \bmod P$ frees the block. In this situation, a single block could be produced by processor 0 and conceptually flow through each of the processors, as it is freed and then allocated again by each processor until it reaches processor 0. Thus, while an ideal system might allocate and reuse a single block for an entire round-trip, private heaps with ownership will allocate P blocks of memory, one for each processor. This factor of P increase is significant. For example, on a 16-processor machine with a 32-bit address space, each processor would only be able to allocate a modest 128 MB of memory before running out of virtual memory.

- Some memory allocators induce *false sharing* by allocating memory from the same cache line to different processors. Of course, we know that false sharing can be avoided by padding memory allocations so that their size is a multiple of the cache line size. However, allocators do not perform such padding because it can significantly increase the amount of memory that is allocated.

The Hoard memory allocator solves these problems by applying two principles:

1. **Limit local memory usage.** If one private heap becomes too large, it moves blocks to a global heap, which can be accessed by other heaps. In particular, when a heap is empty, it first attempts to satisfy an allocation request by using memory from the global heap before allocating new blocks.
2. **Manage memory in large blocks.** The use of large blocks reduces false sharing and reduces contention for the global heap.

We have omitted many details, but we can summarize the advantages of Hoard as follows. The use of multiple private heaps provides concurrency that scales with the number of processors; the use of the global heap provides a mechanism for balancing the load, so that the freed pages do not accumulate in private heaps; the use of large blocks follows our general principle of increasing granularity to reduce overhead and contention.

Hoard is commonly used in many existing operating systems, including Solaris, Linux, and Windows, and there are many examples where the use of Hoard dramatically improves program performance through its more efficient use of memory. Moreover, Hoard has provably bounded memory blowup and low synchronization costs.

Trees

Trees are important data structures because they represent hierarchical organizations. For example, *kd*-trees can be used in graphics rendering and in gravitational simulations to partition space into hierarchical cells. The tree structure makes it possible to find items in this space in time that is proportional to the height of the tree.

Trees present several challenges in parallel computation. First, trees are usually constructed using pointers, and in languages that do not provide shared memory, pointers are local only to one process. Second, we typically use trees for their dynamic flexibility, but dynamic behavior often implies extensive performance-limiting communication. Third, the irregular structure of some trees can make it difficult to reason about communication and load balance. But, challenging or not, trees are too useful to ignore.

Allocation by Sub-Tree

Our guideline of maximizing the number of large blocks of independent computation applies to trees as well, as we would like to assign entire sub-trees to individual processes. For example, we could replicate the top of the tree, known as the "cap," and assign a copy of it and a sub-tree to each of P different processes, as shown in Figure 5.18. If there is no communication among the sub-trees, then we have a scalable solution.

Figure 5.18
Cap allocation for a binary tree on $P = 8$ processes. Each process is allocated one of the leaf sub-trees, along with a *copy* of the cap (shaded).

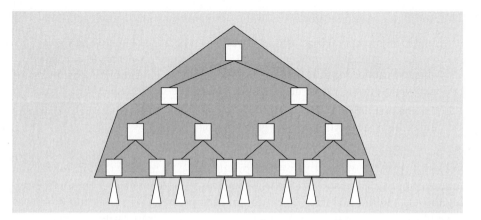

The cap allocation is effective because the cap, being near the root, is small relative to the rest of the tree. Furthermore, because the root and its immediate descendants are available on all processes, interactions that propagate through the root can use local data to identify the correct destination sub-tree. Navigation through the destination sub-tree is typically assigned as a task to its owner. As an additional bonus, in advanced algorithms for gravitational simulations in which large regions of the problem are aggregated into "meta-points," the points around the root tend to be all meta-points and therefore once created are read-only, eliminating communication, race conditions and locking as issues. Of course, as the computation proceeds, changes in the cap must be maintained coherently across processes, which means that all processes must see the same state. If the top of the tree is frequently modified, it could instead be distributed among the processes in various ways.

Such allocations work well when the full tree is enumerated at the start of a computation or when the nodes can be generated in a level-order fashion. For example, Figure 5.19(a) shows how a binary tree could be allocated to eight processes, and Figure 5.19(b) shows how the same tree could be allocated to six processes.

Game Search Example. Allocation by sub-tree works well for problems that can be recursively partitioned into subproblems. For example, suppose we are searching a Tic-Tac-Toe (Naughts and Crosses) game tree on $P = 4$ processes. When symmetries are considered, there are only three initial positions, and we expand one of these to produce the fourth search task (see Figure 5.20). That is, each process will search the game tree descendant from the indicated board position.

Dynamic Allocations

Some trees are allocated dynamically in an unpredictable fashion. Other trees are explored to uneven depths. For example, a search with alpha-beta pruning, which is commonly used in game searches, will prune away portions of the hierarchical

Figure 5.19
Logical tree representations: (a) a binary tree where $P = 8$; (b) a binary tree where $P = 6$.

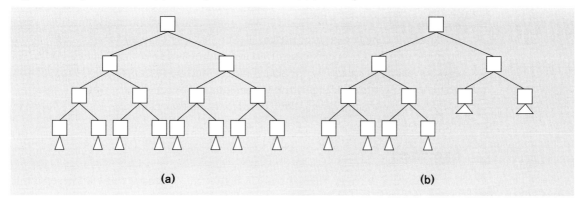

(a) (b)

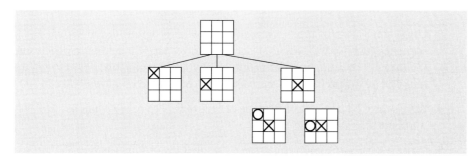

Figure 5.20
Enumerating the Tic-Tac-Toe game tree; a process is assigned to search the games beginning with each of the four initial move sequences.

search space based on previously seen results, leading to a search tree with leaves at different depths. In such cases, a work queue can be used, with the queue entries representing unassigned nodes of the tree. The same trade-offs that were discussed in the section on Assigning Work to Processes Dynamically apply here. Of course, in the case of alpha-beta pruning, there needs to be some mechanism for communicating previous results among processes. These results can either be communicated using shared memory or using some type of combining tree.

Chapter Summary

In this chapter we discussed algorithmic techniques and allocation techniques for the development of scalable parallel computations. We first discussed the power of generalized reduce and scan abstractions. We then discussed various methods of assigning work to processes. Throughout the chapter, we saw the implications of a simple guiding principle—identifying blocks of largely independent computations— and we saw how load balancing issues sometimes interfere with this goal.

Historical Perspective

Community solved problems have been popular for a decade (SETI @ Home is perhaps the most famous, but BOINC lists many others.) Ladner and Fischer [1980] demonstrated the key ideas of the parallel prefix algorithm, and Deitz [2005] developed the four function decomposition for parameterized scans; Blelloch [1996] has also advocated persuasively for scans and general vector operations. Probably the best known partitioning algorithm for irregular grids is Recursive Spectral Bisection of Pothen, Simon, and Liou [1990]. The Hoard memory allocator was developed by Berger *et al* [2000].

Exercises

1. Rework the Schwartz template in Figure 5.2, which uses a binary tree, so that the tree has degree $d > 2$; assume P and d to be powers of 2.

2. Rework the Schwartz template in Figure 5.2 so that it works when P is not a power of 2.

3. Using the Schwartz approach, write a parallel program to determine, for a sequence of binary words that correspond to MIPS machine instructions, the number of branches (defined to be a word in which $bit_{28} == 1$) that are followed by no-op instructions (defined to be a word of all zeroes).

4. Revise the Collatz Conjecture code of Figure 5.17 to process batches of 1,000 numbers.

5. Write a Peril-L program to perform the operations illustrated in Figure 5.5. That is, compute a 4-point stencil computation on a given portion of the data array A. Set up local memory that includes overlap regions, and assume the data is originally allocated to the interior of the local array. Set up global data structures allowing "adjacent" threads to exchange edge elements. Include the logic of the exchanges. *Hint*: Full/empty variables can manage the exchanges between adjacent threads.

6. Write a Peril-L program that computes the `longest_run_of_1s/` A.

7. Write a Peril-L program that computes the `team_standings\` A.

8. Suppose four reductions are to be computed in sequence, as with the bounding box example. Write a Peril-L program that combines the four into one.

9. Using the standard definition for a B+ tree (as given in a sequential algorithms book), implement the data structure using the shared cap.

10. After implementing the B+ data structure with the shared cap, write code so that each of the P processes takes queries from a work queue and either (a) answers the membership question if the request is for the part of the tree managed by that process, or (b) places the query in the queue designated for the process that manages the appropriate part of the tree.

Parallel Programming Languages

In laying the foundations in earlier chapters, we have built intuition abstractly, presenting the concepts in a form that has largely been independent of specific computers or languages. We are now ready to discuss some actual parallel programming languages and to write and run programs. We will present a variety of different approaches, including those that are most commonly used in practice. In particular, we consider two basic approaches—threads and message passing—as well as various higher-level languages.

The notion of threads has its origins in the operating systems community, and today the advent of multi-core chips has greatly increased interest in thread-based programming. We present POSIX Threads, perhaps the most widely used system, and use it to address the main issues in thread-based programming. We also briefly discuss OpenMP and the threading capabilities of Java, two higher level approaches to threads-based programming.

For large parallel computers, message passing is the most widely used programming approach, having emerged from the scientific computing community. The primary attraction of message passing is its applicability to distributed memory parallel computers. There are two message passing libraries in wide use: the Parallel Virtual Machine (PVM) and the Message Passing Interface (MPI). They are different in detail but equivalent in terms of capability, and we present MPI. Additionally, we briefly present three related higher-level languages suitable for programming distributed memory machines: Co-Array Fortran (CAF), Unified Parallel C (UPC), and Titanium.

Currently, there is no high-level parallel programming language in wide use, but one day there will be, which motivates us to study the idea further. Therefore, we present the ZPL language. We are primarily interested in its ability to provide high-level abstract concepts while giving programmers a reasonably detailed understanding of the parallel behavior of their code; this property is one that we hope to see in future high-level parallel languages. We complete the discussion by presenting an even higher level language, NESL.

Finally, having touched on nine different programming systems, we include a short chapter that compares and contrasts the various approaches and serves as a starting point for the further study and development of parallel languages.

Programming with Threads

This chapter discusses ways to write programs for shared address space computers, an important class of machines deserving of special attention because they will soon be everywhere. We begin by discussing in some detail the POSIX Threads interface (Pthreads), which is essentially the interface that we used to implement the Count 3s program in Chapter 1. Our goal is to understand the important concepts and issues that Pthreads programmers face; we will conclude our discussion of Pthreads with three case studies that focus on obtaining good performance. Then we briefly discuss two other thread-programming approaches—Java threads and OpenMP—that attempt to hide some of the complexity of POSIX Threads.

POSIX Threads

Our discussion of POSIX Threads has two goals. The first is to provide sufficient detail about the POSIX Threads standard that readers can begin writing Pthreads programs. The second is to explain that while the facilities of the model are each individually fairly simple, the overall programming model presents a number of important performance and correctness issues, some of which are quite subtle. In keeping with these goals, this chapter will present the Pthreads standard in some depth, though we will not attempt to cover every detail of the POSIX Threads interface. We start by explaining the basic mechanisms for creating threads and controlling the interactions among threads. Then, we discuss issues of safety and performance before looking at some practical aspects of using POSIX Threads.

Online Pthreads Tutorial. For more details, including examples and documentation, see the following Web page at Lawrence Livermore Labs: http://www.llnl.gov/computing/tutorials/pthreads/

Note

Thread Creation and Destruction

Consider the following code:

```
1   #include <pthread.h>
2   int err;
3
4   void main()
5   {
6     pthread_t tid[MAX]; /* Array of Thread IDs, one per */
7                         /* thread that is created */
8
9     for(i=0; i<t; i++)
10    {
11      err=pthread_create(&tid[i], NULL, count3s_thread, i);
12    }
13
14    for(i=0; i<t; i++)
15    {
16      err=pthread_join_(tid[i], (void **)&status[i])
17    }
18  }
```

This code shows a `main()` function, which then creates—and initiates—t threads in the first loop and then waits for the t threads to complete in the second loop. We often refer to the creating thread as the *parent* and the created threads as *children*.

The above code differs from the pseudocode in Chapter 1 in a few details. Line 1 includes the Pthreads header file, which declares the various Pthreads routines and data types. Each thread that is created needs its own thread ID, so these thread IDs are declared on line 6. To create a thread, we invoke the `pthread_create()` routine with four parameters. (See Code Spec 6.1.):

1. A pointer to a thread ID, which will point to a valid thread ID when this thread successfully returns

2. The thread's attributes, which we will discuss shortly; in this case, the NULL value specifies default attributes

3. A pointer to the start function, which the thread will execute once it's created

4. An argument to pass to the start routine; in this case, it represents a unique integer between 0 and t-1 that is associated with each thread.

The loop on line 16 then calls `pthread_join()` to wait for each of the child threads to terminate. If instead of waiting for the child threads to complete, the `main()` routine finishes and exits using `pthread_exit()`, the child threads will continue to execute. Otherwise, the child threads will automatically terminate when `main()` finishes, because the entire process will have terminated. See Code Spec 6.2.

Code Spec 6.1 `pthread_create()`. The POSIX Threads thread creation function.

```
pthread_create()

int pthread_create(          // create a new thread
  pthread_t *tid,            // thread ID
  const pthread_attr_t *attr, // thread attributes
  void *(*start_routine)(void *), // pointer to function to execute
  void *arg                  // argument to function
);
```

Arguments:

- The thread ID of the successfully created thread.

- The thread's attributes, explained below; the NULL value specifies default attributes.

- The function that the new thread will execute once it is created.

- An argument passed to the `start_routine()`.

Return value:

0 if successful. Error code from `<errno.h>` otherwise.

Notes:

Use a structure to pass multiple arguments to the start routine.

Code Spec 6.2 `pthread_join()`. The POSIX Threads rendezvous function.

```
pthread_join()

int pthread_join(            // wait for a thread to terminate
  pthread_t tid,             // thread ID to wait for
  void **status              // exit status
);
```

Arguments:

- The ID of the thread to wait for.

- The completion status of the exiting thread will be copied into `*status` unless `status` is NULL, in which case the completion status is not copied.

Return value:

0 for success. Error code from `<errno.h>` otherwise.

Notes:

Once a thread is joined, the thread no longer exists, its thread ID is no longer valid, and it cannot be joined with any other thread.

Thread IDs. Each thread has a unique ID of type `pthread_t`. As with all Pthreads data types, a thread ID should be treated as an *opaque type*, meaning that individual fields of the structure should never be accessed directly. Child threads do not know their thread ID, but the `pthread_self()` routine allows a thread to determine its thread ID. The `pthread_equal()` routine can be used to compare two thread IDs; see Code Specs 6.3 and 6.4.

Destroying Threads. There are three ways that threads can terminate:

1. A thread can return from the start routine.

2. A thread can call `pthread_exit()`; see Code Spec 6.5.

3. A thread can be *cancelled* by another thread.

In each case, the thread is destroyed and its resources become unavailable.

Thread Attributes. Each thread maintains its own properties, known as *attributes*, which are stored in a structure of type `pthread_attr_t`. For example, threads can be either *detached* or *joinable*. Detached threads cannot be joined with other threads, so they have slightly lower overhead in some implementations of POSIX Threads. For parallel computing, we will rarely need detached threads. Threads can also be either *bound* or *unbound*. Bound threads are scheduled by the

Code Spec 6.3 `pthread_self()`. The POSIX Threads function to fetch a thread's ID.

```
pthread_self()
pthread_t pthread_self();              // Get my thread ID
Return value:
    The ID of the thread that called this function.
```

Code Spec 6.4 `pthread_equal()`. The POSIX Threads function to compare two thread IDs for equality.

```
pthread_equal()
int pthread_equal(                    // Test for equality
  pthread_t t1,                       // First operand thread ID
  pthread_t t2                        // Second operand thread ID
);
Arguments:
    Two thread IDs
Return value:
    ■ Nonzero if the two thread IDs are the same (following the C convention).
    ■ 0 if the two threads are different.
```

Code Spec 6.5 pthread_exit(). The POSIX Threads thread termination function.

```
void pthread_exit()

void pthread_exit(                          // terminate a thread
    void *status                            // completion status
);
```

Arguments:

The completion status of the thread that has exited. This pointer value is available to other threads.

Return value:

None.

Notes:

When a thread exits by simply returning from the start routine, the thread's completion status is set to the start routine's return value.

operating system, whereas unbound threads are scheduled by the Pthreads library. (See the upcoming section on Thread Scheduling.) For parallel computing, we typically use bound threads so that each thread provides physical concurrency. POSIX Threads provides routines to initialize thread attributes, set their attributes, and destroy attributes, as shown in Code Spec 6.6.

A Potential Pitfall. The following example illustrates a potential pitfall that can occur because of the interaction between parent and child threads. The parent thread simply creates a child thread and waits for the child to exit. The child thread

Code Spec 6.6 pthread attributes. An example of how thread attributes are set in the POSIX Threads interface.

```
Thread Attributes

pthread_attr_t attr;                        // Declare a thread attribute
pthread_t tid;
pthread_attr_init(&attr);                   // Initialize a thread attribute
pthread_attr_setdetachstate(&attr,          // Set the thread attribute
        PTHREAD_CREATE_UNDETACHED);
pthread_create(&tid, &attr, start_func, NULL);   // Use the attribute
                                                 // to create a thread
pthread_join(tid, NULL);
pthread_attr_destroy(&attr);                // Destroy the thread attribute
```

Notes:

There are many other thread attributes. See a POSIX Threads manual for details.

does some useful work and then exits, returning an error code. Do you see what's wrong with this code?

```
1   #include <pthread.h>
2
3   void main()
4   {
5      pthread_t tid;
6      int *status;
7
8      pthread_create(&tid, NULL, start, NULL);
9      pthread_join(tid, (void *)&status);
10   }
11
12   void start()
13   {
14      int errorcode;
15      /* do something useful. . . */
16
17      if(. . . )
18      {
19         errorcode=something;
20      }
21      pthread_exit(&errorcode);
22   }
```

The problem occurs in the call to pthread_exit() on line 21, where the child attempts to return an error code to the parent. Unfortunately, because errorcode is declared to be local to the start() function, the memory for errorcode is allocated on the child thread's stack. When the child exits, its call stack is de-allocated, so the parent has a dangling pointer to errorcode. At some point in the future, when a new procedure is invoked, it will overwrite the stack location where errorcode resides, and the value of errorcode will change.

Mutual Exclusion

To allow threads to interact constructively, we need methods of coordinating their interaction. In particular, when two threads share access to memory, it's often useful to employ a lock, called a *mutex*, to provide mutually exclusive access to the variable, also known as *mutual exclusion*. Without mutual exclusion, race conditions can lead to unpredictable results. As we saw in Chapter 1, when multiple threads execute the following code, the count variable, which is shared among all threads, will not be atomically updated.

```
for(i=start; i<start+length_per_thread; i++)
{
  if(array[i]==3)
  {
    count++;
  }
}
```

The solution, of course, is to protect the update of count using a mutex, as follows:

```
1   pthread_mutex_t lock=PTHREAD_MUTEX_INITIALIZER;
      . . .
2    if(array[i]==3)
3    {
4       pthread_mutex_lock(&lock);
5       count++;
6       pthread_mutex_unlock(&lock);
7    }
```

Line 1 shows how a mutex can be statically declared (see Code Spec 6.7). Like threads, mutexes have attributes, and by initializing the mutex to PTHREAD_MUTEX_INITIALIZER, the mutex is assigned default attributes. To use this mutex, its address is passed to the lock and unlock routines on lines 4 and 6, respectively. The appropriate discipline, of course, is to bracket all *critical sections*— that is, code that must be executed atomically by only one thread at a time—by the locking of a mutex upon entrance and the unlocking of a mutex upon exit. Only one thread can acquire the mutex at any one time, so a thread will block if it attempts to acquire a mutex that is already held by another thread. When a mutex is unlocked, or *relinquished*, one of the threads that was blocked while attempting to acquire the lock will become unblocked and will be granted the mutex. The POSIX Threads standard defines no notion of fairness, so the order in which the locks are acquired is *not* guaranteed to match the order in which the threads attempted to acquire the locks.

Code Spec 6.7 The POSIX Threads routines for acquiring and releasing mutexes.

Acquiring and Releasing Mutexes

```
int pthread_mutex_lock(            // Lock a mutex
   pthread_mutex_t *mutex);
int pthread_mutex_unlock(          // Unlock a mutex
   pthread_mutex_t *mutex);
int pthread_mutex_trylock(         // Nonblocking lock
   pthread_mutex_t *mutex);
```

Arguments:
   Each function takes the address of a mutex variable.

Return value:
   0 if successful. Error code from <errno.h> otherwise.

Notes:
   The pthread_mutex_trylock() routine attempts to acquire a mutex but will not block. This routine returns the POSIX Threads constant EBUSY if the mutex is locked.

Mutex Creation and Destruction. In our example, we knew that only one mutex was needed, so we were able to statically allocate it. In cases where the number of required mutexes is not known *a priori*, we can instead allocate and deallocate mutexes dynamically. Code Specs 6.8 and 6.9 show how such a mutex is dynamically allocated, initialized with default attributes, and destroyed.

Code Spec 6.8 The POSIX Threads routines for dynamically creating and destroying mutexes.

Mutex Creation and Destruction

```
int pthread_mutex_init(              // Initialize a mutex
   pthread_mutex_t *mutex,
   pthread_mutexattr_t *attr);
int pthread_mutex_destroy(           // Destroy a mutex
   pthread_mutex_t *mutex);
int pthread_mutexattr_init(          // Initialize a mutex attribute
   pthread_mutexattr_t *attr);
int pthread_mutexattr_destroy(       // Destroy a mutex attribute
   pthread_mutexattr_t *attr);
```

Arguments:

- The pthread_mutex_init() routine takes two arguments, a pointer to a mutex and a pointer to a mutex attribute. The latter is presumed to have already been initialized.

- The pthread_mutexattr_init() and pthread_mutexattr_destroy() routines take a pointer to a mutex attribute as arguments.

Notes:

If the second argument to pthread_mutex_init() is NULL, default attributes will be used.

Code Spec 6.9 An example of how dynamically allocated mutexes are used in the POSIX Threads interface.

Dynamically Allocated Mutexes

```
pthread_mutex_t *lock;                    // Declare a pointer to a lock
lock=(pthread_mutex_lock_t *) malloc(sizeof(pthread_mutex_t));
pthread_mutex_init(lock, NULL);
   /*
    * Code that uses this lock.
    */
pthread_mutex_destroy(lock);
free(lock);
```

Serializability. It's clear that our use of mutexes implements atomicity. The thread that acquires the mutex m will execute the code in the critical section until it relinquishes the mutex. Thus, in our example, the counter will be updated by only one thread at a time. Atomicity is important because it ensures *serializability*. A concurrent execution is *serializable* if the execution is guaranteed to correspond to *some* serial execution of those threads.

Correctness Issues. It is an error to unlock a mutex that has not been locked, and it is an error to lock a mutex that a thread already holds. The latter will lead to *deadlock*, in which the thread cannot make progress because it is blocked waiting for an event that cannot happen. We discuss deadlock and techniques to avoid deadlock in the following sections.

Synchronization

Mutexes are sufficient to provide atomicity for critical sections, but in many situations we would like a thread to synchronize its behavior with that of some other thread. For example, consider a classic bounded buffer problem in which one or more threads put items into a circular buffer while other threads remove items from the same buffer. As shown in Figure 6.1, we would like the producers to stop producing data—to wait—if the consumer is unable to keep up and the buffer becomes full, and we would like the consumers to wait if the buffer is empty.

Such synchronization is supported by *condition variables*, which are a more general form of synchronization than pthread_join(); see Code Specs 6.10 and 6.11. A

Figure 6.1
A bounded buffer with producers and consumers. The Put and Get cursors indicate where the producers will insert the next item and where the consumers will remove its next item, respectively. When the buffer is empty, the consumers must wait. When the buffer is full, the producers must wait.

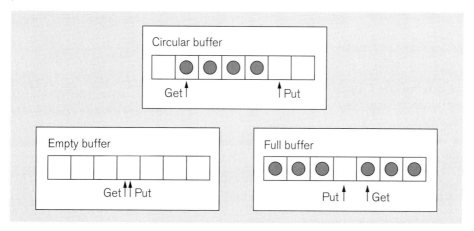

Code Spec 6.10 `pthread_cond_wait()`. The POSIX Thread routines for waiting on condition variables.

`pthread_cond_wait()`

```
int pthread_cond_wait(
  pthread_cond_t *cond,            // Condition to wait on
  pthread_mutex_t *mutex);         // Protecting mutex
int pthread_cond_timedwait(
  pthread_cond_t *cond,
  pthread_mutex_t *mutex,
  const struct timespec *abstime);  // Time-out value
```

Arguments:
- A condition variable to wait on.
- A mutex that protects access to the condition variable. The mutex is released before the thread blocks, and these two actions occur atomically. When this thread is later unblocked, the mutex is reacquired on behalf of this thread.

Return value:
0 if successful. Error code from `<errno.h>` otherwise.

Code Spec 6.11 `pthread_cond_signal()`. The POSIX Threads routines for signaling a condition variable.

`pthread_cond_signal()`

```
int pthread_cond_signal(
  pthread_cond_t *cond);           // Condition to signal
int pthread_cond_broadcast(
  pthread_cond_t *cond);           // Condition to signal
```

Arguments:
A condition variable to signal.

Return value:
0 if successful. Error code from `<errno.h>` otherwise.

Notes:
- These routines have no effect if there are no threads waiting on cond. In particular, there is no memory of the signal when a later call is made to `pthread_cond_wait()`.
- The `pthread_cond_signal()` routine may wake up more than one thread, but only one of these threads will hold the protecting mutex.
- The `pthread_cond_broadcast()` routine wakes up all waiting threads. Only one awakened thread will hold the protecting mutex.

condition variable allows threads to wait until some condition becomes true, at which point one of the waiting threads is nondeterministically chosen to stop waiting. We can think of the condition variable as a gate (see Figure 6.2). Threads wait at the gate until some condition is true. Other threads open the gate to signal that the condition has become true, at which point one of the waiters is allowed to enter the gate and resume execution. If a thread opens the gate when there are no threads waiting, the signal has no effect.

We can solve our bounded buffer problem with two condition variables, `nonempty` and `nonfull`, as shown in Figure 6.3. Of course, since multiple threads will be updating these condition variables, we need to protect their access with a mutex, so line 1 declares a mutex. The remaining declarations define a `buffer` and its two cursors, `put` and `get`, which wrap around when they exceed the bounds of `buffer`, yielding a circular buffer. As we can see from Figure 6.1, the `put` cursor points to the next empty location, and the `get` cursor points to the next element to remove. When the two cursors point to the same location, the buffer is empty, and when the two cursors are a distance of `SIZE-1` apart, the buffer is full. The full buffer actually leaves one location empty because the `put` and `get` cursors use modulo arithmetic to prevent overflow; if we were to allow the buffer to fill completely, we would not be able to distinguish between the full case and the empty case.

Given these data structures, the producer thread executes the `insert()` routine, which first acquires the mutex to access the condition variables. (The figure omits the code for the producer and consumer threads, which are assumed to iteratively invoke the `insert()` and `remove()` routines, respectively.) If the buffer is full, the producer waits on the `nonfull` condition so that it will later be awakened when the buffer becomes nonfull. If the producer thread blocks, the mutex that it holds must be relinquished to avoid deadlock. Because these two events—the releasing of the mutex and the blocking of this waiting thread—must occur atomically, they must be performed by `pthread_cond_wait()`, so the mutex is passed as a parameter to `pthread_cond_wait()`. When the producer resumes execution after returning

Figure 6.2
Condition variables act like a gate. Threads wait outside the gate by calling `pthread_cond_wait()`, and threads open the gate by calling `pthread_cond_signal()`. When the gate is opened, one waiter is allowed through. If there are no waiters when the gate is opened, the signal has no effect.

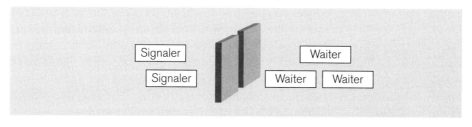

Figure 6.3
Bounded buffer example using condition variables `nonempty` and `nonfull`.

```
1   pthread_mutex_t lock=PTHREAD_MUTEX_INITIALIZER;
2   pthread_cond_t nonempty=PTHREAD_COND_INITIALIZER;
3   pthread_cond_t nonfull=PTHREAD_COND_INITIALIZER;
4   Item buffer[SIZE];
5   int put=0;                          // Buff index for next insert
6   int get=0;                          // Buff index for next remove
7
8   void insert(Item x)                         // Producer thread
9   {
10      pthread_mutex_lock(&lock);
11      while((put>get&&(put-get)==SIZE-1)||    // While buffer is
12              (put<get&&(put+get)==SIZE-1))    // full
13      {
14          pthread_cond_wait(&nonfull, &lock);
15      }
16      buffer[put]=x;
17      put=(put+1)%SIZE;
18      pthread_cond_signal(&nonempty);
19      pthread_mutex_unlock(&lock);
20   }
21
22   Item remove()                              // Consumer thread
23   {
24      Item x;
25      pthread_mutex_lock(&lock);
26      while(put==get)                         // While buffer is empty
27      {
28          pthread_cond_wait(&nonempty, &lock);
29      }
30      x=buffer[get];
31      get=(get+1)%SIZE;
32      pthread_cond_signal(&nonfull);
33      pthread_mutex_unlock(&lock);
34      return x;
35   }
```

from the wait on line 14, the protecting mutex will have been reacquired by the system on behalf of the producer.

In a moment we will explain the need for the `while` loop on line 11, but for now assume that when the producer executes line 16, the buffer is not full, so it is safe to insert a new item and to bump the `put` cursor by one. At this point, the buffer cannot be empty because the producer has just inserted an element, so the producer signals that the buffer is nonempty, waking one or more consumers that may be waiting on an empty buffer. If there are no waiting consumers, the signal is lost. Finally, the producer releases the mutex and exits the routine. The consumer thread executes the `remove()` routine, which operates in a very similar manner.

Protecting Condition Variables. Let us now return to the `while` loop on line 11 of the bounded buffer program. If our system has multiple producer threads, this loop is essential because `pthread_cond_signal()` can wake up multiple waiting threads,[1] of which only one will hold the protecting mutex at any one time; see Code Specs 6.10 and 6.11. Thus, at the time of the signal, the buffer is not full, but when any particular thread acquires the mutex, the buffer may have become full again, in which case the thread should call `pthread_cond_wait()` again. When the producer thread executes line 16, the buffer is necessarily not full, so it is safe to insert a new item and to bump the `put` cursor.

On lines 18 and 32 we see that the call to `pthread_cond_signal()` is also protected by the lock. The example shown in Figure 6.4 shows why this protection is necessary. The waiting thread, in this case the consumer, acquires the protecting mutex and finds that the buffer is empty, so it executes `pthread_cond_wait()`. If the signaling thread, in this case the producer, does not protect the call to `pthread_cond_signal()` with a mutex, it could insert an item into the buffer immediately after the waiting thread found it empty. If the producer then signals that the buffer is nonempty before the waiting thread executes the call to `pthread_cond_wait()`, the signal will be dropped and the consumer thread will not realize that the buffer is actually not empty. In the case that the producer only inserts a single item, the waiting thread will needlessly wait forever.

The problem, of course, is that there is a race condition involving the manipulation of the buffer. The obvious solution is to protect the call to `pthread_cond_signal()` with the same mutex that protects the call to `pthread_cond_wait()`, as shown in the code for our bounded buffer solution. Because both the `insert()` and `remove()` routines are protected by the same mutex, we have three critical sections related to the nonempty buffer, as shown in Figure 6.5, and in no case can the signal be dropped while a waiting thread thinks that the buffer is empty.

Figure 6.4
Example of why a signaling thread needs to be protected by a mutex.

```
            Signaling thread              Waiting thread

                                          while(put==get)

            insert(item);
     Time   pthread_cond_signal(&nonempty);
            // Signal is dropped

                                          pthread_cond_wait(&nonempty, lock);
                                          // Will wait forever
```

[1] These semantics are due to implementation details. In some cases it can be expensive to ensure that exactly one waiter is unblocked by a signal.

Figure 6.5
Proper locking of the signaling code prevents race conditions. By using one mutex to protect three critical sections pertaining to the nonempty buffer, we guarantee that each of A, B, and C will execute atomically, so our problem from Figure 6.3 is avoided: Because B must precede C, there are only three ways that A can be interleaved with respect to B and C, and there is no way for the **insert()** routine's signal to be dropped while a thread executing the **remove()** routine thinks that the buffer is empty.

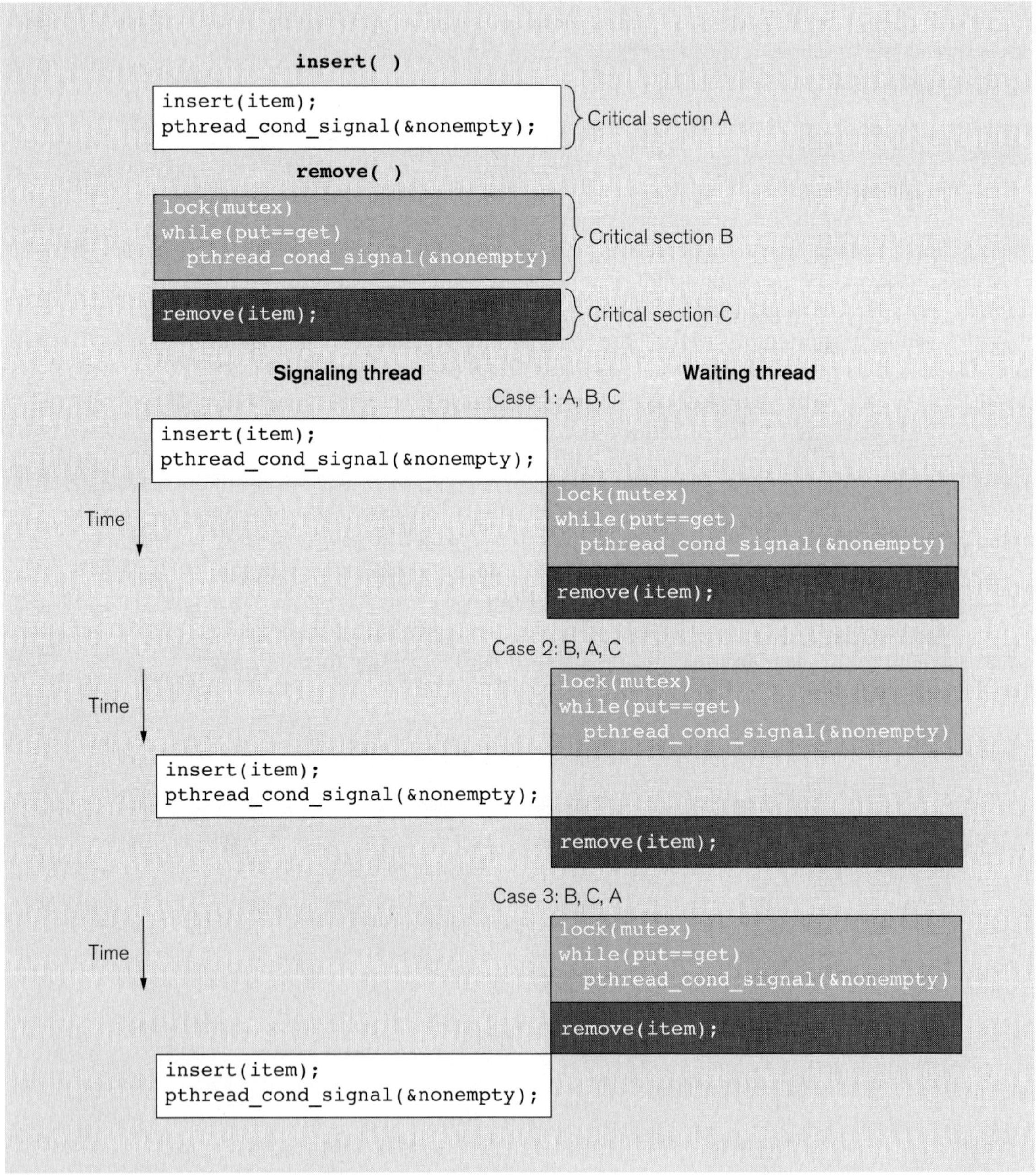

insert( )

```
insert(item);
pthread_cond_signal(&nonempty);
```
Critical section A

remove( )

```
lock(mutex)
while(put==get)
    pthread_cond_signal(&nonempty)
```
Critical section B

```
remove(item);
```
Critical section C

Signaling thread   **Waiting thread**

Case 1: A, B, C

```
insert(item);
pthread_cond_signal(&nonempty);
```

Time

```
lock(mutex)
while(put==get)
    pthread_cond_signal(&nonempty)
```

```
remove(item);
```

Case 2: B, A, C

Time

```
lock(mutex)
while(put==get)
    pthread_cond_signal(&nonempty)
```

```
insert(item);
pthread_cond_signal(&nonempty);
```

```
remove(item);
```

Case 3: B, C, A

Time

```
lock(mutex)
while(put==get)
    pthread_cond_signal(&nonempty)
```

```
remove(item);
```

```
insert(item);
pthread_cond_signal(&nonempty);
```

We have argued that the call to pthread_cond_signal() must be protected by the same mutex that protects the waiting code. However, notice that the race condition occurs not from the signaling of the condition variable, but with the access to the shared buffer. Thus, we could instead simply protect any code that manipulates the shared buffer, which implies that the insert() code could release the mutex immediately after inserting an item into the buffer but before calling pthread_cond_signal(). This new code is not only legal, but also it produces better performance because it reduces the size of the critical section, thereby allowing more concurrency.

Creating and Destroying Condition Variables. Like threads and mutexes, condition variables can be created and destroyed either statically or dynamically. In our bounded buffer example, the static condition variables were both given default attributes by initializing them to PTHREAD_COND_INITIALIZER. Condition variables can be dynamically allocated as indicated in Code Spec 6.12.

Waiting on Multiple Condition Variables. In some cases a piece of code cannot execute unless multiple conditions are met. In these situations, the waiting thread should test all conditions simultaneously, as follows:

```
1   EatJuicyFruit()
2   {
3     pthread_mutex_lock(&lock);
4     while(apples==0||oranges==0)
5     {
6       pthread_cond_wait(&more_apples, &lock);
7       pthread_cond_wait(&more_oranges, &lock);
8     }
9     /* Critical Section: Eat both an apple and an orange */
10    pthread_mutex_unlock(&lock);
11  }
```

Code Spec 6.12 The POSIX Threads routines for dynamically creating and destroying condition variables.

Dynamically Allocated Condition Variables

```
int pthread_cond_init(
  pthread_cond_t *cond,                  // Condition variable
  const pthread_condattr_t *attr);       // Condition attribute

int pthread_cond_destroy(
  pthread_cond_t *cond);                 // Condition to destroy
```

Arguments:
   Default attributes are used if attr is NULL.

Return value:
   0 if successful. Error code from <errno.h> otherwise.

By contrast, the following code, which waits on each condition in turn, fails because there is no guarantee that both conditions will be true at the same time. That is, after returning from the first call to pthread_cond_wait() but before returning from the second call to pthread_cond_wait(), some other thread may have removed an apple, making the first condition false.

```
1   EatJuicyFruit()                    Caution: This code is faulty.
2   {
3       pthread_mutex_lock(&lock);
4       while(apples==0)
5       {
6           pthread_cond_wait(&more_apples, &lock);
7       }
8       while(oranges==0)
9       {
10          pthread_cond_wait(&more_oranges, &lock);
11      }
12
13      /* Eat both an apple and an orange */
14      pthread_mutex_unlock(&lock);
15  }
```

Thread-Specific Data. It is often useful for threads to maintain private data that is not shared. For example, we have seen examples where a thread index is passed to the start function so that the thread knows what portion of an array to work on. This index can be used to give each thread a different element of an array, as follows:

```
1   ...
2
3   for(i=0; i<t; i++)
4   {
5       err=pthread_create(&tid[i], NULL, start_function, i);
6   }
7
8   void* start_function(void*index)
9   {
10      private_count[index]=0;
11  ...
```

A problem occurs, however, if the code that accesses index occurs in a function, foo(), which is buried deep within other code. In such situations, how does foo() get the value of index? One solution is to pass the index parameter to every procedure that calls foo(), including procedures that call foo() indirectly through other procedures. This solution is cumbersome, particularly for those procedures that require the parameter but do not directly use it.

Instead, what we really want is a variable that is global in scope to all code but can have different values for each thread. POSIX Threads supports such a notion in the form of *thread-specific data*, which uses a set of *keys* that is shared by all threads in a process but that maps to different pointer values for each thread (see Figure 6.6).

As a special case, the error values for POSIX Threads routines are returned in thread-specific data, but such data does not use the interface defined by Code Specs 6.13–6.17. Instead, each thread has its own value of `errno`.

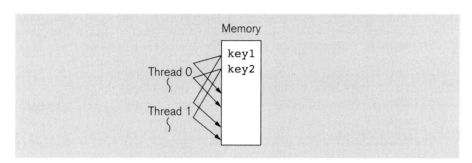

Figure 6.6
Example of thread-specific data in POSIX Threads. Thread-specific data are accessed by keys, which map to different memory locations in different threads.

Code Spec 6.13 Example of how thread-specific data is used. Once initialized with this code, any procedure can access the value of `my_index`.

Thread-Specific Data

```
pthread_key_t *my_index;
#define index(pthread_getspecific(my_index))
main()
{
  ...
  pthread_key_create(&my_index, 0);
  ...
}
void start_routine(int id)
{
  pthread_setspecific(my_index, id);
  ...
}
```

Notes:
   Avoid accessing `index` in a tight inner loop because each access requires a procedure call.

Code Spec 6.14 `pthread_key_create()`. POSIX Thread routine for creating a key for thread-specific data.

`pthread_key_create`

```
int pthread_key_create(
    pthread_key_t*key,                // The key to create
    void(*destructor)(void*));        // Destructor function
```

Arguments:
- A pointer to the key to create.
- A destructor function. NULL indicates no destructor.

Return value:
0 if successful. Error code from <errno.h> otherwise.

Notes:
Avoid accessing index in a tight inner loop because each access requires a procedure call.

Code Spec 6.15 `pthread_key_delete()`. POSIX Thread routine for deleting a key.

`pthread_key_delete`

```
int pthread_key_delete(
    pthread_key_t*key);               // The key to delete
```

Arguments:
A pointer to the key to delete.

Return value:
0 if successful. Error code from <errno.h> otherwise.

Notes:
Destructors will not be called.

Code Spec 6.16 `pthread_setspecific()`. POSIX Thread routine for setting the value of thread-specific data.

`pthread_setspecific`

```
int pthread_setspecific(
    pthread_key_t*key,                // Key to set
    void *value);                     // Value to set
```

Arguments:
- A pointer to the key to be set.
- The value to set.

Return value:
0 if successful. Error code from <errno.h> otherwise.

Notes:
It is an error to call `pthread_setspecific()` before the key has been created or after the key has been deleted.

Code Spec 6.17 `pthread_getspecific()`. POSIX Thread routine for getting the value of some thread-specific data.

---

pthread_getspecific

```
int pthread_getspecific(
  pthread_key_t*key);                    // Key to value
```

Arguments:
  Key whose value is to be retrieved.

Return value:
  Value of `key` for the calling thread.

Notes:
  The behavior is undefined if a thread calls `pthread_getspecific()` before the key is created or after the key is deleted.

Safety Issues

Many types of errors can occur from the improper use of locks and condition variables. We've already mentioned the problem of double-locking, which occurs when a thread attempts to acquire a lock that it already holds. Problems also arise if a thread accesses some shared variable without locking it or if a thread acquires a lock and does not relinquish it. One particularly important problem is that of avoiding deadlock. This section discusses various methods of avoiding deadlock and other potential bugs.

Deadlock. There are four necessary conditions for deadlock:

1. **Mutual exclusion:** a resource can be assigned to at most one thread.
2. **Hold and wait:** threads both hold some resources and request other resources.
3. **No preemption:** a resource that is assigned to a thread can only be released by the thread that holds it.
4. **Circular wait:** a cycle exists in which each thread waits for a resource that is assigned to another thread (see Figure 6.7).

Of course, for threads-based programming, mutexes are resources that can cause

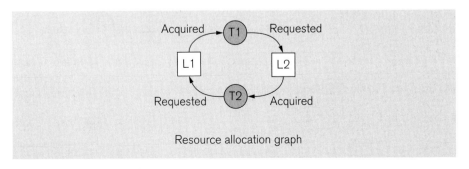

Resource allocation graph

Figure 6.7
Deadlock example. Threads T1 and T2 hold locks L1 and L2, respectively, and each thread attempts to acquire the other lock, which cannot be granted.

deadlock. There are two general approaches to dealing with deadlock: (1) prevent deadlocks, and (2) allow deadlocks to occur, but detect their occurrence and then break the deadlock. We will focus on deadlock avoidance, because POSIX Threads does not provide a mechanism for breaking locks.

Lock Hierarchies. A simple way to prevent deadlocks is to prevent cycles in the resource allocation graph. We can prevent cycles by imposing an ordering on the locks and by requiring that all threads acquire their locks in the same order. Such a discipline is known as a *lock hierarchy.*

A lock hierarchy requires programmers to know *a priori* what locks a thread needs to acquire. Suppose that after acquiring locks L1, L3, and L7, a thread finds that it needs also to acquire lock L2, which would violate the lock hierarchy. One solution would be for the thread to release locks L3 and L7 and to then reacquire locks L2, L3, and L7 in that order. Of course, this strict adherence to the lock hierarchy is expensive. A better solution would be to attempt to lock L2 using `pthread_mutex_trylock()` (see Code Spec 6.7), which either obtains the lock or immediately returns without blocking. If the thread is unable to obtain lock L2, it must resort to the first solution.

Monitors. The use of locks and condition variables is error prone because it relies on programmer discipline. An alternative is to provide language support, which would allow a compiler to enforce mutual exclusion and proper synchronization. A *monitor* is one such language construct, as shown in Figure 6.8. A monitor encapsulates code and data and ensures mutual exclusion. In particular, a monitor has a set of well-defined entry points, its data can only be accessed by code that resides inside the monitor, and only one thread can execute the monitor's code at any time. We can implement monitors in an object-oriented language, such as C++; Figure 6.9 shows a solution using a slightly different approach from that in Figure 6.3.

Monitors not only enforce mutual exclusion, but they also implement an abstraction that simplifies the way that we reason about concurrency. In particular, the

Figure 6.8
Monitors provide an abstraction of synchronization in which only one thread can access the monitor's data at any time. Other threads are blocked either waiting to enter the monitor or waiting on events inside the monitor.

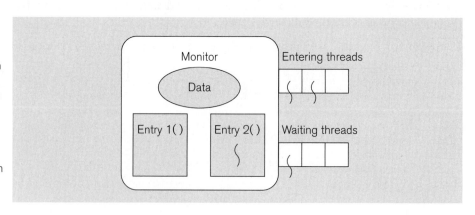

Figure 6.9
Monitor implementation in C++.

```
 1   class BoundedBuffer
 2   {                                            // Implement a monitor
 3     private:
 4       pthread_mutex_t lock;                    // Synchronization variables
 5       pthread_cond_t nonempty, nonfull;
 6       Item *buffer;                            // Shared data
 7       int in, out;                             // Cursors
 8       CheckInvariant();
 9
10     public:
11       BoundedBuffer(int size);                 // Constructor
12       ~BoundedBuffer();                        // Destructor
13       void put(Item x);
14       Item get();
15   }
16
17   // Constructor and Destructor
18   BoundedBuffer::Bounded(int size)
19   {
20     // Initialize synchronization variables
21     pthread_mutex_init(&lock, NULL);
22     pthread_cond_init(&nonempty, NULL);
23     pthread_cond_init(&nonfull, NULL);
24
25     // Initialize the buffer
26     buffer=new Item[size];
27     in=out=0;
28   }
29
30   BoundedBuffer::~BoundedBuffer()
31   {
32     pthread_mutex_destroy(&lock);
33     pthread_cond_destroy(&nonempty);
34     pthread_cond_destroy(&nonfull);
35     delete buffer;
36   }
37
38   // Member functions
39   BoundedBuffer::Put(Item x)
40   {
41     pthread_mutex_lock(&lock);
42     while(in-out==size)                        // while buffer is full
43     {
44       pthread_cond_wait(&nonfull, &lock);
45     }
46     buffer[in%size]=x;
```

(continued)

Figure 6.9 (*continued*)
Monitor implementation in C++.

```
47      in++;
48      pthread_cond_signal(&nonempty);
49      pthread_mutex_unlock(&lock);
50    }
51
52    Item BoundedBuffer::Get()
53    {
54      pthread_mutex_lock(&lock);
55      while(in==out)                              // While buffer is empty
56      {
57        pthread_cond_wait(&nonempty, &lock);
58      }
59      x=buffer[out%size];
60      out++;
61      pthread_cond_signal(&nonfull);
62      pthread_mutex_unlock(&lock);
63      return x;
64    }
```

limited number of entry points facilitates the preservation of invariants. *Invariants* are properties that are assumed to be true upon entry and that must be restored upon exit. As shown in Figure 6.10, these invariants may be violated while the monitor lock is held, but they must be restored before the monitor lock is released.

For example, in our bounded buffer example, we have two invariants:

1. The distance between the In and Out cursors is less than the size of the buffer.

2. The In cursor is not left of the Out cursor. (In Figure 6.1, the Put arrow is not left of the Get arrow.)

Once we have identified our invariants, we can write a routine that checks all invariants, and this routine can be invoked before every entrance to the monitor and after every exit from the monitor. The use of such invariants can be a significant debugging tool. For example, the program in Figure 6.11 checks these invariants to help debug the monitor's implementation. Notice the checks inserted on lines 20 and 22. The check on line 20 is needed because the call to pthread_cond_wait() on line 21 might implicitly release the lock, so it is a potential monitor exit. The check on line 22 is needed because the return from pthread_cond_wait() implicitly reacquires the lock, so it is a monitor entrance.

Re-Entrant Monitors. While monitors help enforce a locking discipline, they do not solve all concurrency problems. For example, if a procedure in a monitor attempts to re-enter the monitor by calling an entry procedure, deadlock will occur. To avoid this problem, the procedure should first restore all invariants, release the

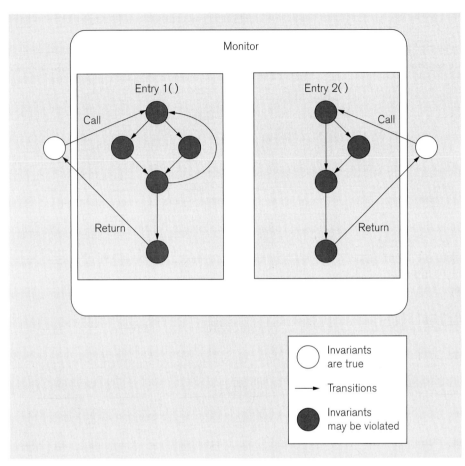

Figure 6.10
Monitors and invariants. The shaded circles represent program states in which the invariants may be violated. The empty circles represent program states in which the invariants are assumed to be true.

monitor lock, and then try to re-enter the monitor. Of course, such a structure means that atomicity is lost. This same problem occurs if a monitor procedure attempts to re-enter the monitor indirectly by calling some external procedure that then tries to enter the monitor. Therefore, monitor procedures should invoke external routines with care.

Monitor functions that take a long time or wait for some outside event will prevent other threads from entering the monitor. To avoid such problems, long-running functions can often be rewritten to wait on a condition, thereby releasing the lock and increasing parallelism. As with re-entrant routines, such functions will need to restore invariants before releasing the lock.

Performance Issues

In Chapter 3 we saw that dependences among threads constrain parallelism. Because locks dynamically impose dependences among threads, the granularity of locking can greatly affect parallelism. At one extreme, the coarsest locking scheme

Figure 6.11
A program to check the invariants in the bounded buffer program, Figure 6.9.

```
1   BoundedBuffer::CheckInvariant()
2   {
3     if(in − out>size)                        // Check invariant (1)
4     {
5       return(0);
6     }
7     if(in<out)                               // Check invariant (2)
8     {
9       return(0);
10    }
11    return(1);
12  }
13
14  Item BoundedBuffer::Get()
15  {
16    pthread_mutex_lock(&lock);
17    assert(CheckInvariant());                // Check on every entrance
18    while(in=out)                            // While buffer is empty
19    {
20       assert(CheckInvariant());             // Check on every exit
21       pthread_cond_wait(&nonempty, &lock);
22       assert(CheckInvariant());
23    }
24    x=buffer[out%size];
25    out++;
26    pthread_cond_signal(&nonfull);
27    assert(CheckInvariant());
28    pthread_mutex_unlock(&lock);
29    return x;
30  }
```

uses a single lock for all shared variables. Such a scheme is simple but severely limits concurrency when there is sharing. At the other extreme, we could associate a lock with each fine-grained sub-structure of a data structure. For example, in our Count 3s example, we might use a different lock to protect each node of the accumulation tree. This scheme not only increases concurrency, but it also increases the latency of acquiring and releasing locks, even when there is no contention for the data structure. Moreover, because each thread has to acquire multiple locks to operate on multiple data structures, the chance for deadlock increases. As an intermediate point, we might use one lock for each accumulation tree. In general, there is a granularity trade-off between parallelism and overhead.

Readers and Writers Example: Granularity Issues. Just as there are different granularities for locking, there are different granularities for using condition variables. Consider a resource that can be shared by multiple readers or accessed exclusively by a single writer (refer to Figure 6.12). To coordinate access to such a

Figure 6.12
Multiple readers, single writer support routines.

```
1   int readers;                            // Neg value=> active writer
2   pthread_mutex_t lock;
3   pthread_cond_t rBusy, wBusy;            // Use separate conditional vars
4                                           // for readers and writers
5   AcquireExclusive()
6   {
7     pthread_mutex_lock(&lock);
8     while(readers !=0)
9     {
10      pthread_cond_wait(&wBusy, &lock);
11    }
12    readers=-1;
13    pthread_mutex_unlock(&lock);
14  }
15
16  AcquireShared()
17  {
18    pthread_mutex_lock(&lock);
19    readWaiters++;
20    while(readers<0)
21    {
22      pthread_cond_wait(&rBusy, &lock);
23    }
24    readWaiters--;
25    pthread_mutex_unlock(&lock);
26  }
27
28  ReleaseExclusive()
29  {
30    pthread_mutex_lock(&lock);
31    readers=0;
32    pthread_cond_broadcast(&rBusy);        // Only wake up readers
33    pthread_mutex_unlock(&lock);
34  }
35
36  ReleaseShared(
37  {
38    int doSignal;
39
40    pthread_mutex_lock(&lock);
41    readers--;
42    doSignal=(readers==0)
43    pthread_mutex_unlock(&lock);
44    if(doSignal)                           // Signal executes outside
45    {                                      // of critical section
46      pthread_cond_signal(&wBusy);         // Wake up a writer
47    }
48  }
```

resource, we can implement four routines that readers and writers can invoke—
AcquireExclusive(), ReleaseExclusive(), AcquireShared(), and
ReleaseShared(). These routines are each protected by a single mutex, and they
collectively use two condition variables. To acquire the resource in exclusive mode, a
thread waits on the wBusy condition variable, which ensures that no reader is still
accessing the resource. When the last reader is done accessing the resource in shared
mode, it signals the wBusy condition to allow a writer to proceed. Likewise, when a
writer is done accessing the resource in exclusive mode, it signals the rBusy condition to allow any number of readers to access the resource; and before accessing the
shared resource, threads wait on the rBusy condition variable.

Two points about this code are noteworthy.

First, the code uses two condition variables, but it's natural to wonder if one condition variable would suffice. In fact, one condition variable could be used, as shown
in Figure 6.13, and the code would be functionally correct. Unfortunately, by using
a single condition variable, the code suffers from *spurious wakeups* in which writers
can be awakened only to go back to sleep immediately. In particular, when
ReleaseExclusive() is called, both readers and writers are signaled, so writers
will suffer spurious wakeups whenever any reader is also waiting on the condition.
Our original solution avoids spurious wakeups by using two condition variables,
which forces exclusive access and shared access to alternate as long as there is
demand for both types of access.

Second, the ReleaseShared() routine signals the wBusy condition variable outside of the critical section to avoid the problem of *spurious lock conflicts*, in which a
thread is awakened by a signal, executes a few instructions, and then immediately
blocks as it attempts to acquire the lock. If the ReleaseShared() were instead to
execute the signal inside of the critical section, as follows, then any awakened writer
would almost immediately block trying to acquire the lock.

```
35  ReleaseShared(
36  {
37    pthread_mutex_lock(&lock);
38    readers--;
39    if(readers==0)
40    {
41      pthread_cond_signal(&wBusy); // Wake up writers
                                                inside of
42    }                              // the critical section
43    pthread_mutex_unlock(&lock);
44  }
```

The decision to move the signal outside of the critical section represents a trade-off.
It reduces spurious lock conflicts, but it allows a new reader to enter the critical section before the ReleaseShared() routine is able to awaken a waiting writer, allowing readers to starve writers, albeit with much less probability than would occur
with a single-condition variable.

Figure 6.13 Multiple readers, single-writer support routines based on a single-condition variable, but subject to spurious wake-ups.

```
1   int readers;                        // Negative value => active writer
2   pthread_mutex_t lock;
3   pthread_cond_t busy;                // Use one condition variable to
4                                       // indicate whether data if busy
5   AcquireExclusive()
6   {
7     pthread_mutex_lock(&lock);        // This code suffers from spurious
8     while(readers!=0)                 // wake-ups!!!
9     {
10       pthread_cond_wait(&busy, &lock);
11    }
12    readers=-1;
13    pthread_mutex_unlock(&lock);
14  }
15
16  AcquireShared()
17  {
18    pthread_mutex_lock(&lock);
19    while(readers<0)
20    {
21       pthread_cond_wait(&busy, &lock);
22    }
23    readers++;
24    pthread_mutex_unlock(&lock);
25  }
26
27  ReleaseExclusive()
28  {
29    pthread_mutex_lock(&lock);
30    readers=0;
31    pthread_cond_broadcast(&busy);
32    pthread_mutex_unlock(&lock);
33  }
34
35  ReleaseShared(
36  {
37    pthread_mutex_lock(&lock);
38    readers--;
39    if(readers==0)
40    {
41       pthread_cond_signal(&busy);
42    }
43    pthread_mutex_unlock(&lock);
44  }
```

Thread Scheduling. So far, we have discussed threads without regard to their interactions with the operating system. Their behavior, however, depends on how they are scheduled. To understand the issues, we need to first define a *kernel thread* to be a unit of scheduling within the kernel, or operating system. The threads that we have been discussing in this chapter can then be mapped to kernel threads in different ways. There are two primary approaches:

1. We could map multiple threads to a single-kernel thread, which would imply that the operating system is unaware of these multiple threads. Such threads, which are sometimes referred to as user-level threads, are efficient because they can be created and destroyed without operating system intervention. One problem, however, is that if one thread blocks—perhaps to wait for an I/O operation—the entire kernel thread blocks, and none of the other threads that have been mapped to that kernel thread can execute. In Pthreads, such threads are known as *unbound threads*.

2. An alternative approach is to map each thread to its own kernel thread. In this case, the operating system is aware of all threads, so when one thread blocks, another thread can be scheduled to execute in its place. Such threads are known as *bound threads*. When threads are used for performance reasons, we typically use bound threads.

In the first approach, each thread competes for resources within a single process, while in the second approach, each thread competes for system resources as doled out by the operating system. In POSIX Threads, the scheduling approach is specified by setting a thread attribute known as the scope contention attribute (see Code Spec 6.18).

Code Spec 6.18 POSIX Thread routine for setting thread scheduling attributes.

Thread Scheduling Attributes

```
int pthread_attr_setscope(
   pthread_attr_t *attr,
   int contentionscope);
```

Arguments:
- Pointer to attribute to set.
- `PTHREAD_SCOPE_PROCESS` for unbound threads and `PTHREAD_SCOPE_SYSTEM` for bound threads.

Return value:
0 for success. Error code from `<errno.h>` otherwise.

Notes:
Thread scheduling is often operating system-specific, and some operating systems do not support both scheduling approaches.

Priority Inversion. There are many scheduling details that we will not discuss in this book. For example, threads can use various scheduling policies, and threads can have different priorities. In this section, we focus on a common scheduling issue that can arise, namely, *priority inversion*.

Priority inversion occurs when a low-priority thread holds a lock that a high-priority thread wishes to acquire. Because the high-priority thread must block while the low-priority thread holds the mutex, the high-priority thread essentially has lower priority than the low-priority thread. With just two threads, the situation is temporary, assuming that the low-priority thread eventually relinquishes the lock. And if critical sections are kept small, then the problem is minimized. A more serious case occurs if a third thread is created with a priority that is between the low- and high-priority threads. This medium-priority thread will preempt the low-priority thread, preventing the low-priority thread from executing and relinquishing its lock. Thus, the high-priority thread must block as long as the medium-priority thread executes.

There are two common solutions to this problem. One solution is to use a *priority ceiling*, which is the highest possible thread priority. Any thread that acquires a lock executes at this highest possible priority, which prevents some medium-level thread from preempting it. Another solution is to use *priority inheritance*. When a thread acquires a mutex, it temporarily inherits the priority of the highest thread that is blocked waiting for that mutex, unless of course doing so would lower its priority. When the thread releases the mutex, its priority reverts to its original priority. Thus, any thread that acquires a mutex inherits the priority of the highest-priority blocked thread because it is in effect making progress on behalf of that blocked thread.

Gang Scheduling. Because the number of processes in a system is typically larger than the number of available processors, modern operating systems must share physical resources by time-slicing the processors; that is, the OS must have a policy for scheduling processes to processors. Poor scheduling can adversely affect performance when two interacting processes are scheduled to execute in different time slices. In particular, if a process p interacts with a process that is not scheduled to execute in the same time quantum, then process p can spend its entire time quantum waiting for an event that will never occur. The solution to this problem is known as gang scheduling or *co-scheduling*: The idea is that P interacting processes should be scheduled on P processors at the same time.

On large parallel computers, gang scheduling is a systems issue that most applications programmers need not concern themselves with, but there is a related issue that more commonly pertains to thread scheduling: If a parallel program uses $P + k$ interacting threads to execute on P processors, performance typically suffers if $k > 0$. We conclude that it's best to write code for some fixed but unspecified number of processors, as suggested by the Scalable Parallelism approach presented in Chapter 4.

Note

Case Study: Successive Over-Relaxation

In Chapter 5 we discussed several methods of assigning work to threads, and in this chapter we have seen how to use Threads to express parallelism. We now put both concepts to work as we reason about the creation of a specific parallel computation. We focus on issues that affect performance, leaving the programming details as an exercise.

Our problem is to compute a 2D successive over-relaxation (SOR) program, which can be used—often in 3D form—to solve systems of differential equations, such as the Navier-Stokes equations for fluid flow. Our computation starts with a 2D array of n values. At each iteration, the computation replaces each value of the array with the average of its four nearest neighbor values. Those values on the edge of the array use some predetermined constant values, known as *boundary values*, as the missing neighbor values. We will assume that the boundary values along the left edge contain 1s, that all other boundary values are 0s, and that each value in the 2D array begins with a value of 0.

The simplest way to handle the boundary values is to allocate space for them in the 2D array and to initialize them with their constant value, giving us the situation as shown in Figure 6.14.

To help formulate our parallel solution, it's useful to examine the data dependences that are present in the computation. Postulate an array containing the values of the current state (old) and an array to be filled with the next iteration's state (new); we will swap pointers to these two at the end of each iteration to perform the update. In each iteration, each element of the old array is read four times, because it is a neighbor to four other array elements. Thus, the old array can only induce input depen-

Figure 6.14
A 2D relaxation replaces—on each iteration—all interior values by the average of their four nearest neighbors.

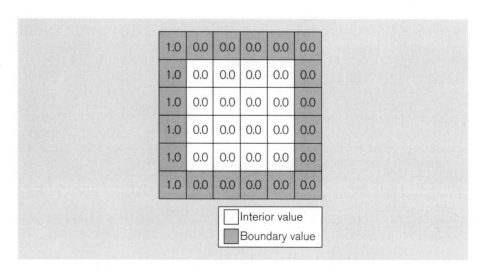

dences. In each iteration, each element of the new array is modified. So with respect to the array elements, there are no true dependences within a single iteration because reads and writes are to different data. There are, however, true dependences across iterations of the computation because we cannot swap the pointers to old and new until all of the new values have been updated.

With this understanding of the problem and its data dependences, we can now ask a simple question, "Should we assign work statically or dynamically?" We can always assign work dynamically using a work queue, but in this case such a solution would have two disadvantages. First, we would have to pay the overhead of accessing a work queue, and second, we might see diminished spatial locality because each processor, which has its own L1 cache, will likely be assigned different parts of the array on different iterations. Since the work is extremely regular—the data structure is a 2D array, the amount of work per array element is roughly constant, and the amount of work does not change over time—and since the work can be fairly divided, a static allocation makes more sense.

Because the work is regular and static, it makes sense to use as few threads as possible, thereby minimizing thread overhead. We will thus spawn t threads at the beginning of our program, we will allocate roughly $1/t$ of the work to each thread, and we will not destroy the threads until the computation has completed. We will also assume that t can be set to match the number of available processors, thus maximizing our parallelism.

Given this static allocation of work to threads, we can ensure that dependences across iterations are preserved by placing a barrier synchronization at the end of each iteration. These barriers preserve all program dependences, so there is no need for any other locks or condition variables.

How exactly should we assign work to each thread? As mentioned in Chapter 5, we could allocate large chunks of work using a block decomposition, or we could interleave the work in a cyclic decomposition. Because the problem iterates over all elements of the array on each iteration, the load balance depends on the amount of work assigned to each thread, so the load balancing advantage of a cyclic decomposition is minimal. By contrast, a block decomposition has the advantage of improving locality because for a given number of elements, a cyclic decomposition has a larger number of neighbors—and thus touches more data—than a block decomposition.

Finally, should we use a 1D or 2D block decomposition? To answer this question, realize that while there are no true dependences within an iteration, there is still the possibility of false sharing, which can be minimized by using a vertical 1D block decomposition; Figure 6.15 shows how such a strategy minimizes the number of points where two threads might falsely share data. In fact, with the suggested block decomposition, false sharing can be eliminated by padding the left or right boundary values. The program is shown in Figure 6.16.

Figure 6.15
(Left) A vertical 1D block decomposition minimizes the potential for false sharing if we assume a row-major memory allocation. (Right) A horizontal 1D block decomposition increases the potential for false sharing. A 2D block decomposition (not shown) would further increase the potential for false sharing, and a cyclic decomposition would be even worse.

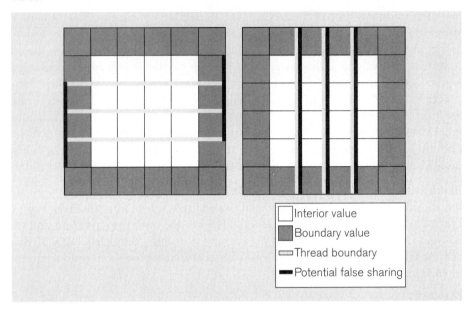

Figure 6.16
2D Sucessive over-relaxation program written using POSIX Threads.

```
 1    #include <pthread.h>
 2    #include <limits.h>
 3    #define MAXTHREADS 16         /* maximum number of threads */
 4    void* thread_main(void *);
 5    void InitializeData();
 6    void barrier();
 7
 8    pthread_mutex_t update_lock;
 9    pthread_mutex_t barrier_lock; /* mutex for the barrier */
10    pthread_cond_t all_here;      /* condition variable for barrier */
11    int count=0;                  /* counter for barrier */
12
13    int n, t, threshold, rowsPerThread;
14    double myDelta;
15    double **val, **new;
16    double delta=0.0;
17
```

```
18   /*
19     Command line args: matrix size, number of threads, threshold
20   */
21
22   int main(int argc, char *argv[])
23   {
24     /* thread ids and attributes */
25     pthread_t tid[MAXTHREADS];
26     pthread_attr_t attr;
27     int i, j;
28
29     /* set global thread attributes */
30     pthread_attr_init(&attr);
31     pthread_attr_setscope(&attr, PTHREAD_SCOPE_SYSTEM);
32
33     /* initialize mutex and condition variable */
34     pthread_mutex_init(&update_lock, NULL);
35     pthread_mutex_init(&barrier_lock, NULL);
36     pthread_cond_init(&all_here, NULL);
37
38     /* read command line arguments */
39     n=atoi(argv[1]);
40     t=atoi(argv[2]);
41     threshold=atof(argv[3]);
42     rowsPerThread=n/t;
43     InitializeData();
44
45     for(i=0; i<t; i++)
46     {
47       pthread_create(&tid[i], &attr, thread_main, (void *) i);
48     }
49     for(i=0; i<t; i++)
50     {
51       pthread_join(tid[i], NULL);
52     }
53
54     printf("maximum difference:  %e\n", delta);
55   }
56
57   void* thread_main(void *arg)
58   {
59     int id=(int) arg;
60     double average;
61     double **myVal, **myNew;
62     double **temp;
63     int i, j;
64     int start;
65
```

(continued)

Figure 6.16 (*continued*)
2D Successive over-relaxation program written using POSIX Threads.

```
66      /* determine first row that this thread owns */
67      start=id*rowsPerThread+1;
68      myVal=val;
69      myNew=new;
70
71      do
72      {
73        myDelta=0.0;
74        if(id==0)
75        {
76          delta=0.0;                   /* reset shared value of delta */
77        }
78        barrier();
79
80        /* update each point */
81        for(i=start; i<start+rowsPerThread; i++)
82        {
83          for(j=1; j<n+1; j++)
84          {
85            average=(myVal[i-1][j] + myVal[i][j+1] +
86                       myVal[i+1][j] + myVal[i][j-1])/4;
87            myDelta=Max(myDelta, Abs(average-myVal[i][j]));
88            myNew[i][j]=average;
89          }
90        }
91        temp=myNew;                /* prepare for next iteration */
92        myNew=myVal;
93        myVal=temp;
94
95        pthread_mutex_lock(&update_lock);
96        if(myDelta>delta)
97        {
98          delta=myDelta;           /* update delta */
99        }
100       pthread_mutex_unlock(&update_lock);
101
102       barrier();
103     } while(delta < threshold);
104   }
105
106   void InitializeData()
107   {
108     int i, j;
109
110     new=(double **) malloc((n+2)*sizeof(float *));
111     val=(double **) malloc((n+2)*sizeof(float *));
```

```
112      for(i=0;  i<n+2;  i++)
113      {
114        new[i]=(double *) malloc((n+2)*sizeof(float));
115        val[i]=(double *) malloc((n+2)*sizeof(float));
116      }
117
118      /* initialize to 0.0 except to 1.0 along the left boundary */
119      for(j=0;  j<n+2;  j++)
120      {
121        val[0][j]=1.0;
122        new[0][j]=1.0;
123      }
124      for(i=1;  i<n+2;  i++)
125      {
126        for(j=0;  j<n+2;  j++)
127        {
128          val[i][j]=0.0;
129          new[i][j]=0.0;
130        }
131      }
132  }
133
134  void barrier()
135  {
136      pthread_mutex_lock(&barrier_lock);
137      count++;
138      if(count==t)
139      {
140        count=0;
141        pthread_cond_broadcast(&all_here);
142      }
143      else
144      {
145        pthread_cond_wait(&all_here, &barrier_lock);
146      }
147      pthread_mutex_unlock(&barrier_lock);
148  }
```

Case Study: Overlapping Synchronization with Computation

As we mentioned in Chapter 4, it is often useful to overlap long-latency operations with independent computation. For example, in Figure 6.17 Thread 0 reaches the barrier well before Thread 1, so it would be profitable for Thread 0 to do some useful work rather than simply sit idle. To take advantage of such opportunities, we typically need to create *split-phase operations*, which separate an operation into two phases: initiation and completion, as shown in Figure 6.18.

Figure 6.17
It's often profitable to do useful work while waiting for some long-latency operation to complete.

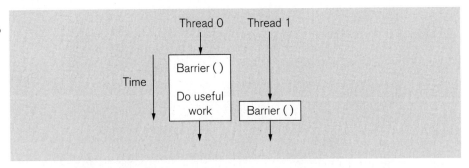

Figure 6.18
A split-phase barrier allows a thread to do useful work while waiting for the other threads to arrive at the barrier.

```
// Initiate synchronization
barrier.arrived();

// Do useful work

// Complete synchronization
barrier.wait();
```

To see a concrete example of how split-phase operations can help, consider a 1D successive over-relaxation program in which our array holds $n + 2$ values: n interior values and 2 boundary values. Analogous to our previous case study, at each iteration the computation will replace each interior value with the average of its two neighbor values, as shown in Figure 6.19. The code for computing a 1D over-relaxation with a single-phase barrier is shown in Figure 6.20. Here, we assume we have t threads, where each is responsible for computing the over-relaxation of n/t values. With a split-phase barrier, the main routine is changed as shown in Figure 6.21.

The code to implement the split-phase barrier seems straightforward enough. As shown in Figure 6.22, we can implement a Barrier class that keeps a count of the number of threads that should arrive at the barrier. To initiate the synchronization, each thread calls the arrived() routine, which increments the counter. The last thread to arrive at the barrier (line 32) then signals all waiters to wake up and resume execution; the last thread also sets the counter to 0 in preparation for the

Figure 6.19
A 1D over-relaxation replaces—on each iteration—all interior values by the average of their two nearest neighbors.

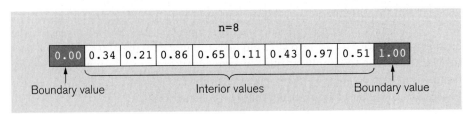

Figure 6.20
Program for 1D successive over-relaxation using a single-phase barrier.

```
1   double *val, *new;              // Hold n values
2   int n;                          // Number of interior values
3   int t;                          // Number of threads
4   int iterations;                 // Number of iterations to perform
5
6   void* thread_main(void *arg)
7   {
8     int index=(int) arg;
9     double *myVal=val;
10    double *myNew=new;
11    int n_per_thread=n/t;
12    int start=index*n_per_thread;
13
14    for(int i=0; i<iterations, i++)
15    {
16      // Update values
17      for(int j=start; j<start+n_per_thread; j++)
18      {
19        myNew[j]=(myVal[j-1]+myVal[j+1])/2.0;
20      }
21      swap(myNew, myVal);
22      barrier();                   // Synchronize
23    }
24  }
```

Figure 6.21
Program for 1D successive over-relaxation using a split-phase barrier.

```
1   double *val, *new;              // Hold n values
2   int n;                          // Number of interior values
3   int t;                          // Number of threads
4   int iterations;                 // Number of iterations to perform
5
6   void* thread_main(void *arg)
7   {
8     int index=(int) arg;
9     double *myVal=val;
10    double *myNew=new;
11    int n_per_thread=n/t;
12    int start=index*n_per_thread;
13
14    for(int i=0; i<iterations, i++)
15    {
16      // Update local boundary values
```

(continued)

Figure 6.21 (*continued*)
Program for 1D successive over-relaxation using a split-phase barrier.

```
17          int j=start;
18          myNew[j]=(myVal[j-1]+myVal[j+1])/2.0;
19          j=start+n_pre_thread -1;
20          myNew[j]=(myVal[j-1]+myVal[j+1])/2.0;
21
22          // Start barrier
23          barrier.arrived();
24
25          // Update local interior values
26          for(j=start+1; j<start+n_per_thread-1; j++)
27          {
28             myNew[j]=(myVal[j-1]+myVal[j+1])/2.0;
29          }
30          swap(myNew, myVal);
31
32          // Complete barrier
33          barrier.wait();
34       }
35   }
```

Figure 6.22
Initial split-phase barrier implementation that keeps a count of the number of arrivals.

```
1    class Barrier
2    {
3      int nThreads;                    // Number of threads
4      int count;                       // Number of threads participating
5      pthread_mutex_t lock;
6      pthread_cond_t all_here;
7      public:
8        Barrier(int t);
9        ~Barrier(void);
10       void arrived(void);            // Initiate a barrier
11       int done(void);                // Check for completion
12       void wait(void);               // Wait for completion
13   }
14
15   int Barrier::done(void)
16   {
17     int rval;
18     pthread_mutex_lock(&lock);
19
20     rval=!count;                     // Done if the count is zero
21
22     pthread_mutex_unlock(&unlock);
23     return rval;
```

```
24   }
25
26   void Barrier::arrived(void)
27   {
28      pthread_mutex_lock(&lock);
29      count++                          // Another thread has arrived
30
31      // If last thread to arrive, then wake up any waiters
32      if(count==nThreads)
33      {
34         count=0;
35         pthread_cond_broadcast(&all_here);
36      }
37
38      pthread_mutex_unlock(&lock);
39   }
40
41   void Barrier::wait(void)
42   {
43      pthread_mutex_lock(&lock);
44
45      // If not done, then wait
46      if(count !=0)
47      {
48         pthread_cond_wait(&all_here, &lock);
49      }
50
51      pthread_mutex_lock(&lock);
52   }
```

next use of the barrier. To complete the synchronization, the wait() routine checks to see if the counter is nonzero, in which case it waits for the last thread to arrive. Of course, a lock is used to provide mutual exclusion, and a condition variable is used to implement synchronization.

Unfortunately, the code presented does not work correctly! In particular, consider an execution with two threads and two iterations, as shown in Figure 6.23. Initially, the counter is 0, and Thread 0's arrival increments the value to 1. Thread 1's arrival increments the counter to 2, and because Thread 1 is the last thread to arrive at the barrier, it resets the counter to 0 and wakes up any waiting threads, of which there are none. The problem arises when Thread 1 gets ahead of Thread 0 and executes its next iteration—and hence its next calls to arrive() and wait()—before Thread 0 invokes wait() from its first iteration. In this case, Thread 1 will increment the counter to 1, and when Thread 0 arrives at the wait, it will block. At this point, Thread 0 is blocked waiting for the completion of the barrier in the first iteration, while Thread 1 is blocked waiting for the completion of the second iteration, result-

Figure 6.23
Deadlock with our initial implementation of a split-phase barrier; Thread0 and Thread1 each waits for different instances of the barrier.

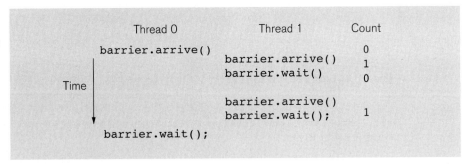

ing in deadlock. Of course, the first barrier has completed, but Thread 0 is unaware of this important fact.

Of course, we seem to have become quite unlucky to have Thread 0 execute so slowly relative to Thread 1, but because our barrier needs to work in all cases, we need to handle this race condition.

The problem in Figure 6.23 occurs because Thread 0 was looking at the state of the counter for the wrong invocation of the barrier. A solution then is to keep track of the current phase of the barrier. In particular, the `arrived()` method returns a phase number, which is then passed to the `done()` and `wait()` methods. The correct code is shown in Figure 6.24. Since the interface to the barrier routines have changed, we need to modify our relaxation code, as shown in Figure 6.25.

Figure 6.24
A correct barrier implementation that keeps track of the correct phase.

```
1    class Barrier
2    {
3       int nThreads;              // Number of threads
4       int count;                 // Number of threads participating
5       int phase;                 // Phase # of this barrier
6       pthread_mutex_t lock;
7       pthread_cond_t all_here;
8       public:
9          Barrier(int t);
10         ~Barrier(void);
11         void arrived(void);     // Initiate a barrier
12         int done(int p);        // Check for completion of phase p
13         void wait(int p);       // Wait for completion of phase p
14   }
15
16   int Barrier::done(int p)
17   {
18      int rval;
```

```
19    pthread_mutex_lock(&lock);
20
21    rval=(phase!=p);                      // Done if the phase # has changed
22
23    pthread_mutex_unlock(&lock);
24    return rval;
25  }
26
27  int Barrier::arrived(void)
28  {
29    int p;
30    pthread_mutex_lock(&lock);
31
32    p=phase;                              // Get phase number
33    count++                              // Another thread has arrived
34
35    // If last thread, then wake up any waiters, go to next phase
36    if(count==nThreads)
37    {
38       count=0;
39       pthread_cond_broadcast(&all_here);
40       phase=1 - phase;
41    }
42
43    pthread_mutex_unlock(&lock);
44    return p;
45  }
46
47  void Barrier::wait(int p)
48  {
49    pthread_mutex_lock(&lock);
50
51    // If not done, then wait
52    while(p==phase)
53    {
54       pthread_cond_wait(&all_here, &lock);
55    }
56
57    pthread_mutex_unlock(&lock);
58  }
```

With this new barrier implementation, the situation in Figure 6.23 no longer results in deadlock. As shown in Figure 6.26, Thread 0's invocation of wait(0) explicitly waits for the completion of the first invocation of the barrier, so when it executes line 50 in the wait() routine, it falls out of the while loop and never calls pthread_cond_wait(). Thus, deadlock is avoided.

Figure 6.25

Program for 1D successive over-relaxation solution of Figure 6.19 with the split-phase barrier code.

```
1    double *val, *new;              // Hold n values
2    int n;                          // Number of interior values
3    int t;                          // Number of threads
4    int iterations                  // Number of iterations to perform
5
6    thread_main(int index)
7    {
8        int n_per_thread=n/t;
9        int start=index*n_per_thread;
10       int phase;
11
12       for(int i=0; i<iterations; i++)
13       {
14           // Update local boundary values
15           int j=start;
16           new[j]=(val[j-1]+val[j+1])/2.0;
17           j=start+n_per_thread -1;
18           new[j]=(val[j-1]+val[j+1])/2.0;
19
20           // Start barrier
21           phase=barrier.arrived();
22
23           // Update local interior values
24           for(j=start+1; j<start+n_per_thread-1; j++)
25           {
26               new[j]=(val[j-1]+val[j+1])/2.0;    // Compute average
27           }
28           swap(new, val);
29
30           // Complete barrier
31           barrier.wait(phase);
32       }
33   }
```

Figure 6.26

Deadlock does not occur with our new split-phase barrier.

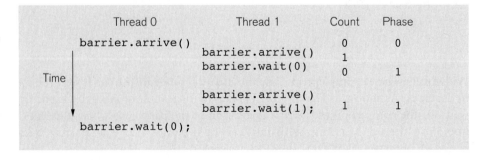

	Thread 0	Thread 1	Count	Phase
	barrier.arrive()		0	0
		barrier.arrive()	1	
		barrier.wait(0)	0	1
		barrier.arrive()		
		barrier.wait(1);	1	1
	barrier.wait(0);			

Case Study: Streaming Computations on a Multi-Core Chip

To understand how a solution for a multi-core chip might differ from a more traditional symmetric multi-processor (SMP), consider the task of designing a parallel program to compress a movie, and focus on identifying the appropriate granularity of parallelism. Assume that the process is compute-intensive and has high bandwidth requirements. Assume further that a movie simply consists of a series of frames, where each frame is a 2D image.

There is a spectrum of possible solutions:

1. **Assign each process its own frame.** We can parallelize the solution at a large granularity by having each process operate on a separate frame, writing the compressed frame back to memory when it's done. This solution is simple, with no communication among processes, but of our possible solutions, it requires the most bandwidth to memory, significant on-chip cache, and it does not parallelize the actual compression process, which is often quite CPU-intensive.

2. **Assign each process a portion of a single frame.** For example, each process could compress 1/P of a frame. Such a solution uses all processes to collectively compress each frame, so it has lower memory bandwidth requirements. However, depending on the compression algorithm, this solution might require communication among processes.

3. **Have multiple processes collaborate on each portion of a frame.** We could take an even finer-grained approach by having all processes cooperate on the processing of a portion of a frame. For example, we could load 1/k of a frame to on-chip cache and then have all P processes cooperatively compress that portion of the frame. Of course, whether this approach is viable depends heavily on whether the compression can use multiple processes. For example, if the algorithm consists of, say, four stages, it's possible to take a task parallel approach in which each process performs one of the four stages in a pipeline.

The best choice depends on the specifics of the computation's bandwidth and computation requirements, as well as the specifics of the target hardware. If the compression is compute-bound, then one of the finer-grained approaches is attractive, particularly if the multi-core chip has low on-chip communication latencies. If on the other hand the compression is memory bound, then the multi-core chip may have insufficient bandwidth to support the first solution; it might be feasible on an SMP, because each processor comes with its own interface to main memory and its own on-chip cache. The third strategy helps minimize both total bandwidth and peak bandwidth.

Java Threads

Java is probably the most widely used programming language that explicitly supports parallelism. This section highlights the main features of Java threads, assuming that the reader has read the previous section on POSIX Threads. We assume that readers are familiar with Java and basic object-oriented concepts.

Java presents interesting support for threading. At its core, it provides the same conceptual features as POSIX Threads, but because of its object-oriented setting, it can also supply higher-level abstractions that are simpler to use. At the same time, it also supports low-level features that can be used as the basis for building new concurrent data structures.

A thread in Java is an instance of the Thread class, which has methods to run and synchronize with the thread. (See Code Spec 6.19 for some of the most important methods.) Thus, Java programmers can use threads by extending the Thread class with specialized forms of threads. This approach is limiting, however, because a class that extends the Thread class cannot extend any other class, since Java only supports single inheritance.

Code Spec 6.19 Java's Thread class methods.

The Java Thread Class

```
public synchronized void start()
```
- Starts this Thread and returns immediately after invoking the run()method.
- Throws IllegalThreadStateException if the thread was already started.

```
public void run()
```
- The body of this Thread, which is invoked after the thread is started.

```
public final synchronized void join(long millis)
  throws InterruptedException
```
- Waits for this Thread to die. A timeout in milliseconds can be specified, with a timeout of 0 milliseconds indicating that the thread will wait forever.

```
public static void yield()
```
- Causes the currently executing Thread object to yield the processor so that some other runnable Thread can be scheduled.

```
public final int getPriority()
```
- Returns the thread's priority.

```
public final void setPriority(int newPriority)
```
- Sets the thread's priority.

Notes:
   For a complete list of public methods for the Thread class, see
   java.lang.Thread.

Fortunately, we typically don't want to modify the core thread facilities. Instead, we merely want to implement a new `thread_main` routine. In such cases, it's preferable to define a new class that implements the `Runnable` interface and instantiates one or more threads inside its main method. This approach is more flexible because it allows the new class to extend other classes; this approach also makes it clear that the basic `Thread` functionality is not being altered.

Synchronized Methods

In addition to the basic `Thread` object, Java supports a simple way to define a monitor using a construct known as a *synchronized method*. For example, we can define a synchronized counter as follows:

```
public class SynchronizedCounter
{
  public synchronized void update(int x)
  {
    count +=x;
  }
  public synchronized void reset()
  {
    count=0;
  }
}
```

With such a definition, an instance of the `SynchronizedCounter` class becomes a monitor, and only one thread can execute any of this instance's synchronized methods at any time; other threads must wait for that thread to exit the monitor. These monitors are extremely convenient because they do not expose the mutex that protects the monitor. Instead, the hidden mutex is implicitly acquired by any thread that enters the monitor, and the mutex is implicitly released when the thread exits the monitor.

Note that locks are owned by threads, so a thread can acquire a lock that it already owns, which allows synchronized methods to be recursive.

Synchronized Statements

Java also provides synchronized statements, which support finer-grained synchronization than monitors. Unlike POSIX Threads, there is no specific mutex data structure, instead, any Java object can be used to specify the synchronization. Thus, we can define a critical section as follows:

```
Object lock;
synchronized(lock)
{
  /* critical section */
}
```

Synchronized statements are finer-grained than synchronized methods in two ways. First, the critical sections can be smaller, consisting of a single block within a method. Second, two pieces of code that do not interact can be synchronized on independent objects, yielding greater parallelism.

Both synchronized methods and synchronized statements have another effect besides implementing mutual exclusion. To understand this point, we need to realize that for performance reasons threads can keep a cached copy of variables and that the values of these cached copies can differ from the value in main memory that is visible to other threads.[2] A synchronized statement or method flushes all of a thread's cached values to main memory, making them visible to all other threads at that point. Of course, this flushing of variables incurs a performance penalty.

The Count 3s Example

With these basic notions of threads and synchronized statements, we are now ready to implement the Count 3s problem using Java threads as shown in Figure 6.27. We see the use of the Runnable interface, and on line 73 we see the use of a synchronized statement to update the count variable atomically; this synchronized statement uses a generic Object named lock to provide synchronization.

Figure 6.27
Count 3s solution in Java.

```
1   import java.util.*;
2   import java.util.concurrent.*;
3
4   public class CountThrees implements Runnable
5   {
6       private static final int ARRAY_LENGTH=1000000;
7       private static final int MAX_THREADS=10;
8       private static final int MAX_RANGE=100;
9       private static final Random random=new Random();
10      private static int count=0;
11      private static Object lock=new Object();
12      private static int[] array;
13      private static Thread[] t;
14
15      public static void main(String[] args)
16      {
17          array=new int[ARRAY_LENGTH];
18
19          //initialize the elements in the array
20          for(int i=0; i<array.length; i++)
```

[2]This memory incoherence is just one of many idiosyncrasies of the Java memory model that can lead to unexpected results. For more details, see Java Specification Request (JSR) 133.

```
21        {
22           array[i]=random.nextInt(MAX_RANGE);
23        }
24
25        //create the threads
26        CountThrees[] counters=new CountThrees[MAX_THREADS];
27        int lengthPerThread=ARRAY_LENGTH/MAX_THREADS;
28
29        for(int i=0; i<counters.length; i++)
30        {
31           counters[i]=new CountThrees(i*lengthPerThread,
32                                       lengthPerThread);
33        }
34
35        //run the threads
36        for(int i=0; i<counters.length; i++)
37        {
38           t[i]=new Thread(counters[i]);
39           t[i].start();
40        }
41        for(int i=0; i<counters.length; i++)
42        {
43           try
44           {
45              t[i].join();
46           }
47           catch(InterruptedException e)
48           { /*do nothing*/ }
49        }
50
51        //print the number of threes
52        System.out.println("Number of threes: " + count);
53     }
54
55     private int startIndex;
56     private int elements;
57     private int myCount=0;
58
59     public CountThrees(int start, int elem)
60     {
61        startIndex=start;
62        elements=elem;
63     }
64
65     //Overload of run method in the Thread class
66     public void run()
67     {
68        //count the number of threes
```

(continued)

Figure 6.27 (*continued*)
Count 3s solution in Java

```
69        for(int i=0; i<elements; i++)
70        {
71          if(array[startIndex+i]==3)
72          {
73            myCount++;
74          }
75        }
76        synchronized(lock)
77        {
78          count+=myCount;
79        }
80      }
81  }
```

Volatile Memory

Java supports a lighter-weight option for synchronizing variables through the use of the `volatile` field modifier, which tells the language implementation that a specific variable cannot have a separate cached value in a register because the value must be consistent with the value that other threads see. Thus, a volatile variable is kept consistent across all threads at all times. The use of volatile variables is efficient because unlike synchronized methods or synchronized statements, the use of volatile variables does not flush the values of the thread's other variables.

Atomic Objects

Java 5.0 supports *atomic objects*, which implement atomic operations on individual objects without the need to use locks (see Code Spec 6.20). For example, the `java.util.concurrent.atomic` package implements classes such as

Code Spec 6.20 Examples of Java's atomic objects.

Sample Operations for AtomicInteger

`boolean compareAndSet(expectedValue, updateValue);`
  ■ Atomically sets the value to `updateValue` if the current value is the same as `expectedValue`.
`int getAndIncrement();`
  ■ Atomically reads the current value and increments the current value by one.

`AtomicBoolean`, `AtomicInteger`, `AtomicLong`, and `AtomicReference`. These classes support operations that both read and update variables atomically, so atomic objects can be used as building blocks for the creation of higher-level nonblocking data structures.

Lock Objects

Java 5.0 provides explicit lock objects in the `java.util.concurrent.locks` package. One problem with implicit locks is that it's not possible to back out of them. Lock objects provide this capability, which is useful for preventing deadlock. In particular, the `tryLock()` method provides a time-out mechanism.

Executors

Java 5.0 also has *executors*, which separate thread management from the actual work that is done by a thread. Unlike the Pthreads interface, the `Executor` interface allows threads to return values to their parent threads, and the `Executor` interface supports more flexible scheduling of work—for example, allowing a thread to be invoked periodically with some given frequency. Executors support the notion of thread pools, allowing a program to reuse threads, which is cheaper than continually spawning and destroying them.

Concurrent Collections

Finally, Java 5.0 supports a set of concurrent data structures that can be accessed by multiple threads simultaneously. These data structures include the following:

- BlockingQueues
- ConcurrentMap
- ConcurrentSkipListMap

Consult online resources for others.

With such extensive support, Java is a convenient alternative to Pthreads.

OpenMP

The OpenMP interface was developed in the late 1990s to give programmers a convenient way to obtain parallelism on shared address space machines. The basic idea is to augment sequential programs in minor ways to identify code that can be executed in parallel. The OpenMP model is significantly simpler to use than Pthreads, but it is also significantly more restrictive in terms of the types of parallel interactions that can be described. The OpenMP standard supports C, C++, and Fortran, and in this section we present a brief introduction to OpenMP using examples in C. More complete information can be found at http://www.openmp.org.

The Count 3s Example

OpenMP is introduced into a C or C++ program using pragmas and into a Fortran program using comments. For example, we could add three pragmas and a declaration to our original Count 3s program from Chapter 1, as shown in Figure 6.28. We see that the pragmas take the following form:

    #pragma omp <specifications>

An OpenMP-compliant C compiler will recognize the construct and generate appropriate multithreaded code using the <specification>. Compilers that don't accept OpenMP simply ignore the pragmas, yielding standard sequential execution. In Figure 6.28, we see that if the pragmas are treated like white space, then the result is a program equivalent to the first Count 3s program in Chapter 1 but with a bit of extra computation, which any reasonable compiler would eliminate. Thus, adding the pragmas to a program can have benefit when using a compliant compiler, but it produces no significant cost otherwise.

The declaration on line 3 of Figure 6.28 introduces the private count_p variable. Its role is to provide a thread-specific location into which each thread of the for loop can accumulate its result. The first pragma (line 5) specifies that its body can execute in parallel, and it identifies the variables used in the body as either shared or private. If left unspecified, all variables are assumed to be shared. The number of threads created is left to the system and is not usually under programmer control.

The second pragma (line 9) specifies that the iterations of the for loop can execute in any order, meaning that the iterations can execute in parallel. Accordingly, OpenMP will apportion to each thread

$$totalIterations \, / \, numThreads$$

iterations, though programmers are provided some control over batch size, as explained below. Of course, if the pragma is incorrect because there *are* dependences, then the results of the parallel execution can be unpredictable. Even if the pragmas are semantically correct, not all for loops can be legally parallelized in OpenMP. Constraints described in Code Spec 6.21 are placed on the loop specification to allow the compiler to predict the number of iterations that will execute and to assign them to threads.

In our Count 3s solution of Figure 6.28, each thread performs a batch of iterations; the number of threes found is accumulated into each thread's private count_p variable. When a thread completes the for loop, it proceeds to the critical section specified by the third pragma (line 17). The compiler protects the critical section with a lock to ensure that at most one thread enters the critical section at any time, allowing the private count_p values to be properly combined into the global count. When all threads have exited the critical section and reached the end of the parallel block of the first pragma, they are joined, resulting in a single thread of control. The result is returned to the calling program.

Figure 6.28 OpenMP applied to the sequential Count 3s program of Chapter 1. The first pragma (line 5) identifies that lines 7–21 will be parallelized; the second pragma (line 9) states that the `for` loop can be multithreaded; the final pragma (line 17) combines in a critical section the private counts created in the multi-threaded `for` loop.

```
1   int count3s()
2   {
3      int i, count_p;
4      count=0;
5      #pragma omp parallel shared(array, count, length)\
6         private(count_p)
7      {
8         count_p=0;
9         #pragma omp parallel for private(i)
10        for(i=0; i<length; i++)
11        {
12           if(array[i]==3)
13           {
14              count_p++;
15           }
16        }
17        #pragma omp critical
18        {
19           count+=count_p;
20        }
21     }
22     return count;
23  }
```

Semantic Limitations on `parallel for`

While the `parallel for` is a convenient tool for introducing parallelism to a sequential program, programmers must be careful that the specified loop iterations are in fact independent. For example, we could have written the Count 3s iteration as follows:

```
#pragma omp parallel for private(i)          Caution: wrong code
for(i=0; i<length; i++)
{
   if(array[i]==3)
   {
      count++;
   }
}
```

However, because the count variable is shared, there is a flow dependence between the uses of count in the different iterations, which implies flow dependences among the uses of count in the different threads. With all threads modifying count simultaneously, a meaningless result is produced. The code in Figure 6.28 fixes the problem by using a private count_p variable and by accumulating those private counts into count after the loops complete. In addition to making variables private, dependences can be handled in OpenMP using atomic, critical, and barrier pragmas (see Code Spec 6.21).

Reduction

OpenMP's reduction pragma can simplify computations that need to combine variables globally. The programmer uses the reduction keyword and gives both the combining operator and the accumulation variable, as described in Code Spec 6.22. Thus, the best OpenMP Count 3s solution is probably as follows:

```
count=0;
#pragma omp parallel for reduction(+,count)
for(i=0; i<length; i++)
{
   count +=(array[i]==3)?1:0;
}
```

The compiler will split the loop iterations among several threads, which will accumulate counts locally, and then *automatically* combine the results.

Code Spec 6.21 OpenMP parallel for statement.

```
parallel for

#pragma omp parallel for
   for(<var>=<expr1>;  <var> <relop> <expr2>;  <var>=<expr3>)(<body> }
```
   Conditions:
   - <var> must be a signed integer variable and the same in each instance.
   - <relop> must be one of <, <=, =>, >.
   - <expr2>, <expr3> must be a loop-invariant integer expression.
   - if <relop> is < or <=, <expr3> must increment each iteration; if <relop> is >, >=, <expr3> must decrement each iteration.
   - <body> must be a basic block, that is, it has no other entries or exits.

Notes:
   - Optional specifications on the pragma line include private and nowait.
   - A set of threads created for a parallel for will join at completion, implying a barrier synchronization.

Code Spec 6.22 OpenMP reduce operation. The `<op>` choice comes from the accompanying table.

`reduction`

reduction(*<op>*:*<list>*)

Conditions:
- *<op>* is one of the operators in the accompanying table; its identity is the value that is used as the left operand for the first step of the reduce operation.
- *<list>* is a set of variables into which the reduce accumulates; for example, `count` in the Count 3s example.

Notes:
Fortran has several more *<op>* choices, including `min` and `max`.

<op>	Identity
+	0
*	1
–	0
&	~0
|	0
^	0
&&	1
||	0

Thread Behavior and Interaction

In OpenMP, threads are generally created in response to a `parallel for`. At the completion of the `parallel for`, the threads join together to resume as a single thread. This join and the implied barrier at the end of a `parallel for` can be avoided by placing the `nowait` pragma in the `parallel for` pragma:

```
#pragma omp parallel for nowait
```

At the end of the loop, the threads simply continue executing beyond the `parallel for`. Notice that the main advantage comes when the next statement is also a `parallel for`.

To ensure that threads that modify a common variable do not interfere with each other, the `atomic` designation can be used:

```
#pragma omp atomic
    score +=3;
```

The `atomic` designation guarantees that the memory update is noninterruptible. That is, the sequence of machine instructions that (1) loads the variable from memory, (2) adds to it, and (3) returns it to memory, is always performed as a single unit. (Other variable updates are possible, as shown in Code Spec 6.23.) Of course, if such an instruction were repeatedly performed in a loop, then performance could suffer because the threads must serialize their accesses to the variable.

To create critical sections that are more complex than a simple variable update, there is the `exclusive` program:

```
#pragma omp exclusive(oneAtATime)
{
    ...only one thread is ever here at any one time...
}
```

which allows a whole block to be executed without conflict because only one thread is allowed to execute the critical section at any time. The name in parentheses (`oneAtATime`) is an optional name for the critical section; if the same name is used in multiple places in a program, a thread executing any one of them excludes all threads from all of the other sites. When no name is given, it is equivalent to using one name for all unnamed critical sections.

Code Spec 6.23 Atomic specification in OpenMP.

```
atomic
```

```
#pragma omp atomic
    <var> <op> <expr> | <expr>++ | <expr>-- | ++<expr> | --<expr>
```

Result:
The statement following the pragma becomes uninterruptible.

Conditions:
- `<var>` is a program variable.
- `<op>` is one of the operations: `+=`, `-=`, `*=`, `/=`, `<<=`, `>>=`, `&=`, `|=`, `^=`.
- `<expr>` is any legal expression.

Notes:
Use of atomic in a loop can have serious performance implications.

Sections

OpenMP can express task parallelism with the `sections` pragma. For example, if three independent tasks, `Task_A()`, `Task_B()`, and `Task_C()` can be executed in parallel and have no dependences among them, then they can be specified to execute in parallel as follows:

```
#pragma omp sections
{
  #pragma omp section
  {
    Task_A();
  }
  #pragma omp section
  {
    Task_B();
  }
  # pragma omp section
  {
    Task_C();
  }
}
```

The block following `sections` lists the parallel tasks, which can be an arbitrary block of C code, including a function call; any number of tasks is allowed. The semantics are that each section is a thread of control and is executed to completion independently of the others. The order is not specified. Notice that the block following each pragma must begin on its own line.

Summary of OpenMP

This brief tour of OpenMP illustrates that the approach is simple and easy to use. Its convenience comes from restricting the programmer's control of parallelism and limiting the amount of information provided. Nevertheless, it can be handy when "a little parallelism" is enough. See the OpenMP Web site for further information, and see Chapter 9 for a critique that compares OpenMP to other programming techniques.

Shared Virtual Memory. Why can't threads-based programs execute on machines that do not support shared memory? Why can't we use software to provide a virtually shared address space on top of such machines? This question was heavily studied in the 1980s and 1990s. The basic issue is that the Shared Virtual Memory system needs to handle all data movement, and it is difficult to do this efficiently without knowledge of the application's sharing behavior. In particular, there is a trade-off regarding the granularity of sharing: A large granularity can amortize inter-processor communication costs at the expense of false sharing. A small granularity can reduce false sharing but increase the

Note

overhead of moving data. In general, we'd ideally like the Shared Virtual Memory system's granularity of sharing to match the application's logical granularity of sharing. Of course, even if the underlying shared virtual memory system were extremely efficient, there is still the question of whether threads-based programming is the best programming model.

Chapter Summary

POSIX Threads are a powerful parallel programming tool that places enormous potential in the hands of programmers. On the plus side, there are few limits to the sophistication of thread-based programs, as programmers are empowered to produce efficient and effective parallel solutions. On the negative side, the power comes with considerable risks; such programs demand deep and careful engineering to be correct and free of race conditions, deadlocks, and subtle performance bottlenecks.

Java provides a simpler thread interface by providing support for monitors and higher-level concurrent data structures. But because these interfaces are not sufficiently general, Java also provides lower-level interfaces that offer much of the functionality of POSIX Threads. OpenMP shows how restrictions can be made to provide a significantly simpler but less general programming model. As we look to the future, an open question is whether we can identify a set of high-level abstractions that falls somewhere between OpenMP and POSIX Threads in terms of programming convenience and flexibility, as well as extreme performance. The question is intriguing.

Historical Perspective

The four necessary conditions for deadlock were first identified by Coffman, et al. [1971]. Hoare [1974] and Brinch Hansen [1975] proposed slightly different variations of monitors in the mid-1970s. The many implementations of POSIX threads are based on the IEEE POSIX 1003.1c-1995 standard; there are numerous books and tutorials available covering advanced techniques. OpenMP was created in the late 1990s by a consortium of vendors and academics.

Exercises

1. Write a simple C program that determines whether a multi-core chip maintains coherent caches. (Remember that there can be multiple levels of caches.) Will your program definitively provide the correct information on every execution? If you were allowed to write your program in assembly language (from which you could invoke Pthreads calls), could you improve upon your program?

2. Our bounded buffer example uses a single mutex to protect both the `nonempty` and `nonfull` condition variables. Could we instead use one mutex for each condition variable? What are the trade-offs?

3. The `pthread_cond_wait()` routine takes the address of the protecting mutex as a parameter so that the routine can atomically block the waiting thread and release the lock that is held by the waiting thread. Explain why these two operations must be performed atomically.

4. For our bounded buffer example of Figure 6.1, specify an invariant about the buffer that must hold outside of the monitor but that is sometimes violated inside the monitor. *Hint*: The answer may be an invariant that cannot be checked with C code.

5. Modify the bounded buffer code to allow the buffer's capacity to use every location. Do this without introducing any extra variables.

6. Use Pthreads to implement a version of the 2D successive over-relaxation program that uses split-phase barriers. Explore different data decompositions and see if there is any significant performance difference.

7. Test the OpenMP Count 3s program given in Figure 6.27, measure its performance, and determine its efficiency for the number of processors on your computer.

8. Write an OpenMP program to solve the Red/Blue simulation (see Exercise 10 in Chapter 4).

9. Experiment with variations on your solution to Exercise 8. Try to improve performance by improving locality of reference.

10. Using Java threads, write a program to solve the Red/Blue simulation (see Exercise 10 in Chapter 4).

7

MPI and Other Local View Languages

Chapter 6 focused on languages for shared address space computers; this chapter and the next will discuss programming approaches that can be mapped to any parallel computer. We divide such languages into two categories: *local view languages*—the subject of this chapter—and *global view languages*—the subject of Chapter 8. We will define these notions in Chapter 9, but for now it suffices to know that global view languages provide some conceptual conveniences that local view languages do not.

As in Chapter 6, we will use the term "language" to include libraries. The main topic of this chapter is the Message Passing Interface (MPI), a library that has become the standard among local view languages. We then briefly discuss three recently developed languages—Co-Array Fortran, Unified Parallel C, and Titanium—which show how local view languages can raise the level of abstraction above MPI.

MPI: The Message Passing Interface

The MPI programming model is extremely simple. MPI presents a distributed memory programming model in which a collection of processes communicates by sending messages. Process management is performed externally to MPI, and MPI execution is initiated with a static number of processes, typically with each process assigned to a different processor. Because each process has its own address space, programmers must formulate their programs so instances can operate on separate portions of a distributed data structure.

While the concepts are simple, MPI provides over a hundred routines. In this section, we will focus on the main ideas upon which all of these routines are built. We start by using the Count 3s example to introduce the basic structure of an MPI program. Here, we use C bindings for MPI, but the standard also provides bindings for Fortran and C++. We then explain the core MPI concepts in more detail and discuss a set of the most commonly used MPI functions.

Online MPI Tutorial. For more details about MPI, including examples and documentation, see the following Web page at Lawrence Livermore Labs:
http://www.llnl.gov/computing/tutorials/mpi/

The Count 3s Example

Figure 7.1 shows an MPI program that solves the Count 3s problem. Lines 12–14 and 66 of the figure show uses of the four essential MPI routines that are common to all MPI programs.

Figure 7.1
An MPI solution to the Count 3s problem.

```
 1   #include <stdio.h>
 2   #include "mpi.h"
 3   #include "globals.h"
 4
 5   int main(argc, argv)
 6   int argc;
 7   char **argv;
 8   {
 9     int myID, value, numProcs;
10     MPI_Status status;
11
12     MPI_Init(&argc, &argv);
13     MPI_Comm_size(MPI_COMM_WORLD, &numProcs);
14     MPI_Comm_rank(MPI_COMM_WORLD, &myID);
15
16     length_per_process=length/numProcs;
17     myArray=(int *) malloc(length_per_process*sizeof(int));
18
19     /* Read the data, distribute it among the various processes */
20     if(myID==RootProcess)
21     {
22       if((fp=fopen(*argv, "r"))==NULL )
23       {
24         printf("fopen failed on %s\n", filename);
25         exit(0);
26       }
27       fscanf(fp,"%d", &length);      /* read input size */
28
29       for(p=0; p<numProcs-1; p++)    /* read data on behalf of each */
30       {                              /* of the other processes */
31         for(i=0; i<length_per_process; i++)
32         {
33           fscanf(fp,"%d", myArray+i);
34         }
35         MPI_Send(myArray, length_per_process, MPI_INT, p+1,
36                 tag, MPI_COMM_WORLD);
```

(continued)

Figure 7.1 (*continued*)
An MPI solution to the Count 3s problem.

```
37          }
38
39          for(i=0; i<length_per_process; i++)  /* Now read my data */
40          {
41             fscanf(fp,"%d", myArray+i);
42          }
43       }
44       else
45       {
46          MPI_Recv(myArray, length_per_process, MPI_INT, RootProcess,
47                   tag, MPI_COMM_WORLD, &status);
48       }
49
50       /* Do the actual work */
51       for(i=0; i<length_per_process; i++)
52       {
53          if(myArray[i]==3)
54          {
55             myCount++;                             /* Update local count */
56          }
57       }
58
59       MPI_Reduce(&myCount,&globalCount, 1, MPI_INT, MPI_SUM,
60                  RootProcess, MPI_COMM_WORLD);
61
62       if(myID==RootProcess)
63       {
64          printf("Number of 3's: %d\n", globalCount);
65       }
66       MPI_Finalize()
67       return 0;
68    }
```

MPI_Init() (line 12) initializes MPI data structures and should be called by each process before any other MPI routines are invoked. MPI_Finalize() (line 66) cleans up MPI data structures and should be the last MPI routine invoked by a process.

MPI_Comm_size() (line 13) determines the number of processes in a particular MPI *communicator*. We discuss the notion of communicators more in the next section, but for now it suffices to know that the default communicator, MPI_COMM_WORLD, includes all processes.

MPI_Comm_rank() (line 14) returns the *rank* of the executing process within a communicator. This rank serves as a unique identifier that distinguishes each process within a communicator, allowing processes to specify the process with which they wish to communicate. The rank is an integer between 0 and $P - 1$, inclusive, where P is the number of processes in the communicator (see Code Spec 7.1–7.4).

Code Spec 7.1 `MPI_Init()`.

```
MPI_Init()
int MPI_Init(                      // Initialize MPI
  int *argc,                       // Number of command line arguments
  char ***argv,                    // Command line arguments
);
```

Arguments:

■ Number of command line arguments.

■ Command line arguments.

Notes:

This routine must be called in every MPI process before any other MPI routine is called. It is an error to call this routine more than once in a process unless a subsequent `MPI_Finalize()` is called.

Return value:

An MPI error code.

Code Spec 7.2 `MPI_Finalize()`.

```
MPI_Finalize()
int MPI_Finalize(
);
```

Notes:

This routine should be the last MPI routine called in each process, and it should only be invoked after all other MPI routines have completed. In particular, any pending communication operations should complete before this routine is called.

Return value:

An MPI error code.

To understand the body of the code, assume that the file `globals.h` includes the following lines:

```
#define RootProcess 0
int length;
int length_per_process;
int myStart;
int myCount=0;
int globalCount;
MPI_Status status;
int tag=1;
```

Code Spec 7.3 `MPI_Comm_Size()`.

```
MPI_Comm_Size()
int MPI_Comm_Size(              // Retrieve the number of tasks in
  MPI_Comm comm,                // the specified communicator
  int *size,                    // The number of tasks
);
```

Arguments:

- The communicator of interest.
- A pointer to the size, whose target will contain the number of tasks in the specified communicator.

Notes:

This routine obtains the number of processes in a communicator.

Return value:

An MPI error code.

Code Spec 7.4 `MPI_Comm_Rank()`.

```
MPI_Comm_Rank()
int MPI_Comm_Rank(              // Retrieve rank of a communicator
  MPI_Comm comm,                // Communicator
  int *rank,                    // Rank
);
```

Notes:

This routine obtains a process' rank within a communicator.

Arguments:

- The communicator of interest.
- A pointer to the rank, whose target will contain the rank of the specified communicator.

Return value:

An MPI error code

Lines 19–48 show how *point-to-point* communication—which sends data from one process to another—is used to distribute the data among the various processes. (We will see shortly how this distribution can be performed more succinctly.) This code starts by having a single process, designated as the RootProcess, read the contents of an array from a file and distribute this data to the other processes. On lines 22–27, the RootProcess opens the specified file name, which is passed through a com-

mand line argument, and then reads the size of the file. On lines 29–37, the
`RootProcess` reads the file contents in `numProcs` chunks, sending the first
`numProcs-1` of these chunks to the other processes and then keeping the last chunk
for its own use.

In particular, the data is sent to other processes on line 35 using the `MPI_Send()`
routine. In MPI, such communication is specified redundantly by both the sender
and the receiver, so lines 44–48 show that each of the `numProcs-1` non-root
processes invoke `MPI_Recv()` to accept the data. We see that there are many details
required to specify such a message, as there are six parameters to `MPI_Send()` and
seven for `MPI_Recv()`. These parameters specify the other process that are involved
in the communication operation, the type and length of the message, and a *tag*,
which is a message identifier. Code Specs 7.5 and 7.6 provide full details.

Code Spec 7.5 `MPI_Send()`.

```
MPI_Send()
int MPI_Send(                          // Blocking Send routine
   void          *buffer,              // Address of the data to send
   int           count,                // Number of data elements to send
   MPI_Datatype  type,                 // Type of data elements to send
   int           dest,                 // ID of destination process
   int           tag,                  // Tag to distinguish this message
   MPI_Comm      *comm                 // An MPI communicator
);
```

Arguments:

- The address of the data to send.
- The number of data elements to send.
- The type of data elements to send.
- The ID of the process that should receive this message.
- A message tag that distinguishes this message from others that may be sent
  to the same process.
- The MPI communicator to use.

Notes:

This routine sends data to another process. This routine has blocking
semantics, which means that the routine does not return until the message
has been sent. `MPI_Isend()` is a non-blocking version of the send operation; it takes a seventh parameter of type `MPI_Request` that is used to
differentiate this send from other invocations of `MPI_Isend()` when waiting for completion.

Return value:

An MPI error code.

Code Spec 7.6 `MPI_Recv()`.

```
MPI_Recv()
int MPI_Recv(                          // Blocking Receive routine
   void          *buffer,              // Address at which to receive data
   int           count,                // Number of elements to receive
   MPI_Datatype  type,                 // Type of each element
   int           source,               // ID of sending process
   int           tag,                  // Identifier to distinguish message
   MPI_Comm      comm,                 // MPI communicator
   MPI_Status    *status               // Status of this receive operation
);
```

Arguments:

- The first six arguments correspond to `MPI_Send()`
- To receive a message from any other process, use `MPI_ANY_SOURCE` as the source.
- To match on any tag, use `MPI_ANY_TAG` as the fifth parameter.

Notes:

This routine receives data from another process. This routine has blocking semantics—it does not return until the message is received. `MPI_Irecv()` is a non-blocking version of the receive operation; it takes a seventh parameter of type `MPI_Request` that is used to differentiate this receive from other invocations of `MPI_Irecv()` when waiting for completion.

Return value:

An MPI error code.

The actual work is performed on lines 50–57, where each process counts the number of 3s in its portion of the array. Finally, each of the local values of count is reduced to a single value by summing them with the call to `MPI_Reduce()`. `MPI_Reduce()` is an example of a *collective communication operation* that involves multiple members of a communicator (see Code Spec 7.7). In this case, each process provides a single integer, and all of these values are summed and returned to the `Root Process` at the address that is specified by the second parameter. Notice how naturally the private variable concept enters in message passing.

Collective communication operations can be significantly easier to use than point-to-point communication operations. For example, the distribution of the array data that was performed with point-to-point communication on lines 35 and 46 could have been performed more succinctly using `MPI_Scatter()`, a collective communication operation that distributes data from one process to all other processes (see Code Spec 7.8). As shown in Figure 7.2, the entire input array can be read into a single array, which is then scattered among all of the processes in the `MPI_COMM_WORLD` communicator using the `MPI_Scatter()` routine. Note that `MPI_Scatter()` is

Code Spec 7.7 `MPI_Reduce()`.

```
MPI_Reduce()
int MPI_Reduce(                        // Reduce routine
   void           *sendBuffer,         // Address at which to receive data
   void           *recvBuffer,         // Number of elements to receive
   int            count,               // Type of each element
   MPI_Datatype   datatype,            // ID of sending process
   MPI_OP         op,                  // MPI operator
   int            root,                // Process that will contain result
   MPI_Comm       comm                 // MPI communicator
);
```

Notes:

This routine implements a reduce operation. A special form of this routine, `MPI_Allreduce()`, treats all processes as if they were the root, meaning that the reduced value will be passed to all processes at the address specified by the second argument. `MPI_Allreduce()` is equivalent to a call to `MPI_Reduce()` followed by a call to `MPI_Bcast()`, which broadcasts values to all processes within a communicator.

Return value:

An MPI error code.

Code Spec 7.8 `MPI_Scatter()`.

```
MPI_Scatter()
int MPI_Scatter(                       // Scatter routine
   void           *sendbuffer,         // Address of the data to send
   int            sendcount,           // Number of data elements to send
   MPI_Datatype   sendtype,            // Type of data elements to send
   int            destbuffer,          // Address of buffer to receive data
   int            destcount,           // Number of data elements to receive
   MPI_Datatype   desttype,            // Type of data elements to receive
   int            root,                // Rank of the root process
   MPI_Comm       *comm                // An MPI communicator
);
```

Arguments:

- The first three arguments specify the address, size, and type of the data elements to send to each process. These arguments only have meaning for the root process.

- The second three arguments specify the address, size, and type of the data elements for each receiving process. The size and type of the sending data and the receiving data may differ as a means of converting data types.

(continued)

Code Spec 7.8 `MPI_Scatter()`. (*continued*)

> ■ The seventh argument specifies the root process that is the source of the
>   data.
> ■ The eighth argument specifies the MPI communicator to use.
>
> **Notes:**
>
> This routine distributes data from the root process to all other processes,
> including the root. A more sophisticated version of the routine,
> `MPI_Scatterv()`, allows the root process to send different amounts of
> data to the various processes. Details can be found in the MPI standard.
>
> **Return value:**
>
> An MPI error code.

Figure 7.2
Replacement code (for lines 16–48 of Figure 7.1) to distribute data using a scatter operation.

```
16   length_per_process=length/size;
17   myArray=(int *) malloc(length_per_process*sizeof(int));
18
19   array=(int *) malloc(length*sizeof(int));
20
21   /* Read the data, distribute it among the various processes */
22   if(myID==RootProcess)
23   {
24     if((fp=fopen(*argv, "r"))==NULL)
25     {
26       printf("fopen failed on %s\n", filename);
27       exit(0);
28     }
29     fscanf(fp,"%d", &length);          /* read input size */
30
31     for(i=0; i<length-1; i++)          /* read entire input file */
32     {
33       fscanf(fp,"%d", myArray+i);
34     }
35   }
36
37   MPI_Scatter(Array, length_per_process, MPI_INT,
38               myArray, length_per_process, MPI_INT,
39               RootProcess, MPI_COMM_WORLD);
```

invoked by all participating processes. A related routine, `MPI_Gather()`, collects
data from multiple processes, leaving it on one process (see Code Spec 7.9).

Code Spec 7.9 `MPI_Gather()`.

```
MPI_Gather()
int MPI_Gather(                          // Gather routine
   void          *sendbuffer,            // Address of the data to send
   int           sendcount,              // Number of data elements to send
   MPI_Datatype  sendtype,               // Type of data elements to send
   int           recvbuffer,             // Address of buffer to receive data
   int           recvcount,              // Number of data elements to receive
   MPI_Datatype  recvtype,               // Type of data elements to receive
   int           root,                   // Rank of the root process
   MPI_Comm      *comm                    // An MPI communicator
);
```

Arguments:

- The first three arguments specify the address, size, and type of the data elements that will be sent from each process.

- The second three arguments specify the address, size, and type of the data elements of the receiving process, also known as the root process. The size and type of the sending data and the receiving data may differ as a means of converting data types.

- The seventh argument specifies the root process that will receive the data.

- The eighth argument specifies the MPI communicator to use.

Notes:

This routine gathers data from all processes in a communicator, leaving the result in the root process. A more sophisticated version of the routine, `MPI_Gcatterv()`, allows the root process to send different amounts of data to the various processes. Details can be found in the MPI standard.

Return value:

An MPI error code.

Groups and Communicators

In MPI, a *communicator* is a scoping mechanism that defines a set of processes that can communicate with one another. For example, to keep messages from library routines distinct from application-level routines, we can define a separate communicator for the library routines.

A *group* is an ordered set of processes that is useful for, among other things, defining collective communication operations. Each process in the group is assigned a unique rank, or ID, whose value is between 0 and $P - 1$, inclusive, where P is the number of processes in the group. A process can belong to multiple groups. For example, consider a program in which we can view the processes as a 2D array of processes. In such a computation, a process could belong to a group that defines a row of processes in a 2D array of processes, and this same process could belong to another group that defines a column of processes in the same 2D array of processes. With these two groups defined, a process can scatter data among either its row or column of processes, or it can perform other collective communication operations among these groups.

Communicators and groups can be dynamically created and destroyed, and we will show an example of their use when we discuss the details of collective communication. There are many routines for manipulating groups and communicators. For details, we refer the reader to an MPI manual.

Point-to-Point Communication

In MPI, point-to-point communication is specified redundantly by both the sending process and the receiving process. Messages are matched based on the operations' specified source/destination process and the specified message *tag*, which is a user-defined non-negative integer. Thus, tags can be used to distinguish logically different messages between the same pairs of processes. In some cases, a process may not statically know which process it wishes to communicate with, in which case it can specify MPI_ANY as its source or destination process.

MPI guarantees that messages between the same source and destination processes will be delivered in order. However, nothing can be said about the ordering of messages that involve more than two processes.

MPI provides many flavors of point-to-point communication. To understand why, realize that there is significant synchronization and data copying that must occur; for each message, the data must be copied across four address spaces, as shown in Figure 7.3. Note that this figure focuses on only the most basic data transfer operations; it ignores implementation-specific details that might require additional buffering and handshaking.

To allow programmers to hide some of this latency, the interface provides different versions of Sends and Receives that expose some of these details. For example, nonblocking versions allow a process to perform some other independent work while it waits for a message to be transmitted. Such overlapping of communication and computation is analogous to the split-phase barrier that we saw in Chapter 6, so it improves performance at the expense of added program complexity.

We now discuss the many variations of point-to-point communication operations.

Standard Send and Receive. The standard Send and Receive operations are *blocking* in the sense that they do not return until transmission is *locally complete*: A message transmission is said to be *locally complete* if the part of the transmission that executes in the local process has completed. A message is said to be *globally complete* if the entire transmission has completed. Thus, it is safe for the sending

Figure 7.3
Each message must be copied as it moves across four address spaces, each contributing to the overall latency.

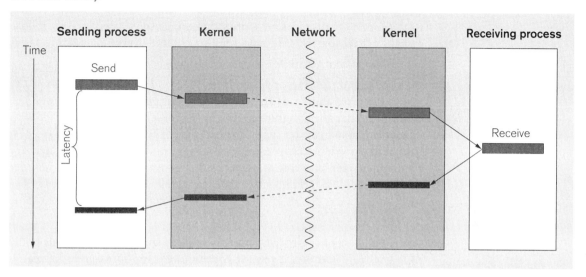

process to overwrite the buffer as soon as `MPI_Send()` returns, and it is safe for the receiving process to use the value in the buffer as soon as `MPI_Recv()` returns.

Non-Blocking Communication. To hide communication latency, it is often useful to overlap communication and computation, so MPI provides non-blocking communication. `MPI_Isend()` and `MPI_Irecv()` are non-blocking versions of the standard Send and Receive routines. Each of them returns immediately, before the operation has completed locally. (Here, I is short for *immediate* mode.)

With `MPI_Isend()`, the sending process does not know when the data in the buffer will actually be transmitted to the receiving process, so it is unsafe to overwrite the buffer until there's some indication that the message has been completed. To wait for the completion of a non-blocking operation, a process can invoke the `MPI_Wait()` routine, which blocks until the specified operation completes globally. To test whether a non-blocking operation has completed, the `MPI_Test()` routine returns immediately, setting the value pointed to by its second parameter to either true or false depending on the status of the message completion.

Similarly, for `MPI_Irecv()`, the data in the buffer is not valid until the operation has completed globally, so `MPI_Wait()` and `MPI_Test()` are useful operations for the receiving process as well.

Other Communication Modes. In addition to the standard Send operation, MPI provides three other modes with related semantics. Each of these types of

Sends can be performed as a blocking or non-blocking operation, and any of the Send routines can be matched with any of the Receive routines.

- **Synchronous Send.** A synchronous send (`MPI_Ssend()` and `MPI_Issend()`) provides semantics that are close to a rendezvous in languages such as Ada: the sender does not return until the receiving process has begun to receive its message.

- **Buffered Send.** A buffered send (`MPI_Bsend()` and `MPI_Ibsend()`) allows the programmer to supply the required buffer space for a message, which insulates the program against any problems that might arise with insufficient system buffer space. Depending on the implementation of MPI, this mode is particularly useful for programs that have large memory requirements for buffering messages or that have an unusually large number of messages in flight at any time. For these routines, the `MPI_Buffer_attach()` and `MPI_Buffer_detach()` routines should be used to specify the allocated memory.

- **Ready Send.** For improved performance on many parallel computers, the `MPI_Rsend()` and `MPI_Irsend()` routines allow a message to be placed directly into a memory location, avoiding handshaking and buffering costs. To use these routines, the programmer must guarantee that the Receive operation has been initiated before the message arrives. If these timing assumptions are violated, an error will be flagged when the Receive operation is performed. Of course, because of the additional assumptions, this mode can be quite error-prone.

While these more sophisticated versions of Send and Receive can improve performance, they can hurt *performance portability*. As machine characteristics change, the trade-offs among the various versions also change. Moreover, the use of some of these routines can severely complicate the program text.

Collective Communication

Collective communication operations are higher-level communication operations that involve multiple processes. In addition to the scatter and reduce routines, which we saw in the Count 3s example, these include a scan routine, a broadcast routine, a barrier routine, and a gather routine that takes distributed data and collects it onto a single process. See Code Specs 7.9–7.13 for the interfaces to these routines.

Our previous examples applied collective communication operations to all processes. We now sketch an example that shows how we can set up multiple groups, in this case one for each row of a 2D array of processes. Having set up these groups, we show how we can then broadcast a different value across each row of processes.

Code Spec 7.10 `MPI_Scan()`.

```
MPI_Scan()
int MPI_Scan(                        // Scan routine
   void          *sendBuffer,        // Address at which to receive data
   void          *recvBuffer,        // Number of elements to receive
   int           count,              // Type of each element
   MPI_Datatype  datatype,           // ID of sending process
   MPI_OP        op,                 // MPI operator
   MPI_Comm      comm                // MPI communicator
);
```

Notes:

This routine has the same interface as the reduce operation except it does not require a root process.

Return value:

An MPI error code.

Code Spec 7.11 `MPI_Bcast()`. MPI routine to broadcast data from one root process to all other processes in the communicator.

```
MPI_Bcast()
int MPI_Bcast(                       // Broadcast routine
   void          *buffer,            // Address of the data to send
   int           count,              // Number of data elements to send
   MPI_Datatype  datatype,           // Type of data elements to send
   int           root,               // Rank of the root task
   MPI_Comm      *comm               // An MPI communicator
);
```

Arguments:

- The first three arguments specify the address, size, and type of the data elements to send to each process.
- The fourth argument specifies the rank of the root, or sending, process.
- The fifth argument specifies MPI communicator to use.

Notes:

This routine broadcasts data from the root process to all other processes in the communicator. Unlike `MPI_Scatter()` and `MPI_Gather()`, the number of elements and the types of the elements must be the same for the root process and the receiving processes.

Return value:

An MPI error code.

Code Spec 7.12 `MPI_Barrier()`.

```
MPI_Barrier()
int MPI_Barrier(                          // Barrier
    MPI_Comm      *comm                    // An MPI communicator
);
```

Arguments:

This argument specifies the MPI communicator to use.

Notes:

This routine blocks until all processes in the communicator have arrived at this point.

Return value:

An MPI error code.

Code Spec 7.13 `MPI_Wtime()`.

```
MPI_Wtime()
double MPI_Wtime(                          // Timing routine
);
```

Notes:

This routine returns the current time in seconds.

Return value:

An MPI error code.

Figure 7.4 shows the code to set up these groups. We assume that there is a global integer, numCols, that holds the number of columns of processes. For brevity, we have taken some liberties with C to enable us to statically initialize a dynamically allocated array.

On line 20, the `MPI_Comm_group()` routine (see Code Spec 7.14) returns a handle to the group that is associated with the existing `MPI_COMM_WORLD` communicator. We then define a new group using the `MPI_Group_incl()` routine: The first parameter selects a set of groups, as specified by the `ranks[][]` array, from the `globalGroup`, where the size of the new group is `P/numCols`, and the new group is named `newGroup` (see Code Spec 7.15).

Figure 7.4
Example of collective communication within a group.

```
1   int numCols;                    /* initialized elsewhere */
2
3   void broadcast_example()
4   {
5     int **ranks;                  /* the ranks that belong to each group */
6     int myRank;
7     int rowNumber;                /* row number of this process */
8     int random;                   /* value that we would like to broadcast */
9     rowNumber=myRank/numCols;
10    MPI_Group globalGroup, newGroup;
11    MPI_Comm rowComm[numCols];
12
13    /* initialize ranks[][] array */
14    ranks[0]={0,1,2,3};  /* not legal C */
15    ranks[1]={4,5,6,7};
16    ranks[2]={8,9,10,11};
17    ranks[3]={12,13,14,15};
18
19    /* Extract the original group handle */
20    MPI_Comm_group(MPI_COMM_WORLD, &globalGroup);
21
22    /* Define the new group */
23    MPI_Group_incl(globalGroup, P/numCols, ranks[rowNumber], &newGroup);
24
25    /* Create new communicator */
26    MPI_Comm_create(MPI_COMM_WORLD, newGroup, &newComm);
27
28    random=rand();
29
30    /* Broadcast 'random' across rows */
31    MPI_Bcast(&random, 1, MPI_, rowNumber*numCols, newComm);
32  }
```

Code Spec 7.14 `MPI_Comm_group()`.

```
MPI_Comm_group()
int MPI_Comm_group(
  MPI_Comm          comm,           // An MPI communicator
  MPI_Group         *group          // Group associated with comm
);
```

Notes:

Returns the group handle associated with a communicator.

Return value:

An MPI error code.

Code Spec 7.15 `MPI_Group_incl()`.

```
MPI_Group_incl()
int MPI_Group_incl(
   MPI_Group  group,           // Existing group
   int        size,            // Size of the new group
   int        *ranks,          // ranks of the processes to include
   MPI_Group  *newGroup        // New group to create
);
```
Notes:

   Creates a new group by selecting processes from an existing group.

Return value:

   An MPI error code.

On line 26, the `MPI_Comm_create()` routine creates a new communicator for the new group that can then be passed to `MPI_Bcast()` on line 31 (see Code Spec 7.16). In this case, the broadcast sends a single randomly generated integer from the leftmost process in a row to all processes in the same row.

This example has manually created a 2D array of process groups, but MPI also provides the notion of virtual topologies, allowing such topologies to be defined and reused. In particular, MPI defines a Cartesian grid and a graph topology. For this advanced topic, we refer readers to the MPI tutorial.

Code Spec 7.16 `MPI_Comm_create()`.

```
MPI_Comm_create()
int MPI_Comm_create(
   MPI_Comm   origComm,        // Existing communicator
   MPI_Group  newGroup,        // New group
   MPI_Comm   *newComm         // Newly created communicator
);
```
Notes:

   Creates a new communicator for a given group.

Return value:

   An MPI error code.

Example: Successive Over-Relaxation

To gain experience in implementing a parallel program in MPI, consider the creation of a 2D successive over-relaxation (SOR) program.

Problem Statement. SOR is often used to solve systems of differential equations, such as the Navier-Stokes equations for fluid flow. In our formulation, the computation will start with a 2D array of n values. In each iteration, the computation replaces each value of the array with the average of its four nearest neighbor values. Those values on the edge of the array use some predetermined constant values, known as *boundary values,* as the missing neighbor values. Assume that the boundary values along the left edge contain 1s, that all other boundary values are 0s, and that each value in the 2D array begins with a value of 0.

The simplest way to handle the boundary values is to allocate space for them in the 2D array and to initialize them with their constant value, giving us a situation as shown in Figure 7.5.

MPI Solution. The problem is defined on a 2D array, with the amount of computation per array element constant per iteration, so the computation is regular and balanced. Thus, a static allocation of work is possible, with each process being assigned roughly $1/P$ of the array elements. Because the value at each array element depends on the values of its four nearest neighbors, a block allocation achieves better locality than a cyclic or block-cyclic distribution. In particular, we choose a 2D block allocation because it minimizes communication volume compared to a 1D allocation.

Figure 7.5
A 2D relaxation replaces—on each iteration—all interior values by the average of their four nearest neighbors.

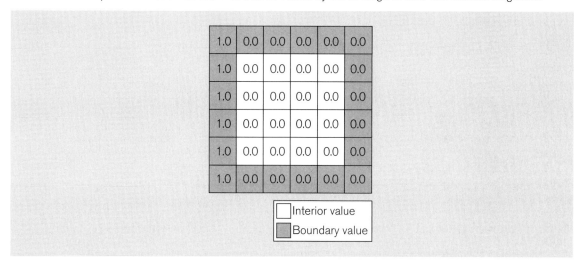

Figure 7.6 shows the main loop of the 2D SOR solution. This code assumes that we are using a Rows × Cols array of processes and that each process owns a Height × Width array of data, including the extra rows and columns to hold the overlap regions. The use of these overlap regions allows the main loop of the computation to proceed without special cases for the non-local values—we simply make sure that their values have been correctly set by the communication operations. In each itera-

Figure 7.6
MPI code for the main loop of the 2D SOR computation.

```
1    #define Top        0
2    #define Left       0
3    #define Right      (Cols-1)
4    #define Bottom     (Rows-1)
5
6    #define NorthPE(i)         ((i)-Cols)
7    #define SouthPE(i)         ((i)+Cols)
8    #define EastPE(i)          ((i)+1)
9    #define WestPE(i)          ((i)-1)
...
101  do
102  { /*
103    * Send data to four neighbors
104    */
105    if(row !=Top)                              /* Send North */
106    {
107       MPI_Send(&val[1][1], Width-2, MPI_FLOAT,
108               NorthPE(myID), tag, MPI_COMM_WORLD);
109    }
110
111    if(col !=Right)                            /* Send East */
112    {
113       for(i=1; i<Height-1; i++)
114       {
115          buffer[i-1]=val[i][Width-2];
116       }
117       MPI_Send(buffer, Height-2, MPI_FLOAT,
118               EastPE(myID), tag, MPI_COMM_WORLD);
119    }
120
121    if(row !=Bottom)                           /* Send South */
122    {
123       MPI_Send(&val[Height-2][1], Width-2, MPI_FLOAT,
124               SouthPE(myID), tag, MPI_COMM_WORLD);
125    }
126
127    if(col !=Left)                             /* Send West */
128    {
```

```
129      for(i=1; i<Height-1; i++)
130      {
131        buffer[i-1]=val[i][1];
132      }
133      MPI_Send(buffer, Height-2, MPI_FLOAT,
134              WestPE(myID), tag, MPI_COMM_WORLD);
135    }
136
137    /*
138     * Receive messages
139     */
140    if(row !=Top)                        /* Receive from North */
141    {
142      MPI_Recv(&val[0][1], Width-2, MPI_FLOAT,
143              NorthPE(myID), tag, MPI_COMM_WORLD, &status);
144    }
145
146    if(col !=Right)                      /* Receive from East */
147    {
148      MPI_Recv(&buffer, Height-2, MPI_FLOAT,
149              EastPE(myID), tag, MPI_COMM_WORLD, &status);
150      for(i=1; i<Height-1; i++)
151      {
152        val[i][Width-1]=buffer[i-1];
153      }
154    }
155
156    if(row !=Bottom)                     /* Receive from South */
157    {
158      MPI_Recv(&val[0][Height-1], Width-2, MPI_FLOAT,
159              SouthPE(myID), tag, MPI_COMM_WORLD, &status);
160    }
161
162    if(col !=Left)                       /* Receive from West */
163    {
164      MPI_Recv(&buffer, Height-2, MPI_FLOAT,
165              WestPE(myID), tag, MPI_COMM_WORLD, &status);
166      for(i=1; i<Height-1; i++)
167      {
168        val[i][0]=buffer[i-1];
169      }
170    }
171
172    delta=0.0; /* Calculate average, delta for all points */
173    for(i=1; i<Height-1; i++)
174    {
175      for(j=1; j<Width-1; j++)
176      {
```

(continued)

Figure 7.6 (*continued*)
MPI code for the main loop of the 2D SOR computation.

```
177                average=(val[i-1][j]+val[i][j+1]+
178                      val[i+1][j]+val[i][j-1])/4;
179            delta=Max(delta, Abs(average-val[i][j]));
180            new[i][j]=average;
181          }
182        }
183
184        /* Find maximum diff */
185        MPI_Reduce(&delta, &globalDelta, 1, MPI_FLOAT, MPI_MIN,
186                   RootProcess, MPI_COMM_WORLD);
187        Swap(val, new);
188    } while(globalDelta < THRESHOLD);
```

tion, the code reads from the val array and writes to the new array. At the end of each iteration, the pointers to these two arrays are swapped in preparation for the next iteration. Notice that to send data to the East and West neighbors, the columns of the array are first copied into a contiguous buffer before being sent as a single message.

Performance Issues

Regardless of the latency of the underlying hardware communication infrastructure, MPI messages incur a large overhead for each message sent. Thus, we typically want to reduce the number of messages sent by (1) choosing algorithms that produce few cross-process dependences, and (2) combining multiple messages into a single larger message.

We saw an example of the second point in lines 113–116 of our 2D SOR solution (Figure 7.6), where we copied the values along the right side of the local array into an array called buffer. The situation becomes a bit more complex if we wish to send the elements of an arbitrary-length linked list. Here, there are some details to work out, namely, how do the sender and receiver agree on the message length when only the sender knows the length? One solution is to use a protocol in which the sender first sends the length to the receiver, but this doubles the number of messages. Another solution might be to block the messages into some large fixed-size chunks and to include in the message an indication of whether there is more data to send. A disadvantage of this second solution is that short messages will be padded to the larger fixed-size.

The large overhead of messages and the fixed set of MPI processes imply that MPI programs are static in nature. However, as Figure 7.7 illustrates, MPI programs *can* perform dynamic work distribution. The figure shows a set of four processes that periodically exchange information about the state of each process' workload, use

Figure 7.7
Depiction of dynamic work redistribution in MPI.

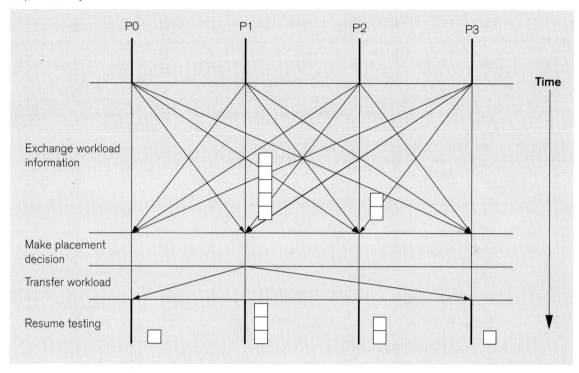

this information to locally compute the desired work distribution for the next set of iterations, transfer work accordingly (perhaps receiving work), and then continue with the computation. The key, of course, is that such work distribution is only feasible if it represents a relatively small fraction of the overall computation and if the benefit of the improved load balance outweighs the cost of this expensive work redistribution protocol.

Overlapping Communication with Computation. Because of the large startup cost associated with each message, it is often useful to overlap communication with computation. As a concrete example of how this optimization can be performed using non-blocking communication, Figure 7.8 shows how we can modify our 2D SOR program from Figure 7.6 to hide the latency of communication. We see that there are a few main differences in the code. First, we use MPI_Isend() and MPI_Irecv() in place of their blocking versions. Second, while these communication operations are underway, we compute the successive over-relaxation for all of the values in the array that can be computed completely locally, that is, for all computations that do not reference any non-local values of the array. Thus, the nested for loops on lines 173–182 do not iterate over the edges of the local array because the edge values depend on values from neighboring processes. We have also added

Figure 7.8
A 2D SOR MPI program using non-blocking sends and receives.

```
101  do
102  {  /*
103      * Send data to four neighbors
104      */
105     if(row!=Top)                      /* Send North */
106     {
107       MPI_ISend(&val[1][1], Width-2, MPI_FLOAT,
108               NorthPE(myID), tag, MPI_COMM_WORLD, &requests[0]);
109     }
110
111     if(col!=Right)                    /* Send East */
112     {
113       for(i=1; i<Height-1; i++)
114       {
115         buffer[i-1]=val[i][Width-2];
116       }
117       MPI_ISend(buffer, Height-2, MPI_FLOAT,
118               EastPE(myID), tag, MPI_COMM_WORLD, &requests[1]);
119     }
120
121     if(row!=Bottom)                   /* Send South */
122     {
123       MPI_ISend(&val[Height-2][1], Width-2, MPI_FLOAT,
124               SouthPE(myID), tag, MPI_COMM_WORLD, &requests[2]);
125     }
126
127     if(col!=Left)                     /* Send West */
128     {
129       for(i=1; i<Height-1; i++)
130       {
131         buffer[i-1]=val[i][1];
132       }
133       MPI_ISend(buffer, Height-2, MPI_FLOAT,
134               WestPE(myID), tag, MPI_COMM_WORLD, &requests[3]);
135     }
136
137     /*
138      * Receive messages
139      */
140     if(row!=Top)                      /* Receive from North */
141     {
142       MPI_IRecv(&val[0][1], Width-2, MPI_FLOAT,
143               NorthPE(myID), tag, MPI_COMM_WORLD, &requests[4]);
144     }
145
146     if(col!=Right)                    /* Receive from East */
147     {
```

```
148      MPI_IRecv(&buffer, Height-2, MPI_FLOAT,
149                EastPE(myID), tag, MPI_COMM_WORLD, &requests[5]);
150      for(i=1; i<Height-1; i++)
151      {
152        val[i][Width-1]=buffer[i-1];
153      }
154    }
155
156    if(row!=Bottom)                   /* Receive from South */
157    {
158      MPI_IRecv(&val[0][Height-1], Width-2, MPI_FLOAT,
159                SouthPE(myID), tag, MPI_COMM_WORLD, &requests[6]);
160    }
161
162    if(col!=Left)                     /* Receive from West */
163    {
164      MPI_IRecv(&buffer, Height-2, MPI_FLOAT,
165                WestPE(myID), tag, MPI_COMM_WORLD, &requests[7]);
166      for(i=1; i<Height-1; i++)
167      {
168        val[i][0]=buffer[i-1];
169      }
170    }
171
172    delta=0.0; /* Calculate average, delta for all points */
173    for(i=2; i<Height-2; i++)
174    {
175      for(j=2; j<Width-2; j++)
176      {
177        average=(val[i-1][j]+val[i][j+1]+
178                val[i+1][j]+val[i][j-1])/4;
179        delta=Max(delta, Abs(average - val[i][j]));
180        new[i][j]=average;
181      }
182    }
183    MPI_Waitall(8, requests, status);
184
185    /* update top and bottom edges, including corners */
186    for(j=1; j<Width-1; j++)
187    {
188      i=1;
189      average=(val[i-1][j]+val[i][j+1]+
190              val[i+1][j]+val[i][j-1])/4;
191      delta=Max(delta, Abs(average-val[i][j]));
192      new[i][j]=average;
193
194      i=Height-2;
195      average=(val[i-1][j]+val[i][j+1]+
196              val[i+1][j]+val[i][j-1])/4;
```

(continued)

Figure 7.8 (*continued*)
A 2D SOR MPI program using non-blocking sends and receives

```
197          delta=Max(delta, Abs(average-val[i][j]));
198          new[i][j]=average;
199      }
200
201      /* update left and right edges, excluding corners */
202      for(i=2; i<Height-2; i++)
203      {
204        j=1;
205        average=(val[i-1][j]+val[i][j+1]+
206                 val[i+1][j]+val[i][j-1])/4;
207        delta=Max(delta, Abs(average - val[i][j]));
208        new[i][j]=average;
209
210        j=Width-2;
211        average=(val[i-1][j]+val[i][j+1]+
212                 val[i+1][j]+val[i][j-1])/4;
213        delta=Max(delta, Abs(average-val[i][j]));
214        new[i][j]=average;
215      }
216      /* Find maximum diff */
217      MPI_Reduce(&delta, &globalDelta, 1, MPI_FLOAT, MPI_MIN,
218                 RootProcess, MPI_COMM_WORLD);
219      Swap(val, new);
220  } while(globalDelta < THRESHOLD);
```

the call to `MPI_Wait_all()` on line 183 (see Code Spec 7.17), which will block until all eight non-blocking calls have completed, at which point we can complete the computation of the remaining values on the edge (lines 185–215).

As we can see, the primary cost of overlapping communication with computation is the need to separate the computation of local averages into two pieces, one that can be performed independently of the communication and the other that relies on the results of the communication, which obscures the overall logic of the computation and significantly lengthens the code.

Derived Data Types. The marshaling of data into contiguous buffers is not always as straightforward as with the 2D SOR program. For example, the data might consist of heterogeneous types. For these situations, MPI provides the notion of a *derived data type* that allows programmers to transfer data from non-contiguous buffers or from buffers that contain heterogeneous types.

The idea is to register a new data type dynamically, which requires that we inform the MPI runtime system of the types, sizes, and offsets of the various components of the derived type. We can use `MPI_Type_struct()` to define this new data type and

Code Spec 7.17 `MPI_Waitall()`.

```
MPI_Waitall()
int MPI_Waitall(                        // Wait routine
   int              count,              // Address at which to receive data
   MPI_Request      *requests,          // Array of requests to wait for
   MPI_Status       *status,            // Array of status values
);
```

Notes:

- This routine blocks until all `count` operations have completed. The second and third parameters should each have `count` entries, and each entry in the `status` array is passed the return status of the corresponding entry in the `requests` array.

- There are many variants of the wait call. For example, `MPI_Wait()` will wait for a single request, `MPI_Waitany()` will wait for any outstanding request to complete, and `MPI_Waitsome()` will wait for any of a list of outstanding requests to complete.

Return value:

An MPI error code.

then we use `MPI_Type_commit()` to register this type with the system. It is good programming practice to call `MPI_Type_free()` to unregister the derived data type and to avoid memory leaks, as `MPI_Type_commit()` will build new runtime structures.

For example, suppose we wish to broadcast a `Person`, which is a structure that consists of the name and age of some person. Figure 7.9 shows how an instance of this `Person struct` can be broadcast to the other processes in the system. In particular, in our `BuildPersonType()` function, lines 14–15 define the types of each field of our derived data type, and lines 16–17 define the number of such variables in each field.

We then get the addresses of each field so that we can compute their offsets. Finally, we call `MPI_Type_struct()` to inform the MPI runtime system of this new data type, and we then call `MPI_Type_commit()` to register this data type.

Given this new routine to define a derived type, we can invoke it as follows and then pass the resulting derived type as a parameter to `MPI_Bcast()`:

```
Person* p=malloc(sizeof(Person));
p->age=44;
strcpy(p->name, "Nelson");
BuildPersonType(p, &newType);
MPI_Bcast(p, count, newType, RootProcess,
          MPI_COMM_WORLD);
```

Figure 7.9
Creating a derived data type.

```
1    struct Person
2    {
3       int age;
4       char[6] name;
5    }
6
7    void buildPersonType(Person* p, MPI_Datatype* newType)
8    {
9       MPI_Datatype types[2];           /* The types of each field */
10      MPI_Aint   offsets[2];           /* Offsets of each field */
11      MPI_Aint   addresses[3];         /* Addresses of each field */
12      int block_lengths[2];            /* The lengths of each field */
13
14      types[0]=MPI_INT;
15      types[1]=MPI_CHAR;
16      block_lengths[0]=1;
17      block_lengths[1]=6;
18
19      /* Get the address of each field in a portable manner */
20      MPI_Address(p, &addresses[0]);
21      MPI_Address(&(p->age), &addresses[1]);
22      MPI_Address(&(p->name), &addresses[2]);
23
24      /* Compute offsets of each field */
25      offsets[0]=addresses[1]-addresses[0];
26      offsets[1]=addresses[2]-addresses[0];
27
28      /* Define and register the new type */
29      MPI_Type_struct(2, block_lengths, offsets, types, newType);
30      MPI_Type_commit(newType);
31   }
```

> **Note**
>
> **Profiling.** Vampir is a well-known commercial performance analysis tool for MPI programs. Developed in Europe, it provides graphical reports that show both per process and aggregate behavior.

Performance Analysis Tools. Over the years, a number of debugging and performance analysis tools have been developed for MPI. A list of these tools can be found at the following Web site: http://www-unix.mcs.anl.gov/mpi/tools.html

Safety Issues

In MPI, there is no shared data, so there is no need to provide explicit mutual exclusion as there is with Pthreads. Nevertheless, MPI programs can be difficult to write because so many low-level details are left to the programmer. For example, programmers must specify messages redundantly at both the sending and receiving processes. Thus, programmers must ensure that sends and receives are properly matched, which includes both the ordering of messages and the details of the message lengths, types, and tags. Moreover, the more efficient variants of messages, such as non-blocking or non-buffered messages are typically the more difficult ones to use. They make additional assumptions about the timing and buffering of messages, assumptions that must be enforced by the programmer. Of course, there are still the issues of deadlock and livelock to deal with.

Message Passing Summary. Because it provides a set of basic facilities that can be supported by almost any parallel computer, MPI has been widely adopted despite the fact that it that forces the programmer to deal with many low-level details and despite the fact that it presents a static process model. Indeed, the MPI-2 standard supports dynamic process creation, among other features, but years after its definition, it still has few implementations. The primary obstacles to its implementation and adoption are the huge number of functions—there are over 500—and the more involved runtime system.

Partitioned Global Address Space Languages

Distributed memory programming has often been equated with message passing. But as we mentioned in Chapter 2, it is possible to build higher-level abstractions on top of a distributed memory machine. Over the past decade, several research groups have built such abstractions, producing a family of languages known as *partitioned global address space* languages, or *PGAS* languages.

The global address space refers to the fact that the languages overlay a single address space on the virtual memories of the distributed machines. These languages do not provide shared memory, because there is no expectation that the hardware will keep it coherent. But a global address space does give programmers the ability to define global data structures, an improvement over a distributed memory model in which the programmer must mentally maintain a collection of separate data structures that act as a global data structure. In PGAS languages, programmers focus on the behavior of a single process and must still distinguish between data that is local and data that is non-local, but the languages simplify programming by eliminating the details of message passing; the compilers generate all communication calls in response to programmer-specified non-local references. Furthermore, they use a one-sided communication substrate, which is potentially more efficient than message passing.

The three main PGAS languages are Co-Array Fortran, Unified Parallel C, and Titanium, which extend Fortran, C, and Java, respectively. We now consider each in turn.

Co-Array Fortran

The first of the PGAS languages was Co-Array Fortran (CAF), a language extension to Fortran developed in the late 1990s by Numrich and Reid; CAF, which was initially named F--, is notable for its elegance and simplicity. The principle idea is to add to Fortran a single language extension called a *co-array*. The co-array is the mechanism for interprocessor communication ("co" is short for communication). Exploiting the fact that Fortran uses parentheses for all array references, CAF appends square brackets to variable names to refer to co-arrays. For example, the following code defines three array variables with co-arrays, which are shown in bold:

```
real, dimension(n,n)[p,*]:: a,b,c
...

do k=1,n
  do q=1,p
    c(i,j)[myP,myQ]=c(i,j)[myP,myQ]+
                    a(i,k)[myP, q]*b(k,j)[q,myQ]
  enddo
enddo
```

The co-array specification indicates that the memory for the variable is distributed across each process, which in CAF is called an *image*. Thus, in the example, each process is assigned portions of the a, b, and c arrays, as defined by the dimension statement. Furthermore, the fact that the co-array is declared to have two dimensions specifies that the processes are to be arranged in a *logical* 2D organization of p rows and q columns. (The * means that each row of processes should be filled as completely as possible; so if num_images()= pq, then there are p rows and q columns of processes.) Each process will find its place in the 2D arrangement by invoking the this_image() routine and by defining the two parameters, myP and myQ, to refer to a specific portion of the final array. The management of the data partitioning, including the initialization of their values, is the responsibility of the CAF programmer.

In the following illustration, myP = 2, myQ = 3:

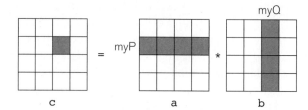

The above matrix multiplication code shows that each process, defined by [myP, myQ], updates its portion of the array as it computes a dot-product. To reference the rows, it accesses data in processes [myP, q], and to reference columns, it accesses data in processes [q, myQ]. The communication calls for these remote references are generated by the compiler, greatly simplifying the programming. The original CAF implementation used a Cray-proprietary, one-sided communication library called Shmem, but more recent implementations have used ARMCI and GASNet, both standard one-sided communication libraries.

CAF presents a clean and elegant interface to user-specified communication for distributed memory parallel computers.

Unified Parallel C

Developed around 2000 by the team of El-Ghazawi, Carlson, and Draper, Unified Parallel C (UPC) gives the programmer a global view of the address space. Unlike CAF, however, when UPC array variables are declared "shared" they are distributed across the memories of the program instances such that the linearly ordered array elements are distributed in a *cyclic* or *block cyclic* arrangement. Recall from Chapter 5 that cyclic and block cyclic distributions can be advantageous when load balancing is a concern, but they generally reduce locality. The UPC programmer can regain locality by directly allocating portions of the arrays to the processes, thereby ensuring that dense neighborhoods are allocated.

Since UPC extends the C language, it supports pointers. UPC pointers can either be private (local to the thread) or shared. Because pointers can be either private or shared and because what they point to can be either private or shared, there are four types of pointers:

		Property of the pointer	
		Private	**Shared**
Property of	**Private**	Private-Private, p1	Private-Shared, p2
the reference	**Shared**	Shared-Private, p3	Shared-Shared, p4

These properties are associated with the language's type system, as their declarations indicate:

```
int *p1;  /* private pointer pointing locally */
shared int *p2;
        /* private pointer pointing into shared space */
int *shared p3; /* shared  pointer pointing locally */
shared int *shared p4;
        /* shared  pointer pointing into shared space */
```

The following vector-vector addition code illustrates the use of the second case, a private pointer pointing into shared space:

```
shared int v1[N], v2[N], v1v2sum[N];

void main()
{
  int i;
  shared int *p1, *p2;
```

```
       p1=v1;
       p2=v2;
       upc_forall(i=0; i<N; i++, p1++, p2++; i)
       {
          v1v2sum[i]=*p1+*p2;
       }
   }
```

The code also illustrates the use of another of UPC's features, the `upc_forall` statement. This abstraction distributes normal C `for` loop iterations across processes using an affinity clause, which is the fourth clause in the `upc_forall` specification. The loop's affinity clause indicates where the iterations are to be performed. In this case, the process that executes the `i`th iteration is the one associated with `i`(the owner). The `upc_forall` statement is a global operation, whereas most UPC code executes locally within a process.

Titanium

The Titatium (Ti) language, developed by a team headed by Kathy Yelick at UC Berkeley, is an extension of Java that executes on distributed memory parallel computers. It has a memory model similar to UPC, and like the other PGAS languages, it generates communication code based on a one-sided communication library. The first obvious quality of Ti that distinguishes it from its predecessors is its object-oriented nature. It also distinguishes itself from Java by adding *regions*, which support safe performance-oriented memory management as an alternative to garbage collection. Several other Java features have been restricted or limited, but more typically features have been added. For example, 2D arrays have been added to make Ti more appropriate for scientific computation.

An important efficiency feature of Ti is its *unordered iteration*, `foreach`, which simplifies both the programmer's and the compiler's job. The key feature is a *point*, a tuple of integers that can range over the *domain* of a variable, that is, its indices. Notice its uses here in matrix multiplication with the names `ij` and `k`:

```
   public static void matMul(double [2d] a,
                             double [2d] b,
                             double [2d] c)
   {
      foreach (ij in c.domain())
      {
         double [1d] aRowi=a.slice(1, ij[1]);
         double [1d] bColj=b.slice(2, ij[2]);
         foreach (k in aRowi.domain())
         {
            c[ij]+=aRowi[k]*bColj[k];
         }
      }
   }
```

Thus, compared to a `forall`, the `foreach` allows concurrency over multiple indices within a single block.

Titanium enforces global synchronization using barriers and the concept of a shared variable called a *single* that is shared across all processes. For example, it is common in a simulation for each process to compute on local data and to periodically coordinate its actions. The barrier ensures that all processes stop computing at the same time to update or read memory. The use of "single" variables with coherent values guarantees that all processes are in the same phase of the computation. For example, a particle simulation might use this concept as follows:

```
int single stepCount=0;
int single endCount=100;
for (; stepCount<endCount; stepCount++)
{
    Read remote particles
    Compute forces on mine
    Ti.barrier();
    Write my particles using new forces
    Ti.barrier();
}
```

Processes cannot get out of sync because they are all controlled by the same value.

Chapter Summary

Without a doubt, the greatest strength of MPI and other message passing libraries is their universality. The ability to transfer a block of memory from one process to another is fundamental to parallel computers, and message passing libraries give programmers access to that facility. It must exist on all parallel machines, so these libraries can in principle—and do in practice—run on any parallel machine. This universality is an essential component of the libraries' popularity and success.

With similar certainty, the greatest weakness of MPI and other message passing facilities is their low level of abstraction. Parallel programming is difficult and benefits greatly from computational abstractions as described in earlier chapters. MPI provides only rudimentary support for a few of these. For example, the basic reduce operation supports the global combination of a single item on each process; the task of combining values locally—that is, the elevation of the reduce concept to an entire distributed data structure—is left to the programmer. Moreover, MPI supports only a small set of basic reduce operators, but as we saw in Chapter 5, the abstraction applies much more generally.

By making the fewest assumptions about the underlying hardware, message passing has the distinction of being the least common denominator: It can execute on any platform. While higher-level languages, such as the PGAS languages, continue to be developed, MPI currently remains the language of choice for programmers who wish to write large, long-lived applications.

Historical Perspective

Early distributed memory computers each came with their own message passing library, preventing the programs from being portable. PVM, the Parallel Virtual Machine, was described by Sunderam [1990] as a means of performing parallel computing on networked machines. With the success of PVM, the MPI standard soon followed and quickly came into widespread use. Recognizing the issues with the low-level nature of MPI, CAF [Numerich 1998], and Titanium [Yelick 1998] were first defined in 1998, with UPC [El-Ghazawi 2001] following shortly thereafter. The MPI 2.0 standard, which was developed in the late '90s to add support for dynamic process management and parallel I/O, has not been widely adopted, possibly because the new features significantly complicate its implementation.

Exercises

1. Execute the Count 3s MPI program (Figure 7.1) and analyze its scalability between 250,000 elements and 10,000,000 for a fixed number of processors P.

2. Revise the Count 3s program to replace the call to `MPI-reduce()` by a custom tree based on the structure in Figure 5.1. Is there a performance difference when compared against the solution for Exercise 1?

3. Execute the SOR computation (Figure 7.6) for 20 iterations on an array large enough to exhibit measurable behavior; execute for the same number of iterations and the same size array the version that overlaps communication and computation (Figure 7.17). Compare their performance.

4. Write an MPI program in which one processor generates a sufficiently large set (at least 1 million) of unique random keys and distributes them to the other processors.

5. Use MPI to implement the Red/Blue computation of Exercise 10 in Chapter 4.

6. Locate an SMP or other shared memory multiprocessor on which you gathered timings for the Red/Blue simulation in Chapter 6, using either OpenMP (Exercise 8 in Chapter 6) or Java Threads (Exercise 10 in Chapter 6). Compare timings with your solution in Exercise 5. Explain the performance differences.

7. Use MPI to implement Batcher's Bitonic Sort, described in Chapter 4, and use blocking send/receive. Use the result of Exercise 4 to initialize the computation.

8. Revise the Batcher Bitonic Sort of Exercise 7 to overlap communication and computation by using non-blocking sends/receives. Compare the performance with that of Exercise 7.

9. Familiarize yourself with the SUMMA matrix multiplication algorithm described in the Matrix Multiplication section of Chapter 8. Apply the concept of groups in the row broadcast and the column broadcast to implement an MPI program for SUMMA.

10. Use the concept of derived data type and the program from Exercise 4 to create a program in which the random numbers, having been distributed to the processors, are paired with a random four-letter string and returned to the master processor.

ZPL and Other Global View Languages

As we have discussed, Pthreads and MPI support parallel programming through libraries that extend a standard sequential programming language. The advantages of such an approach are significant: Programmers are already familiar with the base language, so they can concentrate on learning the library facilities; libraries allow programmers to use familiar tools and development environments; and libraries can be implemented relatively quickly compared to compilers. The main drawback to libraries is that they do not provide any syntactic support for parallel programming nor do they benefit from language or compiler support.

This chapter describes global view parallel programming languages—languages in which programmers "see" the whole computation rather than focusing on the constituent parts. such as individual processes. Such high-level languages can support implicit parallelism, in which the compiler manages process creation, communication, and synchronization, greatly simplifying the programmer's task.

Despite decades of research, no general-purpose, high-level parallel language is in widespread use. In this chapter we present one high-level language, ZPL, which will illustrate some of the benefits of language and compiler support. We conclude the chapter by taking a brief look at the NESL language, another global view programming language with different goals and characteristics than ZPL.

The ZPL Programming Language

ZPL encourages a different way of thinking, one that focuses on arrays and their manipulation. ZPL also provides implicit parallelism, so the compiler generates all parallel processes or threads, inserts all necessary communication calls, and attends to synchronization. For example, the Count 3s task from Chapter 1 is solved in ZPL by a few declarations and the single statement:

```
[1..n] count:=+<<(array==3);    ZPL code for the Count 3s computation
```

Its parallel solution, capable of executing on any parallel computer and comparable to Try 4 in performance, is created from this statement by the compiler; the explanation of the statement follows shortly.

One goal of ZPL is to allow programmers to reason about parallelism and parallel performance, including communication costs, yet be freed from the low-level details of writing the communication and synchronization statements. For example, ZPL programmers never have to concern themselves with race conditions. Another goal of ZPL is to provide performance portability, and again, language support is essential. Finally, we will see how ZPL's syntax plays an important role in achieving its goals.

Our introduction to ZPL begins by describing its core concepts, culminating in an example program for Conway's Game of Life. With this introduction, we then step back and reflect upon the language and its design goals. We resume our presentation of ZPL by describing a few of the more advanced features, and we conclude by explaining how ZPL provides a performance model that allows programmers to reason about performance.

Get the Software. The ZPL compiler and documentation are available as open source at http://www.cs.washington.edu/research/zpl/. The compiler runs on Unix/Linux systems and is easily re-targeted to new parallel machines.

Basic Concepts of ZPL

ZPL is an array language, meaning that entire arrays are operated upon as a unit. Thus, to increment all elements of an array A, we write

```
A:=A+1;
```

or equivalently,

```
A+=1;
```

The updates to the individual array elements are logically performed in parallel. Notice that ZPL's assignment operation is := rather than simply =.

Regions

It is common to modify all elements of an array, and it is equally common to limit the modification to particular elements. To specify the elements that are manipulated in an array expression, ZPL requires that all array operations be executed in the context of a region, as follows:

```
[1..n] A:=A+1;
```

The bracketed text is a *region*, which is a set of indices. As we will see, regions are a central idea in ZPL with many uses. Assuming A is declared to have n elements, indexed 1 to n, then the above statement modifies them all, as the region [1..n] specifies the indices for all arrays in the statement. The statement

```
[1..n/2] A:=A+1;
```

modifies only the first half of A's elements.

> **Notation:** As a convention, ZPL programmers capitalize the names of arrays and regions to emphasize that they reference many elements, and they use lower case for everything else.

Region Form. Regions take several forms. In the common form shown, the lower limit, *ll*, and the upper limit, *ul*, can have any value such that $ll \le ul$; the bounds are separated by double dots for each dimension, and dimensions are separated by commas, as in the following examples:

```
[-100..100]       A linear array of 201 indices
[1..8, 1..8]      A square array for a chessboard
[1..4, 1..4, 1]   A plane in 3D, equivalent to [1..4, 1..4, 1..1]
```

As shown in the last case, a dimension can consist of a single value, in which case it is called a *collapsed dimension*. The limits *ll* and *ul* do not have to be constants; they can also be integer expressions, as in

```
[min/2..2*max]
```

where min and max are *scalar* variables, that is, single numeric values.

Regions Can Describe Sub-Arrays. Because regions specify the array indices that participate in a computation, the specified indices must exist for all arrays appearing in the statement, but the arrays need not have the same dimensions. For example, suppose B is $m \times n$ and E is $m \times m$, $m < n$; then

```
[1..m, 1..m] E:=1/B;
```

references all of E but only the $m \times m$ subarray of B; the other elements of B are not referenced by the statement.

Of course, it is possible, though not common, to change individual elements of an array by simply referencing a degenerate region in which each dimension has been collapsed, as in

```
[x,y]  D:=sqrt(2);
```

which sets the single element D[x,y] to 1.414 . . . .

Regions in Declarations. In addition to specifying the elements of an array that participate in a computation, regions are also used to declare the size of arrays.

For example, three $m \times n$ arrays, B, C, and D, are declared as follows:

```
    var B, C, D : [1..m,1..n] float;
```

These are floating point arrays. Code Spec 8.1 lists all of the primitive types supported by ZPL.

Naming Regions. It is cumbersome to repeatedly write the same regions throughout the program, so they can be named using a `region` declaration as follows:

```
    region R=[1..m, 1..n];
```

Thereafter, the region's name can be used wherever regions can appear. They can be used in declarations, such as

```
    var B, C, D : [R] float;
```

and they can be used to specify indices for array operations:

```
    [R] B:=2*C+D;
```

Brackets are required around the region name.

Region Scoping. Finally, regions are lexically *scoped*. That is, the region that applies to a statement is the region specification on the closest enclosing statement. For example, in the following code fragment the region [R] prefixes the `repeat` statement, which itself encloses four statements; region [R] applies to statements *s1*, *s2*, and *s4*, and a different region applies to statement *s3*:

```
              [R] repeat
                        s1;
                        s2;
    [2..m-1, 1..n]      s3;
                        s4;
                  until condition;
```

Code Spec 8.1 Primitive data types available in ZPL.

Byte Types	2-Byte Types	4-Byte Types	8-Byte Types	16-Byte Types
boolean				
sbyte	shortint	integer	longint	
ubyte	ushortint	uinteger	ulongint	
		float	double	quad
		complex	dcomplex	qcomplex

The prefix 'u' indicates that the representation is unsigned, giving it an additional bit of precision. The `quad` type is available only if it is available in C on the target architecture; otherwise it defaults to `double`. A k-byte complex type uses k bytes for the real and k bytes for the imaginary parts of the number.

(Code Spec 8.2 lists ZPL's available control flow structures.) Because it is common for programs to operate over many arrays with the same shape, it is typical for a program to declare a single region and to prefix the main program block with that region, which causes all statements to operate on arrays of that shape, unless otherwise specified by another region.

Array Computation

ZPL's primitive operators, which are listed in Code Spec 8.3, can be applied to either scalar or array operands. When given array operands, the operator is applied element-wise to corresponding elements of the operands, which must have the same rank. For example, the statement (from a program we will discuss below)

```
[R] TW:=(TW&NN=2)|(NN=3);
```

is applied to corresponding array elements for all indices in R as if many statements of the form

```
TW[1,1]:=(TW[1,1]&NN[1,1]=2)|(NN[1,1]=3)
TW[1,2]:=(TW[1,2]&NN[1,2]=2)|(NN[1,2]=3)
TW[1,3]:=(TW[1,3]&NN[1,3]=2)|(NN[1,3]=3)
            . . .
TW[m,n]:=(TW[m,n]&NN[m,n]=2)|(NN[m,n]=3)
```

were executed simultaneously. (Notice in Code Spec 8.3 that the = operator tests for equality and is not an assignment operator.)

@-translation. Until now, our examples of array computations have applied identical regions to each array operand. To allow programmers to shift the indices for individual array operands, ZPL provides the @ operator which takes an array and a *direction* as operands. A direction is a vector of the same rank as the array operand. For example, to allow each element of A to reference the elements to its left and right, we could declare two directions:

```
direction left=[-1];  right=[1];
```

Code Spec 8.2 Syntax of control statements in ZPL.

ZPL Control-Flow Statements

```
if logical-expression then statements {else statements} end;
for var := low to high {by step} do statements end;
while logical-expression do statements end;
repeat statements until logical-expression;
return {expression};
begin statements end;
```

Text in braces is optional; text in italics must be replaced by program constructs of the indicted kind.

Code Spec 8.3 ZPL's primitive operators and operator-assignments.

Datatype	Operators
Numeric	+ (unary), – (unary), +, –, *, /, ^, % (modulus)
Logical	!, &, |
Relational	=, !=, <, >, <=, >=
Bit-wise	`bnot(a)`, `band(a,b)`, `bor(a,b)`, `bxor(a,b)`,
	`bsl(s,a)` (shift a's bits s places left, fill with 0s),
	`bsr(s,a)` (shift a's bits right s places, fill with 0s)

Exponentiation (^) is optimized to multiplication for small powers, for example, 2, but generally compiles to a call on C's `pow()` function.
The operator assignments recognized are: `+=`, `–=`, `*=`, `/=`, `%=`, `&=`, `|=`

When used with the @ operator, the direction translates the array's region by the specified vector. For example, in the statement

```
[2..n-1] A:=(A+A@left+A@right)/3;
```

A uses the indices given by the region; `A@left` uses the set of indices one less than the indices in the region, that is, 1 to $n – 2$; and `A@right` uses the set of indices one larger than the indices in the region, that is 3 to n. As with other array languages, the semantics of the assignment statement evaluate the entire right-hand side before applying the result to the left-hand side. Accordingly, the statement has the effect of replacing each element in the interior of the array with the average of itself, its left neighbor, and its right neighbor.

As another example, we can declare the eight compass directions:

```
direction nw=[-1,-1]; no=[-1, 0]; ne=[-1, 1];
         we=[ 0,-1];              ea=[ 0, 1];
         sw=[ 1,-1]; so=[ 1, 0]; se=[ 1, 1];
```

If TW is a 2-dimensional array of 0s and 1s, then the expression

```
TW@nw + TW@no + TW@ne +
TW@we +           TW@ea +
TW@sw + TW@so + TW@se
```

computes an array whose value in each position is the number of its neighbors in TW that are 1. (White space is ignored in ZPL, so the arrangement of the terms in both the declaration and the expression is intended to suggest the direction of the translation.) In a moment, we will use this computation in an example program, but first we need to explain one more concept.

Reduce. Recall from previous chapters that a reduce operation combines the elements of an array using a primitive operator; we say we have "used the operator to reduce the array to a single value." ZPL's reduce operation is given by the form

```
op<<A
```

where *op* is one of the primitive associative and commutative operators: +, *, &, |, max, min. To sum the interior elements of A, we write

```
[2..n-1] total:=+<<A;
```

and note that like all operations on arrays in ZPL, it is essential to specify a region.

Reduce can be applied to arrays of any rank. Therefore, to find the largest element in a 2-dimensional array B, we write the following:

```
[R] biggest:=max<<B;
```

It is not necessary to store the scalar result. So the following is legal:

```
[R] span:=(max<<A)-(min<<A)+1;
```

The reduce operation is implemented using Schwartz's algorithm, discussed in Chapter 4. ZPL also has a scan operator that uses the syntax +||A for +-scan.

Life, an Example

To illustrate the concepts introduced so far, Conway's Game of Life, which is a trivial computation often used as a screensaver, serves as a clean, simple example.

The Problem

The game simulates generations of organisms on a 2-dimensional grid, with the initial configuration being generation 0. The rules are as follows:

- An organism lives to generation $i + 1$ if in generation i it has at least two neighbor organisms and no more than three;
- An organism is born into generation $i + 1$ if its position is empty and it has exactly three neighbor organisms in generation i;
- All other organisms die before generation $i + 1$

The rules can be simplified to a single condition that says an organism exists in generation $i + 1$ either because it exists in generation i and has exactly two neighbors or because its position—whether occupied by an existing organism or not—has exactly three neighbors in generation i.

The Solution

We solve the problem in a rectangular world by the array TW, *the world*. Organisms are represented as 1-bits. To know how many neighbors exist for a position, we sum their eight nearest neighbors, as previously discussed, into a variable NN, *neighbor number*. We use the logic shown in Figure 8.1.

Figure 8.1
ZPL program that implements Conway's Game of Life.

```
1    program Life;
2    config const n : integer = 50;
3
4    region
5       R   =[1..n,    1..n  ];
6       BigR=[0..n+1,  0..n+1];
7
8    var
9       TW:[BigR]      boolean = 0;        -- The World
10      NN:[R]         integer;            -- Number of Neighbors
11
12   direction
13      nw=[-1, -1]; no=[-1,  0]; ne=[-1, 1];
14      we=[ 0, -1];              ea=[ 0, 1];
15      sw=[ 1, -1]; so=[ 1,  0]; se=[ 1, 1];
16
17   procedure Life();
18   begin
19      --Initialize the world
20   [R] repeat
21      NN:=TW@nw+TW@no+TW@ne+
22          TW@we+        TW@ea+
23          TW@sw+TW@so+TW@se;
24      TW:=(TW & NN = 2) |(NN = 3);
25   until !(|<< TW);
26   end;
```

How It Works

The first half of the program consists of declarations:

- Line 2 specifies the array bound, n, as a *configuration constant*, meaning that its value does not change after initially being set, and the initial setting is either the default value of 50 or a value specified on the command line.

- Lines 4-6 declare two regions, with BigR being larger than R so that it can hold the boundary values; these boundaries will be uninhabited, that is, assigned 0s, and are required so that the @-references refer to defined values.

- Lines 8-10 declare the problem representation (TW), which is initialized to 0, and the intermediate count of neighbors (NN).

- Lines 12-15 define the eight compass directions needed to reference the nearest neighbors.

The two regions declared by this program were used a combined three times, so it might be tempting to not name them. Nevertheless, we encourage the use of named regions, as they have the same benefit as named constants in other programming languages, namely, they provide additional meaning to the constant, which makes programs easier to understand, modify, and maintain.

The program has a single procedure named `Life` (see Code Spec 8.4). After the world is initialized—we assume a random configuration is created or an input file is read—the computation enters a repeat-loop over array computations. The first line

```
NN:=TW@nw+TW@no+TW@ne+
    TW@we+        TW@ea+
    TW@sw+TW@so+TW@se;
```

computes the number of living neighbors for each array position by type-casting the Boolean arrays into integer arrays and adding. This line could be read, "Add element-wise the array of northwest neighbors in TW to the array of north neighbors in TW to the array of northeast neighbors in TW ....." That is, ZPL programmers think of such operations from the global array viewpoint rather than the local index viewpoint.

The next line creates the next generation by applying Conway's rules. Combining the rules into one statement, we have

```
TW:=(TW&NN=2)|(NN=3);
```

which computes the element-wise logical-or of two arrays, namely, the array of organisms with exactly two neighbors, and the array of positions with exactly three neighbors.

When an iteration of the loop is complete, the termination test checks to see if there are organisms still living, and if not, it exits. In particular, the termination condition

```
!(|<<TW);
```

computes an or-reduce over the world array, TW, which is `false` if no organisms exist, and it negates the result to control the repeat loop.

Code Spec 8.4 Specifying the entry procedure for ZPL.

Entry Point

ZPL requires that some procedure have the same name as the program, that is, matching the word following `program` on the first line. That procedure is the entry point for the ZPL computation.

The Philosophy of Life

The Life game is simple, and the ZPL program for it is also simple. Most of the program consists of declarations, and once the regions and directions have been declared, the actual computation is both concise (two statements) and clear. The conciseness comes from the use of array operations, which can manipulate entire arrays at a time. The clarity comes from abstractions such as regions and directions, which allow programmers to refer to arrays as `TW@nw` instead of forcing them to deal with each of the individual elements directly. The use of array operators also provides a source of implicit parallelism, as the compiler translates the Life program into a highly parallel program with virtually all of the low level details hidden from the programmer.

With this introduction to ZPL, we are now ready to take a closer look at the language's core ideas and design philosophy.

Distinguishing Features of ZPL

ZPL's goals are to provide programming convenience and performance portability. How does it achieve these goals? As we have seen, some of its convenience derives from its ability to manipulate entire arrays at once. But there are many other array languages, including APL and Fortran 90, so how is ZPL different? This section answers these questions as we discuss the core ideas behind ZPL that distinguish it from other languages, including other array languages.

Regions

ZPL's region construct allows programmers to perform array indexing at an abstract level. Thus, sets of indices can be named and reused. Moreover, regions can be manipulated using operators, such as the @ operator, which emphasize the relationship among different array references.

Statement-Level Indexing

Unlike most other languages, regions are applied to entire statements instead of to individual arrays. There is a syntactic benefit to this approach, as it factors out the commonality among the various array expressions in a statement, while at the same time highlighting the differences among the different expressions. For example, in our Life program, the line

```
NN:=TW@nw+TW@no+TW@ne+
    TW@we+        TW@ea+
    TW@sw+TW@so+TW@se;
```

makes it clear that each of the 8 references to the TW array refers to a different offset of the array as defined by the 8 directions. The programmer must declare the 8 directions properly but thereafter can use their names and their implied meaning. By contrast, in languages that do not have regions and that apply indices directly to individual arrays, the programmer must repeat the detailed index calculations for every array reference, as might be done in Fortran 90:

```
NN(1:n;  1:n)=TW(0:n-1;  0:n-1)+TW(0:n-1;  1:n)+TW(0:n-1,  2:n+1)+
              TW(1:n;    0:n-1)+                  TW(1:n,    2:n+1)+
              TW(2:n+1;  0:n-1)+TW(2:n+1;  1:n)+TW(2:n+1,  2:n+1)
```

In addition to the syntactic benefits of regions, there is a more subtle and more profound semantic benefit that pertains to parallel performance. To understand this benefit, first recognize the restrictions imposed by ZPL's use of regions.

Restrictions Imposed by Regions

ZPL's statement-level indexing restricts the types of array computations that can be expressed. For example, with just the index translation operation provided by the @ operator, it is impossible to transpose the elements of a matrix, which in almost any other language can be expressed quite simply by using direct array indexing:

```
for(i=1;  i<n;  i++)
{
  for(j=1;  i<n;  i++)
  {
    Atranspose[i][j]=A[j][i];
  }
}
```

These restrictions are imposed intentionally to enforce a programming discipline that distinguishes expensive operations—in terms of communication in a parallel execution—from inexpensive operations. This discipline in turn facilitates the definition of a parallel performance model, which is essential to achieving the goal of performance portability. (ZPL has another operator, remap, to perform transpose; see below.)

Performance Model

The basic idea behind ZPL's performance model is to specify a data distribution that is based on the program's declared regions. This distribution in turn dictates the data movement that is required for every ZPL operation, which allows programmers to syntactically identify communication costs. Thus, ZPL programmers must pay close attention to the relationship among regions and their ranks, as these relationships imply communication in the parallel execution of the program. In exchange, ZPL programmers do not need to worry about the low-level details of synchronization or communication; moreover, the ZPL compiler is supplied with important information that facilitates its ability to perform various communication optimizations.

To understand the need for ZPL's restrictions, contrast the preceding transpose code with the following loop nest:

```
for(i=1; i<n; i++)
{
  for(j=1; i<n; i++)
  {
    Atranspose[i][j]=A[i][j];
  }
}
```

The codes are identical except for the transposition of the indices on the right hand side of the statement. Yet in terms of data movement, the two codes represent polar opposites, with the former requiring significant communication involving every process, and the latter requiring no communication at all. Thus, languages that allow such code cannot provide a meaningful performance model, because there is no easy way to distinguish expensive operations from inexpensive operations.

Addition by Subtraction

ZPL programmers thus benefit from the removal of certain liberties. In particular, the language replaces overly general operators that can have widely differing costs—in this case direct array indexing—with less general operations whose costs are better defined.

We have also seen restrictions on the ranks of arrays, as the primitive operators can take array operands as long as the arrays have the same rank. For example, if A is a 1-dimensional array declared to have indices [1..n], then it cannot be added to the first row of the 2-dimensional array C:

```
[1, 1..n] C:=C+A;          ILLEGAL: A and C have different ranks
```

This restriction is necessary to preserve ZPL's performance model. Otherwise, the communication cost of the assignment statement could vary greatly depending on whether the C array is distributed across the row dimension, across the column dimension, or across both dimensions.

In the next two sections we introduce features of ZPL that change the ranks of arrays. For example, we will see how to implement a matrix transpose. We will then explain ZPL's performance model, which is the key to achieving performance portability.

Manipulating Arrays of Different Ranks

In ZPL the region that defines an array specifies not only its number of dimensions, its number of elements, and its indices, it also specifies its allocation. Different rank arrays will generally have different allocations, which significantly affect the communication induced by various ZPL operators. Thus, in the common case, ZPL requires that all arrays in a statement have the same rank. But in some situations, computations produce arrays of different rank, and in other cases, arrays of different ranks must be operated on together. For these cases two basic ideas can be used:

- **Use the larger rank:** The array with smaller rank can be declared to have the same rank as the other array. The lower rank array becomes a higher ranked array with one or more collapsed dimensions. For example, to operate on arrays whose regions are `[1..n, 1..p]` and `[1..m, 1..n, 1..p]`, the first region can be changed to `[1, 1..n, 1..p]`.

- **Replicate elements:** When values of lower rank arrays are used repeatedly with elements of higher ranked arrays, the elements of the lower ranked array can be replicated so that they can be manipulated with the elements of the other array. ZPL's *flood* operator efficiently performs this replication without literally representing each replicated element.

Later in this section, we will see these two ideas merge in the concept of the "flood dimension." We now introduce operators that change rank, such as partial reduce, and operators that accommodate rank differences, such as flood.

Partial Reduce

The reduce operation converts an array into a scalar. That is,

```
sum:=+<<A;
```

sums the elements of array `A` to produce a single value. If this result is seen as "reducing" or combining *all* of the dimensions of an array, then a partial reduce can be viewed as combining *some* of the dimensions of an array. For an $m \times n$ array `B`, we could reduce the first dimension by combining the columns of values to produce a single row, or we could reduce the second dimension by combining the rows of values to produce a single column. Here `B` is known as the *source array* and the resulting row or column is known as the *target array*.

Not surprisingly, ZPL's partial reduce uses two regions *with the same rank*, one to specify the source indices for the operand array and one to specify the target indices of the result array. The source region is specified as an operand to the reduce operator; the target region is the region that applies to the statement. To partially reduce `B` along the first dimension using the add operator—that is, to add the columns of numbers to produce a row—we write

```
[1, 1..n] C:=+<< [1..m, 1..n] B;
```

where the "operand region," `[1..m, 1..n]` specifies the indices of `B` that participate in the reduce (the source), and the statement region `[1, 1..n]` specifies the indices of the result (the target). For example, for $m = 3$ and $n = 4$,

```
[1, 1..4] 7765   ⇔   +<<[1..3, 1..4] 3 1 4 1
                                      1 4 1 4
                                      3 2 1 0
```

We see that the regions differ in the first dimension, so this operation reduces the first dimension from 3 elements to one, leaving the second dimension unchanged.

To reduce B in the second dimension using the multiplication operator—that is, to multiply the rows of values to produce a column—we can write

```
[1..m, 1] D:=*<< [1..m, 1..n] B;
```

and for $m = 3$ and $n = 4$ the result will be

```
[1..3, 1] 12   ⇔   *<<[1..3, 1..4] 3 1 4 1
          16                        1 4 1 4
           0                        3 2 1 0
```

In this case, the two regions differ in the second dimension, so the 3×4 array is reduced to a single three-element column.

Notice that the region on the statement is really just defining the prevailing context for the computation. The closest applicable region might be specified as the operand of another operation, as in the more complex operation on the $p \times m \times n$ array F,

```
[1,1,1..n] G :=max<<[1,1..m,1..n](min<<[1..p,1..m,1..n] F);
```

which finds the plane of minimum values over the first dimension and then finds the row of maximums over the columns of the plane. Thus, for $m = 3$, $n = 4$ and $p = 2$, an example is

```
[1,1..3,1..4] 2 1 3 1   ⇔   min<<[1..2,1..3,1..4] 3 1 4 1
              1 3 1 2                              1 4 1 4
              0 2 0 0                              3 2 1 0

                                                  2 4 3 4
                                                  1 3 2 2
                                                  0 5 0 3

[1,1,1..4]    2 3 3 2   ⇔   max<<[1, 1..3, 1..4]  2 1 3 1
                                                  1 3 1 2
                                                  0 2 0 0
```

Here, the min-reduce combines the first dimension, and the max-reduce combines the second dimension.

Flooding

Just as it is possible to reduce an array dimension, it should be possible to expand an array dimension. ZPL's flood operator (>>) expands one or more dimensions of an array by replicating values across the specified dimensions. Because flood is effectively an inverse of partial reduce—and therefore has the opposite effect on array size as the partial reduce—flood has a similar syntax. So,

```
[1..m, 1..n] B:=>>[1, 1..n] C;
```

fills the array B with copies of the first row of C. For $m = 3$ and $n = 4$, an explicit example is

$$[1..3, 1..4] \begin{array}{cccc} 7 & 7 & 6 & 5 \\ 7 & 7 & 6 & 5 \\ 7 & 7 & 6 & 5 \end{array} \iff >>[1, 1..4] \begin{array}{cccc} 7 & 7 & 6 & 5 \end{array}$$

$$\neq$$

As with partial reduce, the dimensions to flood are indicated by the differences between the source and target regions.

Of course, flooding can apply to any dimension, including the second dimension, as in

```
[1..m, 1..n] C:=>>[1..m,1] D;
```

which can be illustrated by an example in which $m = 3$ and $n = 4$:

$$[1..3, 1..4] \begin{array}{ccc} 12 & 12 & 12 \\ 16 & 16 & 16 \\ 0 & 0 & 0 \end{array} \iff >>[1..3,1] \begin{array}{c} 12 \\ 16 \\ 0 \end{array}$$

In addition, it is possible to flood only a portion of a dimension with replicated values.

The Flooding Principle

What is the point of flooding; why copy values? Flooding is necessary because the element-wise operators assume that their operands have the same dimensions, and these operators take a single region to specify indices for both of their array operands. Suppose, for example, that we wish to scale every column of a matrix by the values in the matrix's second column. The matrix is 2-dimensional and the column is in concept 1-dimensional, so we replicate the column values, producing a second dimension for the array, enabling an element-wise divide operator. Specifically, we write

```
[1..m,1..n] B:=B/(>>[1..m, 2] B);
```

The expression in parentheses evaluates to an $m \times n$ array composed of n copies of column two; the result of the statement is that every column is scaled by the values in column two. Specifically, let $m = 3$ and $n = 4$:

$$[1..3, 1..4] \begin{array}{cccc} 3.00 & 1.00 & 4.00 & 1.00 \\ 0.25 & 1.00 & 0.25 & 1.00 \\ 1.50 & 1.00 & 0.50 & 0.00 \end{array} \iff \begin{array}{c} 3\ 1\ 4\ 1 / 1\ 1\ 1\ 1 \\ 1\ 4\ 1\ 4\ \ 4\ 4\ 4\ 4 \\ 3\ 2\ 1\ 0\ \ 2\ 2\ 2\ 2 \end{array}$$

The values are only *logically* replicated. The compiler does not create the fully replicated array; it only replicates as many values as necessary, in this case, one column per process. Thus, the flood operation is quite efficient, with minimal data movement, and there is good locality when referencing values of a flooded array.

Data Manipulation, an Example

Imagine a dataset consisting of *n* observations, say cups of coffee consumed in a day, for *m* subjects. We can represent such data using an array D with dimensions [1..m, 0..n], where the array has been given an additional 0th column to record summary data. Now consider some illustrative computations on this data.

The most coffee consumed on any day by any subject is the max-reduce over the data portion of the entire array:

```
[1..m,1..n] most:=max<<D;              -- Compute top score
```

The variable most is a scalar.

The maximum for each subject is the partial reduction across the rows, which we store in the 0th column:

```
[1..m, 0] D:=max<<[1..m, 1..n] D;      -- Record individual maxima
```

The computation produces a column of values.

To determine if there are non-coffee drinkers, we can check for a 0 in the summary column, and compute the or-reduce over that column:

```
[1..m, 0] tFans:=|<<(D = 0);           -- Does anyone not like coffee?
```

The variable tFans is a scalar. (Of course, a simple and-reduce &<<D would also work, but it may be less clear.)

In the case where everyone is a coffee drinker, we can scale everyone's coffee habit to be in the range [0,1] relative to their biggest day by flooding the first column across the array and dividing the result into the data array:

```
if !tFans then
   [1..m,1..n] D:=D/(>>[1..m, 0] D);   --Scale by maximum
end;
```

Finally, we can determine the percentage of days of the study that each person achieved his or her maximum. We begin by comparing the whole data array to 1, then partially reducing each row using addition, which produces a count of max days for each person, and then dividing the results by n.

```
[1..m, 0] D:=100*(+<<[1..m,1..n](D=1)) / n; --Pct days@max
```

Instead of using column 0 to hold summary values, some programmers might prefer to declare the dataset to have its proper dimensions [1..m, 1..n] and use a separate array `Score [1..m, 1]` to store summary results. Of course, we require `Score` to be 2-dimensional, because it will be used in expressions involving the 2-dimensional array D. With this approach the foregoing computations become:

```
[1..m,1..n]  most   :=max<<D;
  [1..m, 1]  Score  :=max<<[1..m, 1..n] D;
  [1..m, 1]  tFans  :=|<<(Score=0);
             if !tFans then
[1..m,1..n]    D    :=D/(>>[1..m, 1] Score);
             end;
  [1..m, 1]  Score  :=100*(+<<[1..m,1..n](D = 1))/n;
```

By such computations, ZPL programmers perform routine data manipulation, switching back and forth among various data sizes but remaining within a given rank.

Flood Regions

The use of the `Score` variable in our last example illustrates a curiosity in our use of ZPL. Although it made sense perhaps in our first solution to place the summary column in the 0th position, why do we specify the array `Score` to have its second index be 1? Could it be 0 or 9 or n? The answer is yes. The actual consequences of this decision for memory allocation will be explained below, but our point now is that the choice will generally be arbitrary. To see the arbitrariness, notice that one of the operations on `Score` is to flood it, that is, replicate it in all column positions.

ZPL provides the concept of a flood dimension, denoted by an asterisk (*) in the region expression. The flood dimension indicates that we don't care what the index is because all values in that dimension have the same value. So the best way to define the summary array from the last example is

```
var Score : [1..m, *] float;
```

which specifies that the data is flooded in the second dimension. The final four statements from the earlier example now become:

```
  [1..m, *]  Score  :=max<<[1..m, 1..n] D;
  [1..m, *]  tFans  :=|<<(Score=0);
             if !tFans then
[1..m,1..n]    D    :=D/Score);
             end;
  [1..m, *]  Score  :=100*(+<<[1..m,1..n](D=1))/n;
```

There is no need to flood `Score` in the third line because the data has already been declared to be flooded by the properties of flood dimensions. Thus, there are values to correspond element-wise with the *n* elements of D's second dimension. How many elements does `Score` have in its second dimension? Any number needed with any needed indices. Graphically, the values of `Score` can be visualized as follows:

$$..., v_1, v_1, v_1, v_1, ...$$
$$..., v_2, v_2, v_2, v_2, ...$$
$$..., v_3, v_3, v_3, v_3, ...$$
$$..., v_4, v_4, v_4, v_4, ...$$
$$...$$
$$..., v_m, v_m, v_m, v_m, ...$$

So Score matches arrays of any size in the second dimension.

Flood dimensions are sensible, based on the principle that programmers should never be asked to specify more than they mean. But there is another important reason for their use. Flood dimensions enable the compiler to use efficient data representations—complete data replication is avoided—and efficient communication protocols—multicast is often possible. As a result, it is generally better to select a flood dimension than it is to make an arbitrary choice of a collapsed index value.

Matrix Multiplication

To apply the ideas of this section, consider computing the product of two dense matrices, C = AB, where A is $m \times n$ and B is $n \times p$. This computation is most simply programmed in sequential programming languages as a triply nested loop:

```
for(i=0; i<m; i++)
{
   for(j=0; j<p; j++)
   {
      C[i,j]=0;
      for(k=0; k<n; k++)
      {
         C[i,j]+=A[i,k]*B[k,j];
      }
   }
}
```

The inner most loop computes the *dot product*, in which the ith row of A is multiplied by the jth column of B and reduced to produce C[i,j].

While this code is simple, it is not the right way to think about a *parallel* matrix product. Indeed, van de Geijn and Watts argue that computing the dot products separately, that is, a row of A times column of B, is exactly backwards. In their SUMMA (Scalable Universal Matrix Multiplication Algorithm) approach, they bring the initialization and the *k*-loop to the outside, effectively computing all of the *k*th terms of all of the dot-products at once. This contrary way of thinking produces an extremely efficient algorithm because it uses regular communication patterns. It is also the easiest ZPL matrix multiplication algorithm because it exploits flooding.

To understand the key idea of SUMMA and why flooding is so fundamental to it, notice that in the computation $C = AB$ for 3×3 matrices, the first two columns of the result are as follows:

$$C_{1,1} = A_{1,1} \times B_{1,1} + A_{1,2} \times B_{2,1} + A_{1,3} \times B_{3,1} \qquad C_{1,2} = A_{1,1} \times B_{1,2} + A_{1,2} \times B_{2,2} + A_{1,3} \times B_{3,2} \cdots$$
$$C_{2,1} = A_{2,1} \times B_{1,1} + A_{2,2} \times B_{2,1} + A_{2,3} \times B_{3,1} \qquad C_{2,2} = A_{2,1} \times B_{1,2} + A_{2,2} \times B_{2,2} + A_{2,3} \times B_{3,2} \cdots$$
$$C_{3,1} = A_{3,1} \times B_{1,1} + A_{3,2} \times B_{2,1} + A_{3,3} \times B_{3,1} \qquad C_{3,2} = A_{3,1} \times B_{1,2} + A_{3,2} \times B_{2,2} + A_{3,3} \times B_{3,2} \cdots$$

We see that the first term of each of these equations can be computed by replicating the first *column* of A across a 3 × 3 array, and replicating the first *row* of B down a 3 × 3 array, that is, by flooding A's first column and B's first row, and then multiplying corresponding elements; the second term results from replicating A's second column and B's second row and multiplying, and similarly for the third term.

The ZPL implementation of the SUMMA algorithm is shown in Figure 8.2. The program begins with the obvious variable declarations. The Col variable will be used to flood columns of A, and Row will be used to flood rows of B. In the body of the procedure, the entire computation is executed in the context of the result array C's dimensions. The result array is initialized to 0, and the computation enters the k-loop that processes the n terms of the dot product.

In the body of the loop the next column of A is flooded across Col and the next row of B is flooded down Row. In the final statement of the loop the two flooded arrays are multiplied element-wise and accumulated into the result array, C. Then the next term of the dot-product is considered.

Figure 8.2
The SUMMA matrix multiplication algorithm in ZPL.

```
var A     : [1..m, 1..n] double;
    B     : [1..n, 1..p] double;
    C     : [1..m, 1..p] double;
    Col   : [1..m, *]    double;
    Row   : [*, 1..p]    double;
    k     :              integer;

procedure MM();
[1..m, 1..p] begin
            C:=0;
            for k:=1 to n do
    [1..m, *]     Col:=>> [1..m, k] A;
    [*, 1..p]     Row:=>> [k, 1..p] B;
            C+=Col*Row;
        end;
    end;
```

Notice that the use of the temporary arrays Col and Row was actually unnecessary. The procedure body could have been written as follows using the flood operator:

```
[1..m, 1..p] begin
            C:=0;
            for k:=1 to n do
              C +=(>>[1..m, k] A )*(>>[k, 1..p] B);
            end;
          end;
```

In fact, the compiler will generate temporaries corresponding to Col and Row for the above code anyway, but it saves the programmer a few lines of typing. The SUMMA algorithm is both extremely efficient and easy to write.

The constraints on partial reduce and flood are summarized in Code Spec 8.5.

Reordering Data with Remap

ZPL encourages computation on local data, but data often has to be moved around to become local. The remap operator performs arbitrary restructuring of data, which can include changes to its rank. Before learning about the remap operator, we must introduce the notion of Index Arrays.

Index Arrays

As a programming convenience, ZPL provides a set of pre-defined constant arrays whose contents hold the index values of the relevant region. These arrays, which are known as *Index Arrays*, are denoted as Index<*dimension number*>, as in Index1,

Code Spec 8.5 Requirements of ZPL's partial reduce and flood operators.

Partial Reduce (<<) and Flood (>>)

These operations require two regions, a source region (included as an operand) and a target region (applied to the statement), as in the following examples:

```
[1, 1..3]      ...  +<<[1..3, 1..5] A ...  // reduce
[1..3,1..5]    ...    >>[1, 1..3]   A ...  // flood
```

For each dimension in the two regions, the index ranges are either identical or one is a collapsed dimension (singleton value). For partial reduces, which are indicated by collapsed dimensions on the target region, the elements of the operand are combined and assigned to the collapsed dimension; for flood operations, indicated by collapsed dimensions on the source region, the element is replicated across the range of the collapsed dimension.

`Index2`, `Index3`, and so on. For example

```
[1..3,1..3]  ... Index1 ...  ⟺    1   1   1
                                   2   2   2
                                   3   3   3
```

is an array of the first dimension indices, and

```
[1..3,1..3]  ... Index2 ...  ⟺    1   2   3
                                   1   2   3
                                   1   2   3
```

is an array of second dimension indices. The only constraint on the use of Index Arrays is that the statement's region have a sufficient number of dimensions.

Index Arrays which are efficiently implemented because their values are already available within the compiled code, are used frequently in ZPL programs, as in

```
[1..n,1..n]  Diag:=Index1=Index2;
```

for constructing an array with 1s down the diagonal, and

```
[1..n,1..n]  RMO:=n*(Index1-1)+Index2;
```

for computing the row-major order index of elements of a 2D array. They are also used frequently with the remap operator.

Remap

The remap operator, denoted by the # symbol, defines a reordering of an array. It takes two arguments: a source array and a list of *remap arrays*, where the remap arrays contain indices that define the re-ordering. The remap operator has two forms, known as *gather* and *scatter*.

Gather. If the remap operator appears as a right-hand side, that is, as an expression, then the remap specifies a gather operation and the result array will select values from the source array as indicated by the remap arrays. For example, suppose that A and P are declared over the region [1..7] and have the values

```
A ⟺ d d e e o r r
P ⟺ 5 6 1 3 7 4 2
```

then in the statement

```
B=A#[P]
```

A is the source array and P is the remap array, and the statement assigns to B the value

```
B ⟺ o r d e r e d
```

because the first element of B will be the 5th element of A, the second element of B will be the 6th element of A, and so forth.

Scatter. If the remap operator appears on the left-hand side of an assignment, then the remap operator performs a scatter operation, as values of the source array are placed in the result array as specified by the remap arrays. For example, the statement

```
C#[P]=A
```

will produce

$$B \iff e\ r\ e\ r\ d\ d\ o$$

as the first element of A will be placed in the 5th element of C, and so forth.

It is common for remap arrays to use expressions based on the values of the Index Arrays. For example,

```
A#[8-Index1]
```

reverses the source operand because the remap array contains the index values in descending order, producing

$$r\ r\ o\ e\ e\ d\ d \iff d\ d\ e\ e\ o\ r\ r\ \#\ [7\ 6\ 5\ 4\ 3\ 2\ 1]$$

To spell *ordered* backwards, we can write `A#[P#[8-Index1]]`.

Repeated Values in Remap Arrays. The values in the remap arrays do not have to be unique, although that is the most common case. For example, the gather `A#[1 1 1 1 1 1 1]` is

$$d\ d\ d\ d\ d\ d\ d \iff d\ d\ e\ e\ o\ r\ r\ \#\ [1\ 1\ 1\ 1\ 1\ 1\ 1]$$

is a cumbersome (and expensive) way to copy the first element of A. For scatter the issue is more curious. Because scatter assigns values, an index value appearing multiple times in the remap array can result in different orders of assignments, resulting in unpredictable results. So the scatter form `A#[ 1 1 1 1 1 1 1 ]:=A`

$$?\ d\ e\ e\ o\ r\ r \iff d\ d\ e\ e\ o\ r\ r\ \#[1\ 1\ 1\ 1\ 1\ 1\ 1]$$

will result in one of *d, e, o* or *r* being assigned to the first index position, but which one is undefined. Different parallel executions can produce different results.

Higher Dimensions. Higher dimension arrays require multiple remap arrays in the brackets, with the array in the *i*th dimension specifying the index values for that dimension. For example, in

```
B#[C,D]
```

the elements of B are reordered using C as the remap array for the first dimension and D as the remap array for the second dimension. For example,

```
[1..n, 1..m] Btranspose:=B#[Index2, Index1];
```

is a standard idiom for computing the transpose of an array, because the indices of the two dimensions are interchanged. For Btranspose declared over region [1..n, 1..m] and for $m = 3$ and $n = 2$ the transpose is illustrated below:

$$
\begin{array}{l}
a\ c\ e \\
b\ d\ f
\end{array}
\iff
\begin{array}{l}
a\ b \\
c\ d \\
e\ f
\end{array}
\ \#[1\ 2\ 3, \quad 1\ 1\ 1 \\
1\ 2\ 3 \quad 2\ 2\ 2]
$$

The operation of this gather is clear: Item i, j in the result comes from the $C_{i,j}$, $D_{i,j}$ position of the operand (see Code Spec 8.6).

Ordering Example

Remap is used regularly in ZPL. An excellent example of its use is to reorder rows of a 2-dimensional matrix. We will illustrate such a computation in this section.

Recall the "coffee drinkers" data array from the section on Data Manipulation. The array was defined over the region [1..m, 0..n], recording the number of cups of coffee consumed by m people over n days; the first column was used for summary statistics. For example, we know that we can compute the average coffee consumption of the participants by using a partial reduce:

```
[1..m, 0] D:=(+<<[1..m,1..n] D)/n;
```

Now, suppose we want to order the coffee drinkers by their average consumption, least to greatest. We can solve this problem by reordering the rows of the D array

Code Spec 8.6 Requirements of ZPL's remap operator.

Remap

Arrays are restructured by the remap operator (#), which takes two operands: the array to restructure and, in brackets, arrays for each dimension of the result. So the remapping of a 2-dimensional array A would be written as A#[C,D], as in A#[Index2, Index1] to compute the transpose of A. Remap has two forms:

Gather is used on the right-hand side of an assignment statement: Item i, j in the result *comes from* the $C_{i,j}$, $D_{i,j}$ position of the operand.

$$
\begin{array}{l}
a\ c\ e \\
b\ d\ f
\end{array}
\iff
\begin{array}{l}
a\ b \\
c\ d \\
e\ f
\end{array}
\ \#[1\ 2\ 3, \quad 1\ 1\ 1 \\
1\ 2\ 3 \quad 2\ 2\ 2]
$$

Scatter is used on the left-hand side of an assignment statement: Item i, j of the operand *goes to* position $C_{i,j} D_{i,j}$ position in the result.

$$
\begin{array}{l}
e\ c\ a \\
f\ d\ b
\end{array}
\#[1\ 1\ 1,\ 3\ 2\ 1] \ := \
\begin{array}{l}
a\ c\ e \\
b\ d\ f
\end{array}
\\
2\ 2\ 2,\ 3\ 2\ 1
$$

based on the value in column 0, which means that we need to compute each coffee drinker's ranking based on the 0th column. Our strategy is to break the task into three parts:

1. Use the flood operator to make all comparisons and compute the rankings.

2. Use the reduce operator to find the ranking.

3. Use the remap operator to put the rows of the array into the right order.

For convenience, we will assume that the averages are unique, but it is simple to handle duplicates.

All Comparisons Ranking Algorithm. To compare every element with every other element of a sequence, we flood a 2D array with the averages stored in the 0th column, which gives us one of the operands for the comparison. To get the other operand, we transpose the array and flood it in the other dimension. An element-wise comparison of the two arrays yields an array of bits.

We begin with the declarations:

```
RepC : [1..m, *] float;        --Temp for replicated columns
RepR : [*, 1..m] float;        --Temp for replicated rows
```

We then use the averages in column 0 of D to flood the arrays. For RepC the flood is direct because the two arrays are oriented properly. For RepR column 0 must first be transposed to be a row before flooding:

```
[1..m,*] RepC:=>>[1..m, 0] D;            --Replicate Ave Col
[*,1..m] RepR:=>>[*, 1..m] D#[Index2, 0];   --Repl Ave as a Row
```

Performing all of the comparisons is a simple matter:

```
[1..m, 1..m]  ... RepC>=RepR;        --Make an array of bits
```

Obviously, care must be taken to choose the right relational operator. In the row corresponding to the smallest item, the >= operator will set only one bit; in the row containing the maximum item, all of the bits will be set.

Find the Ranking. To find the ranking of the drinkers, we simply add the 1s in each row using a partial reduce. This will produce a column of results, but because we will be using the result in a remap, we don't want just a column; we want an array flooded with the rankings. So, we include the declaration

```
var Rank : [1..m, *] integer;
```

which makes the second dimension a flood dimension.

With the Rank variable declared operator, we can perform the partial reduce followed by the flood

```
[1..m, *] Rank:= >>[1..m,*](+<< [1..m,1..m](RepC >= RepR));
```

producing the desired result.

Figure 8.3
ZPL program for ranking coffee drinker data.

```
...
var RepC : [1..m, *] float;       -- Temp for replicated columns
var RepR : [*, 1..m] float;       -- Temp for replicated rows
var Rank : [1..m, *] integer;     -- Replicated ordering
...

procedure rankingData();
  begin
        [1..m, 0]  D     :=(+<<[1..m,1..n] D)/n;              -- Figure averages
        [1..m,*]   RepC  :=>>[1..m, 0] D;                    -- Replicate ave col
        [*,1..m]   RepR  :=>>[*, 1..m] D#[Index2, 0];        -- Replicate ave as row
        [1..m, *]  Ran   :=>>[1..m,*](+<<[1..m,1..m](RepC >= RepR));
                                                             -- Compute ordering
      [1..m, 0..n]  D#[Rank, Index2] := D;                   -- Reorder
  end;
```

Sort with the Rank Array. Now, using the values in Rank we can reorder the rows of D using the remap operator

```
[1..m, 0..n] D#[Rank, Index2]:=D;
```

which orders the rows by the value in the 0th column. The final program is shown in Figure 8.3.

This reordering operation seems complicated when considered for the first time, but it is a standard ZPL paradigm. It quickly becomes second nature, especially once the apparatus has been set up.

Parallel Execution of ZPL Programs

Having described the main features of ZPL, we are almost ready to present the language's unique performance model, but we first need to understand ZPL's parallel execution model. The parallelism in ZPL programs derives from its array language semantics in which the elements of arrays are manipulated simultaneously. Thus, arrays can be distributed across multiple processes and manipulated concurrently.

Role of the Compiler

The ZPL compiler converts array statements into loop nests. For example, the following statement

```
[R] TW:=(TW&NN=2)|(NN=3);
```

is translated into code equivalent to the following C code

```
for(i=myLo1-1; i<myHi1; i++)
{
  for(j=myLo2-1; j<myHi2; j++)
  {
    TW[i,j]=(TW[i,j]&&NN[i,j]==2)||(NN[i,j]== 3);
  }
}
```

where we assume that the loop bounds, myLo1, etc., have been properly initialized for each process. If there are uses of the @ operator, the compiler will insert the necessary communication before the loop nest. The reduce operators are translated to code similar to the generalized reduce code given in Chapter 5, and so forth.

To produce efficient code, the compiler performs numerous optimizations, including the following:

- It fuses—or combines—loop nests, which can greatly reduce memory requirements by converting array temporaries into scalar temporaries.

- It can combine communication operations for messages between the same pairs of processes.

- It can overlap communication and computation.

- It efficiently implements flood arrays. Because all elements of a flooded dimension are identical, only one value is needed per process.

- It efficiently implements Index Arrays. Because array indices are already represented by the compiler to iterate over loop nests, no extra memory is needed to represent Index Arrays.

Many other, more complex, optimizations are applied, as well as standard sequential optimizations.

The remainder of this section describes the details of ZPL's data distribution, which are critical to understanding ZPL's performance model.

Specifying the Number of Processes

Because the parallelism in a ZPL program is implicit, the amount of physical parallelism available is specified externally to the program. In particular, users specify a logical grid of processes—typically a 2D grid—when the program is invoked on the command line. For example, we might wish to specify that sixteen processes be arranged logically in two rows of eight, which we refer to as a 2×8 grid of processes.

Assigning Regions to Processes

In ZPL, the first step in assigning arrays to processes is to assign regions to processes. The regions of a program are distributed so that for all regions, the same index is assigned to the same process. To achieve this effect, think of all regions being superimposed so that their indices align, as shown in Figure 8.4. From this superimposition, their bounding region—the smallest region that includes all of the indices of the superimposed regions—is computed.

Once computed, the bounding region can be allocated to the specified process grid. The allocation is a block allocation using an assignment that is as balanced in each dimension as possible. The indices are allocated to processes indexed in the obvious way: low index to high index in row major order. Thus, the allocation of the bounding region in Figure 8.4 to a 2×2 grid of processes is shown in Figure 8.5. We can see that the decision to allocate regions so that all indices align can result in a slightly suboptimal allocation. The effect is generally small and arises only occasionally. As another example, the allocation in Figure 5.9(b) is achieved for a 16×16 region by specifying a 16×1 process grid.

Array Allocation

Given the distribution of regions to processes, the distribution of arrays is trivial, as arrays inherit the allocations of their declared regions. As with the C language, memory for the arrays is allocated in row-major order, and of course the compiler can allocate additional overlap regions where necessary.

For example, the arrays

```
var B, C, D : [1..8, 1..8] float;
```

allocated to a 2×2 process grid, would assign process p_0 the subregion [1..4,1..4], implying that those indices for arrays B, C, and D are also allocated to it; p_1 would be allocated the subregion [1..4, 5..8], and so on.

Figure 8.4
Bounding region. Regions used in the program are superimposed so that their indices align; the black square has the same index in all regions. Once aligned, the bounding region is the smallest region containing the indices of the superimposed regions.

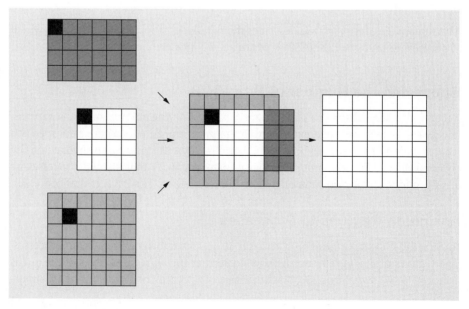

Figure 8.5
Block allocation of the bounding region. The bounding region (a) is partitioned using a balanced allocation (b), which assigns a set of indices (c). The contributing regions' indices are inherited from those indices (d).

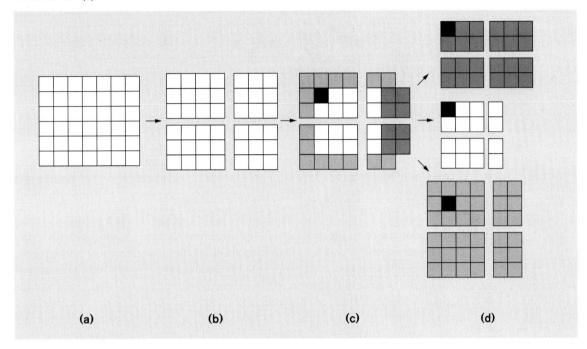

(a)   (b)   (c)   (d)

Scalar Allocation

Non-array variables are redundantly allocated so that each process has a copy of all scalars. Thus, scalar computation, such as

```
i:=i+1;
```

is redundantly computed by each process. This redundancy eliminates communication (recall the random number example of Chapter 2). On the other hand, scalar computation is not a source of improved performance through parallelism.

Work Assignment

With the arrays allocated, the work assignment is easily specified using the owner computes rule: Each process computes the values for the elements allocated to it. So the region that states the indices to be used in an array statement also defines the process that will perform the actual computation. For the statement

```
[1..8, 1..8]  B:=C+D;
```

process p_0 would perform the update to the subregion [1..4, 1..4] of B using the local elements of C and D. By implication, when the data is well balanced among the processes, the work for such statements will be well balanced. Thus, the work to update this array will be distributed among the four processes evenly enough that a speedup approaching four can be anticipated.

 Region Allocation Policy. The policy of aligning the regions so that index $[i, j, ..., k]$ of any region is assigned to the same process guarantees that when element-wise operations are performed on arrays, such as A+B, all of the computation is local to the process. There is no communication.

Performance Model

Given the previous description of how regions, arrays, and work are allocated to processes, it is easy to see how a program with only element-wise computations would perform in parallel: It exhibits essentially perfect speedup. But what about the other ZPL constructs? In fact, they are almost as easy to understand.

ZPL's performance model is based on the element-wise specification plus an overhead communication cost for those operations, such as @-references and remaps, that require values from other processes. The model rests on the idea that these two costs—basic work and communication overhead—constitute a good first approximation to the performance of any algorithm on any CTA platform. The model is easy to use because programmers can syntactically identify the places in their code where communication costs are incurred. Code Spec 8.7 shows a brief summary of these costs.

Code Spec 8.7 ZPL performance model.

ZPL's performance model specifications for worst-case behavior; the actual performance is influenced by n, P, process arrangement, and compiler optimizations, in addition to the physical features of the computer.

Syntactic Cue	Example	Parallelism (P)	Communication Cost	Remarks
[R] *array ops*	[R] ... A+B ...	full; work/P	—	
@ *array transl.*	... A@east ...	—	1 point-to-point	xmit "surface" only
<< *reduction*	... +<<A ...	work/P + log P	2log P point-to-point	fan-in/out trees
<< *partial red*	... +<<[ ] A ...	work/P + log P	log P point-to-point	
|| *scan*	... +|| ...	work/P + log P	2log P point-to-point	parallel prefix trees
>> *flood*	... >>[ ] A...	—	multicast in dimension	data not replicated
# *remap*	... A# [I1,I2] ...	—	2 all-to-all, potentially	general data reorg.

To amplify further on the cost model, consider the following operations:

- **@-translations:** The @-modifier on operands implies the transmission of data from adjacent processes to local overlap regions. Only edge elements are transferred, so by the CTA model, these point-to-point communication operations will in general require a communication delay of λ for the entire edge.

- **<< reduces:** The reduce operators use the Schwartz algorithm to combine the array values into a scalar, followed by a broadcast to distribute the scalar value back to all processes. Thus, the communication pattern is a combining tree followed by a broadcast tree, each of which is at most $\log P$ height, resulting in $2\lambda \log P$ communication cost.

- **<< partial reduces:** The partial reduces follow the combining concepts of full reduces but without the broadcast and restricted to a dimension.

- **|| scan:** Scan operators use the parallel prefix operation and therefore have two traversals of a $\log P$ height tree, one up and one down, resulting in a $2\lambda \log P$ communication expense.

- **>> flood:** The flood operator distributes stored values to other processes; a multicast—a broadcast to a subset of the processes—can be used if available. (Special hardware is generally fast, but even without it broadcast can be performed with a tree, resulting in $\log P$ concurrent transmissions.) The primary feature of the flood operator that bounds its communication complexity is that if processes are assigned to more than one dimension, only a small subset of the processes will be recipients of any flood.

- **# remap:** The remap operator is ZPL's most expensive because it entails two communication cycles: one to distribute the pattern of communication (the remap arrays) and one to distribute the data itself. Potentially, these are both all-to-all communications, meaning that each process might have to communicate with every other process. ZPL attempts to optimize remap to reduce its expense: Examples include the use of constant arguments that occur, say, in transpose (`A#[Index2, Index1]`) or the reuse of remap arrays that have not changed since the last remap.

Using this information, it is possible to know roughly how a statement will perform.

Applying the Performance Model: Life

When we wrote the Life program we focused on producing the proper computation, but we could also know in approximate terms how the program would perform. Recall that the main computation was

```
20  [R] repeat
21         NN:= TW@nw+TW@no+TW@ne+
22              TW@we+        TW@ea+
23              TW@sw+TW@so+TW@se;
24         TW:=(TW&NN=2)|(NN=3);
25      until !(|<<TW);
```

The loop contains essentially three computations: the calculation of NN, the calculation of TW, and the reduce for the loop-termination test. We analyze each as follows:

- **Calculating NN:** This statement involves eight @-translations followed by local computation. According to Code Spec 8.7, each @-translation requires a λ delay, because a CTA computer can be expected to perform many such point-to-point communications at once. So we charge constant communication plus local computation.

- **Calculating TW:** This statement requires only local computation on the array elements; there is no communication charge.

- **Or Reduce:** The loop termination expression requires the $2\lambda \log P$ time for the Schwartz algorithm.

Furthermore, the default block allocation will result in reasonably balanced work, implying a factor of P speedup on the computation. So asymptotically, as n increases, the problem continues to enjoy full speedup with $O(\log P)$ communication overhead per iteration; if P grows, the increase in communication overhead remains modest.

Applying the Performance Model: SUMMA

The matrix multiplication algorithm of Figure 8.2 has as its main computation the following statement:

```
[1..m, 1..p] begin
        C:=0;
        for k:=1 to n do
          C+=(>>[1..m, k] A )*(>>[k, 1..p] B);
        end;
      end;
```

Ignoring the one-time initialization of array C, which is perfectly parallel, the loop has for each of the n iterations two flood operations and then multiply-add computations on the local elements. Again, the default block operation will result in a reasonably balanced allocation, so the multiply-add computations will be fully parallel. If we arrange the P processes into a $\sqrt{P} \times \sqrt{P}$ grid, then each multicast tree implementing a flood will have height $\log P/2$. Thus, the communication overhead for the two iterations can be estimated to be $O(\log P)$ per iteration, making it an efficient parallel matrix product solution.[1]

Summary of the Performance Model

We have described estimates of the worst-case time complexity of a computation based on how the model describes ZPL's execution on a CTA computer. As program-

---

[1] This type of analysis can be used to compare algorithms. The original paper announcing the computation model compared SUMMA with Canon's algorithm and found SUMMA to be better, a prediction that was confirmed by experimentation.

mers, we can depend on it as a reliable machine-independent bound. Though certain ZPL compiler optimizations can lead to better performance, the model guarantees that the program will realize at least this level of performance. For example, the compiler can move communication calls, allowing it to overlap communication with computation. If successful, the communication overhead might be entirely invisible; but if unsuccessful, the performance is still what the model predicts.

It would seem that any language could define a performance model by simply providing performance bounds for every operation. But recall the difficulty presented by the transpose code that uses direct array indexing: a minor syntactic change can lead to a significant difference in communication costs. Thus, for languages that support direct array indexing, every array assignment would have its communication costs bounded by the cost of a transpose, producing extremely imprecise bounds. Communication costs are even more difficult to predict when programmers are allowed to distribute different arrays in different ways. So we can see that a central aspect of ZPL's performance model is the set of restrictions that the language imposes on the programmer. Thus, if a language is to have a meaningful parallel performance model, the model must be designed into the language from the start.

NESL Parallel Language

The Nested Parallel Language (NESL) is a high-level data parallel language implemented in the mid 1990s at Carnegie Mellon by a team headed by Guy Blelloch. NESL, which is loosely based on the language ML, uses a functional approach that is quite intuitive. Our interest in NESL is two-fold: First, NESL is another high-level global view language built expressly for data parallel computing. Second, NESL has a complexity model that allows programmers to assess the behavior of their programs.

Language Concepts

The basic data type in NESL is a sequence, written in square brackets,

```
[6, 14, 0 -5]
```

which is 0-origin indexed. Sequences can be characters,

```
"NESL allows sequences of characters"
```

written in shorthand inside double quotes. And sequences can contain subsequences

```
["a" "sequence" "can be made of" "sequences"]
```

provided all elements are of the same atomic type.

The basic operation of NESL is the parallel *apply-to-each* operation expressed in set braces. For example,

```
{a+1 : a in [6, 14, 0, -5]};
```

applies the increment operation a+1 to each element in the sequence in parallel, which produces [7, 15, 1, -4]. Apply-to-each can take multiple same-length sequences

```
{a+b : a in [6, 14, 0, -5]; b in [4, -4, 10, 15]}
```

which produces [10, 10, 10, 10]. There is a substantial set of primitive operators, and functions can also be defined. The following code illustrates function definition, function application and +-reduce:

```
function dotprod(a, b) =
  sum({x*y : x in a; y in b});
dotprod([2, 3, 1], [6, 1, 4]);
```

Matrix Product Using Nested Parallelism

Nested parallelism is defined to be the ability to apply in parallel a function to each element of a collection of data, along with the ability to nest such parallel calls. The concept is illustrated in a simple form by the matrix multiplication function shown in Figure 8.6.

To understand how the NESL code works, observe that an $m \times n$ matrix would be represented as a sequence of m row sequences, each consisting of n items, so that the first sequence is the top row, and so on. A transpose of such a matrix reorders the items in the obvious way: The first row sequence contributes the first item in each of n new row sequences of the output, and so on.

Looking at the code in Figure 8.6, we notice that there are three nested apply-to-each braces: The outer apply-to-each is applied over the rows of the input array A, that is, each row is processed independently. The next apply-to-each is applied over the columns, converted into sequence items by transposing the input array B; so for each row of A each of the columns of B will be paired and processed in parallel. The result of these two apply-to-each operations is to create n^2 parallel tasks, one corresponding to each element in the result matrix. Finally, the innermost apply-to-each performs the dot-product computation on corresponding items in the argument sequences in parallel. Thus, there is n^3 parallelism in this nested use of the apply-to-each construct.

Figure 8.6
A NESL matrix multiplication function.

```
function matrix_multiply(A,B)=
  {{sum({x*y : x in rowA; y in columnB})
    : columnB in transpose(B)}
    : rowA in A}
```

This solution can be considered to be a parallelization of the triple-nested loop shown previously, rather than, say, the SUMMA approach.

NESL Complexity Model

NESL uses two measures to determine an expression's complexity: work and depth. *Work* is simply the number of basic operations, so our matrix multiplication computation embodies $O(n^3)$ work. Depth is the longest chain of dependences in the computation; the apply-to-each has a depth of 1, because the operations can all be performed in parallel. A sum, which is implemented as a binary tree, has a depth of $O(\log_2 n)$, because the levels must be performed in leaves-to-root order, which introduces a logarithmic-length chain of dependences.

As a functional language, NESL exposes substantial concurrency and provides programming convenience by abstracting away the notion of memory locations and memory references. The complexity model captures the best-case work and minimum delay. At the same time, the functional abstraction prevents the NESL complexity model from describing machine-level details such as locality and data motion, so the model does not allow the programmer to reason about *parallel* program performance.

Chapter Summary

We have introduced the high-level array programming language ZPL. There is more to ZPL than presented here—we have presented only the so called ZPL Classic—and greater control is available for more complex computations. ZPL's implicit parallelism frees the programmer from dealing with many low-level details pertaining to communication, synchronization, and data distribution. At the same time, its features have been carefully designed to support an accurate parallel performance model that is applicable to any parallel computer that embodies the CTA. Thus, ZPL is significant because it shows how powerful high-level abstractions can be used to create efficient and portable parallel programs.

NESL is an even higher-level language that exploits the functional programming style to express parallelism. It also has a clean and simple syntax that allows programmers to specify parallelism without introducing dependences.

Historical Perspective

The ZPL language was developed at the University of Washington by the authors and a stellar team of colleagues; it was the first high-level language to achieve high performance across all (MIMD) parallel platforms, that is, to achieve performance portability. One of its primary contributions was the WYSIWYG performance model [Chamberlain 1998]. Other citations can be found at the ZPL Web site. NESL [Blelloch 1996] has been the basis for a large number of elegant algorithms; the NESL Web site provides examples and a brief tutorial.

Exercises

1. Using a 3×3 data array, manually compute example values for the ZPL computations in the section on Data Manipulation.

2. Revise the row rank ordering of the coffee data to handle duplicates.

3. Using the ZPL program for Conway's Game of Life as a specification, write an MPI program to implement the Game of Life, assuming a 2-dimensional array decomposition.

4. Write a ZPL program to implement the Red/Blue computation specified in Exercise 10 of Chapter 4.

5. Using ZPL's performance model, analyze the performance of the Red/Blue computation of Exercise 4. Notice that the solution may share many features with the analysis of Conway's Game of Life.

6. Reasoning by analogy to the SUMMA algorithm, apply the flood operation to solve the all-pairs shortest path problem. The n-vertex graph input will be represented as an $n \times n$ adjacency matrix, with "infinity" values in those positions not directly connected.

7. Use ZPL's performance model to analyze the performance of the all-pairs shortest path computation of Exercise 6.

8. Use the flood operator to produce a 3D matrix multiplication in ZPL; flood the A and B matrices to be cubes of replicated values, perform all of the pairwise multiplications, and reduce one dimension to produce the result to be assigned to the C matrix. Notice that the remap operator will be needed to reorient the arrays from their input orientation.

9. Apply the ZPL performance model to analyze the program from Exercise 8. In considering the performance, use a 3D process grid.

10. Following Exercise 9, analyze the performance of the solution when a 2D process grid is used so that arrays are allocated in their "normal" orientation.

11. Write a NESL program to implement the Red/Blue computation, described in Exercise 10 of Chapter 4.

12. Explain the issues that arise when trying to implement the SUMMA algorithm in NESL.

Assessing the
State of the Art

As we mentioned in Chapter 1, the parallel computing community does not yet have all of the answers when it comes to parallel programming. As a result, this book initially concentrated on fundamental principles before exploring specific programming approaches. In this chapter, we take a broad view of the state of the art in parallel programming. We first evaluate existing approaches and then collect lessons from these languages as we look to the future.

Four Important Properties of Parallel Languages

Before evaluating different programming approaches, we identify four important properties that will frame our discussion:

- Correctness
- Performance
- Scalability
- Portability

This list is not exhaustive. There are other qualities that are desirable, but these four address the most critical needs for parallel programmers.

Correctness

Though it is nontrivial to write correct programs of any type, the problem is exacerbated for parallel programs, which are often sensitive to timing features of the program execution. Sequential programs are generally reproducible, so two executions with the same input produce the same output; but parallel programs can vary wildly in their behavior depending on timing variations. So the first question to ask about any parallel programming system is whether this sensitivity can be removed? If so, then the correctness aspect of parallel programming might be simplified to approximate that of sequential programming.

P-Independence. Such considerations have motivated the concept of P-independence.

> **Definition**
>
> **P-independence:** A parallel program is P-independent if and only if it always produces the same output on the same input regardless of the number or arrangement of processes on which it is run; otherwise a program is P-dependent.

P-independence does not address the imprecision of floating point arithmetic; different runs of a P-independent program can produce floating point answers that differ in some bit positions. Rather, P-independence speaks to control-flow reproducibility in the presence of varying amounts of parallelism.

A parallel "Hello, World" program is trivially P-independent if it prints the salutation only once. At the other end of the spectrum, a parallel program that outputs the number of processes on which it is executing is trivially P-dependent.

The notion of P-independence is significant because we believe that programmers generally intend to write P-independent programs; but when a language's abstractions are P-dependent, the burden is on the programmer to neutralize the sensitivity to the number of processes. Thus, P-dependence complicates the construction of parallel programs.

Global View and Local View Abstractions. The notion of P-independence can be translated to languages by classifying programming abstractions into two groups:

- **Global view abstractions:** A language construct that preserves P-independent program behavior presents a global view abstraction
- **Local view abstractions:** A language construct that does not preserve P-independent program behavior presents a local view abstraction

Accordingly, languages that use global view abstractions are known as *global view languages,* and those that use local view abstractions are known as *local view languages.* Global view languages are easier to debug because they can be debugged based on a sequential execution instead of any particular instance of a parallel execution.

Examples. Consider a few programming abstractions from earlier chapters.

- **Locks:** Two threads that use locks can potentially lead to deadlock (see Chapter 6), but the same program executed with one thread generally will not result in deadlock, so locks are a local view abstraction.

- **Send/Receive:** A program that uses a blocking receive operation can execute correctly on multiple processes but will deadlock when executed on a single process, so receive operations are a local view abstraction.

- **`forall` loops:** A parallel loop, such as those used in OpenMP, provides the same result regardless of the number of threads that are used to execute the loop, so `forall` loops are a global view abstraction.

- **Barrier:** A barrier synchronizes the execution of all threads or processes. While the latency of executing the barrier depends on the number of participating threads or processes, the operation produces no side effects that depend on the number of threads or processes, so a barrier is a global view abstraction.

- **Reduce and Scan:** The semantics of reduce and scan are defined on the elements of an array, independent of the number of threads or processes on which that array resides, so reduce and scan operations are global view abstractions. However, if user-defined reduces and scans have side effects, then such operations are local view abstractions because the side effects can depend on the number of processes that participate in the operation.

Examples. Consider the following languages.

- **ZPL Classic:** The core of the ZPL language, which is the portion presented in Chapter 8 and which is known as ZPL Classic, is a global view language.

- **NESL:** NESL is a global view language.

- **Message Passing Libraries:** Obviously, message passing is a *local view language*, as is Co-Array Fortran and most other parallel programming facilities.

Performance

How much performance is enough? Although we have implied throughout this book that P-fold parallelism is the goal, the answer depends on the context. For example, on a 2-processor multi-core system, there are different situations where programmers might be content with speedups of 1.2, 1.9, or 2.1:

- A modest speedup of 1.2 may be satisfactory in cases when the application in question has little inherent parallelism, and the goal was to exploit an otherwise idle processor. The net result is a non-negligible 20% performance improvement, which is not so easy to achieve by other means.

- A speedup closer to 2 is reasonable when a programmer has carefully structured the program to eliminate most parallel overheads and to exploit available concurrency.

- Superlinear speedup is possible when the computation exhibits good locality of reference. Because the two cores collectively have more L1 cache than either does alone, the system can accommodate a larger working set.

However, it is typically more difficult to obtain superlinear speedup on a multi-core chip than on other multi-processor systems because the two cores share some memory resources (the L2 cache in the case of the Core Duo and memory bandwidth for all multi-core chips).

The point is that in evaluating performance, we need to understand the situation and have reasonable performance expectations.

Scalability

Performance is not only application-dependent, but it is also hardware-dependent. In particular, as we increase the number of processors, it is typically harder to sustain the same level of speedup. Thus, in many cases scalable parallelism might appear to be an unnecessary goal, particularly when the short-term objective is to run on a specific hardware platform, such as a multi-core chip that has a fixed number of processors.

But the number of cores per multi-core chip is likely to grow quickly over time, roughly doubling every 18 months if Moore's Law continues to be tracked by vendors. Accordingly, any long-lived software—that is, any successful software—should be scalable to stay on this performance curve. Once a scalable program is written, it can track the hardware advances without significant programmer intervention, just as sequential software did in the years when clock speed was increasing rapidly.

Portability

In addition to scalability, portability is important for long-lived software because parallel hardware has always exhibited considerable diversity. Of particular importance is the notion of *performance portability*, which is the ability of a program to obtain good performance, perhaps with some modest amount of tuning, on a wide range of parallel computers.

Performance portability is achieved by designing algorithms predicated on a realistic abstract machine model, which was why the CTA was introduced. The abstract model limits assumptions to universal concepts and suggests costs that are realistically achievable on machines that scale. By programming to a realistic abstract machine model, programmers can move their code to different architectures with the expectation that the program's core properties will be compatible with the new hardware; tuning may be needed, but the algorithms do not need to be completely rethought.

By contrast, programmers who program directly to some specific target hardware may be forced to make algorithmic changes when retargeting to a different platform, as the code may depend on features that are no longer available or may exploit idiosyncratic performance characteristics of the original hardware. Programmers must assume *some* platform as they develop algorithms, so it might as well be a realistic abstract model.

The use of a portable substrate—say MPI—is by itself insufficient to ensure performance portability; if the portable substrate provides low-level constructs, they are likely to have different performance characteristics on different hardware.

Evaluating Existing Approaches

We are now ready to evaluate the programming approaches that we have discussed in Chapters 6 through 8.

POSIX Threads

Pthreads and other lock-based approaches provide great power and flexibility, but there's a sense in which these approaches, which are clearly *P*-dependent, provide too much flexibility. This flexibility has implications for both correctness and performance.

Part of the problem is the broad interface across which threads can interact. Because of the shared address space, any statement can potentially interact with any other statement. In particular, any memory reference can potentially induce a dependence with any other thread. For example, when debugging a race condition in a Pthreads program, the problem could involve any statement in the program. By contrast, when debugging a race condition in an MPI program, the problem can only involve MPI routines, which are the only way for processes to interact. (Of course, MPI presents its own difficulties, as we will discuss shortly.)

The broad interface also affects performance. We've argued that it is important to recognize cross-thread dependences to reason about parallel performance, but because cross-thread dependences look no different from other reads and writes to memory, the shared address space does nothing to encourage locality.

The specifics of locks and condition variables are also problematic. Their use forces programmers to reason about all possible interactions and interleavings because these constructs are based on the timing of state changes. More specifically, these constructs defeat the goals of modularity and abstraction in two ways: (1) Lock-based code is not composable, and (2) locking is a global property with respect to both performance and correctness. Two pieces of code that each operate correctly in isolation might exhibit problems when used in combination. For example, if the two codes do not protect shared data with locks, a race condition can occur; if they each acquire the same set of locks in different order, deadlock can occur; and if they happen to access variables that reside on the same cache line, false sharing can occur. For performance reasons, it is also important to reason about locks globally, because the granularity of locking can affect parallelism and performance. For example, a data structure that provides mutually exclusive access might be appropriate in one situation, but when the data structure is composed with other structures, we might want a coarser granularity of locking.

Not only is it impossible to hide the details of locking behavior inside of a module, but it is also difficult to summarize the locking requirements in an interface. It is not enough to know what locks are used. To avoid deadlock, we need to know the order in which these locks are acquired. To optimize performance, we need to know where the locks are being used. In short, locks and condition variables are at odds with modularity.

One argument for a shared address space approach is that its similarity to sequential programming allows for an incremental migration of sequential programs to parallel platforms. The more cynical view is that such a model encourages programmers to create inefficient parallel programs—ones that are too similar to sequential programs—which then require considerable effort to transform into efficient parallel programs. Given our view that parallel programming is significantly different from sequential programming, we do not favor the "slow migration" approach.

Java Threads

Java Threads provides multiple levels at which to program. One level is very similar to POSIX Threads, so it has most of the same advantages and disadvantages as POSIX Threads. The higher-level interfaces create synchronized objects and methods, along with concurrent data structures, which hide much of the complexity of the lower-level interface. The higher-level interfaces present a number of performance problems because they limit the programmer's ability to control the granularity of parallelism and to perform optimizations that hide latency. Although there are cases where these issues do not matter, better control is generally needed to achieve the performance and scalability goals discussed.

OpenMP

OpenMP is a global view language that constrains the programmer to the simplest forms of parallelism, so it is extremely easy to use. But there are many forms of parallelism that are not expressible in OpenMP. In terms of our Peril-L language, OpenMP only provides the ability to use `forall` statements, barriers, and reduce. It disallows such forms of concurrency as fine-grained synchronized operations.

MPI

MPI only allows processes to interact with one another through MPI calls, so MPI provides a thinner interface than Pthreads, and thinner interfaces are generally easier to reason about than fatter interfaces. However, with MPI the programmer must specify so many low level details that the specification is onerous and error prone. In particular, because the programmer must specify each communication operation redundantly at each participating process, there are many opportunities for errors.

MPI's point-to-point communication routines are P-dependent, but MPI does provide communication abstractions in the form of collective communication operations, including reduce, scan, and user-defined reduces and scans. These collective operations are heavily used in MPI programs, perhaps because they are one of the few ways that programmers can view the computation more globally.

As a distributed memory programming model, MPI forces programmers to think about multiple disjoint address spaces simultaneously. Thus, programmers sometimes reason about a local block of computation executing on one process, but other times they need to make a mental translation that relates this block of computation to those on other processes. By contrast, Pthreads, OpenMP, and ZPL provide a single address space, which requires fewer mental translations by the programmer.

From a performance perspective, the large software overhead of message passing encourages course-grain parallelism, which frequently has significant performance advantages. From an algorithmic point of view, MPI is best suited toward solutions with a static number of processes, contrasting with POSIX Threads, which allow threads to be created dynamically.

Finally, while MPI programs are portable in the sense that they can be compiled and run on almost any parallel computer, MPI programs do not necessarily achieve performance portability because the interface is so low-level that it implicitly exposes assumptions about the underlying hardware. In particular, optimizations that favor specific point-to-point communication modes for one parallel computer are often not optimal for other parallel computers. Of course, just as Java threads provides simpler interfaces above Pthreads, other higher-level languages can be built on top of MPI, so we can view MPI as a communication substrate for higher level languages. With this view, the question becomes, what is the right language to build on top of MPI?

PGAS Languages

The PGAS languages improve upon MPI by providing a higher-level mechanism for specifying communication that can be efficiently implemented on distributed memory parallel computers. The key advancement of these languages is the view presented to the programmers, who are allowed to think beyond the confines of an individual process because the global address space overlaid on the separate memories supports the definition of global data structures.

The three languages have also introduced a series of clever ideas to simplify programming. To pick one from each language: The co-array of CAF is an elegant mechanism to refer to non-local memory; it fits into the language cleanly and needs few added concepts. UPC's `upc-forall` statement distributes iterations according to a programmer-specified affinity, giving the programmer some control over a compiler-generated global operation. And Titanium's unordered `foreach` iterator is a significant simplification for both programmers and the compiler when multi-dimensional arrays are involved.

Despite their global address space, the primary problem with PGAS languages is that they all strongly retain the local view of the computation. Programmers still focus on writing a local program that is then replicated across all processes, and programmers must still manage the computation as a piece of the larger solution. For example, the responsibility for handling all of the "edge cases" falls to the programmer. The consequence of such localized computation is that many low-level details remain. The mechanics of message-passing are gone, but the obligations and burdens of a local perspective remain.

ZPL

ZPL simplifies programming by raising the level of abstraction to provide a global view of the program. Classic ZPL is a global view language.[1] ZPL provides a rich set of higher-level parallel abstractions, including array language semantics, regions, flooding, reduces, and scans. These constructs hide the low level details of communication and synchronization, and as a result of these abstractions, ZPL programs are quite succinct.

ZPL encourages programmers to think in a parallel style through the use of array operations; its new abstractions like flooding have promoted new programming techniques such as Problem Space Promotion (see Chapter 10). Although ZPL presents a high level of abstraction, it provides performance portability by building on a realistic machine model (CTA). From that machine model, a performance model was developed to describe the execution cost of the ZPL operations, allowing programmers to reason about performance in a machine-independent fashion. ZPL also encourages the creation of scalable programs through its scalable parallel abstractions.

Among ZPL's serious shortcomings are its unfamiliar concepts (regions, flooding, remap, array programming, and so on), its lack of pointer-based data structures, and its limited dynamic memory allocation facilities. It also does not support modern programming methodologies, such as, object-oriented programming.

NESL

As with other functional languages, NESL's referential transparency makes programs more mathematical and easier to reason about. Its global view abstractions effectively hide parallelism. However, like other functional languages that abstract away memory references, NESL programs are difficult to analyze with respect to data motion and locality, key features for achieving good parallel performance. In a similar vein, NESL encourages the Unlimited Parallelism approach to algorithm design. For example, it leads naturally to the triply nested loop implementation of matrix multiplication, which admits the maximum potential parallelism. By con-

---

[1]Some of the more sophisticated language constructs, not described in this book, can produce results that are not *P*-independent.

trast, the SUMMA algorithm, which is a superior practical parallel algorithm, is more difficult to specify in NESL.

Lessons for the Future

Because the ideal parallel programming facility has not yet been created, we consider features that future systems should have, based on our lessons from the past.

Hidden Parallelism

Chapters 6 through 8 clearly show that parallel programming is difficult. Readers probably asked, "Is it necessary to program like this in order to enjoy the benefits of parallelism?" The answer is both "yes" and "no."

Parallelism has long been successful because it has been underground and hidden from programmers. The prime example is the parallelism exploited by the micro-architecture of contemporary processors. Consider the following features that deliver hidden parallelism, listed roughly in chronological order:

- Bit-parallel functional units
- Multiple functional units
- Pipelined execution
- Out of order execution
- Increasingly wide data-paths
- DMA controllers
- Prefetch units
- Trace caches
- Simultaneous multi-threading
- *Vector processors*
- *Chip multi-processors*
- *Co-processors: I/O controllers, network controllers, graphics co-processors*

The italicized items in the list expose parallelism to the software. All others are largely hidden from the programmer. We say "largely" because there are times when programmers or compilers wish to reason about the effects of caches, prefetching, or some other aspect of hardware parallelism, and there are cases where some of these features are exposed to the software, for example, through a prefetch instruction or performance anomaly.

We see that over time the trend has been toward ever-larger units of parallelism, to the point that we are no longer able to hide parallelism within the hardware, which explains why it is now exposed to the software in the form of multi-core chips.

Of course, there are different ways to hide parallelism. For example, we have seen how ZPL provides sequential semantics while encouraging programmers to think in terms of regions, which implicitly express parallelism. Another example is the Cilk language, which extends the C language with a set of explicitly parallel constructs for spawning parallelism. Cilk retains sequential semantics using a definition called *serial elision*. In particular, the semantics of a Cilk program are the same as those of the sequential C program that results from removing all Cilk constructs.

Hidden parallelism is important because it hides complexity, which is a powerful tool in system design. The trick, of course, is to hide complexity without obscuring performance costs.

Transparent Performance

It is important to allow programmers to reason accurately about performance as they develop their algorithms and programs. We have seen that languages of any level can hinder this ability to reason about performance, as illustrated by Pthreads and NESL. Likewise, the ability to reason about performance can be supported by either low level or high level approaches, as demonstrated by MPI, Co-Array Fortran, and ZPL.

Locality

We have argued that global view abstractions are desirable, but it is also important that our programming abstractions encourage locality and minimize data movement. MPI encourages locality by making communication explicit and difficult. To differing degrees, the PGAS languages and ZPL encourage locality without introducing as much programming difficulty. As we look to the future, it is important that we develop languages that encourage locality while still providing convenience.

Constrained Parallelism

Language designers are often tempted to provide powerful constructs that offer programming convenience. However, in a parallel language, too much power, or too much programmer flexibility, can be detrimental:

- Flexibility can have correctness implications because it can allow interactions that are difficult to reason about. For example, it is convenient to allow threads to reference and modify any memory location at any time, but this convenience makes it difficult to limit unwanted interactions.
- Flexibility can have performance implications because it can obscure the performance model. For example, locks introduce the possibility of resource contention, which can be difficult to reason about without understanding the costs of various machine-specific operations, such as memory latencies, instruction latencies, and the number of competing threads.
- Flexibility may exist to expose maximal parallelism, but maximal parallelism is not the goal. The goal is to make effective use of the available parallelism, which often implies the need to exploit locality, to limit the interdependence of threads, and to reason about data movement and synchronization.

Thus, the important property of a parallel language may not be what it allows but what it disallows. For example, in comparing POSIX Threads against higher-level approaches, such as OpenMP and ZPL, we see that Pthreads allows threads to interact with great freedom, which forces the programmer to specify what interactions should *not* occur. By contrast, OpenMP and ZPL constrain the available parallelism from the beginning, which is much less dangerous from a correctness point of view and which makes behavior more predictable from a performance point of view. The key, of course, is to find the right balance between freedom and restraint, and the answer is likely to differ depending on the problem domain.

Implicit versus Explicit Parallelism

Given our desire to use constrained parallelism to offer programming convenience, to make performance transparent, and to encourage locality, we might ask the question: What is the right level at which to expose parallelism? Should we expose parallelism through libraries, in languages, or in the hardware interface (ISA)? Based on the idea that parallelism belongs underground, the right level is as low as possible without impacting our ability to reason about performance and to achieve good performance.

Different problem domains have different requirements. Until recently, general-purpose microprocessors have been able to hide parallelism from the software, but even the early graphics processors found it important to expose parallelism. Today's GPUs have managed to expose parallelism in a very benign way: programmers typically write customized shading routines that are sequential code fragments; the parallelism is managed by code that is written by the hardware vendors. Other problem domains, such as digital signal processing, are sufficiently restrictive that successful domain-specific languages have emerged that can be effectively compiled to produce extremely efficient code.

The tension between generality and convenience is a challenging one. General solutions tend to provide general mechanisms, while domain-specific solutions manage to hide parallelism through higher-level abstractions. The tension can be viewed as a trade-off between explicit parallelism and implicit parallelism, the former being more general and the latter being more convenient. If abstractions that deliver implicit parallelism could be related to lower-level, more explicit parallelism forms, then programmers could strike the balance, choosing a level that matched their programming efforts with the performance needed.

The goal then is to provide programming systems that coherently support a range of levels of abstraction :

- At the higher levels, abstractions provide convenience without full generality, that is, constrained parallelism.
- At the lower levels, there are more general features.

The keys to such systems would be (1) to provide convenient ways for experts to create appropriate abstractions, particularly domain-specific ones, (2) to provide mechanisms by which programs specified at the different levels of abstraction can conveniently interact, and (3) to provide optimization tools that can leverage the assumptions of the higher-level abstractions.

Chapter Summary

In this chapter we have critiqued the programming approaches of Chapters 6 through 8. Our goal was not to pick winners and losers but rather to make explicit the characteristics that readers will already have noticed about each approach. Every programming facility presented has advantages and disadvantages, and they all have a loyal following of programmers who will argue enthusiastically for the approach. We concluded this chapter by summarizing some of the lessons of this book to suggest a few important desirable properties that future languages should have.

Given the current state of the art, we can be sure that the future holds new languages and new programming abstractions that will simplify the parallel programmer's task. Chapter 10 looks briefly at some promising new ideas.

Historical Perspective

Deitz [2004] introduced P-independence, though the idea without the name has long been claimed as an advantage of functional parallel languages. Cilk was developed at MIT by a group headed by Leiserson [1995].

Exercises

1. Using the concept of user-defined reduce from Chapter 5, write a P-dependent parallel reduce that has the property that it computes the number of processors that participated in the computation.

2. Find a description of a parallel programming language in the literature and determine if it is P-independent.

3. Find five parallel programming abstractions described in this book but not analyzed in this chapter, and decide whether they are global view abstractions or local view abstractions; include at least one from each group.

4. Return to the Count 3s computation in Chapter 1, and review the reasons why it did not achieve 8-fold parallelism. Under what circumstances could the program achieve greater speedup?

Looking Forward

Having learned the general principles of parallel computation and having learned specific details of various languages, we now look to the future, both as a community and individually. The rapidly developing field presents us with many new opportunities.

As parallel programmers, we are keenly interested in new research that can simplify our program development efforts. Abstractions like Transactional Memory and new parallel programming languages fall into this category and are the topic of Chapter 10. We are also interested in hardware systems that present significant opportunities for applying parallelism, and we consider some of the popular ones, such as attached processors for personal computation, and enormous systems, typified by the Grid. Finally, we conclude Chapter 10 by exploring emerging computing paradigms, such as MapReduce, and three emerging programming languages whose goal is to boost programmer productivity.

Moving from the general to the personal, we present guidelines for writing, debugging, and measuring parallel programs. Chapter 11 is the final chapter, but we recommend that students read it early in their study of parallel computation. The guidelines—designed with a capstone project in mind—nevertheless apply to even the simple programs found in the exercises at the end of the chapters.

10 Future Directions in Parallel Programming

The great Neils Bohr once said "Prediction is very difficult, especially about the future." This is particularly true in parallel computation because it is common for researchers and vendors to tout "silver bullet" solutions, which ultimately do not succeed. In this chapter we consider a small selection of ideas that are being developed. Because, as Bohr said, it is difficult to predict the future, we make no claim that these are the most promising topics. However, they have received a lot of "buzz," so readers will want to be familiar with them.

Attached Processors

While general purpose microprocessors have become increasingly sophisticated and power hungry, there has long been a realization that pouring so much effort into general purpose microprocessors can be inefficient. Instead, special purpose processors can be much more power and space efficient, so it makes sense to offload as much work as possible to special purpose *attached processors*. The use of attached processors is not new, as early microprocessors offloaded work to floating point co-processors. The modern term "attached processor" hints at the asymmetric nature of the two processors, indicating that the attached processor is performing work on behalf of the host processor (see Figure 10.1).

Like floating point co-processors, today's attached processors can be thought of as specialized engines for solving computationally intensive tasks. The fact that the

Figure 10.1
Attached processors.

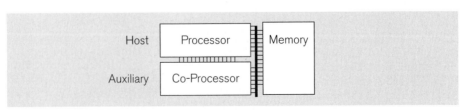

host processor runs concurrently with the attached processor is typically not a significant source of parallelism. Instead, there is generally significant parallelism embedded in the attached processor.

While other instances of this structure have been proposed—including Field Programmable Gate Arrays (FPGAs) attached to a general purpose processor—this section focuses on two architectures:

- Graphics Processing Units attached to a standard processor
- The Cell Processor with eight attached processors and an embedded Power PC host

Graphics Processing Units

The idea of performing general purpose computing on graphical processing units (GPGPU) has gained recent popularity because of the tremendous performance and price/performance of GPUs. For example, in comparing the nVidia GeForce 8800 and the Intel Core2 Duo, we see that the GPU has roughly ten times the floating point CPU power (367 GFLOPS versus 32 GFLOPS) and roughly ten times the memory bandwidth (86.48 GB/s versus 8.4 GB/s). Moreover, improvements in GPU performance have been increasing at a faster rate than improvements in general purpose microprocessors, roughly doubling performance every six months, which is significantly faster than improvements to general purpose processors, as shown in Figure 10.2. As GPUs become increasingly programmable, it is prudent to understand their strengths, weaknesses, and prospects for general purpose computing.

There are several reasons why GPUs offer such good performance. Economically, the performance of GPUs is driven by the large video game industry. Technically, a GPU is specialized for graphics rendering, a compute-intensive application with large amounts of data parallelism. As such, GPUs can fairly easily improve floating point performance by adding more processing cores. Furthermore, GPUs can largely ignore many issues that general purpose processors must deal with, including the need to keep pipelines full for sequential codes. Thus, GPUs avoid spending transistors on matters such as branch prediction, caching, and instruction scheduling.

GPUs implement hardware support for the *graphics pipeline*, which takes as input a list of vertices that define geometry and emits as output an image in a framebuffer. As its name suggests, there are several intermediate stages in this pipeline, all performing graphics-related steps (see Figure 10.3). Typically, one stage maps vertices from object space to screen space; another stage rasterizes triangles, producing fragments that contribute to the value of a pixel; and another stage performs shading and texturing. Of course, this discussion simplifies the actual process, which has varied over time.

Early GPUs focused exclusively on supporting graphics, and such systems had a fixed-function hardware realization of the graphics pipeline. These early GPUs only

Figure 10.2
GPU versus CPU
performance over
time.

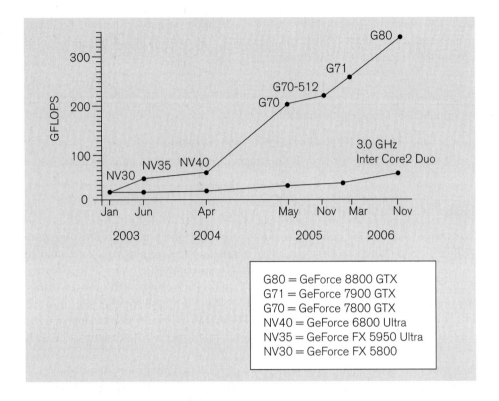

G80 = GeForce 8800 GTX
G71 = GeForce 7900 GTX
G70 = GeForce 7800 GTX
NV40 = GeForce 6800 Ultra
NV35 = GeForce FX 5950 Ultra
NV30 = GeForce FX 5800

Figure 10.3
The graphics pipeline.

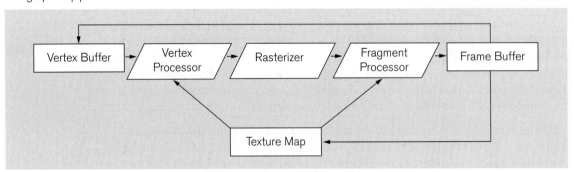

supported single precision floating point operations, with no double precision
operations, no integer operations, and no bit manipulation operations. Over time,
however, the hardware has become increasingly programmable, as game developers
seek to use the hardware in different ways. As a result, the trend is for GPUs to support more general purpose computing. For example, the next nVidia GeForce card
will support double precision floating point and integer operations.

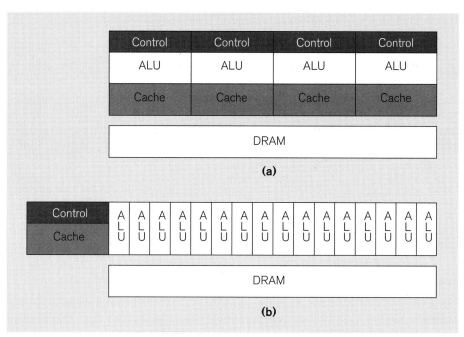

Figure 10.4
A simplified diagram of (a) conventional four core multi-core system, and (b) a (single) GPU core containing 16 processing ALUs; the core will be replicated on the chip.

If we strip away some of the terminology, a modern GPU looks like a massively parallel fine-grained multi-core chip, with its own on-chip DRAM (see Figure 10.4). As an example, the nVidia GeForce 8800 has eight cores (copies of Figure 10.4(b)) that each consist of 16 SIMD processors, which means that these processors operate in lock step.

While the hardware implementation is typically SIMD, the programming model is not, as languages such as Compute Unified Device Architecture (CUDA) are close to complete subsets of the C programming language. Nevertheless, the power of GPUs lies in their ability to perform massively parallel floating point computations. As with other multi-core chips, a standard paradigm is to bring in a block of data and use the multiple processors to do as much processing on it as possible before loading in a new block of data.

As an indication of the variety of applications that can be written for GPUs, the CUDA developer's kit (see http://developer.nvidia.com/object/cuda.html) gives examples of the following programs written in CUDA:

- Parallel bitonic sort
- Matrix multiplication
- Matrix transpose
- Parallel prefix sum (scan) of large arrays
- Image convolution

- 1D Discrete Wavelet Transform using Haar wavelet
- CUDA BLAS and FFT library usage examples
- Binomial Option Pricing
- Black-Scholes Option Pricing
- Monte-Carlo Option Pricing
- Parallel Mersenne Twister (random number generation)
- Parallel Histogram
- Image Denoising
- Sobel Edge Detection Filter

To summarize, the use of GPUs for general purpose computing is extremely promising, with a growing community of users (see www.gpgpu.org) and increasing support for mainstream computing.

Cell Processors

The Cell processor is a joint project of Sony, Toshiba, and IBM whose goal is to produce a powerful device for supporting interactive video games. The Cell architecture, shown in Figure 10.5, contains a standard PowerPC, including L1 and L2 caches, and eight SPEs or "synergistic processing elements." These SPEs are powerful SIMD machines capable of executing four single-precision floating-point operations per cycle. The EIB or "element interconnect bus" supports an enormous amount of on-chip communication, nominally capable of more than 300 GB/s, though with snooping, it is limited to somewhat more than 200 GB/s. Finally, the Cell system has excellent bandwidth to main memory.

The Cell is programmed using C/C++ under Linux. Presently, the tools supporting Cell programmers are limited. For standard computations such as matrix multiplication, early experiments with the Cell have shown that it is possible to extract most of the theoretical performance from the chip. However, the programming effort to achieve such performance is daunting. The SPEs have no cache memory, so the programmer must carefully manage the timing and movement of data to and from the chip using DMA commands. Therefore, the notion of double-buffering, in which one block of data is transferred while another is being computed on—a form of overlapping communication latency with computation—is important for achieving good performance. Efforts to automate such data movement in the compiler have so far proven to be unsuccessful. One challenge for the community is to develop tools and languages that make it easier to program such distinctive processors.

Attached Processors Summary

Attached processors are attractive because their specialized nature can offer great performance, offloading both computation and memory traffic from the main processor. However, attached processors complicate the programming model—it is

Figure 10.5
The floor plan of the Cell processor.

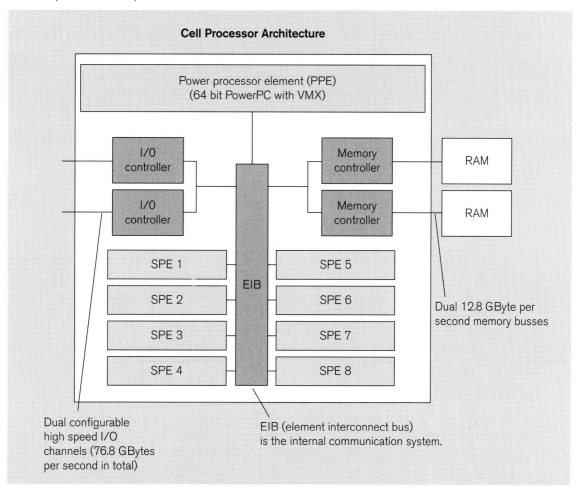

Cell Processor Architecture

Power processor element (PPE)
(64 bit PowerPC with VMX)

I/O controller

I/O controller

Memory controller

Memory controller

RAM

RAM

SPE 1

SPE 2

SPE 3

SPE 4

EIB

SPE 5

SPE 6

SPE 7

SPE 8

Dual 12.8 GByte per
second memory busses

Dual configurable
high speed I/O
channels (76.8 GBytes
per second in total)

EIB (element interconnect bus)
is the internal communication system.

not a CTA—by asking the programmer to partition the computation, to reason carefully about memory traffic between the attached processors and the host processor, and often to program at a low hardware-specific level of abstraction.

Though the programming regime for attached processors seems very different from the other approaches in this book, there is evidence that the two worlds are converging. For example, researchers at Microsoft have produced the Accelerator language, which translates an array language into fragment code for a GPU. There are necessarily some restrictions on the expressiveness of the array language at this early date, but the idea shows promise. As another example, the languages for programming GPUs continue to approach those for general purpose processors.

Grid Computing

As high performance computing becomes increasingly relevant to a wider range of enterprises, such as financial services, manufacturing, and gaming, an increasing number of organizations are motivated to use large-scale parallel computers. However, as computer maintenance and administration become increasingly expensive, it is often not cost effective for an organization to own and maintain its own supercomputer, particularly for organizations whose computing needs vary over time. In these cases it often makes sense to outsource computing.

In keeping with these trends, the notion of a computing grid arose in the early 1990s. The term "computing grid" suggests an analogy to the power grid, where power is a resource that anyone can tap into without worrying about the details of how the power is obtained and transmitted. A computing grid would similarly provide compute power while hiding many of the details from its users. Because of the potential cost effectiveness that comes from economies of scale, at least a dozen countries now have national grid computing projects.

Of course, computing grids come in many different sizes, perhaps operating within a company, across multiple companies, or across a region or country. One goal is to create a computing resource that is greater than the sum of its parts. For example, we can imagine a computing grid that includes a variety of special hardware—everything from huge storage banks to powerful scientific instruments such as telescopes—that would be far too expensive for any single organization to purchase. Even without including special purpose hardware, a grid can provide peak computing power that far exceeds what any individual organization could afford.

To achieve economies of scale, grids often consist of computing resources that are physically distributed across large geographic areas and that span multiple administrative domains—for example, resources may be owned by different organizations. Until now, much of the activity has been in building infrastructure and defining standards that allow grids to be created and used. The issues are much more complex than for the power grid, of course, because the interface to computing services is much broader than the interface to electricity.

To improve overall system utilization, most computing grids are multiprogrammed with dynamic resource allocation. This situation contrasts with typical supercomputing environments that run client programs in batch mode with gang scheduling to minimize interference among client computations.

As distributed systems, computing grids face many of the same issues that the distributed computing community addresses:

- Resource management
- Availability
- Transparency
- Heterogeneity

- Scalability
- Fault tolerance
- Security
- Privacy

However, because users of grid computing are interested in parallel computations, the additional issues of performance and application scalability also come into play. This confluence of parallel and distributed computing introduces some interesting technical problems related to the efficiency of the grid and of its applications, including the following:

- How much does interference among different client programs degrade each program's efficiency? In particular, interference that degrades one process can have a rippling effect on other processes that must interact with the degraded process. In the worst case, we get a situation in which some processes sit idle while waiting for events on some heavily loaded processor. What techniques can be used to minimize such performance degradation?

- Can programmers produce efficient parallel programs without knowing the details of the target platform? With current practice, many programs are written specifically for a particular hardware platform (we don't recommend this), and at a minimum there is typically some amount of target-specific tuning that occurs before programs are put into production mode.

- How can programmers debug, develop, and tune their programs if they cannot see a consistent repeatable set of computing resources? Of course, the use of P-independent languages would help, but such languages are not yet the norm.

- How does a user know if low efficiency is caused by a problem with the grid or by inefficiencies in the user's program?

- How can we simplify the creation of introspective programs that tune and reconfigure themselves to adapt to a changing computing environment?

The notion of computing grids is clearly important, and we can see that there are many open issues to address before they can reach their full potential.

Transactional Memory

For decades, databases have dealt with concurrency issues by using the notion of *transactions*, so it makes sense to ask whether similar ideas can be applied to the memory operations of a shared memory parallel program. Active research in the area of *transactional memory* (TM) has recently begun to address this question. In this section, we introduce the main concepts behind transactional memory, we explain how TM can address many of the shortcomings of lock-based programs, and we identify some important unresolved issues.

A database *transaction* modifies data to ensure four properties, known as ACID (atomicity, consistency, isolation, and durability). *Atomicity* means that all operations in the transaction complete or none completes. *Consistency* is an application-dependent concept that means that storage is updated as if the operations were performed in some serial order. *Isolation* means that the effects of the transaction are equivalent to an isolated execution in which no other transactions are present. *Durability* means that the changes made by a transaction persist. Durability is not needed by programs whose memory states disappear when they exit, so a transaction in a TM system has atomicity, consistency, and isolation.

In a TM system, the programmer identifies transactions, and the system—implemented in either hardware or software—enforces the semantics of transactions by tracking their loads and stores to memory and detecting any conflicts that would violate the transactional properties. If a transaction completes successfully, it is said to have *committed*; otherwise the transaction *aborts* and none of its side effects is visible.

Transactional memory simplifies programming because a transaction gives the illusion of serial execution without the possibility of interactions from other threads. When compared against lock-based programs, TM provides many benefits. In particular, transctions are scalable, composable, deadlock free, and easy to use.

Concretely, transactions are identified by some language construct, such as an *atomic* region, which delimits the extent of a transaction. For example, in our Count 3s example, the update of the shared `count` variable might be implemented as follows:

```
atomic
{
   count+=private_count;
}
```

This `atomic` region bears a striking resemblance to the `synchronized` statement in Java (see Chapter 6):

```
synchronized
{
   count+=private_count;
}
```

Here, the `synchronized` keyword identifies the statement as a critical section that will be executed with mutual exclusion. This trivial example is too simple to illustrate the distinction, but the next section will explain the benefits of transactions by contrasting it with lock-based critical sections.

Comparison with Locks

Recall from Chapter 9 that lock-based programming suffers from several problems. We now recap the problems and explain how transactional memory addresses them.

First, locks can lead to deadlock. Transactions cannot deadlock; they either commit or abort. Of course, livelock, in which a transaction makes no progress because it repeatedly aborts, is a possibility.

Second, locks are too strict. They enforce sequential execution even in two situations where it is not needed: (1) concurrent reads to a shared memory location, and (2) concurrent writes (or concurrent writes and reads) to different memory locations. By contrast, a transactional memory system detects these two situations and allows them to execute concurrently.

Third, locks face a granularity trade-off: Coarse-grained locks limit concurrency, which limits scalability, while fine-grained locks are difficult to reason about because of the possibility of deadlock. With transactional memory, if programmers define large atomic sections, the system will allow multiple threads to execute as long as their memory accesses do not interfere, so transactions have the potential to scale better than locks. Of course, large transactions are not completely free, since they force the TM system to track a larger number of load and store operations.

We can now see the difference between an atomic section and Java's synchronized statement. If we want to provide mutual exclusion to an existing method, which could represent some arbitrarily large amount of code, the synchronized statement serializes the execution of the entire method, whereas the atomic region asks the system to disallow memory accesses that interfere within that region. Thus, transactions can better modulate the granularity of concurrency than locks.

Fourth, locks do not compose well. For example, if two methods that access shared data acquire fine-grained locks in different orders, using them together can cause deadlock. With transactional memory, all dependences are dynamically detected and resolved, so there is no notion of statically ordered lock acquisition.

Fundamentally, we see that locks statically specify an implementation strategy, which is suboptimal because the actual interleaving of threads is not known until runtime. Although recent work has proposed hardware that detects situations when locks can be ignored at runtime—known as Speculative Lock Elision—the reasoning that goes into using locks is static, complex, and does not compose. By contrast, transactional memory asks the programmer to provide the desired semantics statically but allows the system to make implementation decisions dynamically. Of course, given the proper language support, static analysis by compilers can provide potentially valuable information to the dynamic system, so static information need not be ignored.

Implementation Issues

We have argued that transactional memory is simpler to use than locks and offers potential performance benefits. The key question is how efficiently a TM system can implement transactions. It is too early to answer this question fully, but we will briefly summarize the space of design issues, before concluding with some open problems.

A TM system must perform two basic operations: it must detect when memory accesses from different threads conflict, and it must provide a mechanism for isolating the effects of a transaction until it either commits or aborts. These are known as *conflict detection* and *data versioning,* respectively.

Conflict detection checks whether two threads access the same memory location, with at least one of the operations being a modification of that location. To detect such conflicts, the TM system must keep track of the read set and write set for each transaction. Conflict detection can be performed either pessimistically or optimistically.

A *pessimistic conflict detection* scheme detects conflicts as early as possible, so that it can avoid wasted work. Upon detecting a conflict, it can either abort a transaction immediately, or it can stall one of the transactions—preventing it from performing the offending access in hopes that there will be no conflict later. On the other hand, a pessimistic approach may face cycles of recurring conflicts and be unable to make forward progress.

An *optimistic conflict detection* scheme assumes that conflicts are rare, so it delays conflict checks until the end of a transaction, at which point the transaction either commits or aborts. Such a scheme performs wasted work if a conflict could have been detected earlier. It also precludes the option of stalling a thread as a means of conflict resolution, because the threads will most likely have progressed past the first potential conflict. On the other hand, the optimistic approach can guarantee progress by simply committing the first completed transaction.

The second basic mechanism maintains multiple versions of data so that transactions can be either rolled back or committed. Again, there are two basic approaches: eager and lazy.

With *eager versioning* the system saves copies of the old version of data so that it can write the new values to main memory. This approach is fast if the likelihood of a commit is high, but aborts are slower because they must restore the transaction's state by walking over the list of saved values.

With *lazy versioning* new values are saved to a write buffer while the old version is left untouched. Aborts are thus fast, while commits must copy values from the write buffer. This approach has the added expense of searching the write buffer to retrieve new values when reads are performed.

A separate dimension in the design space is the *granularity of conflict detection*, which can be performed at an object level, a cache line level, or a word level. These choices present different trade-offs in terms of (1) the overhead of conflict detection and data versioning and (2) the likelihood of false conflicts, which are analogous to false sharing.

Open Research Issues

Aside from the many implementation issues that we have just mentioned, we now touch on a few other open research problems with transactional memory.

- I/O operations are problematic because I/O devices fall outside of a TM system's rollback mechanism, so their operations cannot be undone. Similarly, interactions with legacy codes are problematic because such codes have not been decomposed into transactions.

- Conflict detection is defined on low-level operations, namely, loads and stores, so TM systems cannot distinguish *structural conflicts* from *semantic conflicts*. To understand the issue, consider two transactions that each increment a counter. Semantically, the two transactions can legally interleave their increments as long as each operation actually updates the counter (as opposed to updating a value in a register). However, the TM system will disallow many of these semantically legal interleavings because the ordering of loads and stores will appear to indicate a conflict. Thus the distinction forces TM systems to abort many more transactions than necessary.

- *Open Nested Transactions* have been proposed as a mechanism for dealing with both of the above problems. Open Nested Transactions essentially provide a mechanism for stepping outside of the TM system, but they introduce complex and fundamental issues with the interaction between the open nested transactions and the TM system.

- Long-running transactions are problematic. Under some implementation policies they are likely never to commit. On the other hand, if they are given priority over shorter-running transactions, they can severely degrade performance for many other threads. In the database community, long-running transactions are often handled by processing them with special semantics or by running them on separate systems. It is unclear how these solutions translate to transactional memory.

- There are subtle but fundamental differences in the semantics of Software Transactional Memory (STM) and Hardware Transactional Memory (HTM), which means that STM is not a simple migration path to HTM. Practically speaking, this dichotomy is significant because ideally we would use STM to build the software base, both to gain experience with transactional memory and to guide the development of HTM. But because of their differences in semantics, this migration path is not possible.

- Of course, transactional memory does not pretend to solve all problems related to parallel performance. It does not address issues of locality or of reducing interactions among threads, so another open area is the integration of transactional memory with parallel programming models or parallel languages that can facilitate good locality and data movement.

In summary, transactional memory is a rich and interesting research area with potential benefits and some fundamental unsolved problems.

> **Dynamic Optimistic Parallelization.** Just as Transactional Memory has built on the database notion of serializable execution—an execution that is equivalent to *some* sequential execution—the Galois system applies the idea at a higher semantic level. In particular, the Galois system is geared toward parallelizing codes whose data dependences cannot be statically known, as is the case with many graph-based algorithms, such as Delauney triangulation. The language supports optimistic parallelization in which the application assumes that different parts of the computation can proceed independently. The notion of independence is based on commutativity, as defined by operations on abstract data structures, and an execution is rolled back if a conflict is found. One important aspect of the Galois system is its higher-level data structure-specific notion of commutativity. For example, for operations on a shared set, the definition of commutativity is based on abstract set operations rather than on low-level loads and stores.

MapReduce

An important development in parallel computation is the enormous increase in scale in cluster-based computations typified by the MapReduce facility developed at Google. Described by Dean and Ghemawat in 2004, MapReduce is a tool for searching huge data archives using a standardized plug-in style framework. Google used MapReduce to replace its *ad hoc* index-building software for operations like computing PageRank. The idea is being applied elsewhere, and there are several implementations. The name comes from the map and reduce operations found in LISP and other functional languages: The map operator applies some function to each element of a list, while the reduce operator combines elements of a list, as we've seen discussed throughout this book. The term MapReduce is now generic, applying also to descendent systems.

Except for scale, the MapReduce framework shares much with Schwartz's algorithm of Chapter 4 and the customized reduce of Chapter 5. But scale is critical here, causing a more stream-based view to be adopted. Thus, imagine a tree in which the leaves are the disks of a distributed file system of, say, Web pages. The computations of interest sometimes produce a single output value, like the reduce computations we have seen. But more generally they produce tables of values—as is more typical of databases—such as a table of words and the count of the number times each occurs in the file system.

The data, streamed from the disks, is filtered using the *map* function, producing an output stream of key/value pairs. For example, if the task is to count word occurrences, then the data in the file would be converted to a stream of pairs such as `<'dog', 1>` when 'dog' is encountered in the input. The key/value pairs are streamed to another computer called an *aggregator* (see Figure 10.6), which sorts the key/value pairs. The aggregators then apply the *reduce* function to the streams,

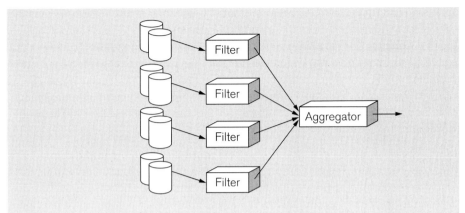

Figure 10.6
Schematic diagram
of a MapReduce
system.

producing summary streams. For the counting words example, lists with their word/count pairs are merged (two counts of a word are added), producing another list of word/count pairs that may participate in more aggregation. Merging is a typical reduce operation, but there are other more complex reduce functions. The outputs of the reduce operation can be aggregated with others, producing a hierarchical structure that can process enormous amounts of data.

To use the system, programmers write simple scripts that define the map and the reduce operations; these plug into the MapReduce framework. Consider an example that processes a collection of many files containing records that consist of a single floating point number, perhaps the results of scientific experiments or observed data. The desired output is the number of records (`count`), the sum of the floats (`total`), and the sum of the squares of the floats (`sum_of_squares`). A Sawzall (MapReduce descendant) program for this computation is as follows:

```
count: table sum of int;
total: table sum of float;
sum_of_squares: table sum of float;
x: float=input;
emit count <- 1;
emit total <- x;
emit sum_of_squares <- x*x;
```

The first three lines declare the necessary reduce functions for the aggregators that sum the data coming from the filters; the reserved word `table` is an aggregator type; however, in this case it represents only singleton values.

The remaining statements specify the map operation for the filters. The first of these processes the file's records (untyped byte strings bound to `input`) by converting them to floating point and assigning them to x. The filter then emits three key/value pairs to the aggregators to be processed. The filter code is instantiated for each record in all of the files.

In many instances, there is an opportunity for an intermediate optimization between the filtering and the first round of aggregation, which has the potential of greatly reducing the amount of data transferred. For example, the previous word count example emitted a key/value pair for each occurrence of a word in the distributed file system, but there are likely far fewer unique words than occurrences. So we can imagine a *combining* operation that merges values to implement a data reduction. As a result, each filter might simply send to the aggregator a list of the unique words and their counts.

MapReduce is both a parallel computation and a distributed computation. It utilizes many computers to compute a specific result efficiently, but because of its scale, distributed computing issues of reliability, availability, and so on, are critical. Perhaps the best way to emphasize the balance between the computational power derived from its parallelism and the distributed computing challenges is to quote Pike [2005]:

> We monitored [Sawzall's] *use during the month of March 2005. During that time, on one dedicated Workqueue cluster with 1500 Xeon CPUs, there were 32,580 Sawzall jobs launched, using an average of 220 machines each. While running those jobs, 18,636 failures occurred (application failure, network outage, system crash, etc.) that triggered rerunning some portion of the job. The jobs read a total of 3.2×10^{15} bytes of data (2.8PB) and wrote 9.9×10^{12} bytes (9.3TB) (demonstrating that the term "data reduction" has some resonance). The average job therefore processed about 100GB. The jobs collectively consumed almost exactly one machine-century.*

In addition to merging concepts from parallel and distributed computing, MapReduce shows an elegant way to process large volumes of data in which disk access time is a dominant component of the computation.

Problem Space Promotion

Algorithmic techniques such as divide-and-conquer guide us in finding effective solutions to problems. As parallel programming advances, we expect that new programming techniques specialized to parallel computing will be invented. Problem Space Promotion is one recent example.

Problem Space Promotion (PSP) is a parallel solution technique for problems involving combinatorial interactions of array data. PSP reformulates algorithms that operate over d-dimensional data as computations in a higher dimensional problem space. The goal of PSP is to replicate data in one or more dimensions to increase parallelism and to reduce communication and synchronization requirements, that is, to remove dependences. To see how this might be achieved, consider a problem in which n array values must all interact pair wise. One solution is to keep two copies of the array, to operate on corresponding elements of the two arrays, and then to cyclically shift one of the arrays; after n shifts all n^2 pairs will have been processed. (The shifting formulation is suitable for a distributed memory setting, but in a shared memory setting separate array references in a doubly nested loop achieve the same effect.) Alternatively—and with greater parallelism—two new operands can be created, formed by replicating the data of the array as rows, and replicating the transpose of the array as columns; corresponding pairs of elements of these arrays can be combined and operated on all at once.

As a concrete illustration, consider the problem of sorting a sequence, S, of n unique numbers:

> $C \leftarrow S^T \le S$ *compare all pairs of numbers, (1 if true, 0 otherwise)*
> $P \leftarrow sum\_cols(C)$ *column sums give sorted index positions*
> $S \leftarrow S[P]$ *permute elements of S into order*

The solution requires quadratic work because it performs n^2 comparisons. Though the input is 1-dimensional, the operations are performed over 2-dimensional arrays, such as C. The advantage of the PSP approach is that it specifies that all comparisons can be performed independently and that all columns can be summed independently, which increases concurrency dramatically compared, say, to the odd-even transposition sort of Chapter 4. Observant readers will recognize this computation as the ordering technique used in Chapter 8 to rank the coffee drinkers in the ZPL program; ZPL's flood and reduce operators are well suited to the use of the PSP technique.

In addition to sorting, many $O(n^2)$ operations can be expressed as PSP computations with correspondingly fewer dependences. N-body computations are one example, as is the identification of the mode of an input set. Also, for matrix multiplication the "dot-product step" of the SUMMA algorithm shown in Figure 8.2 is an instance of the PSP; indeed, SUMMA is simply an iteration of n PSP operations. More generally, matrix product can be seen as a 3-dimensional PSP computation. The 2-dimensional input arrays are replicated (flooded, in the terminology of Chapter 8) into a 3-dimensional "box," bringing all n^3 pairs of values together. These boxes are multiplied together element-wise and then summed along the third dimension to produce the resulting matrix product.

We emphasize that "raising the dimension" is only a logical concept, a programming abstraction giving the programmer a means of specifying a computation in a way that does not introduce dependences. The elimination of dependences by the PSP specification leads to substantial performance improvements over other techniques that define computation in lower-level, more primitive terms.

Emerging Languages

Early work with supercomputers focused much of the effort on the hardware, with the software often being the product of heroic programming efforts. Realizing that programmer productivity is at least as important as a machine's peak performance, the DARPA-funded High Productivity Computing (HPC) Program seeks to develop parallel programming languages focused on improving programmer productivity.

After several rounds of competition, the HPC program has produced the emergence of three new parallel languages (as well as proposed new hardware):

- Chapel (Cascade High Productivity Language) from Cray Inc.
- Fortress from Sun Microsystems Inc.
- X10 from IBM Watson Research Center

These languages are not yet completely designed or implemented, but they offer promising ideas that can truly contribute to parallel programming productivity. They are open source efforts, and their design specifications are available. We now give a short sketch of each language.

Chapel

The Cray Inc. team that is designing the Cascade High Productivity Language criticizes the low-level "fragmented" programming approaches (chiefly message passing) that have reigned in high-performance computing. Their goal is to achieve object code performance comparable to low-level techniques while promoting productivity through the use of proven high level abstractions supported by advanced compilation techniques (see Figure 10.7). As they describe it,

> Chapel supports a multithreaded parallel programming model at a high level by supporting abstractions for data parallelism, task parallelism, and nested parallelism. It supports optimization for the locality of data and computation in the program via abstractions for data distribution and data-driven placement of subcomputations. It supports code reuse and generality via object-oriented concepts and generic programming features. While Chapel borrows concepts from many preceding languages, its parallel concepts are most closely based on ideas from High-Performance Fortran (HPF), ZPL, and the Cray MTA's extensions to Fortran/C.

The design of Chapel is guided by four key areas of language technology: multi-threading, locality-awareness, object-orientation, and generic programming.[1]

Fortress

The team at Sun Microsystems has placed great emphasis on innovative ways to address the productivity problem. For example, certain expressions closely resemble standard mathematical notation (see Figure 10.8). The result is a language that steps outside of much of our conventional thinking about parallel languages. As they describe it,[2]

> [W]e are able to support features in Fortress such as transactions, specification of locality, and implicit parallel computation, as integral features built into the core

[1] http://chapel.cs.washington.edu/spec-0.750.pdf
[2] http://research.sun.com/projects/plrg/faq/index.html

Figure 10.7

1-dimensional radix-4 FFT in Chapel;
complete code at http://chapel.cs.washington.edu/hpccOverview.pdf.

```
for (str, span) in genDFTPhases(numElements, radix) {
  forall (bankStart, twidIndex) in (ADom by 2*span, 0..) {
    var  wk2=W(twidIndex),
         wk1=W(2*twidIndex),
         wk3=(wk1.re-2*wk2.im*wk1.im,
              2*wk2.im*wk1.re-wk1.im):elemType;
    forall lo in bankStart+[0..str) do
      butterfly(wk1, wk2, wk3, A[[0..radix)*str+lo]);
         wk1=W(2*twidIndex+1);
         wk3=(wk1.re-2*wk2.re*wk1.im,
              2*wk2.re*wk1.re-wk1.im):elemType;
         wk2*=1.0i;
    forall lo in bankStart+span+[0..str) do
      butterfly(wk1, wk2, wk3, A[[0..radix)*str+lo]);
  }
}
. . .
def butterfly(wk1, wk2, wk3, inout A:[1..radix]) { . . . }
```

$conjGrad$[Elt **extends** Number, **nat** N,
    Mat **extends** Matrix [Elt, $N \times N$],
    Vec **extends** Vector [Elt, N]
    ]$(A: \text{Mat}, x: \text{Vec}):(\text{Vec}, \text{Elt})$

$cgit_{max} = 25$

$z : \text{Vec} = 0$

$r : \text{Vec} = x$

$p : \text{Vec} = r$

$r : \text{Elt} = r^T r$

for $j \leftarrow$ **seq**$(1: cgit_{max})$ **do**

   $q = Ap$

   $\alpha = \dfrac{\rho}{p^T q}$

   $z := z + \alpha\, p$

   $r := r - \alpha\, q$

   $\rho_0 = \rho$

   $\rho := r^T r$

   $\beta = \dfrac{\rho}{\rho_0}$

   $p := r + \beta\, p$

end

$(z, \|x - A\, z\|)$

Figure 10.8

Fortress code for the Conjugate Gradient computation from the NAS parallel benchmark suite.

of the language. Features such as the Fortress component system and test frame-work facilitate program assembly and testing, and enable powerful compiler opti-mizations across library boundaries. Even the syntax and type system of Fortress are custom-tailored to modern HPC programming, supporting mathematical notation and static checking of properties such as physical units and dimensions, static type checking of multidimensional arrays and matrices, and definitions of domain-specific language syntax in libraries. Moreover, Fortress has been designed with the intent that it be a "growable" language, gracefully supporting the addition of future language features. In fact, much of the Fortress language itself (even the definition of arrays and other basic types) is encoded in libraries atop a relatively small core language.

By looking for novel ways to express computation, the Fortress language challenges us to think about how best to describe the parallelism in a problem.

X10

The IBM team that is designing X10 is doing so as part of IBM's PERCS project (Productive Easy-to-use Reliable Computer Systems). Though it is a new language (see Figure 10.9), X10 is extremely close to Java,[3] and because it is also a PGAS lan-guage, it is possible to compare with the Titanium approach. This is what the X10 team says about their approach:

X10 aims to contribute to this productivity improvement by developing a new programming model, combined with a new set of tools integrated into Eclipse and new implementation techniques for delivering optimized scalable parallelism in a managed runtime environment. X10 is a type-safe, modern, parallel, distrib-uted object-oriented language intended to be very easily accessible to Java ™ pro-grammers. It is targeted to future low-end and high-end systems with nodes that are built out of multi-core SMP chips with non-uniform memory hierarchies, and interconnected in scalable cluster configurations. A member of the Partitioned Global Address Space (PGAS) family of languages, X10 highlights the explicit reification of locality in the form of places; lightweight activities embod-ied in async, future, foreach, and ateach constructs; constructs for termination detection (finish) and phased computation (clocks); the use of lock-free synchro-nization (atomic blocks); and the manipulation of global arrays and data structures.

X10 incorporates a wide range of parallel programming concepts that target both multi-core and clusters of multi-core machines, which are likely to be typical of future parallel architectures.

---

[3]http://domino.research.ibm.com/comm/research_projects.nsf/pages/x10.index.html/$FILE/ATTH4YZ4.pdf

Figure 10.9

X10 code to compute the 2D Jacobi iteration.

```
public class Jacobi {
  const int N=6;
  const double epsilon = 0.002;
  const double epsilon2 = 0.000000001;
  const region R = [0:N+1, 0:N+1];
  const region RInner= [1:N, 1:N];
  const distribution D = distribution.factory.block(R);
  const distribution DInner = D | RInner;
  const distribution DBoundary = D - RInner;
  const int EXPECTED ITERS=97;
  const double EXPECTED ERR=0.0018673382039402497;
  double[D] B = new double[D] (point p[i,j])
                  {return DBoundary.contains(p)
                  ? (N-1)/2 : N*(i-1)+(j-1); };
  public boolean run()   {
    int iters = 0;
    double err;
    while(true) {
      double[.] Temp =
            new double[DInner] (point [i,j])
            {return (read(i+1,j)+read(i-1,j)
            +read(i,j+1)+read(i,j-1))/4.0; };
      if((err=((B | DInner) - Temp).abs().sum())
         < epsilon)
      break;
      B.update(Temp);
      iters++;
    }
    System.out.println("Error="+err);
    System.out.println("Iterations="+iters);
    return Math.abs(err-EXPECTED ERR)<epsilon2
        && iters==EXPECTED ITERS;
  }
  public double read(final int i, final int j) {
    return future(D[i,j]) B[i,j].force();
  }
  public static void main(String args[]) {
    boolean b= (new Jacobi()).run();
    System.out.println("++++++ "
        + (b? "Test succeeded."
        :"Test failed."));
    System.exit(b?0:1);
  }
}
```

Chapter Summary

This chapter has discussed several diverse methods of exploiting parallelism. These methods vary in scale from the use of the Cell's SPEs to the Internet-scale computations supported by the MapReduce model. The issues they address vary as well, including correctness and convenience (Transactional Memory and the Chapel, Fortress, and X10 languages), price/performance at the chip level (GPGPU), price/performance at the enterprise level (Grids), and the programmability of large-scale computations. Finally, we see in both grid computing and MapReduce a confluence of parallel and distributed computation.

Historical Perspective

The Cell project is described by IBM [2006]. nVidia's CG language [Mark et al.] began the migration to general purpose languages computing on GPUs. The more recent Accelerator language [Tarditi 2006] is based on array computations. Lock Elision was described by Rajwar and Goodman [2001]. Foster and Kesselman [2003] present the grid computing concepts. Herlihy and Moss [1986] popularized the concept of hardware transactional memory; Shavit and Touitou [1995] proposed a software only approach. MapReduce is described by Dean and Ghemawat [2004], and Problem Space Promotion is described by Chamberlain, et al. [1999].

Exercises

1. Suppose a MapReduce that takes 220 processors and processes 100 GB of data is solved not on a Xeon cluster, but rather with Grid computing techniques. Explain how the computation might have to be changed; in your answer, consider whether more or fewer processors should be used.

2. Using Peril-L, write a pseudo-code algorithm for matrix multiplication on the Cell. Select an algorithm that is amenable to the use of exactly eight processors, and concentrate on the data motion among the processors.

3. Consider how a sort can be implemented using a Cell processor. Assume the logic of Batcher's Bitonic algorithm; also assume that the problem exceeds the memory capacity of the Cell processors, so data must be transferred back and forth between the attached processor and main memory. Assuming data transfer is the only constraint, estimate the execution time to sort 2^{35} quadwords.

4. Suppose a large data structure such as a B-tree or AVL-tree is to be modified concurrently. Explain how transactions can be used to guarantee that the integrity of the tree's structure is preserved. Explain the consequences of changing the granularity of the solution.

5. Compare the solution in Exercise 4 with a solution that uses conventional locking. Which solution would be preferred if in addition to minimizing the time to completion for inserts, an added design goal is to minimize the variation in completion time?

Writing Parallel Programs

The best way to learn parallel programming is to do it. Previous chapters treated concepts related to parallel programming. This chapter concerns the programming activity itself.

We recognize two opportunities for parallel programming practice associated with this book. Small programming exercises, like the examples and the end-of-chapter exercises, provide an opportunity to explore new algorithmic concepts or learn a new parallel programming language. They are an excellent means for understanding specific material. The other activity, which is covered in later sections of this chapter, is a substantial term project spanning many weeks. A term project provides an opportunity to design entirely new algorithms and to deal with the full spectrum of complexities surrounding parallel programming. Both activities are essential to understanding the material clearly.

Of necessity, this chapter treats the writing of a parallel program in a general, machine- and language-independent manner, though you, of course, have to use a specific language and specific computer. Most topics are relevant to all parallel programming situations, but occasionally some issues may not apply.

Getting Started

Even before considering parallel programming, we recommend that you become familiar with the access and practical use of the target parallel computer.

Access and Software

The parallelism available with single-user systems is often limited to a few processors, but they tend to be convenient to access. For these systems, the mechanics of writing parallel programs is not substantially different from that of writing any other kind of program. Many-processor systems, by contrast, are often multiuser systems that are typically used "at a distance." In order to program them, it may be necessary to get permission or guidance in the proper access protocol. For systems that serve a community, such information is usually posted on a Web page; for the cluster computer in the next lab, access might be arranged on a less formal basis.

Another issue that should be addressed when arranging access is to verify that the programming language and software tools that you intend to use are available on the target platform. In this regard, multiuser systems are often more convenient because someone may have already installed the desired system. For personal systems, it may be necessary to find and install the desired software. Notice that tools such as debuggers, performance profilers, may be installed at the same time.

Hello, World

Traditionally, the first program written in a new language or for a new system is a trivial computation, such as the "Hello, World" program—it simply prints the greeting—which tests the activities of compiling, linking, loading, queuing (if necessary) and running a parallel program on a parallel platform.

Once "Hello, World" is running, the next task is to run a similarly trivial program that executes on multiple processors, combines results from all processes, and outputs the results. Such computations resolve the difficulties of spawning threads or processes and communicating among them. Though usually straightforward, it is best to verify that these fundamental operations are fully understood before proceeding with more ambitious tasks.

Finally, before starting in earnest with the programming, it is prudent to test that the program execution can be measured. A key part of working with parallel computations is measuring their performance, so it is critical that you know how to get accurate timings. Since the two previous test programs are too trivial to execute for a measurable amount of time, add code to the threads to iterate 10^8 times on some memory operation, such as exchanging the values of two variables:

```
temp=x;
x=y;
y=temp;
```

Verify that you can detect a change in performance when the iteration count is increased, say, to 10^9.

Optimizing Compilers. When checking the timing facilities, be sure to print some value (other than the timings) that is referenced in the timed code. Optimizing compilers often analyze a program to determine which statements can contribute to the final output; then they eliminate all code that does not contribute. By printing some value from the timed portion, you ensure that the compiler will not eliminate it.

With these preliminaries resolved, we are ready to develop parallel programs.

Parallel Programming Recommendations

Most readers of this book are already experienced programmers and do not need help in writing successful sequential programs. Accordingly, we focus on those issues that are unique to parallelism or apply significantly to the parallel programming activity. We subscribe to software engineering principle, but expertise in software engineering is not assumed. Perhaps the best advice is to proceed thoughtfully.

Incremental Development

Parallel programs are usually complex, making them difficult to create and understand, so a practical methodology is helpful. We recommend an incremental approach that moves from one working version of the program to another. For example, it might begin with a program that only initializes the parallel data structures. This initial program can then be incrementally modified with small improvements, being careful to test the new program thoroughly at each step to verify that it continues to work properly. This same methodology can be used to independently design, implement, and unit-test significant new modules before they are integrated and tested with the main program. This technique places a premium on finding good test cases and in keeping a careful development history so that when problems are discovered it is possible to roll back to a previous working version. (We recommend the use of a version control system such as Subversion.)

How large is a "small improvement"? It is not measured in lines of code, of course, but rather in terms of the amount of complexity it adds to the program and in terms of our confidence in its correctness. Even a few lines of program that affect thread interactions can be hugely complex, requiring careful examination. On the other hand, blocks of program text, especially procedures that have no interactions with other threads, could be easy additions even though they might represent a considerable amount of code.

Focus on the Parallel Structure

We advocate building the parallel structure first and then inserting the functional components later. This may seem roundabout, but it is often easier to recognize difficult-to-find parallel errors when they are not obscured by the functional parts of the computation.

Another reason to adopt this view is that it focuses on "top level parallelism," that is, the primary decomposition of the computation into parallel components. This macro view leads us to see, for example, matrix multiplication as combining rows and columns rather than as many scalar multiplies and adds, even though we may ultimately apply parallelism at many levels. This macro view usually identifies the places where parallelism has the biggest payoff.

To illustrate the idea of a parallel superstructure, imagine that our intended program does the following:

- Initializes data structures
- Spawns a set of threads that each iterates over a part of the data structure and interacts with other threads at the end of each cycle
- Summarizes the data with a reduction
- Prints the result
- Exits

Figure 11.1 shows a schematic diagram of the superstructure of this imagined computation.

These steps, which reflect the basic parallel structure of the program, can be written and debugged prior to specifying the actual functionality of the computation. By getting the basic structure working in this skeletal form, there are fewer places for the parallelism-related bugs to hide.

Testing the Parallel Structure

One complication is that the functional portion often determines how the parallel portion behaves, which is significant because thread interaction is a primary source of complexity and potential bugs. If, as in Batcher's Bitonic Sort (described in Chapter 4), the thread schedule is predetermined, then it is easy to test. If the thread interaction is data dependent or dynamic, then some mechanism must be built to reproduce typical schedules so that the interactions can be tested. Of course, the

Figure 11.1
The parallel super-structure of a sample computation. Control flows from the top; the gray band identifies the position in each thread where interactions with the other threads are concentrated.

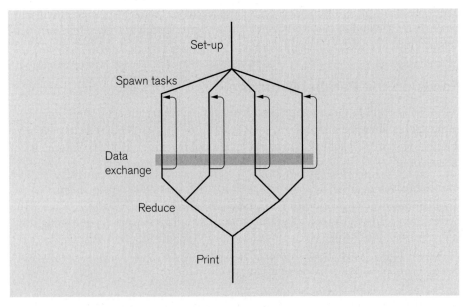

functionality that determines the schedule could be programmed and used, but it may be too unpredictable for efficient program development. So we suggest first checking interactions under controlled conditions—either inputting a test schedule or programming a predictable schedule—to verify that the interactions are right. These "test jigs" can be adjusted to check different schedules and to increase confidence in the result.

Sequential Programming

Sequential programming is much better supported by program development tools than is parallel programming, so it makes sense to exploit this fact. We recommend writing as much sequential code as possible, which fits well with our suggestion of inserting sequential code into a parallel superstructure. Code that can be developed and tested independently of the main parallel program can generally be included with confidence. The functional components of the program will often fall into this category.

Be Willing to Write Extra Code

With parallel programming, it is very easy to write buggy code, so the rush is not to produce a large volume of code but to produce correct and efficient code. Even the emphasis on efficiency can be misguided, as performance optimizations often complicate the code and introduce bugs. It is important to be willing to write extra code for the purposes of testing, debugging, and understanding the main parallel program. There are many examples where extra code or tools can be useful:

- To help eliminate race conditions, which are notoriously difficult to identify, it is sometimes possible to create a test harness that systematically stresses a large set of thread interactions for a varying number of threads. Such a harness might require hooks into the parallel program to make it possible to control different execution interleavings. The hooks might invoke artificial delays to certain parts of the program, or, in a threaded system they might relinquish the processor.

- To facilitate testing, it may be useful to create a program that generates a wide variety of program inputs. Often, just the act of thinking about different program inputs reveals implicit assumptions in the code that are not valid.

- Often, it is useful to create small tools for inspecting the state of various data structures. For example, if a data structure is distributed across multiple processes on a distributed memory machine, it is useful to have a print routine that prints a globally coherent view of the data structure, as opposed to having each process independently print its own local view of the data structure. Such a routine will likely pass a token among the processes to synchronize the various print statements.

- To debug long-running programs, it is useful to implement a checkpointing facility that periodically saves the state of the execution on all processes so that subsequent executions can resume from some point in the execution that is close to the manifestation of the bug. Checkpoints should be placed carefully so that they represent a point in time that could actually have occurred. For example, consider a message sent from process p to process q. If a checkpoint saves p's state before it sends the message, and saves q's state after it received the message, then the state is inconsistent, because it is not possible for the message to have been received but not yet sent. The simplest way to avoid such problems is to place checkpoints at barriers or other global synchronization points.

- To understand parallel performance and performance bottlenecks, it is often useful to include instrumentation code that can be turned on or off. Such code might measure the amount of work that a thread performs, or it might make timing measurements. Of course, timing measurements can be problematic when trying to measure short events.

As with sequential programs, the liberal use of assertions can be helpful for quickly identifying places in the code where assumptions are violated.

Controlling Parameters during Testing

When testing programs there is a general tendency to create tiny test cases, and for many computations this approach may be sufficient. Parallel computation has the property, however, that test cases must be sufficiently large that when the work is distributed among the processes there is enough work for them to do so that they exhibit representative interactions. Thus, if n data items are sufficient to test a sequential computation, we should expect a t-thread parallel computation to require at least tn items, more when the issue of divisibilities is considered. Additionally, we need to use enough processors to induce a rich set of interactions. Unfortunately, there is no universal rule for how many data items are sufficient; each situation is unique.

Finally, assuming that there are sufficiently many data items, we need to consider various schedules of interactions for them. As previously noted, synthetic schedules have the advantage that they can be controlled to a large degree. Testing should include the kinds of interactions anticipated, of course, remembering that even if the schedule is predictable like Batcher's sort, the actual time when threads reach synchronizing points is not. If the interactions are data dependent or dynamic, the test schedules should include a selection of extreme schedules—all tasks waiting on the same task, or a series of tasks each waiting on its predecessor, and so on.

Functional Debugging

The primary way to determine if the right answer is being computed is to compare the parallel program's output to another computation, usually a sequential one. The strategy works well for programs manipulating discrete objects but is less reliable when floating point arithmetic is involved. Because the parallel program will have a different—or even unpredictable—order of execution, the inherent imprecision of floating point can lead to results that are not bit-for-bit identical. In such cases, it is usually appropriate to use a threshold of correctness, as in "correct to d-digits of precision."

As the preceding sections have implied, we advise minimizing the number of bugs introduced by using a careful development process. But bugs are inevitable. Unfortunately, effective parallel debugging tools are nearly nonexistent. Most programmers capture data and inspect it, inevitably affecting the timing characteristics and often the actual functionality of their programs.

Capstone Project Ideas

The previous chapters have emphasized small exercises to teach specific topics. But a larger project teaches many things beyond the concepts of parallel programming, such as managing complexity, developing effective programming methodologies, and practicing proper experimental procedures. Developing expertise in these areas on a project of your choosing is excellent preparation for future challenges. There is a parallel computer near you—it is time to write a substantial program for it!

Several kinds of computations are possible as a capstone project. In selecting a problem it is best to focus on what the computation solves rather than on its parallel behavior. Problems chosen because they are "very parallel" or have an obvious parallel implementation are usually less engaging than projects whose answer is personally interesting. Obviously, it is best if the problem requires enormous amounts of computation, but that really isn't a necessity when the goal is to learn.[1] We divide potential projects into three classes, as we now discuss.

Implementing Existing Parallel Algorithms

Because parallelism is a long-studied topic, there are many parallel algorithms described in the literature. These are usually described informally or written in an *ad hoc* pseudo-code rather than being given as a production program. As an illustration, Batcher's Bitonic Sort was written in Peril-L (for the alphabetization task) in Chapter 4 to illustrate scalable parallel computations. The goal of such a project would be to produce a working implementation for a specific platform and to characterize its behavior.

At first sight, this project appears to be quite easy because it seems simple to find an algorithm in a book and to implement it in a production programming language for a contemporary machine. But there is one caution: Published parallel algo-

---

[1] Problems whose sequential complexity is $O(n^2)$ or higher are preferred.

rithms often make assumptions that may not apply to the available language and computer. As an extreme example, there is a huge literature on PRAM algorithms, but as explained in Chapter 2, the PRAM model is unrealistic for scalable parallelism. The best advice is to check the paper carefully and understand the assumptions that the authors are making. If they are compatible with the available machine, language, and goals, then proceed; otherwise, keep looking. The components of such a project would be as follows:

- Locate an algorithm of interest.
- Identify any computational assumptions on which the algorithm is based.
- Formulate representative test inputs for measuring the program.
- Develop a program using the methodology given earlier.
- Measure the overall performance, including the performance of specific subcomputations.
- Based on the evidence of the test measurements and the topics covered earlier in this book (for example, Chapter 3), revise the program to improve its performance.
- Report the results of the project.

The possibility of improving a published algorithm may seem unlikely, but it is possible. More likely, the implementation will usually have many chances for improvement even if the base algorithm remains unchanged.

The list of components (and the lists in the next two sections) appears to be a simple set of steps. However, there are potential complications in each step, the list may not be exhaustive, and the steps cannot always be performed strictly in the given order.

Competing with Standard Benchmarks

A second class of projects—related to the first—is to implement a standard parallel benchmark for a new setting and to compare how the solution performs.

There have been a variety of parallel benchmark suites over the years—consult the Web for details. One highly respected suite is the NAS Parallel Benchmarks (NPB), (https://www.nas.nasa.gov/Resources/Software/swdescriptions.html), produced by researchers at NASA. The benefit of benchmark programs is that they are generally well written (often ingeniously so), are widely understood, and typically have published performance numbers. Accordingly, if a new version of the benchmark is written, say, in a new language or with some other new feature, then the results of the project program can be compared to the published results. Such competition can be fun.

The components of such a project would be as follows:

- Review the programs in a benchmark suite, and identify one program of interest.

- Locate papers reporting experiments with that benchmark, noting details such as the platforms and implementation language.

- Develop a program using the methodology given previously.

- Following the standard methodology used in the papers, including test data, measure the overall performance, and compare with published results. This step can be deceptively difficult. For example, the NAS Parallel Benchmarks provide a collection of inputs of different sizes, each appropriate for platforms with different amounts of memory. If your benchmark suite has not been so carefully designed, you may need to modify the test inputs.

- Based on the measurements and topics covered in Chapter 3, determine why the observed performance differs from the published results. Again, this step can be difficult, as it often requires an understanding of how architectural differences, program inputs, and programming techniques interact. Moreover, many papers do not offer sufficient details to yield repeatable experiments.

- Report the results of the project.

A variation on this theme is to consider the whole suite, not rewriting the programs, but simply changing them to exploit an architectural feature, such as changing message passing commands into one-sided or shared memory references. As a caution, this variation's simplicity is probably deceptive for most architectural features.

Developing New Parallel Computations

The most interesting type of project is to solve a new problem in parallel. By applying your own knowledge and creativity to the task, you earn the satisfaction of having built a working parallel program and having resolved all of the parallel issues yourself, which can be extremely rewarding.

The main requirement is to be familiar enough with a computation that you can express its components in a different form—a parallel one—and obtain the correct solution. As a source of ideas, Table 11.1 gives the titles of project reports for several courses on Parallel Computation. Obviously, without the report we cannot be sure what specific computation was implemented, but the titles do suggest areas that present significant computational problems worthy of parallel solution.

The primary steps in such a project would be as follows:

- Review the literature on the computation, if it is not already completely familiar.

- Develop a plan that begins with a limited, achievable goal of parallelizing the kernel computation and then adds additional layers of functionality as needed. While the development approach is incremental, be sure that the overall plan makes sense. In particular, avoid the pitfall of only parallelizing the kernel and discovering later that much of the time is spent in non-parallelizable portions of the code.

Table 11.1 Titles from Project Reports from Parallel Computation courses.

Chess-End Games	3-Satisfiability Problems	Gene Sequence Alignment
Segmented Least-Squares	Video Motion Detection	A* Path-Finding for Games
Audio Analysis with a GPU	KD-Tree Construction	Image Convolution
Exact String Matching	MP3 Fast Fourier Transformation	Boid Simulation
Kohonen Maps	Ray Tracing	Galaxy Simulation
Prime Factorization	Rectangular Partitioning	Kenser-Ney Smoothing
Data Encryption	Checkers Min/Max Search	Artificial Neural Nets
Ray Casting	Julia Sets	Constraint Satisfaction
Sample Sort	Traveling Salesman Problem	Collaborative Filtering

- Develop a program for the kernel using the methodology described previously.
- Analyze the behavior of the solution to understand how its performance changes as the problem size and the number processors increase.
- Based on the analysis, improve the performance of any bottlenecks.
- Add the next layers of functionality as outlined in the plan, parallelizing where necessary.
- Report the results of the project.

The point of formulating a plan before starting is to contain your tendency to be overly ambitious (we all do it!) and to focus your enthusiasm on the key goal: creating a parallel solution to a personally interesting problem.

Notice that in using the first two approaches for selecting a project—program a published algorithm or compete with a benchmark—code may exist that can be used directly, especially for the functional components. Even in the third approach, there is often open source software that provides the required functionality, albeit in sequential form. To the extent that correct working program segments can be acquired easily and honestly, it makes sense to use them.

Performance Measurement

Typically, the purpose of writing a parallel program is to solve a problem more rapidly. It follows that after getting a computation to produce the correct results, the next task is to measure its performance. The use of timers has already been tested—it was the next preliminary step after "Hello, World"—so all that remains is to consider how to apply them to understand the program's performance. Many topics directly relevant to this section are covered in the Chapter 3 section, *Performance Measurement*; this section assumes familiarity with those topics.

Comparing against a Sequential Solution

The first question everyone asks about a parallel program is, "How much does it improve on the sequential program?" The question implies that the execution time—by which most people mean elapsed time or "wall clock" time—of the parallel and sequential computations be compared. Call this quantity *overall performance*.

What parts of the program should we include in measuring overall performance? Should we include initialization and cleanup costs when timing the program? Because we care about overall execution time, it makes sense to time the entire program. However, initialization and cleanup are one-time costs that are not representative of the core of the computation, particularly if they will be dwarfed by the core computation in longer production runs. Probably the best answer is to understand the behavior of the various program components and to be very clear about what is being measured when reporting results.

It is important to understand the individual costs of each phase of a program because Amdahl's Law tells us that if certain costs, such as initialization, are inherently sequential, then they will limit speedup. For example, if time is dominated by disk I/O, then we know that there's no profit to parallelizing the core computation. Moreover, such an understanding will allow us to reason about the potential benefits of moving to some other hardware, perhaps one that supports parallel I/O with lower initialization costs.

Finally, the sequential program that is the basis of the comparison should be either the "obvious" competition or the fastest known sequential program. The first case refers to programs that are in wide use and are therefore familiar to those interested in the comparison. The second case applies when there is interest in how much the computation can be improved through parallelism. The sequential program should *not* be the parallel program restricted to one processor, unless it also happens to be the fastest known sequential computation (it does happen!). Whichever applies, it should be specified when the results are reported.

Maintaining a Fair Experimental Setting

For any comparison to be meaningful, many variables must be controlled. As mentioned in Chapter 3, these include the hardware on which the programs execute, the languages and compilers used, the optimization settings used to produce the compiled code, and the program input. For example, both programs should be run on the same computer, implying that the sequential program should be run on one processor of the parallel machine.

Another complication is the difficulty of producing repeatable results. Because modern computers are multi-programmed, other programs and unrelated tasks can be executing while the measured program is running. These can range from background security daemons to other users, if, for example, a server cluster is used as the parallel computer. The consequences of such interference can range from minor timing imprecision to completely unreliable results. The main worry is that the other computations use resources—network or bus bandwidth, for example—that unpredictably affect a measured program. Thus, it is clearly best to measure performance as the system's sole user; when that is not possible, then it is important to accumulate a sufficient number of runs that slow outliers can be identified and thrown out.

> **Minimum versus Average.** Many researchers report the average execution time if the normal execution setting for the program is a multiuser system, but the median is probably a better value because it ignores the effects of a few bad outliers. The minimum execution time is also important, since it indicates the performance that is achievable in the best conditions.

One potential source of unpredictability involves the operating system and runtime system. For example, some programs require significant paging to load initial data from disk, and the cost of this paging can vary based on the state of the operating system's virtual memory system. Such behavior can be neutralized and made more predictable by "warming up" the system. The idea is to run the program twice and measure the time of the second execution. (Of course, if a program has conflict misses, they should and will be counted, but the initial heavy paging activity will be avoided.) Similarly, if the system has a dynamically invoked Just In Time (JIT) compiler, which can affect memory system behavior in unpredictable ways, the system can be warmed up so that all methods are compiled before measurements are taken. As another example, garbage collection times can produce widely unpredictable execution times, so in garbage collected languages such as Java, it is often wise to force a garbage collection immediately before measuring performance.

Understanding Parallel Performance

Ultimately, our goal is to obtain good performance, so it is tempting to measure speedup, decide that the speedup curve looks good, and declare success. How do we know, however, whether we've actually been successful? As discussed at the end of Chapter 3, there are many ways in which a speedup curve can be misleading. We might get good speedup because our problem sizes are large relative to the number of available processors; in actuality, our program might be extremely inefficient, so if we were to move to a larger production machine we would see unacceptable speedup. Conversely, speedup may be poor, but the problem itself could admit very little parallelism. For example, if we could speed up a program such as gcc compiler by a factor of 2, we'd be thrilled. Ideally we should compare our results against those of others. Even this approach has problems, because many differences—compiler optimizations, clock speed, cache sizes—can significantly affect the results, making them difficult to compare.

The goal then, is not merely to achieve some level of speedup or efficiency. The goal should be to develop a deep understanding of the program's behavior by answering some of the following questions:

- What are the individual phases of the program? It is often easier to understand the behavior of individual phases than to understand the aggregate behavior of multiple phases.

- How do the individual phases of the program scale? Scalability can be studied by using a variety of input sizes and, if possible, a variety of machine sizes and a variety of types of machines.

- What are the bottlenecks in each phase? What are the sources of overhead, contention, and idle time? These aspects of performance loss can sometimes be difficult to measure directly, so it might be necessary to instrument the code to gather various statistics about the amount of work done per process and the amount of interaction among processes. Of course, as the Heisenberg Uncertainty Principle reminds us, our attempts to examine the behavior often perturb the behavior, so we need to be careful.

- How much parallelism is there in the various phases? This question can sometimes be answered analytically and sometimes empirically. How much communication is there and of what form?

- How much memory is used? What other resources are heavily used?

- What trade-offs can be made to improve performance? With an understanding of the performance bottlenecks, it should be possible to identify trade-offs that improve performance. Is the granularity appropriate? In what ways can the granularity be changed?

Of course, many of these questions can only be answered in the context of a specific machine, so it is often interesting to conduct experiments on multiple machines.

Performance Analysis

It is sometimes possible to understand a program's performance weaknesses entirely by analysis, and though serious parallel programs are likely to be too complex for us to be completely successful at program analysis, it is useful to try. At the very least, it is possible to find a set of potential trouble spots that require experimental study.

It is advisable to check for large portions of the computation that are completely sequential. These have probably been considered and resolved during the programming, but it is wise to revisit the matter. Do there remain portions of the program that are sequential or exhibit little parallelism? If so, are there alternative solutions, possibly involving techniques like parallel prefix?

It is also important to analyze granularity issues. A common problem is for subcomputations to perform too little work relative to the overhead incurred. Examples include such things as queuing and dequeuing tiny tasks that do little work and cause congestion at the queue. Another example is to perform tiny computations in parallel that could be done faster on one process. For example, suppose each of P processes has a value and the computation requires that they be sorted. A parallel sort over P processes will induce considerable inter-process communication, while it could be considerably faster to send the values to one processor to be sorted.

Experimental Methodology

Running experiments to find the sources of performance loss is like solving a mystery. It is essential to have a hypothesis to direct the search; a list of candidates might already be available from the analysis. Other sources are load imbalance, lock contention, excessive communication, and so on, as outlined in Chapter 3. A good approach is to test individual sections of the program, being as focused as possible.

To be successful, it is good to emphasize reproducibility. In normal sequential debugging, it might be possible to place a breakpoint in the code and begin investigating from there. But parallel programs often depend on asynchronous events—especially when they contain bugs—so they cannot be stopped just anywhere. It is common to place a barrier in the code to print values for debugging, only to have the problem disappear. Of course, having a reproducible state available is also critical for reproducing and finding bugs.

To capture a reproducible state in the middle of a computation, we must stop the computation and write a coherent version of the state, as discussed earlier. The preferred case is to find a natural barrier where all processes must wait anyway; these can be actual barriers, or places such as reductions where there are implied barriers. From these places, the program can be stopped and started with minimal perturbation on the timings. If such places are not handy, then experiment with barrier placement so it does not hide the behavior being studied.

For example, the program structure shown in Figure 11.1 does not contain any explicit barriers, though there is an implicit barrier after the reduction, which is probably too late to help us limit the size of our computation. But we notice that in the gray section, the processors are exchanging information, and in all likelihood, they are doing so to update the state *to decide if the iteration should continue*. That is, all control stops until each thread decides whether to continue—based possibly on its local computation or a broadcast value from one process that performs the operation for all. Figure 11.2 shows a schematic of the computation in Figure 11.1. This implied barrier is a place to stop and start the computation.

The protocol is to run the computation up to a barrier, capture the program state immediately after the barrier, and write the data to a file. This approach allows the program to be repeatedly restarted in the post-barrier state. The protocol is not perfect. Barriers are not instantaneous, and they are not always in the most desirable

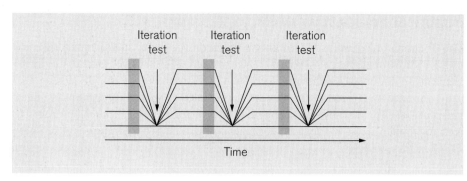

Figure 11.2
Schematic execution for $P = 5$ processes from the structure in Figure 11.1. At each iteration test, processes decide whether to continue iterating based on the data exchanged (gray).

places. Nevertheless, this style of inspection limits the degree to which the test program varies—in the segment of interest—from the actual program.

This methodology may allow us to test a part of the program without running it from the start, which can be a significant simplification. But other simplifications may not be possible. We may need, for example, to execute on sufficiently many processors or run a sufficiently large computation to create the behavior we conjecture is causing our performance loss.

Portability and Tuning

Having written a scalable parallel computation, we often wish to run it on a variety of platforms. If the principles described in Chapters 2 through 5 have been applied judiciously, then the program should run well on most parallel platforms, and similar performance across the platforms can be expected. But because computers are different in detail, it will likely be necessary to tune the program for execution on the new platform.

Chapter Summary

This chapter has focused on the process of writing and debugging parallel programs. Though much of the guidance applies to any parallel programming, the main emphasis has been on larger projects. Such projects can become quite complex, requiring the use of a careful methodology. We have offered general guidelines for programming, functional debugging, and performance debugging that apply to many situations. Every specific case will have its own characteristics and will rely to a great extent on the programmer's intelligence and skill, but these guidelines should help.

Historical Perspective

The discussion of parallel checkpoints is based on the distributed computing community's notion of a *valid recovery line*, which is described in the survey by Elnozahy, et al. [2002]. In the interest of generality, we have not emphasized parallel programming tools because they tend to be coupled to specific programming facilities, such as OpenMP or message passing. Nevertheless, we encourage readers to look for available systems that are compatible with the programming environment in which they work.

Exercises

1. Using Figure 11.1 as a guideline, describe the parallel structure of Batcher's alphabetizing algorithm in Figure 4.7 of Chapter 4.

2. Using Figure 11.1 as a guideline, describe the parallel structure of the Fixed Parallelism alphabetizing algorithm in Figure 4.5 of Chapter 4.

3. Following the guidelines in the Getting Started section, become familiar with a parallel computer and take basic timings measurements.

4. Program the Count 3s computation and run it on the parallel computer of Exercise 3.

5. Using a parallel program of your choice, compute the absolute speedup that the program achieves; plot the values as an increasing number of processors is applied.

Glossary

Amdahl's Law A bound on the possible improvement to a computation using parallelism: If $1/S$ is the computation time devoted to inherently sequential work, then a parallel solution to the problem can provide a maximum speedup of S.

Atomicity The property that a series of operations executes atomically; the execution of the operations is atomic if either all of the operations occur or none of them occur. A common way to ensure atomicity is to protect the series of operations by a mutex; once the mutex is acquired, the code will execute without interruption until the mutex is released.

Cache Coherence A cache management protocol in which the caches of different processors see a consistent value when referencing a given memory location.

Chapel A parallel programming language under development by Cray Inc.

Cilk A language for multithreaded parallel programming based on ANSI C and developed at MIT.

Chip Multiprocessor (CMP) A single chip containing multiple processors; also known as a multi-core chip; present CMPs have fewer than 20 processors.

Cluster A parallel computer made largely from commodity components; such systems can be scalable to many thousands of processors.

Co-Array Fortran A PGAS language extending Fortran and developed at Cray Inc.

Contention The degradation of performance caused by competition for shared resources.

Critical Section A section of code that must access shared data and for which undisciplined access can lead to race conditions.

Data Dependence A relationship between two threads of control arising from a required ordering of memory accesses.

Data Parallelism A computation that applies an operation to different items of data in parallel. With data parallelism, the number of simultaneous operations that can be performed grows with the amount of data.

Dependence An ordering constraint on two events; dependences limit the potential parallelization of a computation; dependences that cross thread or process boundaries require communication and/or synchronization.

Distributed Memory Parallel Computer A parallel computer whose hardware does not implement a shared address space.

Efficiency A performance metric defined as Speedup/P, where P is the number of processors.

Embarrassingly Parallel A computation with few or no dependences among threads or processes.

Erlang A parallel functional language designed by Ericsson Computer Science Laboratory.

F-- The original name of Co-Array Fortran. The name is a pun on the name C++.

False Sharing A phenomenon in which two objects, manipulated privately by independent processes, are allocated on the same cache line, causing the cache coherence protocol (wrongly) to invalidate the cache line in a processor when another processor changes its value, thereby degrading performance even though the references to the data are independent.

FLOPS Floating Point Operations Per Second, a performance metric for scientific computations whose performance is largely dictated by their floating-point performance.

Fortress A parallel programming language designed by researchers at Sun.

Global View Abstractions Programs written using global view abstractions produce the same output—given the same input—regardless of the number or arrangement of processes on which they are run.

GPGPU General Purpose computing on Graphical Processing Units.

High Performance Fortran (HPF) A data parallel language that extends sequential Fortran 77 and Fortran 90 programs through the addition of directives that describe how data is distributed among processes.

Idle Time A source of inefficiency occurring when processes cannot perform useful work, either because they have no work to perform or because they are blocked waiting for some event.

ISA (Instruction Set Architecture) An ISA is the interface to the hardware, defining the instructions and data types that the hardware implements.

Latency A measure of the amount of time that is required to complete a computation. This measure is often contrasted with throughput.

Locality A desirable property of a program's memory references in which they cluster together: *temporal locality* occurs when accesses to a memory location are clustered in time; *spatial locality* occurs when accesses to a memory location are clustered by address.

Load Imbalance A source of inefficiency in which processes perform different amounts of work, causing some processes to complete execution substantially earlier than others, leading to idle processes.

Local View Abstractions Parallel programming facilities producing different output depending on the number or arrangement of processes on which they run.

Memory Controller The interface between the CPU, including its on-chip caches, and DRAM, facilitating the efficient reference of memory; the controller performs operations such as buffering outstanding memory writes to decrease the likelihood that the CPU will stall when waiting to complete memory writes.

MIMD In Flynn's taxonomy, a Multiple Instruction Multiple Data computer, commonly referred to as a parallel computer; its key property is that each ALU executes its own instruction stream.

Moore's Law An observation made by Intel founder Gordon Moore that transistor density doubles roughly every 18 months; as technologies have advanced, the semiconductor industry has repeatedly found ways to adhere to this guideline.

Multi-core Chip A single chip containing multiple processors; also known as a chip multiprocessor or CMP; currently, such chips have fewer than 20 processors.

Mutual Exclusion The property of a code segment guaranteeing that exactly one thread will execute the code at any one time; often used to provide atomicity by exploiting the property that mutually exclusive code cannot be interrupted by another thread.

N$_{1/2}$ The problem size for a given program and machine, required to achieve an efficiency of 1/2.

NESL A parallel functional language providing nested parallelism and developed at Carnegie Mellon University.

NUMA Architecture Non-Uniform Memory Access (NUMA) architecture implements a shared address space, but memory access times are non-uniform because memory is physically distributed; memory local to a processor has lower latency than non-local memory.

Overhead Any cost of a parallel computation that is not also incurred by a corresponding sequential computation. One of four fundamental causes of perfor-mance loss in a parallel program.

P Abbreviation for the processor count of a parallel machine.

Parallel Virtual Machine (PVM) A message passing interface, many of whose ideas were later incorporated into the MPI standard.

PGAS Languages A Partitioned Global Address Space parallel programming language; such languages present a single address space that is shared by all processes. Hence, an object is referred to by the same name in all processes; a global address space does not imply a coherent memory.

P-Independence A parallel program is P-independent if and only if it always produces the same output on the same input regardless of the number or arrangement of processes on which it is run.

Pipelining A form of parallelism in which a computation is divided into a sequence of smaller subcomputations that are performed in order; with enough resources, each of the subcomputations can be performed simultaneously on different problem instances, improving throughput.

PRAM Parallel Random Access Machine, a theoretical model of a parallel computer that assumes unit cost access to a shared memory and synchronous execution.

Process A unit of parallelism that includes its own address space.

Processor A physical unit of concurrency, also known as a CPU (Central Processing Unit).

Race Condition A situation in which the output of a program depends on unpredictable timing behavior.

Reduce An operation that applies a function to a collection of values to produce a single result; typically, the functions are associative and commutative and include addition, multiplication, maximum, and minimum.

Relative Speedup A measure of parallel performance, in which a $P = 1$ processor parallel execution time is used instead of the best sequential time, T_S.

Relaxed Memory Consistency A property of parallel processors in which an execution may produce a result that is not sequentially consistent.

Scan An operation that applies a function to an ordered collection of values, producing all of the prefixes, where the ith prefix is the function applied to the first i items; also known as parallel prefix operator; the functions, like reduce, are typically addition, multiplication, maximum, and minimum.

Sequential Consistency A property of parallel processors in which any execution produces a result that matches an execution in which (1) the operations of all processors were executed in some sequential order, and (2) the operations of each individual processor appear in the order specified by the program.

Shared Address Space Parallel Computer A parallel computer whose hardware allows all processors to access a single shared address space; such machines generally implement cache coherence.

SIMD In Flynn's taxonomy, a Single Instruction Multiple Data computer, also known as a vector processor, in which one instruction controls the execution of multiple ALUs that execute in lockstep.

SISD In Flynn's taxonomy, a Single Instruction Single Data computer, frequently referred to as a sequential or von Neumann computer.

SMP (Symmetric Multiprocessor) A shared address space parallel computer in which memory latency is independent of the issuing processor; hence, the view of memory is symmetric across processors.

Speedup A measure of parallel performance; for a given computation, the time for the fastest sequential program T_S divided by the time for a parallel program on P processors; generally expressed as a curve plotted for values of P on the x-axis.

SPMD A parallel program that is specified as a single program executing on different processors, motivating the name, Single Program Multiple Data; occasionally confused with SIMD, but SIMD is a hardware classification and SPMD is a software classification.

Superlinear Speedup Greater than P-fold speedup on P processors; efficiency exceeding 1.

Task Parallel A task parallel computation is one in which parallelism is obtained by dividing the functions to be performed so that they can be performed concurrently.

Thread A unit of parallelism, logically consisting of program code, a program counter, a call stack, and some modest amount of state including a set of general purpose registers; in threads-based parallel programming, threads share access to memory.

Throughput A measure of the amount of work that can be completed per unit time; this measure is often contrasted with that of latency.

Titanium A PGAS language, extending Java and being developed at UC Berkeley.

Transactional Memory A concurrency control system for the memory operations of a shared memory parallel program, inspired by the notion of transactions in databases.

UMA (Uniform Memory Access) Architecture Shared address space architecture, such as an SMP, in which access to memory is independent of the processor that makes the request, in contrast with NUMA architecture.

Unified Parallel C (UPC) A PGAS language, extending the C language and developed at George Washington University.

X10 A parallel programming language being designed by IBM.

ZPL A data parallel array language developed at the University of Washington.

References

Ali-Reza Adl-Tabatabai, Christos Kozyrakis, and Bratin Saha. "Unlocking Concurrency," *ACM Queue*, 4(10), pp. 24–33, December/January 2006–2007.

G.M. Amdahl. "Validity of the single-processor approach to achieving large scale computing capabilities," in *AFIPS Conference Proceedings*, AFIPS Press 30, pp. 483–485, 1967.

Emery D. Berger, Kathryn S. McKinley, Robert D. Blumofe, and Paul R. Wilson. "Hoard: A Scalable Memory Allocator for Multithreaded Applications," *The Ninth International Conference on Architectural Support for Programming Languages and Operating Systems (ASPLOS-IX)*. November 2000.

Guy Blelloch. "Programming Parallel Algorithms," *Communications of the ACM*, 39(3), March 1996.

Robert D. Blumofe, Christopher F. Joerg, Bradley C. Kuszmaul, Charles E. Leiserson, Keith H. Randall, and Yuli Zhou. "Cilk: An Efficient Multithreaded Runtime System," *Proceedings of the Fifth ACM SIGPLAN Symposium on Principles and Practice of Parallel Programming (PPoPP)*, pp. 207–216, 1995.

W. J. Bouknight, Stewart A. Denenberg, David F. McIntyre, J. M. Randall, Amed H. Sameh, and Daniel L. Slotnick. "The ILLIAC IV System," in *Computer Structures: Principles and Examples*, Daniel Siewiorek, C. Gordon Bell, and Allen Newell, eds., pp. 306–316, McGraw-Hill, 1982.

Bradford L. Chamberlain, E Christopher Lewis, and Lawrence Snyder. "Problem space promotion and its evaluation as a technique for efficient parallel computation," In *Proceedings of the ACM International Conference on Supercomputing*, 1999.

Bradford L. Chamberlain, Sung-Eun Choi, E Christopher Lewis, Calvin Lin, Lawrence Snyder, and W. Derrick Weathersby. "ZPL's WYSIWYG performance model," *Proceedings of the IEEE Workshop on High-Level Parallel Programming Models and Supportive Environments*, 1998.

Edward G. Coffman, Jr., M. J. Elphick, and Arie Shoshani. "System Deadlocks," *ACM Computing Surveys*, 3(2), pp. 67–78, 1971.

Jeffrey Dean and Sanjay Ghemawat. "MapReduce: Simplified Data Processing on Large Clusters," *Sixth Symposium on Operating System Design and Implementation*, pp. 137–149, December 2004.

Steven J. Deitz. "High-Level Programming Language Abstractions for Advanced and Dynamic Parallel Computations," Ph.D. thesis, University of Washington, February 2005.

Michael J. Flynn. "Some computer organizations and their effectiveness," *IEEE Transactions on Computers*, vol. C-21, p. 948, 1972.

Ian Foster and Carl Kesselman. *The Grid: Blueprint for a New Computing Infrastructure*, Morgan Kaufmann, 1999.

K. Gharachorloo, D. Lenoski, J. Laudon, P. Gibbons, A. Gupta, and J. Hennessy. "Memory consistency and event ordering in scalable shared-memory multiprocessors," *Proceedings of the 17th Annual International Symposium on Computer Architecture*, pp. 15–26, May 1990.

Per Brinch Hansen. "Structured multiprogramming," *Communications of the ACM*, 15(7), pp. 574–578, July 1972.

W. Daniel Hillis and Guy L. Steele Jr. "Data parallel algorithms," *Communications of the ACM*, 29(12), pp. 1170–1183, December 1986.

C.A.R. Hoare. "Monitors: an Operating System Structuring Concept," *Communi-cations of the ACM*, 17(10), pp. 549–557, October 1974.

Roger W. Hockney. "Supercomputer Architecture," *Infotech State of the Art Conference: Future Systems*, Infotech Intl. Ltd., 1977.

C.R. Jesshope and Roger W. Hockney. *Parallel Computers 2*, Adam Hilger, 1988.

David J. Kuck. "A Survey of Parallel Machine Organization and Programming," *ACM Computing Surveys*, 9(1), pp. 29–59, March 1977.

Richard E. Ladner and Michael J. Fischer, "Parallel Prefix Computation," *Journal of the ACM*, 24(4), pp. 831–838, October 1980.

Ralf Lämmel. "Google's MapReduce Programming Model—Revisited," *Science of Computer Programming*, 68(3), pp. 208–237, 2007.

L. Lamport. "How to make a multiprocessor computer that correctly executes multiprocess programs," *IEEE Transactions on Computers*, C-28(9), pp. 241–248, September 1979.

James R. Larus and Ravi Rajwar. *Transactional Memory (Synthesis Lectures on Computer Architecture)*, Morgan and Claypool, 2006.

Gil Lerman and Larry Rudolf. *Parallel Evolution of Parallel Processors*, Perseus Publishing, 1994.

William R. Mark, R. Steven Glanville, Kurt Akeley, and Mark J. Kilgard. "Cg: A System for Programming Graphics Hardware in a C-Like Language," *International Conference on Computer Graphics and Interactive Techniques*, pp. 896–907, 2003.

R. W. Numrich and J.K. Reid. "Co-Array Fortran for Parallel Programming," *ACM Fortran Forum*, 17(2), pp. 1–31, 1998.

John D. Owens, David Luebke, Naga Govindaraju, Mark Harris, Jens Kruger, Aaron E. Lefohn, and Timothy J. Purcell. "A Survey of General-Purpose Computation on Graphics Hardware," *Computer Graphics Forum*, 26(1), pp. 80–113, March 2007.

Rob Pike, Sean Dorward, Robert Griesemer, and Sean Quinlan. "Interpreting the Data: Parallel Analysis with Sawzall," *Scientific Programming*, pp. 277–298, 2005.

D. Pothen, H. Simon, and K. P. Liou. "Partitioning sparse matrices with eigenvectors of graphs," *SIAM Journal of Matrix Analysis and Applications*, 11(1990), pp. 430–452.

Ravi Rajwar and James R. Goodman. "Speculative Lock Elision: Enabling Highly Concurrent Multithreaded Execution," *Proceedings of the 34th Annual ACM/IEEE International Symposium on Microarchitecture*, pp. 294–305, 2001.

Burton J. Smith, "A pipelined, shared resource MIMD computer," *International Conference on Parallel Processing, IEEE,* 1978.

Lawrence Snyder. "Type architecture shared memory and the corollary of modest potential," *Annual Review of Computer Science,* 1, 1986.

Lawrence Snyder. "Design and Development of ZPL," *Third History of Programming Languages Conference, ACM,* 2007.

J.T. Schwartz. "Ultracomputers," *ACM Transactions on Programming Languages and Systems,* 2(4), pp. 484–521, 1980.

V.S. Sunderam. "PVM: A Framework for Parallel Distributed Computing," *Concurrency: Practice and Experience,* 2(4), pp. 315–339, December 1990.

Herb Sutter and James Larus. "Software and the Concurrency Revolution," *ACM Queue,* 3(7), pp. 54–62, September 2005.

David Tarditi, Sidd Puri, and Jose Oglesby. "Accelerator: Using Data-Parallelism to Program GPUs for General-Purpose Uses," *The Twelfth International Conference on Architectural Support for Programming Languages and Operating Systems (ASPLOS-XII),* pp. 325–335, November 2006.

Michael Wolfe. *High Performance Compilers for Parallel Computing,* Addison Wesley, 1996.

Special Issue on BlueGene, *IBM Journal of Research and Development,* 49(2/3), 2005.

Index

RAM model in, 44–46
  speedup interpretation and, 79–80
Sequential searches, 45
Serial elision, 280
Serializability
  with mutexes in POSIX Threads, 153
  TM system built on, 296
Servers, parallel and distributed computing, 5
SETI@Home, 142
Shared memory machines
  AMD Dual Core, 33–34
  Intel Core Duo, 31–34
  observations about, 43
  Sun Fire E25K, 35–36
Shared memory parallel programming
  CTA architecture, 49, 53–54
  defined, 62
Shared Virtual Memory, 199–200
shmem (shared memory), 54
SIMD (single instruction, multiple data) computation, 43–44, 287
Simultaneous multithreading (SMT), 35
Single heaps, memory allocation case study, 138
Single-phase barrier, SOR using, 180–183
Single program, multiple data (SPMD) computation, 49
Single variables, Titanium, 233
SISD (single instruction, single data) computation, 43–44
Slow migration approach, 276
SMPs (symmetric multiprocessors)
  architectures, 34–35
  defined, 34
  implementing memory allocator for, 137–139
  Sun Fire E25K, 35–36
  X10 built from, 302
SMT (simultaneous multithreading), 35
Snooping, 34–36
Software
  accessing programming, 305–306
  scalable performance and, 83
Software Transactional Memory (STM), 295
SOR program
  with Message Passing Interface, 219–228
  with POSIX Threads, 174–179

Sorted sequences, merging in Scalable Parallelism, 104
Spatial locality, 73
Speculative Lock Elision, 293
Speedup
  assessing performance, 273
  concerns with, 79–80
  measuring performance using, 78
  measuring using efficiency, 79
  parallel performance and, 316
  scaled vs. fixed-size, 81
  superlinear, 78–79
SPEs (synergistic processing elements), Cell processor, 37–39, 288
Spin locks, 67
Split-phase barriers
  correcting implementation of, 184–186
  deadlock with, 184
  defined, 179
  successive over-relaxation using, 180–181
SPMD (single program, multiple data) computation, 49
Spurious lock conflicts, 170
Spurious wakeups, 170
SRI (System Request Interface), 33–34
Stale values, 32
Standard Send and Receive operations, MPI, 212–213
State of the art assessment, 271–282
  correctness, 271–273
  of Java Threads, 276
  lessons for future, 279–282
  of MPI, 276–277
  of NESL, 278–279
  of OPENMP, 276
  performance, 273–274
  of PGAS languages, 277–278
  portability, 274–275
  of POSIX Threads, 275–276
  scalability, 274
  summary review, 282
  of ZPL, 278
Statement-level indexing, ZPL, 245
Stencil computations, 126–129
STM (Software Transactional Memory), 295
Streaming computations, on multi-core chips, 187
Structural conflicts, vs. semantic, 295
Sub-arrays, 238
Sub-trees, allocation by, 139–141

Substantial subproblems, Scalable Parallelism, 99–100
Subversion, 307
Successive over-relaxation (SOR) program
  with Message Passing Interface, 219–228
  with POSIX Threads, 174–179
SUMMA (Scalable Universal Matrix Multiplication Algorithm)
  NESL difficulties with, 279
  PSP technique used in, 299
  ZPL implementing, 253–255
  ZPL performance model, 266–267
Sums, 9–14
  expressing parallel, 13
  iterative computation, 9–12
  pair-wise computation, 12–13
  parallel prefix, 13–14
Sun Fire E25K symmetric multiprocessor
  estimates for λ, 52
  overview of, 35–36
  shared memory of, 43
Supercomputers
  architectures of, 40
  Blue/Gene L, 40–43
  estimates for λ, 52
  parallel programming in, 5
Superlinear speedup, 78–79, 273–274
Symmetric multiprocessors. See SMPs (symmetric multiprocessors)
Synchronization
  overlapping computation with, 179–186
  Peril-L language and, 91–92
  reduce and scan, 96
  as source of parallel overhead, 65
Synchronization, POSIX Threads, 153–163
  creating/destroying condition variables, 159
  overview of, 153–156
  protecting condition variables, 157–159
  thread-specific data, 160–163
  waiting on multiple condition variables, 159–160
Synchronized memory, and full/empty variables, 94–95
Synchronized methods, Java, 189–190
Synchronized statements, Java, 189–190, 292–293